RACING TIME

A Memoir of Love, Loss and Liberation

PATRICK SMITHWICK

Illustrations by
SAM ROBINSON

Published by
DEMENTI MILESTONE PUBLISHING

First Printing

Copyright © 2019 by Patrick Smithwick

Patrick Smithwick, Author

Wayne Dementi, Publisher
Dementi Milestone Publishing, Inc.
Manakin-Sabot, VA 23103
www.dementimilestonepublishing.com

Cataloging-in-publication data for this book is available from The Library of Congress.

ISBN: 978-1-7330268-0-2

Printed in the USA

The book team extends its apology for any errors or omissions and encourages copyright owners inadvertently missed to contact the publisher.

To Tom

THOMAS HORNE VOSS

19 September 1950 – 21 January 2014

Contents

PART FIVE

ILLUSTRATIONS
by Sam Robinson

Distilling the Moment

Sam Robinson paints landscapes and portraits, but mostly he paints the Mid-Atlantic steeplechase racing scene, combining the three motifs in an exciting blend of horses, riders and weather. The families and farms devoted to this pursuit preserve their traditions fiercely. To do the subject justice, it is necessary to be there with easel, sketchbook and camera to record, but also to be a part of the experience.

A few pages into the manuscript of *Racing Time*, it was clear to Robinson that this was an insider's view, a personal record of a deep history that informed much of what the artist aimed to depict on canvas. After experimenting with pencil and wash, Robinson concluded that nothing less than full-sized oil paintings in the tradition of the great artists of the Golden Age of American Illustration would do the subject justice. He would work on large canvasses, saturated with color, which could then be reduced to bookplates. As the narrative of the book developed through the telescoping of time, the images would emerge, drawn upon sources that vary from places still in existence, people still with us, and photographs of times past.

Robinson sincerely hopes that each plate succeeds in distilling a moment of significance from *Racing Time* in a way that rings true for those who knew it, and extends the imagination of those who are learning of it.

RACING TIME

DIGGING

Between my finger and my thumb
The squat pen rests; snug as a gun.

Under my window, a clean rasping sound
When the spade sinks into gravelly ground:
My father, digging. I look down

Till his straining rump among the flowerbeds
Bends low, comes up twenty years away
Stooping in rhythm through potato drills
Where he was digging.

The coarse boot nestled on the lug, the shaft
Against the inside knee was levered firmly.
He rooted out tall tops, buried the bright edge deep
To scatter new potatoes that we picked,
Loving their cool hardness in our hands.

By God, the old man could handle a spade.
Just like his old man.

My grandfather cut more turf in a day
Than any other man on Toner's bog.
Once I carried him milk in a bottle
Corked sloppily with paper. He straightened up
To drink it, then fell to right away
Nicking and slicing neatly, heaving sods
Over his shoulder, going down and down
For the good turf. Digging.

The cold smell of potato mould, the squelch and slap
Of soggy peat, the curt cuts of an edge
Through living roots awaken in my head.
But I've no spade to follow men like them.

Between my finger and my thumb
The squat pens rests.
I'll dig with it.
                              — Seamus Heaney

PROLOGUE

The Reality of Sisyphus

Fork the rounded edge of the shovel just inside the rut of the stream, where the grass is growing. It makes a nice slice sound of shovel tip penetrating turf, then dirt, then a thick layer of sandy soil. It hasn't rained for a month. A drought. Two of the four springs running along this quarter mile of stream are dried up. You know it will rain again; it will rain soon. The odds are, it has to rain soon, and when it does you want the water to flow down through your recently hand-dug channel—to open up, deepen and widen the channel, and not to spread out into an infinity of rivulets and underground tunnels and roundabouts that never return to the main stream, turning the bottom of this paddock into a marsh.

You try to balance it out so that sixty percent of the time you have the right hand down close to the lug of the spade and the left hand at the end of the shaft because your natural inclination is to do it the other way around which puts too much strain on your right hand, right arm, right side. The tip of the spade slices through turf, dirt, grit. Water flows into the quarter-moon shaped cut in the earth. Yes, this is a stream, not a dried out ditch. It will flow again.

This stretch of the stream is one hundred yards long and at a shovel width at a time—and often several thrusts to be made in that half-foot width—you have a ways to go but you don't think of that. You might've cheated once or twice, stood up straight, leaned on the shovel, stretched out your back, and eyeballed the entire length of the stream to come, turned and looked down at

3

the length of the stream completed, but you know this is not a good way to get the job done. Just as you don't write five pages—skipping lines on a yellow legal pad—and then stop, count the number completed, and the number, twelve, to go to fulfill the morning's quota.

You pull the shaft to your left hip, and using the heel of the shovel as a lever against the edge of turf, push the handle down. The turf and muck strains to maintain all that it has gained in the year since you last dug it out. It holds together, grass roots fighting not to lose their grip, muck stuck to itself, water appearing from nowhere filling the gradually growing opening, the mud sucking, sucking to itself, hissing, trying to hold, then separating with a *th-swash*, and now, the part that can get to your back. You push in hard, and pull up, straightening your legs, straightening your back, pull the shovel filled with a thick pie of sod and muck, water escaping off the edges of the shovel, and either swing it back and around your right hip, dumping it by your side—the easier move—or, straining your back, triceps and stomach muscles, pull it straight up and thrust the shovel out, away from you, dumping the sod and muck on the other side of the stream.

Slice, slosh, sucking-th-wash, strain, fulfillment.

Slice, slosh, sucking-th-wash, strain, fulfillment.

Fulfillment: I've shown the completed and freshly dug-out stream—clean and clear water for the horses to drink now flowing freely—to my wife as we and the dogs have crossed it on the way out for a walk, to my son as we've ridden alongside it on horses, to my daughter as she's driven her truck over the stream and to the spring and the marshy area in which, while mowing, I've gotten the tractor stuck, and out of which she will pull me. On the evening after completing the digging, I've soliloquized at dinner to wife and sons and daughter about the engineering feat I had pulled off that late afternoon, but no matter. No one understands. With one exception—my mother always did. How she would rant in the winter when the stream became blocked, the water rose along its banks, funneled into a maze of sluiceways, then froze, forming an archipelago of iced-over, dangerous rinks hidden by tufts of tall grass, or in the spring when the grass grew too tall on the stream's sides, thick weeds and multiflora rose crept in, the current came to a stop, the rains fell and the field became a marsh which the horses would tear through, their hooves scooping out divots, trampling the grass that was left, turning half an acre into a mud hole. And how she would rhapsodize when its banks were mowed and its channel was open and she could watch her three Thoroughbreds standing side-by-side lower their heads, test the current with their muzzles, and sip the fresh spring water.

I've been digging this stream out since I was a teenager and used to attack it in the heat of the day, engine revved high, working fast and hard, damn the torpedoes, full steam ahead, do or die. I have been digging out this stream in the early spring, struck an odd rock—a rock that sounded different, not the usual clang of steel against stone, but a softer sound, a sound with a hollowness to it, and then witnessed the primordial magic of a feed-tub sized snapping turtle come out of his winter hibernation and slowly shake off his slumber, stick out his powerful legs, lift up his carapace-shielded body, and move smoothly, more gracefully than you'd imagine, stealthily, confidently, powerfully away from me, across the stream, and into the tall grass.

Just last week, I was digging near one of the springs of my youth where as teenagers on summer Sundays Tom Voss and I, after galloping horses in the morning for my father, used to pick mint, bring bags of it back to the house, make buckets of mint juleps, and invite our friends over. Fully into my rhythm of thrust into the mud, stomp foot down on lug of spade, shove deeper with foot, hands, arms, back, lean shaft back, toss muck—suddenly something was wildly, impossibly fast, wriggling out from under my foot causing me to leap into the air higher than Nureyev on his best night, and yell like hell as it elongated, unreeling itself beneath me, slither-swimming away, its body moving in perfect forward S-motion out from under my airborne shadow, its head raised up like that of a python's in the old Tarzan movies. My feet came down, I hesitated for a split-second, thought of thrusting my spear at the point right below his head, then instead high-stepped backwards while watching it whip upstream.

Such an interlude is extremely beneficial to stream digging. It is worth at least twenty yards. It is a gift: the heart races, the pathways of the mind are flushed out and the electric currents of fear flash through. Everything—every blade of grass, tip of a rock, head of a frog—is pulsatingly clear, in highest definition. The body feels limber and strong and fresh again like an eighteen-year-old's. It's that hint of dark primordial danger, and even the possibility of death, that does it: the imagining of two hollow fangs penetrating the rubber of the boots, sinking into your flesh, joining yourself, your humanity, to the reality of one million years of evolution, the pain sharp, like the prongs of a pitch fork entering your foot which you'd experienced as a child, the shock of pain so sudden, so unexpected, and then, wrenching your foot away, the snake-head releasing from your boot. Then the worry: was it poisonous, did it inject its venom, would you have to go to the emergency ward, was there anyone home to go with you, should you pull the boot off, cut the wound with a knife and try to suck the venom out?

And now, for the next half hour of your life, every thrust of the shovel has meaning. You are totally into the digging, beads of sweat roll pleasantly down your sides, dollops of sweat drip off your nose, you can feel the blisters forming on the old callouses under the knuckles, and as much as you've tried to lift with your legs, to be smart, to lean back and swing the shovel with your full body, nevertheless, you can feel the fatigue in your back, but you don't mind it. You can judge from it how hard you've been working and tomorrow, it may be sore, but it will remind you of all that you have accomplished today. Your body is giving out in one way but in another, it has found a rhythm, a comfortable rhythm, like a long, everlasting Grateful Dead riff that is exhausting the band, the deadheads, everyone, but no one wants it to end and it just keeps going and going. The mud splashes up onto the lenses of your protective glasses creating little spots in your vision. Less and less you rely on your arms. Instead—say your shovel clanks against an awkwardly-shaped, cumbersomely heavy rock right there in what you want to be the channel of the stream. It is too late in the day for you to simply put the tip of the shovel beneath the rock, work the spade further and further under the rock, then with arm and stomach muscles, use your body as a crane, lift the rock up and out, and dump it to the side. No—you have to put the shovel down, set it beside the stream. Plant one foot, then the other, into the mud you want to get rid of, bend down, dig with fingers through the grit, wedge one knee against the bank of the stream, claw deeper under the rock searching the ridges for a good grip, lift, strain with entire body, the rock not wanting to leave, the suction holding it in place, and then with a *thwwaaash-clup* it is released. You stand, pressing the cold, wet unchangeable hardness of the druid stone to your thighs and crotch. Covered with mud, straining every muscle in your body, hunched over, feet spread wide, you crab-walk up the bank and over to the landfill area, and fling it onto the other rocks and cinder blocks and chunks of concrete.

The leaden stone doesn't bounce or roll or ricochet off the other rocks. Seeming incredibly lifeless after your wrestling match, it cracks against a cinder block, splits it in half, rolls off the pile onto the grass and is immediately stationery. It lies awkwardly on its side, in the grass, alone and out of place. Feeling badly for this stone wrenched from its century-old demesne of individual respectability and carelessly thrown on this pile of rubble, you take a few steps, pick it up and place it firmly in a gap formed by two respectable rocks.

Walk back to the stream. Cross the area just dug out. Step up the bank. Sit down. Look downstream at the satisfying wave-like rhythm of the black bank, scalloped on one side, a series of rounded shovel thrusts, all the way to the horse crossing. Glance upstream—how many pages to go?—towards the top spring. Fifteen yards. It's 6:30 p.m. In the shade of the spring's trees. You'll reach the spring by 7:00 and then you'll walk out of the shade into the sunlight—no longer an adversary, no longer relentlessly pressing down on you, but now friendly, caressing your mud-splattered arms, massaging your back, drying the sweat of your t-shirt—stroll down along the stream, admiring your work, stopping here and there to remove any blockage of the flow, to the plastic liter tonic bottle that you know still holds two or three good pulls of water. Sit on the bank in the angled sunlight and admire the force of the current while draining the bottle from its wide mouth. Then rise up, grab the shovel, and head in, looking forward to the modern delight of a hot shower—fresh, clean water massaging the back, fresh, clean hot water slapping down hard on the lower back, loosening the muscles, the jets fingering into mud-splattered ears and eye sockets and hair, rinsing away the rank, atavistic, spermy, tad-pole scent you have loved since you were nine or ten and used to spend full days covered in it, your mother and father pleading with you to stop building the dams that backed up the stream.

As a youth, I would work in the lower section where the banks are higher, the slope of the stream is steeper, and the water ran faster. I'd pick a spot that had strong, secure banks. Set rocks—river boulders in my mind—across in a line from bank to bank, the water rippling over their tops and purling through the interstices. Then, smaller rocks in the gaps, the flow slowing. With my short-handled, rust-red Army shovel that my father had given me for Christmas—I loved it; it could become an axe, a hammer, a shovel and even a saw—I'd dig mud out, making a "lake" on the uphill side, and plaster the mud against the upstream wall of the dam. Using the shovel's sharp blade, I'd carve rectangular sections of turf out of the side of the banks and strategically place them against the deep water side, as well as across the top, watching the water level rise, filling the newly cut banks, rise above the grass line, putting more and more pressure on the dam, popping through gaps here and there. I remember rushing off, having to hunt for "boulders" further afield, reaching my fingers deep into the dark water, into the mud and grit, beneath the rock, and, body weary, tiring, but eight-year-old mind not realizing it, I pulled against a cumbersome rock. Squatted over it and heaved against its weight and suction. Dug my heels in, making good gripping spots, and leaned as in a tug-of-war contest. The suction released. I collapsed on the bank, the "boulder," too big for me to handle, in my lap. I found a protrusion beside a slight concavity, a perfect grip. Holding the rock's unforgiving weight and its sharp edges tight against my stomach, I hobbled upstream as it slipped downwards, pressing against my crotch and thighs. Reaching the dam, I halted, gathering all strength and resolve, and stepped, Gulliver-like, over this Lilliputian project. The boulder was inexorably sliding out of my grip—the lives of thousands of dam workers below at stake. I wanted to slowly lower it into just the right spot where it was needed to blunt the growing force of the rushing water but all I could do was step over the dam, the workers looking up in terror, and let it go. It made a Herculean splash, a splash out of *Moby Dick*, coating me with muck. I pulled my red bandana out of my rear pocket, wiped off my face, collapsed on the bank and watched as the dam held back the water, the water level rose, filling the canyons, the stream backed up, the reservoir swelled, and a shimmering, crystalline wave finally flowed in a perfectly formed, smoothly-curved, and constantly-swirling arc over the top of the dam, creating a weir.

That was sixty years ago. And I know that last night I pulled the same rock—the water rushing off it revealing the beauty of its flinty, scarlet-streaked and silver-chinked surface, unseen for five decades, anchored deep below the surface by a handle-like protrusion—out of the stream that sixty years ago I had deposited as the linchpin for my project, to halt the incessant, burrowing, forward-roiling rush of water, of time, to let it rise and form a pond, a lake, a reservoir of the present.

PART ONE

Turning and turning in the widening gyre
The falcon cannot hear the falconer;
Things fall apart; the centre cannot hold;
Mere anarchy is loosed upon the world,
The blood-dimmed tide is loosed, and everywhere
The ceremony of innocence is drowned;
The best lack all conviction, while the worst
Are full of passionate intensity. . . .

— William Butler Yeats,
"The Second Coming

Just Perfect

"Crooks," he told me. "You got ripped off. When will you learn? That whole family is nothing but a pack of thieves. Why didn't you talk to me before building that fence."

It was an unusually hot and muggy Saturday morning in May, and I'd finished galloping seven horses for my cousin and best friend Tom Voss at Atlanta Hall Farm, a mile from my family's farm, Prospect Farm, in Monkton, Maryland, where I'd grown up and where my wife Ansley, daughter Eliza and I had just moved. We'd gone out in sets of four: we hacked one set of two-year-olds to the old rusty starting gate, rode them through the stalls, circled back, stood them quietly in the stalls while Tom, positioned directly in front of us, opened and shut the gates, and then we jogged them out together. We vanned a couple of sets to the nearby Elkridge Harford Hunt Club, where we breezed them on the long uphill mile course Tom has marked off with pylons and keeps harrowed and mowed. We popped a set of three-year-olds over the course of logs by the indoor track, and we schooled two sets of older horses, fast, over the hurdles. A full morning.

I was seated in my late mother's beaten and battered but still-running-strong Ford-150 pickup, pulling off my sweat-soaked boots, socks and leggings. Tom was leaning against the open door. He hadn't shaved for a couple of days and had just asked me who I'd gotten to build our new board fence along the Manor Road edge of the farm. His well-worn Voss Stable baseball cap (an admirer had given him a box of them) was pulled down low over his eyes; his dirty-blonde hair sprouted out the sides and descended out the back of the cap almost to his shoulder blades (unseen was the growing pale bald spot under the cap). Beads of sweat dripped off his whiskery face, making rivulets through the layer of grime and chaff picked up from the bales of straw he'd just unloaded, from this, my truck, which he'd been using all morning (I knew I shouldn't have left the keys in the ignition), just to irk me—driving it fast through fields to watch us gallop and school, and occasionally, when he knew I was looking, leaning forward as if riding a race, over the Labrador and two Norwich terriers vying for position on his lap—the truck rattling and bouncing along—reaching out the window and giving his mount a couple of whacks with my father's old riding whip that I'd left on the dashboard. Stalks of straw were stuck to his sweaty arms and scattered across his wet, sun-bleached, blue polo shirt, which was ripped on both sides between the collar and shoulders.

Suddenly, he was cramming himself into the cab, between the steering wheel and me, his arm brushing across my chest, his powerful shoulder mashing me back against the seat. Wondering what the hell he was doing, I watched him grab the pack of Pall Malls he'd left on the dashboard. He stuck a crumpled cigarette in his mouth, stared at me, giving me a go-to-hell look I'd been receiving for five decades. "How about a light?" he asked.

"No."

"Come on, don't be such a pansy. Where's that lighter you got for your sixteenth birthday."

"Long gone. Light it yourself. Go on, kill yourself."

" 'Long gone.' We're both going to be 'long gone' before we know it."

"Speak for yourself."

"You can't live forever."

"Yes, I realize that."

"We've already lived more than three-quarters of our lives," he said, taking a strong pull and blowing the smoke away from us. "Sometimes, I think about walking away from all this, moving to Vermont."

"Yes, I know what you mean." I took a deep breath, looked around at the barns, the fields, the horses—savored the hard fitness of my body, loving the streamlined feeling, not an ounce of fat on me, every muscle having been pushed to the limit over the morning. "Sometimes I too think of walking away from all this, hanging it up."

Well, that'll be the day, Tom sang out, *when you say goodbye*
Yes, that'll be the day, when you make me cry
You say you're going to leave, you know it's a lie
'Cause that'll be the day when I die. . . .

"Not bad, not bad," I said, impressed with that steel trap of a memory of his and pulling up from my own memory the image of his older brother Ned's compact, one-song-to-a-side, Buddy Holly 45-record spinning around and around on my record player as we sat on the floor in my bedroom, watched the needle make its way to the center, and listened.

He took another pull and stared at me. We'd gotten off track. I'd been telling him about all the money we'd been spending on the farm—roofs, the new well, a new heating system, remodeling the kitchen, trimming trees—and he'd asked who I'd gotten to build the fence.

"Don't deal with that family any more. They don't care about you or your farm. You can build your own fences. On your way home, stop and check in with Johnny Rice, you know, J.B.'s AA friend, on the Jarrettsville Pike. You know where I mean?"

"Yes."

"Look behind his house, where the barn used to be. First, he had the Amish tear the barn down and take away all the chestnut beams. Then, he had them pull out all the old locust posts from the paddocks he no longer uses. He's cutting the posts up, loading them into his pickup, driving downtown and selling them for firewood. It's highway robbery. He'll probably start tearing the house down next, selling bits and pieces. . . ."

I drove over, pulled up beside a barn-sized pile of old locust posts. Johnny stepped out of his house, greeted me. "Sure," he said, "there're some good ones in there. Any friend of J.B. Secor's is a friend of mine. Go in and pick out what you want. Is my man winning any races?"

"Yeah, he's taken a string up to Suffolk Downs, and he's winning one or two a week."

"He'd better watch out up there. Not his turf. The local boys might not appreciate his success."

"That's what Tom says. We called J.B. this morning to congratulate him on his latest win, and Tom told him, "John, you'd better slow it down."

Heavy, unwieldy, much longer than you'd think, difficult to carry, one side covered with rusted and bent nails and sawed off sections of nailed in oak boards, each post was an *artifact* (vocabulary for Medieval History course I'll soon be teaching sixth graders). The posts might have been seventy years old, but they were as solid and strong as if they'd just been cut. Every afternoon for the next four days, I stopped by the *cache* of posts, climbed through the immense pile, picked out the best, wrestled them into the pick-up, drove home, unloaded them in front of the corncrib. Then, Ansley found a farmer who had oak boards he'd cut himself and was selling at a discount if you picked them up yourself. They were new, salted with sawdust, still damp with sap and life, and had no cracks. Counting carefully, I slid them over the tailgate into the back of the truck, drove home, stacked them beside the posts. And there the pile of posts and stack of boards remained through May, June and early July, Ansley intermittently asking what was my "plan" and finally urging me to go ahead and build the fence. "Don't you want the fence finished before you go to Saratoga?" She located two strong young Mexican men to help put the fence up. We were organized, set to go.

Arising at 5:00 a.m., before the heat, on a Sunday in late July, I lay twenty-five sixteen-foot boards, one by one, in a line separating the lawn from the back paddock. Picked out fifty of the best locust posts, pulled and hammered and crowbarred out the old nails and chunks of boards, then carried each awkwardly balanced post—they are tapered, thicker and heavier at the bottom, then funneling up to a narrowed top, something not done anymore—to the line of boards. Dropped the posts, one at a time, at eight-foot intervals onto the brick-hard ground.

At 8:00 a.m., it was warming up. Every other day of the summer, I'd be on my fifth horse of Dickie Small's coming off the track at Pimlico at this time, but Dickie had found a "guest rider" (student at MICA, Maryland Institute College of the Arts, with hour-glass figure, long legs, and swishing blonde pony tail when wearing a helmet), had given me this Sunday off to get the fence up, and had even offered to trailer his tractor and post-hole dig-ger over at 11:00 to dig the holes. I had seen him operate heavy equipment at his family farm, Strathmore Stud, which he was converting into a breeding operation. Fast, furious, an explosion of energy. I'd driven in one afternoon for a tour and there he was in T-shirt, flannel shirt, and thick wool cap pulled down hard on his head, sweat pouring out from around its brim—the chain saw was roaring and he was attacking a barn-sized pile of tree trunks. When he jumped in the front-end loader, and started beeping, spinning and speeding around, moving the logs, I walked care-fully backward and left the premises. *No help needed,* I'd told him.

The fence builders, Carlos and Geraldo, whom we'd paid cash the evening before for ripping the invasive multi-flora rose out of the hedgerow, were due any minute. After they'd left last night, I had taken down seven panels of raggedy-ass wire fence. I had attached a chain—so heavy that I could not pick the whole thing up at once—to one end of the fence, wrapped it around and around the wire, and was preparing to pull out one short sec-tion, two panels, of fence at a time. Put the tractor in gear. It strained. Pushed the power lever, a little more, a little more. The chain was taut. The tractor leaned against it. And then suddenly the tractor took off going way too fast across the paddock, the horses and ponies, who had been grazing and watching me from a safe distance, snorting and bucking and galloping away, and the entire fence, plus a rusted-out steel gate, hopping and dancing and clanging behind us. This, I had not meant to do. I jumped off the tractor, ran to the barn, got a bucket of oats and called the horses and ponies before they realized that if they so desired they could wander onto our lawn and jog out the driveway, through the open gate, and onto Manor Road with its speeding cars. Caught Riderwood, my lackadaisical timber horse, and Warfield. Snapped shanks on their halters. Walked them up through the gate to the top paddock while Saitensohn, my hurdle horse from Germany, and the two fat pure-bred Welsh ponies, Silver Charm and Eloquence, followed. This would be temporary. Not much grass, no shade, too many flies, and no stream for water. Worked until dark, pulling out the weed trees and rusty steel posts along the old fence line, preparing for the two young men.

The morning sun already warming my back, I fussed about,

set up a plumb line, got the tools ready for the three of us. Stepped into the kitchen at 8:30. "Don't hold your breath," Ansley said.

By 9:00, I had drunk too much coffee. Started to dig the holes myself with the rickety sixty-year old hand-held post-hole digger. Hit rock.

Ansley called me in—gave me breakfast: scrambled eggs, crisply fried Virginia ham, buttermilk pancakes with maple syrup, orange juice, melon, English muffins. I topped it off by brewing a fresh pot of coffee. Sipping the coffee, we chatted about the progress we were making on our many farm projects as she straightened the kitchen, and I felt my strength returning.

Everything was ready. Where were my muscular young men who said we did not need a gasoline-powered post-hole digger, who both grinned, showing off the whitest of teeth, held their arms out like body builders and tensed their muscles? Where were they with their thick triceps and deltoids for banging that post-hole digger into the hard clay and then pulling it filled with dirt and rocks out of the hole hundreds and hundreds of times in the debilitating heat? Where were they who said about the heat, "This is nothing."

I sipped my coffee, let my body absorb the breakfast, watched Ansley maneuver around the kitchen in her nightgown. Her back was sore from building a rock wall earlier in the week. I said I had just the right thing, jogged up the stairs, got a small canister of all-natural Amish pain relief ointment that I'd meant to give Tom for Christmas for his sore knee, and a tube of mentholated gel.

She stood before me, placed her hands on the counter, lifted her night gown exposing her fanny and lower back, pointed to the narrow area just above the little patch of soft blonde hairs on her coccyx.

I applied the Amish cure-all. She arched her back at the coldness of it and I couldn't believe the situation and for the first time hoped to hell the Mexican team did not show up all. I was filthy from carrying the posts and the boards, sawdust and rust from old nails and black grit from old boards all over my shorts and arms and bare chest. And there before me was the long strong white marble back narrowing into the slender white marble waist before spreading out to two perfectly smooth gentle white marble cheeks—a life-size sculpture of luxurious, voluptuous curves and I couldn't believe she had agreed to do this. The ointment was quickly absorbed. In case the healthy stuff didn't have much kick, it was now time for the chemicals. I squeezed the green gel that will sometimes come out in a ball and bounce/roll right off your skin. Squeezed an amoeba-shaped blob of it—its fluorescent, eerie, blue-green, radioactive color and its silly-putty texture did make you wonder what it was made of—onto her back and rubbed and massaged it in, leaning into her, putting my weight into it, wanting to draw out that ache, knowing she would soon feel a glowing, burning, icy-hot sensation.

My thoughts drifted off course, here and there, and then to my distant relative Walt Whitman and "I Sing the Body Electric," parts of which I would not be reading to my students.

> This is the female form,
> A divine nimbus exhales from it from head to foot, . . .
> I am drawn by its breath as if I were no more than a helpless
>   vapor . . .all falls aside but myself and it,
> Books, art, religion, time . . the visible and solid earth . . the
>   atmosphere and the fringed clouds . . what was expected
>   of heaven or feared of hell are now consumed, . . .
> Hair, bosom, hips, bend of legs, negligent falling hands—all
>   diffused . . . mine too diffused,
> . . . . loveflesh swelling and deliciously aching,
> Limitless limpid jets of love hot and enormous . . . . quivering
>   jelly of love . . . . white-blow and delirious juice, . . .

"That's good," she said, standing straight, pulling her nightgown down and grinningly looking into my eyes. "Now we've got to build this fence."

"What?" I laughed. "You and me?"

"Yes."

I went out, pulled on my leather gloves and starting digging postholes. Soon, she came out in a pair of my old cut-off khakis and a thread-bare Gilman School T-shirt, her only pair of tennis shoes, and on her little, knobby fingers—now with the arthritis, I must massage those fingers, why not with the Amish ointment?—our emerald engagement ring and diamond wedding ring.

She watched me lift the rickety posthole digger, holding its five-foot long handles, pound the two curved steel plates into the hole, spread the handles wide, clamp the steel plates together, slide my hands half way down the handles, lift the digger out, a handful of dirt and rocks caught in the jaw of the plates, swing it to my side and drop the contents—this one continuous movement being almost an exact replication of the "tonging" for oysters I had done a life-time ago on the Chesapeake Bay before spending the winter dredging for oysters on a skipjack. "You need a heavy-duty post-hole digger," she said. She made some calls, drove up to the hardware store, bought a new post-hole digger; nuts and bolts, gudgeon and pintel for the gate; and a ball of string, returned, and with her bare hands picked up the shockingly heavy six-foot steel bar and started breaking up the clay and rocks two feet down in a hole. She moved to a new site, grabbed a shovel, started to dig, and progressed, as she'd seen me doing, from using the shovel to using the steel bar to using the new post-hole digger. We dug through the morning, through hard-baked clay and omnipresent rocks.

We began to set the posts. I held a post steady while she scooped dirt into the hole. "Is it straight?" she asked.

"Yes, yes, it's fine."

"How do you know it's straight?"

"What do you mean? I can tell."

"No you can't. Where's the level?"

I sighed, released the post and headed for the garage. "We need the ball of string too. It's on the counter in the kitchen."

We set the two posts at either end and one post on the turn. We tied the horizontal string to the two far posts, ran it around the middle post so that the inside of the posts ran down its length. She used the level—making sure every post was perfectly straight, and she eyed the taut string, making sure the posts were in a per-fect row. Down on her bare knees, emeralds and diamond glis-tening on her hands, scooping dirt and stones into a hole while I held the post, beads of sweat dripping from her nose, she looked up at me, blue eyes suddenly sparkling and wide open, dilated, and said, "Do you like my organizing?"

"Yes," I said. "Yes, I love your organizing. I'm looking for-ward to you organizing me tonight."

We laughed and continued with our work. I fell into a role I've learned to adopt over the years, lost focus on the big picture but continued to push myself along, knowing she'd keep me going in

the right direction. My thoughts spun back to New Year's Eve. . .
. "*I love you because you are so cute and so funny,*" *I'd stated, thinking, that was number six; I had to make it to ten. My wife of thirty-five plus years wanted ten reasons why I loved her. It was late. The snow was billowing down; we had just returned from a peaceful and moving New Year's dinner at Atlanta Hall Farm with Tom and Mimi. We were on the couch by the fire.*

"Are you making fun of me?" she'd asked.

"No. No. You are funny. You were so funny tonight and so cute."

"OK, that's number six. What's number seven?"

I heard the rhythms, the peaceful meter of the lines, the first line, the sound of a woman's voice and then parts of a poem being spoken:

How do I love thee? Let me count the ways.
I love thee to the depth and breadth and height
My soul can reach, when feeling out of sight
For the ends of Being and ideal Grace.
I love thee to the level of every day's
Most quiet need, by sun and candlelight.
I love thee freely, as men strive for Right. . . .

"You are organized," I answered.

"Do you like my organizing?"

"I love it. I want you to organize me all night long," I said.

"That's seven, Sweetheart. That's seven. What's number eight?"

"I love your endurance, your strength, your resilience," I said, thinking that these were admirable traits, not ones usually associated with love, but why not, and they were so much a part of her. "I love how you can walk all day and into the night through the streets of Paris, New York or London. I love how you can hike without the slightest sign of fatigue up and down the Adirondack Mountains, along a Florida beach, or through the redwoods of the Big Sur campground just north of the Henry Miller Library."

"That's nice, I like it. Go on."

"I love how you can work. I've never seen anyone get so much accomplished in one day, in one hour, in my life."

I was thinking of the last two years, my mother being sick and dying and Ansley organizing everything: the over-powering wave of doctors' appointments, the dozens of emergency ward visits, the weekly trips to the dialysis nightmare of a clinic—don't remind me of those lazy, careless, do-nothing bastards and that heartless doctor! After Mom died, Ansley kept going, organizing the funeral, the wake. Then, when we bought Prospect Farm from my sisters, our childhood farm with its 200-year-old house and all its aches and pains and anachronisms, and sold our newly purchased, newly built modern house with its modern conveniences, she organized the entire move—the second move in two years—in the heat of the worst drought in fifty years. She packed and moved out of the house we had just settled into; cleaned out, cleaned up, and repaired Mom's house, and commandeered a battalion of plumbers, well-diggers, electricians, carpenters, painters, stone masons, roofers for three months, working from seven in the morning to ten at night, every single day, all June, July, and August.

She hadn't had one day off, one weekend away, one vacation for two straight years, and when that brazen self-proclaimed "landscape architect" sat there in his skid loader and looked out over our farm and house—the well-diggers banging away, the head of the tree crew revving his chain saw high up in his cherry picker and sawing through limbs which his men grabbed and fed into the rip-roaring mouth of the chipper, the prima donna carpenter arriving to work at noon in his fancy van with the carved black walnut shelves and then staying, sawing and hammering and whining about how difficult the job was until 10:00 p.m., the roofers hiking across our fraying asphalt shingles, the stone mason laying the cinder blocks for the entrance to the cellar, the plumbers driving their trucks across the lawn, killing the last vestiges of grass, and lugging the new pump, the new hot water heater and the new water purifier system down through the new Bilco door, down the steep new steps into the cellar which we had just finished reinventing, turning the dirt floor into a concrete floor, taking out the seventy-five-year-old pickup truck size furnace and leaky, rusted, deserted oil tanks, sistering the termite-gnawed beams and jacking the sway-backed house up three inches in some places, six inches in others, money pouring out of our savings accounts, gushing out of our retirement funds, coming from places where we didn't even have money, from credit card accounts, from the sale of old stocks, from the board of horses and ponies we took on—when that landscape architect, feet propped up on the dashboard of his air-conditioned skid loader, not a drop of sweat on him, asserted, "What you really need here is a contractor to organize all this." I replied, "Listen, my wife is smarter, and quicker, and more organized"—yes, there it is again—"than any goddamn contractor on the East Coast, and you'd better get back to work."

The northwest wind was buffeting the house, rattling the old living room windows.

> Learning to love differently is hard,
> love with the hands wide open, love
> with the doors banging on their hinges,
> the cupboard unlocked, the wind
> roaring and whimpering in the rooms
> rustling the sheets and snapping the blinds
> that thwack like rubber bands
> in an open palm.
>
> — "To have without holding," Marge Piercy

I got up off the couch, set a few splintery slices of oak fence board on the dimming flames, then two quarter-sections of a big ash log that had been filled with knots and particularly tough to split. I poured some more wine, sat down. "Do I have endurance?" she asked, taking a sip of the red wine, the glass reflecting the flames of the fire.

"Yes, you do," I said.

Lunch. "That's probably enough for today," I said at 1:00, thinking I had no more left in me, not wanting to overdo it. We could have a well-deserved lunch, retire upstairs, relax on this peaceful Sunday afternoon with no one around. Then, I could read another chapter of Allison Weir's fascinating biography of the indomitable and inspiring Eleanor of Aquitaine and fall asleep.

She grinned knowingly at me. Made sandwiches while I slumped at the counter. Revived, I was out beside her digging and tamping and eyeing the taut horizontal line and the level.

By late afternoon, the sun had swung around the barn so that we were no longer working in the shade. There was no breeze. It'd be nice to walk through our side-paddock, climb the fence, traipse past the neighbors' ducks and duck house on the edge of the pond, cross the lawn, and jump into the cold water of their deep pool. We tamped in the last post, stood back and admired our work: twenty-five posts, like sentries, ready to do their job. "OK," I said. "That's about it for me today. Let's go for a swim."

"I'd love to get these boards up. Come on, we can finish this today."

I laughed at the absurdity of the remark.

"Don't you want to get the horses back out in the big field?"

I walked into the coolness of the kitchen, made an ice-cold drink, sat on the back porch sipping it while watching her water the flowers and listening to her rhapsody about the hummingbird that was zooming back and forth from the water-feeder to her tiny eggs in the nest in the far corner of the porch.

Back out. I was worried my Eleanor of Aquitaine would get splinters. Gave her my gloves. She pulled them on, said they were too big, she couldn't work in them. We lifted two sixteen-foot oak boards. The weight was too much. We carried one board at a time out to the line of posts. I'd already laid one board, which I thought of as the top board, beside each set of three posts—or one panel. We carried twenty-five middle boards out, setting each beside its top board. Then, we carried twenty-five bottom boards out, setting each beside the top and middle board. A three-board fence.

The posts were up in a line—the thin piece of string, the horizontal plumb line, running straight down the row just barely touching each post. The new boards, chestnut colored with darker splotches where the wood was still sappy, were set in a line beneath the string.

"OK, looks good," I said, surveying the pleasingly straight line of securely tamped in posts and ready-to-be nailed boards. I let it hang. Held my breath, waiting for a reply.

She bustled around, stacked some old boards filled with rusty nails away from our work area. "Yup," she said, stopping and giving what we'd accomplished a look, "let's get the hammers and nails."

A sinking sensation enveloped me.

"And we need a tape measure."

Starting at the bottom, we marked every post where the top of each board would be, three marks: one twelve inches up for the bottom board, the second twenty inches up for the middle board, the third forty inches up for the third board. None of our horses or ponies would be trying to jump this fence onto the stone surface of our future patio; we were making it lower than the paddock fences. We wanted the horses to put their heads over this fence. We wanted to be able to sit and look over the fence at the horses and the stream and the field beyond.

The bending over to pick things up, the kneeling down and getting back up, was becoming an effort. Ansley loves making exact measurements. I don't. I stood, held the tape measure as she kneeled on her bare knees in the clay and stones around each post, and with a nail scraped a mark, then—not content with just an inch-long mark—scraped the nail back and forth a few times the full width of the post, first for the bottom board, then the middle, then the top. I watched her hands. The sun's rays danced on the diamond of our wedding ring. Soon, she was holding one end of the board, pushing it against a post. I was holding the other end, leaning my hip, or my knee, or my shoulder into the board, and hammering in the nails.

We continued down the line, not talking now, marking all twenty-five posts. My right hand and wrist—injured in a fall in a steeplechase race that spring—were shot. I could keep on with them but I would pay a price the next day. I started each nail by holding it with my left hand and hammering it with my right until it caught. I finished by hammering with my left, improving my swing as we progressed.

I was content with one nail per spot for now. When I paused to drink some ice-water or to get more nails, Ansley took the other hammer and banged in a second nail.

"These nails are expensive. They're case-hardened nails. You don't need to put so many nails in the boards. It just makes them crack."

"You need at least two," she said. "I don't want the boards to warp."

Good point, good point.

"Besides," she said, "I like hammering."

"Well just remember, they're expensive."

We banged and hammered. I got grumpy when everything didn't go right with hanging the gate.

"Stop, just stop, you're rushing."

I was rushing, leaning into the electric drill, burrowing a hole that I knew was too wide for the pintel. Needed a drill bit one size smaller and didn't have it.

"I am *not* fucking rushing," I said, making a mess, pouring wood glue into the hole. Tried to push the glue into the hole with my pocketknife, a favorite, given me by our middle child, Andrew, back in our camping days. The glue dripped down the post, over the tortoise shell knife handle, across my hands, onto my boots. I pushed the pintel into the hole. The glue gushed back out. My temper was rising. Should've stopped earlier, I thought. Should've stopped earlier but she just had to keep pushing me, and now look…. at any second I could fly off, spin out of control. We were completely finished with the exception of this damn gate that we really didn't need anyway. We had two hundred and fifty feet of board fence up and now these two three-quarter inch holes were making the entire fence ineffective. I was on the verge of throwing the tool chest across the rocks and weeds that would one day be the patio, on the verge of picking up the steel gate and smashing it against the fence.

Out of the house she came, holding a bundle of long wooden matchsticks. She stuck three sticks in one hole, spread them apart into a triangular shape. They stuck out too far. "Give me your knife. I handed her the knife covered in quickly drying glue. She gave me a look, shook her head, wiped the glue off the blade. She handed me the matchsticks. I held them against the top of the board, in a line. She cut each one at just the right spot. She stuck three in the top hole. I pushed the pintel into the hole, tapped it with a hammer, then screwed it in the rest of the way. Goal accomplished. We did the same with the other hole.

Finished hanging the gate, she kept moving—putting the tools away, cleaning up. And then, we looked and we marveled. Neat, its lines crisp, the boards straight and parallel to one another, looking like something you'd love to gallop into and soar over, the entire fence line was up and we could not stop admiring it. "Hold on," I said. I jogged over to the side paddock, opened the gate. Warfield burst into the field, Saitensohn and Riderwood came galloping out, then the plump ponies, Silver Charm and Eloquence. All five tore around, jumped the stream, came to a simultaneous and sudden stop. The horses reared and bucked and farted, dug with their front feet and started rolling while the ponies immediately put their heads down and began to graze.

We watched and laughed. "OK, let's take a shower."

"Yes," she said, surprising me, and strode to the house, into the kitchen. I could hear the washing machine start to whirl and swash and wash. I heard the French jazz CD she likes start up. I stood there, half of me headed for the house, the other half leaning toward the garage, wondering what I would decide. The vertical posts were jutting three to four inches above the horizontal top boards of the fence. They were like uneven teeth, like fangs where a smooth white row should be.

I wondered if I had the strength and steadiness and cool-headedness to finish it—to get the chain saw out, hold the saw sideways and roar-buzz an even, level cut along the edge of each horizontal oak board and through each locust post. I sat for a few seconds, took an inventory of my energy level. Images of what could happen, what could go wrong if I made a mistake, flitted through my mind. I decided I would go slowly, methodically, safely, not rushing, not taking any chances.

I put on safety goggles, pulled leather gloves back on, studied the chain saw, started it, full concentration, total focus. I braced my elbow against my chest, focused on the invisible line I would cut, and began while hearing the earthy, farm rhythms of Robert Frost's voice. Over the spring semester, I'd shown my class of juniors (an all-time favorite—coed—made up of boys from Gilman, and girls from Bryn Mawr and Roland Park Schools, all three within a short walk of each other in northern Baltimore) a short film on Frost during which he'd recited "Out, Out –" I could distinctly hear the low, gravelly, metrical cadence:

> The buzz saw snarled and rattled in the yard
> And made dust and dropped stove-length sticks of wood,
> Sweet-scented stuff when the breeze drew across it.

I could hear his intonation as my saw roared. I pictured a girl up on the porch of a farmhouse calling out for her brother—who was working with his father, proving himself at the end of a chainsaw—to come to dinner. I heard her ringing a bell, and pictured and heard our old porch bell. Then, I heard:

> His sister stood beside them in her apron
> To tell them "Supper." At the word, the saw,
> As if to prove saws knew what supper meant,
> Leaped out of the boy's hand, or seemed to leap –
> He must have given the hand. However it was,

Neither refused the meeting. But the hand!
The boy's first outcry was a rueful laugh…

Lastly, there was that image. I didn't think of any words. I just saw the image:

. . . As he swung toward them holding up the hand
half in appeal, but half as it to keep
the life from spilling. . . .

I leaned into my work, feeling I was a part of this saw, a part of this fence, a part of this farm. I was imagining myself standing in my classroom, trying to bring the synergy—the joining of Shakespeare, Frost, Faulkner—at this exact moment, to life: MacBeth's lines of despair on hearing of Lady MacBeth's suicide—

. . . Out, out, brief candle!
Life's but a walking shadow, a poor player
That struts and frets his hour upon the stage
And then is heard no more. . . .

from which Frost takes the title of his poem; Faulkner writing a novel as if "told by an idiot," the title of which—*The Sound and the Fury*—he takes from the last lines of MacBeth's lament—

. . . It (life) is a tale
Told by an idiot, full of sound and fury
Signifying nothing.

My saw roared. Its oily, smoky exhaust clung to me. Its chain ripped through the posts, spraying sawdust across my chest.

I began to plan how I would make my students feel the power of this moment. I laughed to myself as an image passed through my mind: setting a duffel bag on the battered World War II Army desk, unzipping it, pulling out this chainsaw now in my hands.

Realizing I was getting loopy, I bore down on the saw, pushing the chain through another post. My mind leapt to a scene in the Scandinavian novel *Out Stealing Horses* where Petterson does an artful job showing the pleasure of sawing wood, somehow (using Hemingway's minimalistic "tip-of-the-iceberg" techniques) getting the feel of it down just right—the feel I was now having, ten posts sawed, fifteen to go—while also, between the lines, hinting at the upcoming betrayal and infidelity of the farmer's beautiful wife. . . . I gladly did not have that problem, but the saw was becoming heavier. The sweat was pouring off me. The roar of its engine and the rattle and ripping of its chain was echoing in my skull. I pulled myself together.

Steadily, I marched down the line, cutting off each post at the exact height of the board nailed to it, beveling it so that it was lower on the lawn/future patio side and slanted upward toward the paddock side. Driving me was one thought, one image: walking to the car with Ansley and stopping to show her this work—completely finished.

Into the shower. I could barely move. She energetically soaped her entire body. I'd never seen anything as beautiful as when she put her face in the stream of hot water, pulled her hair back behind her ears and the pellets of water bounced off her face, rivulets ran down over her breasts and stomach and legs taking along the soap and suds and foam. I soaped and scrubbed her broad back. Walt:

> The female contains all qualities and tempers them,
> She is in her place and moves with perfect balance,
> She is all things duly veiled, she is both passive and active,
> She is to conceive daughters as well as sons, and sons as well
>   as daughters.

> As I see my soul reflected in Nature,
> As I see through a mist, One with inexpressible completeness,
>   sanity beauty,
> See the bent head and arms folded over the breast, the Female
>   I see.

We walked out the back door, headed for the car and dinner. I cleared my throat, looking at the fence line in the fading light. She looked. It didn't click immediately, the change. She glanced at me, then back at it again. Her face lit up with a big smile and she said, "Oh Sweetheart—it's perfect now, just perfect."

In Its Own Orbit

Tt's late-June. It's early-July. It's late-July. The race is coming up. The A. P. Smithwick Memorial. Every year the date nears, the pressure increases, the excitement builds, post time is in minutes, gamblers rush to the windows, the tape is dropped and the horses are off and running. August—Thoroughbred racing at Saratoga Springs, New York. The best racing in the world. Each decade ushers in a fresh generation of riders. A few veteran trainers fade away; their sons pick up the trade. New, fresh horses run. New owners with new money stand in the paddock. And the A. P. Smithwick—a bulkhead against the roiling whitewater of time, a celebration of my father "Paddy," Racing Hall of Fame steeplechase legend—remains the same: 2 1/16 miles over hurdles, fast.

Time flows differently at Saratoga. It passes in an unreal, dreamlike state—the town, the lakes, the majestic trees; the horses, Oklahoma training track, the barns, the beauty of the main track and the irreplaceable century-old clubhouse; the betting, the Bentleys, the wads of twenty and hundred dollar bills; the bars, the restaurants, the late nights dancing; the early morning screwdrivers and fresh melons; the early evening scotch, roast beef, perfectly ripened tomatoes and just-picked corn on the cob all remaining consistent, unchanging, pooled in a deep reservoir, while friends, relatives and I launch ourselves, incrementally changed each year, into the current: we marry, have children, introduce them to the Spa, develop careers, leave racing, return

31

to racing, lose the youthful money-making ability to pick winners through hunches, lose the endurance to get by on a few hours sleep per night, gain the wisdom to savor every moment.

When I reflect on past experiences—whether riding my bike around town as an adolescent or riding races as a youth, whether arising at 5:30 and going to the barn with my father or thirty years later arising at 5:30 and going to the barn with my best friend—they are recorded in a different manner from my outside-of-Saratoga memories.

Most of the *time* in my life has seemed to have existed as if time were a steadily flowing river and I am with it, the river and I are one; we don't change much day-to-day or year-to-year, and yet, as we surge and flood, slow and swirl, we see that life and people and places on shore are changing and before we know it, a birthday is coming up, a class reunion is planned, an anniversary is approaching, and it's a big one—a decade has gone by. Two decades have gone by. In September of 2016, four decades will have gone by, and it will be Ansley's and my fortieth anniversary.

But when I look back at Saratoga, I see the year as an oval, like a racetrack, much like the mile and an eighth main track at Saratoga. The oval is stretched out, with winter at the top—white and gray; summer on the bottom—faded green, yellow; spring on the left—a lush green; fall on the right—rust. August is an exception; it is red and it is shimmering, flickering. Down on the bottom, right before the track heads up into fall, it intensifies for four weeks: brighter, even more heat, faster paced, much faster, a daily lifestyle like no other, little sleep, much gaiety, go-go-go, action, meeting new people, seeing old friends, making incredible connections, spending money, dishing out twenty dollar bills like they're ones, and racing—horses, fast horses, the fastest in the world, running day after day as Rolls Royces roll by, actors and millionaire investment bankers step up to the $100 betting window, jockeys head to the jocks' room and the "hot box" to sweat off another three pounds, trainers stand outside their barns talking to owners.

One trainer speaks intently to four septuagenarian Louisville boys, fraternity brothers, who've just bought a yearling at the Fasig Tipton sales the night after my father's race for half a million, then turns and speaks just as intensely to one of the last of the old-time grooms, also a septuagenarian, a slim, fit black man from Camden, South Carolina, who knows more about how to take care of a horse than anyone in the barn—his father rubbed horses, his grandfather rubbed horses—and who doesn't have enough in the bank to retire and who doesn't give a damn, he doesn't want to retire, he doesn't have much time left, he's racing time, and this new half-million-dollar colt in the stall behind him is going to be his big horse next year; this new horse will be taking him to Churchill Downs the first weekend in May.

Saratoga is brighter, hotter—the parts are moving; it's like a Mondrian, like *Broadway Boogie Woogie*, but not still, not stationery; the shapes are moving, they're hopping, they're popping, they're dancing, to jazz, to my father's favorite, Louis Armstrong singing *Mack the Knife*.

The August memories are not part of the gallop around the annual track of time. They are separate. They are sections of the oval, which are taken out, and which exist one on top of the other; they are mini-ovals that exist in the full annual oval of life, and, they are not arranged chronologically. They are pancakes which can be shuffled like a deck of cards in my mind. Records—that's better. Vinyl albums. Each visit to Saratoga is imprinted on a beautiful, black, slick, light-weight, full-frequency 33 1/3 speed LP equipped with stereophonic sound as well as the added feature of full color cinematography. They are on the shelf of my mind, and they are not neatly stacked; they're spread out, and they're out of order. If I want to recall one summer's visit to Saratoga, I put four or five of them from that period on the turnstile, all at once, and start playing them.

There are the great memories: winning a hurdle race on Tote'm Home II at Saratoga, Pop the trainer, Emmett Grayson and Jack the Indian the grooms, when I was eighteen. Two years later, winning again, this time on Wild Amber, Pop the trainer. I can recall in my body how we started to make our move coming around the turn and heading down the stretch into the last fence, how each horse jumped the last fence—this back when there *was* a last fence on the stretch—how we passed the lead horses, and exactly what it felt like going under the wire, in front, pulling up, easing up, standing up in the irons, galloping out, jogging through the gap, out onto the flat track, and then cantering back to Pop waiting for me by the winner's circle.

Then my mind will slip to an album I'd rather forget: the time

I rode eighteen-hands plus Limbo at Saratoga in a maiden hurdle, the tree of the saddle broke, the saddle slid up on his neck, and I got run off with, opened up twelve lengths on the field, my feet banging together under his neck.

Another album—more recent, the summer Jonathan Kiser, Tom Voss's star jockey, died from an accident unrelated to horses, Ansley, our children—Paddy, Andrew, Eliza—and I were up at the Adirondacks on our annual vacation. Ansley encouraged me to ask Tom if he needed help. We pulled up stakes, drove home to Maryland for Jonathan's funeral, then I hopped in the car with Tom, drove back up to Saratoga and first day had the bike crash— cut up my face and forehead. Mimi, Tom's wife, had to take me to the emergency ward. One half of my face, for a week, looked terrible: raw, leaking puss, swollen, stitches on chin, stitches on forehead. When Mimi and I returned from the emergency ward, it was late afternoon and Tom was seated on the edge of his bed looking at his bare feet. He held a small Band-Aid in his hand over his big toe. He looked up at me as if I'd just walked in from a nap, made no recognition of my condition, and asked, "Can you put this Band-Aid on my blister. I can't reach it." Mimi released a four-letter word, and then couldn't help but chuckle.

I galloped Tom's horses for two weeks—he even put me on the payroll, meaning he convinced his bookkeeper (Mimi) that I was worth it, and had her write out the check. I can remember him, beamingly proud and upbeat, sitting across the table from me in Sperry's, pulling the check out of his wallet, signing it and handing it to me.

A decade ago, Tom and I rode out in the morning, criticizing and ridiculing a couple our age (his owners) for drinking, smoking, and partying so late the night before. Then, we both started laughing. What old farts we were becoming! It wasn't long ago that we had gone out and hadn't come back until the sun was coming up. I have had some of the most special Tom-moments in my life ambling back to the Annex on a horse of Tom's, Tom alongside on the "pony"—either retired jumper Mickey Free or retired champion flat horse John's Call—quietly walking, taking in the barns and horses and riders and owners, the panoply of Saratoga, and talking to each other in low voices. I'd be on his horse for the A. P. Smithwick, returning from the main track,

the trainers and riders and handicappers all tipping their hats to him. He'd stop and trade jokes with a few. The old-timer now. The veteran trainer. Billy Turner would jog out, say hi to us both. Jimmy Murphy, Scotty Schulhoffer, Leo O'Brien, Pat Myer—Tom took me past their barns. They were all friends of Pop's. They'd stop work, pat my horse, pat Tom's, have a few words. Share the moment, the shimmering, spinning moment when time for the group of us, different generations, merged; we were on two, three, four spinning records—the disc jockey with fast hands working the turntables, lacing their recordings into one new recording of the present—all brought together by my father.

At Saratoga, when I see the twelve-horse barn just across from the track kitchen in Horse Haven my mind leaps to Pop and Tom and Emmett and Jack the Indian and Mike the Englishman. It seems a lifetime ago, like someone else's life. I can feel it, feel the textured wool of the blue and white checkered blankets we threw over the horses on the chilly mornings after they'd galloped and been washed in steaming soapy water; I can smell it, inhale the dashes of pine oil Emmett poured in the wash water; smell the clean, wet clover after the hay man dropped it off; smell the soaped leather of the saddles and bridles in the tack room mingling with the smoke of Pop's Pall Mall; feel the smooth curvature of the indentation in the dirt one step from the tack room and the worn spot in the old floor board, the first step into the tack room. I can feel the tension of Pop giving me a leg up on Wild Amber knowing we were going out for a school on National Steeplechase and Hunt Day with hundreds of spectators and an announcer there, and the race coming up, and knowing my great friend Mike White just ten barns down, was getting a leg up from his father, and soon we'd be going a turn-of-the-field head-and-head. I can feel the pain and strain in my arms and fear in my body, leaning back, pulling as hard as I can, my irons jacked up higher than usual, the reins covered in sweat and sliding through my fingers, having to reach back, pull my bandana out of my back pocket, slap it across one rein, our pace quickening, quickening, trainers and grooms leaning on the outside rail of Oklahoma watching as the unreal-sized Limbo threw his head, trying to wrench the reins out of my hands, took his gigantic strides, and they all wondered if he would take off, run off, crash through the outside rail with me at any minute. I can remember the early 6:00 a.m.

calm, the faint mist coming up off the wet grass, Emmett and Jack quietly finishing mucking out their stalls. I can taste the steaming hot, raunchy, racetrack kitchen coffee—black—feel it in my mouth and going down into my empty, shrunken stomach as I set out the tack, preparing to get on the first horse of the morning, Pop in the chair outside the tack room, cigarette in mouth, legal pad in lap, writing down the sets. I can smell the sweetness of his cup of coffee, made with sugar and cream, mix with the scent of burning tobacco leaves, as, carrying my tack, I walk past him.

More recently, one morning, after finishing galloping for Tom, I walked into the Racing Hall of Fame on Union Avenue just down and across from the main entrance to the track, checking in before my daughter Eliza—just out of college—and I had a book signing there later in the day. I was in boots, blue jeans, and polo shirt. I stepped through the doors, walked toward the book store, and there before me was a life-size photo of Pop. He is younger than I. I'm older than he lived to be. He is in his twenties. He is in blue jeans, boots and polo shirt, and he is wearing the exact same "tooled" belt, with the western buckle, that I am wearing, a belt given to Pop by Eddie, Tom's father—who loved the west, especially Arizona and Wyoming.

When I was twelve, thirteen and fourteen I worked for Pop and my Uncle Mikey at the Annex, the outcropping of two long barns off Fifth Avenue just across from Oklahoma training track. In those days, there was a jumping race every afternoon, and it was the third race, after the daily double, so post time was 2:30. In my memory is a strong, clear recording—of polishing my shoes, pulling on coat and tie and going to the races with Mom after working all morning at the Annex walking hots, riding the pony, cleaning tack, raking the walking ring. There's the irreplaceable record—that spins forever in my mind—of standing under the trees in the old spacious paddock just a few feet away from the circling, jigging horses, watching Pop in the Old Rose—pink—with the yellow collar and cuff silks of Mrs. Ogden Phipps, or the dark blue silks with cerise cross sashes of Mrs. Theodore Randolph, or the black and green striped silks of June McKnight—listening to Mikey, Mikey giving him a leg up, and then Pop and the horse, and the other horses and riders—Tommy Walsh, Scotty Schulhoffer, Evan Jackson, Jimmy Murphy, each a close friend of my father's and like an uncle to me—filing out under the clubhouse and onto the track as the bugler plays the Call to the Post and then Fred Capossella in his inimitable way calls out, "The horses ... are on ... the track," and ten minutes later, "The fans are moving down to the rail. That can mean only one thing: It is now post time." Pop would win or finish in the money. After the race, we'd hang around outside the jocks' room, buying a lemonade at the little stand run by Sadie, a kind and generous black woman who took interest in our lives. Mom would be relaxed for the first time all day. My sister Sue Sue, a year younger, would be playing tag with the children of other jockeys. Pop would step out of the jocks room, showered, hair perfectly parted, in coat and tie. Mom and Sue Sue would return to the house. I'd hop in the car with Pop and we'd shoot over to the Annex where Pop would check over the horse he'd just ridden, help feed and water, and talk to the men before stopping by Scotty's Paddock for a drink on the way home.

And then, there's this separate track on the LP of those years: Speedy is there at the Annex. Speedy Kiniel, who takes care of me all morning—keeping an eye out for me. He is young, fit, fast, lithe, strong, black. Most grooms rub three horses. Some four. Speedy rubs six. The shedrow in front of his stalls is perfectly raked, not one loose stalk of hay or straw marring the criss-cross patterns he's made in the dirt with his rake. "Don't you touch my rake!" He's customized it, bent each tine just so. The runner—a rubber-sheathed chain at hip height stretching across the opening of the stall—is taut and glistening black. Below the runner, the webbing—with a total of three snaps attached to three screw eyes on either side—is also taut and clean.

Each halter is hanging on a nail high up outside the stall, the leather glistening from the afternoon's cleaning, still damp from the saddle soap and Lexol; the brass fittings are reflecting the afternoon rays and giving off the metallic, sharp, sinus-scouring scent of the cleaning polish.

Each horse had been washed after his gallop that morning, cooled out, and Speedy has rubbed—really rubbed—and brushed each horse's body and legs. The manes lie over on the correct side. Each horse has a set of clean white bandages on the front legs. Not too tight—bad for the tendons. Not too loose—could come off and be dangerous. The shiny safety pins are stuck perfectly on the outside, and those tendons and sesamoids and ankles and knees inside the bandages—Speedy has rubbed and soothed and massaged Bigeloil or rubbing alcohol or Bowie Mud onto them until each of those six horses feels like he has the fresh, never-strained, sizzling-with-the-desire-to-gallop-to-breeze-to-fly legs of a two-year-old. The morning of work, the afternoon of work is over.

Alfonso—Speedy's sleepy-eyed, philosophic, slow-drinking brother—strolls over to the wheelbarrow-load size of damp clover under a tree, pulls out a six-pack of dew-beaded beer bottles. The men sit on bales of straw and drink their cold beers talking about the fights at the rec center that night. Willie Dixon, whose father is a flat trainer, Mike White and I have been talking about these fights for a week.

Speedy has his long jet-black hair in a conk—"A conk, man! You know, a conk – pompadour style"—and a black silk bandana tightly wrapped over it. Junior's there, quiet Junior Tibbs, with his cannonball shoulders. He'll be fighting that night. He sips a beer. Speedy turns the beer down. Sips a vodka concoction. Has to keep his weight down. The Smithwick stable will have two fighters entered on this night.

Junior is quiet and confident. He has known who his opponent will be for a few days and is not concerned. Speedy has just discovered he's been matched against a young Italian hot-shot who works over on the main track and who thinks he's the next Rocky Marciano; the short, muscular Italian has been working out on his speed bag outside the bunk house and has been bragging that he's a fighter, a brawler. He comes at whomever steps into the ring and overwhelms him with body blows and aggression; he will intimidate this tall, lanky skinny black boy; he'll show this black boy who has heart. We've scouted him, watched him working out on his speed bag behind his bunkhouse. He holds both fists high to protect his head, peeks through his arms, and leaves his body open. Speedy listens, listens to the men talk, sips his vodka, and now he's up, no fatigue, no slowing down. He begins to circle, he's shadow-boxing around a water bucket set on top of another bucket, moving in towards his opponent, back-pedaling out, dancing in while jab-jab-jabbing, dancing out, all the while circling around and his fists are moving—*pshw pshw pshw, phsw phsw phsw*—faster, his feet faster, sweat is popping out of his forehead. The men are laughing and drinking their beers, Pop is grazing the horse he rode that afternoon, Uncle Mikey is in a stall feeling a horse's legs, and I'm breaking a sweat just thinking about the fight that night. I can't wait. Mike, Willie and I are going to ride our bikes over. This album spins and spins. The early mornings with my father, the afternoons at the races with my mother, then back at the Annex with my father and the men— and the fights at night. It spins on the self-perpetuating turntable that I don't want to stop.

Yet how about the year Tom trained Mickey Free to win the APS. Gregg Morris rode him. Coming into the last, it looked like Mickey was going to be second. We knew he'd run through the stretch with all his heart but he didn't have a great burst of speed. Galloping into the last, the jockey on the lead horse is very relaxed. Looks like he's counting the purse money. Looks like he's thinking about what his first drink will be that night, what he'll have for dinner—whom he'll be dancing with. He approaches the fence, does not ride the horse into it, lets the horse get in too close, the horse trips up and the jockey falls off. We are standing up, roaring, "Come on Mickey! Come on Mickey!" Gregg picks up the stick, hits him once, twice. Two others are gaining on him. Then Gregg hand-rides Mickey under the wire, pulling away from them. We're dancing in the box. I'd schooled Mickey that morning. Mimi owned Mickey. What a night we had. Late—I hid under Tom and Mimi's bed; they climbed in; Tom started to make a move; I jumped out from under the bed—the paparazzi!— and began snapping away with a bright flash. Afterwards, Mimi opened another bottle of champagne. We sipped it in our pajamas, except for Tom—the pajamas part that is; he never owned a pair of shorts or wore any pajamas. He preferred his boxers, whether it was playing tennis or lying in bed drinking champagne.

Places are connected to the flow of time. In life, we often pass through a place consistently with passing through time. I lived in Talbot County on the Eastern Shore of Maryland, worked there, and then left. Talbot County is being a newlywed with Ansley, not having children, not needing much money, not having responsibilities, staying up late, few expenses, sailing under the stars in my customized eighteen-foot boat; one summer writing in the mornings then commuting by canoe two miles up and across the

Miles River to work in the afternoons as a carpenter rebuilding an old house; another year being a reporter, editor and photographer for *The Star Democrat* and *The Daily Banner*; one winter working on the water as a dredge-hand on a skipjack the worst year of the century, 1975—1976, the year the Bay froze up. Talbot County is both a bright *past* place—and a bright past *time* in my mind.

But, with Pop's race: *we never leave Saratoga*. We always go back. It is always there. The winner's circle beckons. The year cycles back around to it. Some years, I've gone there and been on the wagon. Others, I've gone and raised hell. On returning, it's impossible to explain Saratoga in the rushed shorthand of today's dialogue. I've been working as a reporter on newspapers, or as a teacher, or as a director of public relations, or as a freelance writer and rider, and when I've returned to my colleagues and they've asked, "How was Saratoga?" I am at a loss: images of bright silks flashing down the stretch, lines of men and women reading their programs and *Racing Forms* at the betting windows, svelte jockeys standing at ease in the paddock, older, retired men, standing at the bar at the races, lighting their cigars, savoring that first pull, revelers in their twenties and thirties laughing, dancing, buy-ing rounds, clogging the streets around Sperry's at 1:00 a.m., the sound of bands playing on roof tops and out in gardens filling the air, and most of all, the emotion of standing in the winner's circle one year with my sisters Susan—holding McLean, a baby, in one arm, Collin standing by her side—and Sallie; another year with my children Paddy, Andrew and Eliza; later always with Susan's son McLean; once with Pop's great friend Bobby Burke; and thinking of my father, part of me laughing and celebrating the win and another part of me tearing up, choking up, as I stare out, trying to smile at the phalanx of clicking photographers; and for all those years of the A. P. Smithwick Memorial, the arising at 5:30 every morning, having a coffee by myself, warming and loosening up by pedaling to the Annex, tacking up a horse, riding out to the track alongside the fastidious Englishman Bob Witham and Tom, another year alongside Tom's daughter Elizabeth and Tom, another year alongside Jonathan and Tom, then one year I was galloping head and head with Stowe Burke, Bobby Burke's grandson, generations of Tom's riders and grooms coming and going and moving on, unaware of one another, Tom and I remain-ing, back, there at the same barn, same stalls, same track, every year—the riding every morning, getting more and more fit, and then, one day, having to leave, go back to the office, head back to Maryland, leave the grooms and hot walkers and galloping girls and boys I've come to know. After hearing the question "How was Saratoga?" you just can't sum it up, do it justice; you give it a shot, but you're never satisfied with the results.

Saratoga is unreal. It is an unreal step out of time, more unreal and celebratory back when it was a four-week sprint, versus the six-week marathon of today.

Ansley's first trip to Saratoga was with our son Paddy as a baby. Of that album, I remember staying out late showing her the town, returning to a motel room and paying the babysitter, collapsing on the bed without any energy left, and witnessing the most beautiful scene of her breast-feeding our child.

Pick up another album, any album: I'm walking by the jock's room with son Andrew, a seventeen-year-old, five years younger than Paddy. We watch the jocks walking out, headed for their horses in the paddock. I explain to Andrew that's what I did when I was his age. I tell him what the jocks room is like. It suddenly seems to me as if I'd been walking out of there, in boots, britches and silks, just the day before. The man who runs the jocks room introduces himself; he shakes my hand, Andrew's hand. Tells us he knew my father. Asks if there's anything he can do. Yes, I say, we'd like to go in, look around. OK, he says, as soon as all the jocks have left for this race.

One album is the year of jogging beside Eliza on her bike, helping her cross the streets, teaching her how to ride in town—which was also the year of the beads. Ansley and Susan had taken Eliza and Taylor, Kip Elser's daughter, to the bead store, and several other crafts stores in town, and they were at it, night after night, stringing necklaces and bracelets, making favors for our dinner tables, draping the necklaces around Kip's and my necks, planning on going into the business. Kip—Johns Hopkins classmate, fellow steeplechase jockey, highly focused and disciplined bloodstock agent who buys and sells horses all over the world—was all ears, encouraging them, asking about their business model; when Eliza spoke to him he looked her in the eye, paid attention and even added his own ideas—not so many—about the fashion world of beads and bracelets and necklaces.

The year my memoir *Racing My Father* came out, the New York Racing Association set up a table for me outside the jocks' room. Scotty Schulhoffer, Hall of Fame trainer, known for his training of Lemon Drop Kid and other Grade I winners, and one of Pop's best friends, walked up to me, bought a book, talked about my father, how he loved him, how he'd never have another friend like him, and the memories overloaded, flooded my brain synapses with images of Mom and Pop, and Susan, Sallie, and I, as children, along with Tommy Walsh and Jimmy Murphy and Evan Jackson, eating at DeRossi's, the family restaurant owned by Scotty's wife's family.

Flying—an album spins into my mind out of nowhere: I am galloping horses for Dickie Small in Fort Erie, Canada. At the barn at 4:30 a.m., muck out until 5:15, on first horse at 5:30. Eight to ten a morning. Long mornings. We have few riders. We have few grooms. But we're winning races. Dickie is having a ball. Tom has also brought up a string. Dickie has gotten Ansley and I a cottage on Lake Erie. He's brought his Boston Whaler up behind his pickup, and takes us out water skiing. Ansley stuns us with her elegant Florida slaloming. It's late July. Dickie reads in the paper about the upcoming A. P. Smithwick in Saratoga hundreds of miles away. Hands me a credit card: "You'd better go, Pat. Stay as long as you like." I do go: I meet with Mike White, my child-hood friend. We sit on the curb of a Saratoga side-street, talk about our lives, our ambitions in an unusually intense way. That album spins and spins. The needle gets caught in a scratch; over and over I see us in the shade leaning back onto the grass, talking as we used to do as kids when fishing in Yaddo—the big park behind the main track of Saratoga. The image, the conversation—wasn't there something I could have done?—continues. The turntable spins. That was the last time I saw or spoke to Mike.

I have this stack of Saratoga albums in my brain, and the passage of time does not diminish or change the importance of any one record. One containing the images of Mike—red-headed, tall, thin and gifted with a gritty, quick, sinewy and powerful strength—stepping off his bike and heading into a brawl with a town gang, and me lagging behind but upon seeing Mike go under feeling the ecstasy of rage and loyalty as I dove in. Just as powerful is one years later of Paddy, Andrew and I running in the rec center, stopping to do stretches, and listening and watching as two football coaches berated and threatened and chastised their twelve-year-old players doing calisthenics and it was all I could do not to dive in again, Paddy and Andrew saying, "No Dad, no Dad," and on we ran, at that age, in that era, all three of us loving to run—no plans, no routes, no time-tables, running for the joy and camaraderie and serendipity of where it would take us.

One record on top of another. Memories are pulled out of albums from thirty years ago, from forty years ago, from yesterday. They are vivid. They are alive. They exist out there, spinning and wheeling, on their own, disconnected from the regular flow of time, separated and unattached, in their own orbit.

The Open Road with Eliza

A new Saratoga album: peaceful, cruising, coasting, leaving the Spa, passing Albany, driving down the Northway—the wide swath of black asphalt with the white stripes down the middle foreshortening into the vast mountains of sky-piercing trees ahead, cruising along early Sunday morning with the rest of America headed home after a week's vacation, or, with boat on trailer behind, and kids piled in the back, going out for a day on the water, the sky a gradually brightening blue with a flotilla of staid and dignified east-ward drifting cumulus clouds disregarding us—I was thinking, *that's it*, my last big signing of the summer. The die is cast on this book, *Flying Change*. I will do the upcoming signings and talks, finish up this publication year strong and move on. I had learned from *Racing My Father*, out in 2006, that there is a time when you reach the point of diminishing returns in marketing and promoting a book.

I was leaving the world of racing, I was graduating. I had been there, left, returned, and now, it's time to move on. No longer craving this world, Eliza beside me sleeping, I was feeling independent, self-assured, Whitman-like:

Afoot and light-hearted I take to the open road,
Healthy, free, the world before me,
The long brown path before me leading wherever I choose.

Henceforth I ask not good-fortune, I myself am good-fortune,
Henceforth I whimper no more, postpone no more, need nothing,

Done with indoor complaints, libraries, querulous criticisms,
Strong and content I travel the open road.

All was before me. I was not needy of the approval and the nods of this person or that. It was like the feeling four decades ago of driving the U-Haul in the early morning down Route 81 through the Shenandoah Valley to Hollins College, leaving home and the racetrack. On the way to Hollins to write. And, though I didn't know it, to meet Ansley and to start a new life. To have children, and one of those children, Eliza Whitman Smithwick, was with me at the moment; she had helped me gain the assurance and the desire to break away, as again, I headed off for a fresh start.

So calm, confident—walking, working, planning with me all weekend, she maintained her poise, her composure no matter what the situation. She would pass the Dick Diver repose test from *Tender is the Night* with ease:

> They were at Voisins waiting for Nicole, six of them. . . . They were looking over the other patrons of the restaurant to see if they had repose—Dick said no American men had any repose, except himself. . . . Things looked black for them—not a man had come into the restaurant for ten minutes without raising his hand to his face. . . .

I must tell her. Here she was, or, had been, the one who got nervous and had stomach aches in her early years at college, but in this potboiler, in this hot cement mixer of people, competition, events and emotions, she was calmer than I. She had repose.

That glow, that sense of perspective and sense of humor, that full support when with Eliza—I must keep that, hold it, treasure it, savor it. She doesn't try to control or improve or correct people. She lets them be. When I make a mistake, it is OK. We laugh at it and move on. In that one bookstore, I trusted the clerk on counting the books I'd sold and that was a mistake. (Or so it seemed at the time.) Eliza didn't judge me, scold me, comment on my actions. She knew it would work out. She helped me move on, and it did work out.

Instead of becoming upset at the machinations of others, she laughs. She walks tall, her posture straight. (The first surprise when I got home was Ansley not being my height. I was so used to looking directly into Eliza's eyes.)

That unselfishness—sweltering in the box, a couple of races after the A. P. Smithwick, I had asked Eliza if she wanted to walk back to Kip and his wife Helen's house on Jefferson Street, near Five Points Market, to rest before the next book signing. "Yes," she said. She was having fun and didn't look the least bit tired—but she was going to do whatever I wanted, whatever was best for me.

Gently forceful—at the National Steeplechase Association party at the Reading Room, standing under the tent, I looked over at our signing table, with the poster and stacks of *Flying Change* along with copies of *Racing My Father*, and the empty chair, and the four-foot wide moat of empty space surrounding the table, and I groaned inside, wishing I hadn't lined this up. Eliza, cheerful, exuding positive energy: "Come on Dad. This is fun. We're meeting interesting people and we're eating lobster and drinking champagne." A good-looking, college-aged male waiter approached with a tray of hors d'ouvres. "Look," she said, laughing, "You're having one of those baby lamb chops you love. Let's enjoy the party."

So mature—her insistence that we return and sit at the little table with the stacks of books, something I did not want to do. I was embarrassed, I was humiliated, but she was right, and she kept my spirits up. The waiter followed us, or rather—Eliza. At that moment, Tom appeared. He was recuperating from a tough afternoon: what a heart-breakingly close loss it had been for him in the A. P. Smithwick. He sat in "my" seat, asked Eliza how it was going. He grabbed the attention of the waiter who had been hovering around Eliza, held up a copy of *Flying Change*, asked if he'd read this book, didn't wait for an answer, opened the book up, and on the title page scrawled a dashing, devil-may-care "T H Voss"—as he loved to do, as he had been doing all his life on pads of paper, the initials "THV" carved into trunks of trees, knifed into an old glass panel of the window in our dining room, tattooed into his arms—then handed the book to the waiter. No mention of payment. A pretty waitress headed past us. He signed again, added an inscription to this one, handed it to her. Her eyes sparkled at him; she was laughing; she said she couldn't wait to read it and would tell all her friends.

"How long did it take you to write it?"

He put his hand on the stack of *Racing My Fathers*. "This one . . . took all my life." He moved his hand to a copy of *Flying Change*. "This one, ten years."

"You're so nice to give it to me. I'm going to tell all my friends about it. Thank you..."

Eliza had used her calligraphy skills to make a handsome card: *Flying Change*— $30. *Racing My Father*—$25. Tom slid it under our cigar box.

The cocktail sippers and hangers-on spotted the action. They drifted over, started picking up copies of *Flying Change*, looking through it, asking Tom questions. He signed a couple "A. P. Smithwick," scrawled a note, gave them away. Then there were twenty people lined up at our table. He signed "T H Voss" on the title page, handed the book to me, I inscribed it to the buyer. We had a system. We were selling books. Eliza and Tom were laughing. A pack of young steeplechase jocks shyly meandered over and began flirting with Eliza. She laughed at their awkward comments and kept them—all short arms and deep pockets—on their toes. Tom told inquiring prospects that they'd get a deal if they paid in cash: $80 for a pair of signed books, one *Flying Change*, one *Racing My Father*. They fell for it. $20s, $50s, hundred dollar bills. Eliza stuffed the cash in our cigar box. The party was ending and we couldn't leave. They were demanding more books and more inscriptions and more of a piece of Tom and Eliza. Eliza was laughing and helping Tom sign and hand out book after book.

Flush with cash, Eliza and I drove to First Caroline Street restaurant, sat down with sister Susan, her son McLean, and a group of McLean's childhood friends, bought drinks and dinner. I'll never forget sitting in that far corner chair beside Susan and looking diagonally across at Eliza, long blonde hair, long-limbed, and laughing—that smile, that joy, that self-assurance, that balance, my daughter, my daughter, the miracle of it. We had these moments, a stack of 45's forever spinning in my mind.

I loved her way of relating to Kip—sitting on the couch with him, looking over her portfolio of sketches for Badgley Mischka, the high-end fashion designer, where she had been doing an internship all summer, Kip intently listening to her explanations, studying her design-sketches for cocktail dresses, evening gowns, wild-looking high heels, commenting on them, learning about women's fashion, and then flipping through a Badgley Mischka catalogue: dresses, outfits, overcoats going for $3,000, $5,000, $25,000.

Walking into Saratoga Trunk on Broadway—we're making the rounds, not for my book, but for Eliza now; she's doing some sales and introductions for Badgley Mischka—the manager comes quickly out of her office, can't wait to meet Eliza, talks to her about her career, is happy and cheerful and delighted to be with Eliza.

I love her trust of McLean. Her comfort being with him. Her staying out until 3:00 a.m. with him.

I loved her laughter at the stupidity of the awkward flirtatious remarks and actions of the recently divorced Sebastian Cromwell, up from Pennsylvania, who at the NSA party had asked about her upcoming semester abroad in Paris—would she have time to go to the beaches on the Mediterranean? "I bet you'd look good in a bikini," he'd said, which she wisely did not tell me until later.

Cruising down the Northway in Ansley's sedan that is old enough to have a clutch and five forward gears, I was cutting loose. I was cutting loose from this racing world as a writing topic, as a way of life—"Afoot and lighthearted, I take to the open road, . . ." Driving home to the quiet of Maryland in August, to space on the farm that is not teaming with crowds; leaving the fast-paced Saratoga with its crush of racing fans, and gamblers; traveling down the wide, tree-lined lanes of the Northway—she's beside me, sleeping, curled up. I gently place my faded gray-blue Gilman School cap over her eyes and pat her once on the knee. Leave the radio off. Drive calmly. Look in wonder at her feet.

Her feet are a bit on the rough-looking side. The bottoms of my daughter's feet—crossed, up on the dashboard, in the bright sunlight—are calloused and smudged with dirt. Her insteps and the knuckles of her toes are coated with a film of dust—how in the world did that happen? Had she been dancing in a dust pile? (Days later, back on the farm, I was barefoot most of a day. I walked through some high grass returning from a swim in my neighbor's pool, and looked down, astonished to see my feet looking just as Eliza's had. This is what happened when you went barefoot, I remembered, walking back from the neighbor's pool as I had a thousand times as a boy.)

The sky was huge—*azure* (one of the five colors used in medieval heraldry, according to the textbook on the Middle Ages I'd been studying every night. I'd been hired in July by Su Harris, Head of Harford Day School in Bel Air, Maryland, to teach English, and had recently been excitedly informed that I would be teaching not only English but also, and primarily, Medieval History. "You can do it," Su sang out over the phone on a Sunday morning, sitting out on her dock, her feet dangling over the Susquehanna, her sailboat rigged and ready to be launched. "You can design your own course. The kids will love you. This will be yours. You'll own it.")

A flotilla of cumulus clouds ran before the wind overhead, and I could see for miles on either side of the highway, forests going on forever. We were rolling, 70, 75 miles per hour: tractor trailers; SUVs pulling boats; mini-vans packed with kids stuffed into safety seats staring at mini-screens, bikes hanging off the stern; college sophisticates in beat up Japanese sedans, windows open, music blaring, hair flying; gray-haired couples in big Buicks and Cadillacs; an occasional touring bus; hip outdoors men and women, kayaks dashingly lashed to the roof. Humanity headed south. Headed home.

I thought back on the morning after the race: Eliza was asleep. Kip did his yoga and was off to the track. Helen left early to do errands. I had a coffee, pulled on running shoes and took Helen's lively Jack Russell, Wilbur—you might say he took me—for a jog around Congress Park. Ran up and down some steps. Knocked off thirty sit-ups, thirty push-ups, thirty backwards push-ups. Found a tree limb—thirteen pull-ups. What the hell—stood on my head in the center of the park.

I was thinking off and on about what to do next. Over and over, people had asked, "Are you working on another book?" That's the American way. You're barely finished one project and they want to know—What's next? Hurry up and figure it out. I'd been thinking, "Oh poor me: oh, this tedious marketing, the never-ending promoting, the do-nothing distributor, the bureaucratic bookstore chains, the vacuous and apathetic bookstore employees." I'd been whining!

What was that sign Tom had over the entrance to his office/

tack room: "No Crybabies."

What was that line from "Song of the Open Road"? *"Henceforth I whimper no more, postpone no more, need nothing,"*

I jumped in the shower, rushed to Susan's.

I lie down in just my boxers on a raised massage table. I am in the new building—fifteen by thirty feet—Susan recently had built behind her house to use for her energy and healing work on clients, and for her therapy sessions. Sunlight streams in through the big windows. Two chairs. A lamp. No clutter. Susan and Carrie, a close friend and colleague of Susan's, start to work on me. At first, they're talking. Susan's relaxed, in her element. Talking about this meridian, that energy path, this organ. Susan is at my head, Carrie at my feet.

I look up and Carrie is doing this wild *whoop-whoop* sounding whirligig motion right above my crotch. We laugh. Susan tells me they're working on my "sacral chakra." The whirligigging leads to a hollowing out feeling, a drawing out of energy, a feeling of concavity, as if the area between my hips were a peaceful, open "hollow" in the woods.

Another time I look up and the two of them are doing a scooping, sloughing off motion, as if they are unrolling an endless blanket from me, or digging out the last of a pile of sand that was covering me, starting at my head and going to my foot. Laughing, they explain they're ridding me of negative energy. I lighten. My body becomes lighter. Like floating in salt water. Hovering.

Then, they're tapping into meridians, energy pathways, and I am seeing colors. They are doing "chakra clearing." Earlier, it had been the "Brazilian technique." Now they are linking up meridians, working on radiant circuits, making neuro-vascular connections.

Small puffs of yellow, expanding, blooming, small square puffs are growing, becoming bigger, the inside of the squares hollow, vacant. Purple puffs appear, tiny in the center of the yellow canvas and growing until everything, the entire canvas, all that is visible, is slate-purple.

The purple dissolves. The purple across the top becomes blue, the whole top half of the horizon, and it unrolls from the top, going from a darker to a lighter blue, like pulling down a rolled up shade, lighter lighter, and there's a thin horizontal strip of green going across the bottom, green like the grass of Maryland in the spring, and this long line of green rises, meets the line of blue and then, there is Mikey, my uncle. Handsome and young, in dark blue polo shirt, worn khakis, Irish cap pulled low over his eyes, he's fully alive. He's standing, he's young and he's standing straight. His profile is silhouetted against the sky and he is four horse-lengths away from me in a field, up on a hill in the big field at the farm at Hydes, and he is saying, *Never give up. Never, never, never give up.*

I take it in. I listen to this clear and concise advice.

I wonder about my father and then, click, Pop is there. He is closer than Mikey was; he is very close, I could reach out and grip his shoulder. He is young and handsome. It is before he had the fall. It is a few years before the fall when he was still in his riding prime and his hair is black, glistening with life, parted on the side. The part is clean and straight and you can see the white of his scalp. He is taking up the whole frame, and distinctly, clearly, calmly, as if we'd just been discussing the subject while seated at a booth in Sperry's, he says, *Take it to the next level, Bud.*

Never give up.

Take it to the next level.

There is not one point of advice and then another. There is not a number one and a number two. These two are linked. They are one. They are like two horses galloping down the stretch, head-and-head, and finishing in a dead heat. Or better yet, they are like a horse and a rider galloping down that homestretch, pushing and striving together, working as a well synchronized team, moving as one entity, one being—smoothly, athletically, swiftly, gracefully, gaining, gaining—and at the wire, winning. Or, most of all, they are one, a team, the two brothers, the winning team that had performed with brilliance for over twenty years speaking simultaneously.

Afterwards, shimmering light, high positive energy, brightness—this feeling carries through the day—through a breezy sunny lunch at the Fasig Tipton sales pavilion with Eliza, a few people who've read my books and want to meet me, and Bobby Burke, Pop's great friend, legendary show ring rider—the only rider to be inducted into both the Hall of Fame of Hunter Jumpers and the Hall of Fame of Open Jumpers—notorious hard drinker and lady's man in earlier days and now the most gentle, insightful, thoughtful octogenarian you've ever met who has outlived all his generation.

This high, this positive, clear-headed, crystalline vision of life carries on into the next day, this day, today, when—driving down Interstate 87 I feel released, freed. I am *looking forward* to the future, the open road, spurring on to the next level.

Last Dance at Old Hilltop

Four a.m. sharp the alarm clock perched on a cabinet six steps away in the bathroom starts to beep. It's Sunday, late August. At 5:30, I'll be galloping down the stretch of Pimlico Race Course, twenty miles south of our farm in Monkton, on my first of nine horses. I did most of my riding on this track back when I was a student at Johns Hopkins University forty years ago. Then it was three bucks a horse and we used to call it "gas money." You'd have a salary job galloping full time for one trainer and you'd pick up a few outside horses—say early, before your trainer started, or later, when he was finished, or on Sunday when many of the riders stayed in bed. When you got off a freelance horse, the trainer would take the reins, and stuff a sliver of three folded dollar bills into your back pocket. (One of the few successful freelancers back in those days was Cliff Barrosox, the strongest man to ever gallop a horse. He rode all winter, no matter if the windchill were ten degrees, in a blue jean jacket and no gloves. He rode thirty a day at the track and at farms—undercutting the rest of us by charging only $2 a horse. He worked hard, saving every cent for his later years, and at middle age was crushed by a car he was working under.) Three dollars, or one horse, filled up my black Ford Falcon with the V-8 that would tippy-toe along at 125 mph. Today, freelance riders get from $10 to $12.50 for galloping a horse at a Maryland track, $15 on farms. Gas money? Don't think so. It takes three horses to fill the tank of my old pickup truck that is hard-pressed to go 65. How did I end up back doing this again? It was that e-mail a few springs ago. I'd been working on a book, had it published, and sent out a blitz saying I was looking for a teaching position or a spot as a writer.

"Pat," Dickie Small wrote back. No short cuts in his e-mails. He writes everything just right using caps, using periods, using that Gilman School and University of Pennsylvania education. "We're not offering any professorships here at Pimlico, but if you want your old job back you can have it. I could use a good rider. Short hours. High pay. In case you forgot, we start at 5:00 —Dickie. P.S. You'll have your own valet." In the upper corner, the time of writing: 3:15 a.m. Dickie is R. W. Small, as listed in the program, Richard Watters Small who has trained a stable of thirty to forty horses at Pimlico since the 1970s when slim and fit as a racehorse, the young Green Beret was decommissioned from the Army after returning from Vietnam.

During the week, I gallop for Dickie 5:30 to 8:00, hop in the pickup, drive a few miles to Gilman on the other side of town where I take a shower, change into white collar clothes, and perform my duties directing the publications and public relations department and teaching a junior English class. (The other day, fast-striding to the office at 9:00, I passed the Director of Admissions. He stared at me, shook his head, and mumbled "Bankers' hours.") But this is a Sunday. So simple. Delightful. I'll come straight home after galloping. And it is one of my last. Unlike Gilman, Harford Day, a small K-Prep through eighth grade school, is northeast of Baltimore, far from Pimlico, and I will no longer be able to keep the Pimlico-to-School schedule during the academic year that I maintained through my teenage years at Gilman, undergraduate years—along with classmate Kip Elser—at Johns Hopkins, and off and on through many seasons in my adult years.

It is quiet. I put on a pair of glasses, hobble sideways holding the banister, down the worn wooden stairs, allowing myself the luxury of taking one step at a time at this hour, to the kitchen, push in the button to the coffee machine, drop two slices of bread in the toaster, walk back up the stairs—limbering up now—perform my morning ablutions. Standing out in the hall so as not to awaken Ansley, I pull on jockey shorts, T-shirt, blue jeans. Pull my father's old cowboy belt through the loops. Stuff a red bandana in my right rear pocket and walk back down to the kitchen, the legs loosening. Pour coffee. Spread butter and blackberry jam on one slice, butter and honey on the other, sit at the counter, glance at the glowing digits on the coffee machine: 4:13. I sip the coffee, and taste every bite, every nuance, every differentiated shade of meaning of the toast, and savor every second, every tick of the morning.

I move to the chair by the woodstove, bedecked with a pot of flowers and a fan. Pull on socks. Pull on leggings. Pull on boots. The boots: Kroops—Maryland-made by the renowned boot maker in Laurel. Chucky Gore, one-time show ring rider, and king of the Pimlico freelance riders in the 1980s, told me to get a pair from Charles Turner. That's Chucky, who galloped seventeen a day—who one winter kept right on galloping seventeen a day after breaking four ribs, and who saved and saved, never spent a cent. In the early '90s, one morning he galloped his fourteenth horse, had a heart attack, rode the horse back to the barn, slid off and that was it, died in the tack. Charles Turner had these boots custom made to fit my feet. Charles, black, run-off storyteller, 350-pounder, didn't need sleep —who in the '80s was Dickie's night watchman, hot walker, trouble shooter.

When Dickie saw me handing Charles a check for the boots, he said, "No Pat, that's a business expense. Give me the bill."

That was in 1984 when I left the nicest job teaching English at Oldfields School, the one hundred fifty-year-old all-girls boarding school in Glencoe, twenty miles north of Baltimore, where Ansley was teaching French and history (before she became Chair of the Language Department, Director of Learning, Associate Head, and finally Interim Head), and returned to Pimlico to gallop for Dickie in the mornings and have the afternoons free to write. The boots are light, reaching up over my ankles. They fit like slippers around my feet, conforming to my high instep and high arches, and through years of wear, stretching around the bunions on the inside of each foot. They are zip-up "paddock boots." The zippers gave out years ago. I punched tiny holes along the sides of the broken zippers, threaded in thin leather laces—and the boots are now better than new. They've been resoled twice—thin full leather soles—and they slide easily and efficiently in and out of racetrack stirrups, which are smaller than the stirrups I use at home. If a horse stumbles and falls galloping, or spooks or breaks a leg or rears and is about to go over backwards, or flips out when the starting gate man slams the doors shut behind us—and I either have to disengage or am catapulted from the saddle—my feet will slide freely out of the stirrups. This is important. I've been dragged twice in my life; both times that short distance seemed very long, and I had thought my time was up.

I glance at the clock. 4:20.

I run my hand over the cracks and crevices across the ball of the foot, spreading out like crows' feet from the eyes of a veteran galloping boy. The leather is dry. Too dry, bleached out. I shouldn't do this, it could make me late, but I decide to go ahead anyway. I duck into the cold pantry, dig into my father's old shoe shine kit, pull out a can of cordovan polish, a brush that looks like it's made for lathering on shaving cream, and my father's wooden-handled, gracefully-curved shoe brush. I place one foot on the second step of the steep stairway that spirals up to the back of the house. Can't see. I pull a string attached to a light chain and a bare bulb flashes on illuminating the high walls and half a dozen black and white photos of my father winning races in the 1950s and 1960s at Belmont Park, Saratoga Springs, Monmouth Park on the great Neji, on the great King Commander, on the great Elkridge, but I don't think about that. I apply polish to one boot, rub it into the cracks and crevices, into the seam, set it down, rub the polish into the other boot. Brush and buff and shine the first foot, then the other. My hand whips back and forth across the leather, bringing it to life.

I grab a banana and car keys, step outside with my coffee. Cut through the darkness to the truck.

In the driver's seat. Streamlined. Review the inventory of what I need: My body and what's on it. Mug of coffee and a banana. Wallet in glove compartment. And in the wallet, a small photo of son Andrew in his "dress" Marine uniform. Thinking of him, picturing him safe and sound at his base in Iraq, I close my eyes, say a prayer, and open my eyes while chanting, "He'll be all right. He'll be all right."

I start the engine, turn on the lights, glance at the clock. Twenty-five of five. I feel a lift. I'm looking forward to the quiet trip in. The roads will be empty. It's like getting something for free.

Leaving the door open, I drive toward the top shed—the two beams sweep across the field, falling for a second on Warfield, my light-boned, chestnut hunter, grazing—and coast down to the main aisle-way of the barn. The twin beams swing across the field, showing emptiness, quiet, grass, and then brighten on

Riderwood and Saitensohn, my two steeplechase horses, both bays, across the stream. They raise their heads, pin their ears forward, look questioningly in my direction, and start ambling in.

I step into the feed room. Toss four dippers of feed into a bucket, duck through the board fence, step out into the field. Both horses crowd me. Their shoulders rub against me. They try to stick their heads in the bucket at the same time and neither gets his nose in. I push back, laughing, pour half the bucket into a feed tub on the fence, walk to their shed, pour the rest into a tub in the corner. I duck under a rail, quickstep down the aisle-way—my legs developing a nice spring to them—drop the bucket back in the feed bin. A puffy-gray barn cat leaps off a wall box, scoots ahead of me, and bounces up to the platform holding his bowl. His brother flies from the stall door directly in front of me across to a foot locker, lands, knocks down my Uncle Mikey's Hall of Fame plaque, which I've been meaning for months to hang in the tack room, skitters and claws to get its footing, destroying what was a neat pyramid of rolled bandages, sending them unraveling across the floor, jumps up to the platform and is instantly tranquil, purring and rubbing his body against his partner, awaiting his breakfast.

Returning to the truck, I see Warfield's silhouette twenty yards away up in the top paddock. He's leaning over the fence, watching Riderwood, below me, munching his feed. Silver Charm and Eloquence are beside him. I hesitate. He's really too plump; the ponies are fat; and I'm falling behind schedule. Warfield is licking the sides of his mouth.

Back into the feed room. Fill the dipper. Stride up to the paddock, toss half in Warfield's feed tub, rub him between the eyes. Twenty years old, and he has more guts, more character, more moxie, and more intelligence than any horse I know. I walk three panels down the fence line, pour a handful inside the fence for Eloquence, take a few more steps, pour the rest for Silver Charm.

Out the driveway, take a left and ease the truck through three of its four manual gears down Manor Road. Slow for a fox trotting across, leaving the farm of the late Sidney Watters, Hall of Fame trainer, combat veteran of World War II, best friend of my parents, and Dickie's uncle and mentor. Pull my glasses off so my eyes will acclimate. Haven't yet given in to riding with glasses.

Take a right on the Jarrettsville Pike and turn on the radio.

Relief: the BBC's literary hour. I won't have to hear about the latest news in Iraq. A young female journalist with a sophisticated British accent is interviewing an older black man with a rich and resonating voice. The novel *Things Fall Apart* is mentioned and I am amazed to realize I am listening to the writer Chinua Achebe (His advice to writers: 1. Go for it. 2. Read.) and he and I and the snappy interviewer are cruising along together. Achebe is criticizing Joseph Conrad's depiction of Africans in *Heart of Darkness*, saying the descriptions are racist and demeaning, and for this, he condemns the entire novel. Achebe and I drive through the dark, not a soul on the road, and we agree to disagree on this point. I picture Achebe half a century ago as a young college student in South-Eastern Nigeria going through his late-night lucubrations, coming across "The Second Coming" by Yeats and studying the lines:

Things fall apart; the centre cannot hold;...
The best lack all conviction; while the worst
Are full of passionate intensity.

I let the old campaigner pick up speed heading down the steep hill onto Dulaney Valley Road and across the long and wide and empty bridge—soon to be dedicated to Cpl. Christopher J. Coffland, U. S. Army Afghanistan, Killed in Action—over Loch Raven Reservoir, down through the valley of trees to the Beltway. As the BBC commentator concludes her program, she mentions that the Russian novelist, Alexander Solzhenitsyn, has just died, and I think back on a chapter in *One Day in the Life of Ivan Denisovich* and how inspirational one specific scene, in which Denisovich is building a brick wall, has been to me.

Onto the Beltway. Some tractor-trailers. Only a few cars on Sundays, some with bubbles on rooftops and bicycles hanging off the sterns—families heading off for summer vacation. We shift lanes. Someone lets me in. Everyone is more courteous at this time of day. We pick up speed. NPR plays that exact same mournful melody—it is 5:00 a.m.—and then on a Sunday morning, it's jazz. I listen for a few minutes; it's too jazzy and I turn it off.

Passing under the Charles Street bridge—soon to be dedicated to Marine Capt. Nicholas Lee Ziolkowski, killed in the Iraq War—a full-throated, low-slung, black Mustang approaches from behind, moving right along, and growls by. That's Justine, one of my riding colleagues. She was absent yesterday. Busy working off the vast number of community service hours she was recently awarded for her last speeding ticket. Earlier in the summer, she'd also missed a day, this one for a court appearance: a girl had made the mistake of flirting with Justine's boyfriend. Justine confronted her. The girl screamed at Justine. Justine hit her over the head with a beer bottle.

Off the Beltway, onto the Jones Falls Expressway, then onto Northern Parkway, up the hill, past Sinai Hospital, through a few lights. Instead of proceeding into the heart of Pimlico—sidewalks cracked and littered with beer cans, needles, old newspapers; store and restaurant windows boarded up—where in just a few hours men will be sitting apathetically on door steps staring into space with glassy eyes and sipping out of paper bags, I take a left by the 3/8th's pole of Pimlico Race Course, drive along the tall wire fence. This is where Doug Small, Dickie's father, had his stable in the '50s and '60s, and then Dickie had his in the '70s and '80s, a nice wooden barn with a high ceiling over the long shed-row that stretched all the way down this street, a barn that was torn down ten years ago, along with a dozen others, to be rebuilt one day.

Ease up at the STOP sign, take a left on Winners Avenue, rumble along, the track to my left, row houses on my right. I glance to the left through the ten-foot chain-link fence topped off with a roll of razor-sharp concertina wire. The French expression my wife sometimes uses, *Plus ça change, plus c'est la même chose*, comes to mind. Forty years ago, First Lieutenant R. W. Small and three other members of the Fifth Special Forces Group would crawl through a hole in a fence like this in the middle of the night, board a C-130 or C-123, fly beyond the reach of radar to 15,000 feet, and parachute into the Vietnam jungle for a week of reconnaissance as part of their training for High Altitude Level Opening missions, the HALO operations. When not parachuting and reconnoitering, Dickie had slept and worked inside this same type of wire spiraled around the perimeter of his camps to keep out guerilla units of the Vietcong who would like to cut his throat. Forty years later, back in the U.S.A., he is still working inside the wire, but it is strung to keep out thieves, drug dealers, and gang members who would most likely run the other way if confronted by this six-foot three man who exudes a calm fearlessness no matter what the situation. When driving his horse van up the New Jersey Turnpike a few years ago, Dickie pulled over in a rest stop to "take ten"—rest his eyes. He snapped awake when he noticed he had company. A man was pointing a .22 calibre rifle at him. "You think you can hurt me with that little thing," Dickie said, grabbing the rifle and pushing the would-be robber out of the cab.

Through the fence I see the Receiving Barn—where in May the horses for the Preakness are stabled—and then Dickie's barn. Dickie, in blue jeans, T-shirt and short sleeve checkered shirt, floppy Irish wool cap, is hunched over a steel picnic table writing up the sets for the morning in the jagged yellow light. He gets up at 3:00 a.m. Does his e-mails. Checks the internet for racing news, past performances of horses the day before and for upcoming races. (Never buys the exorbitantly priced *Racing Form*.) Is here at his "office" by 5:00. If it is pouring rain, he'll work at a desk in a closet-sized room beside the tack room. As they say in the Green Berets, "Trained to the point of ruthless efficiency."

I glance at Dickie, pass the eerie blinking-blue crime surveillance camera on the top corner of a row house, and take a left into Pimlico Race Course.

There are only three full-size barns, each with forty stalls, on this side of the track, where there used to be fifteen. Quiet. I drive across the asphalt, and make an effort.

Does anyone care? I will be making decisions like this all morning. Hundreds of opportunities will present themselves where I can do it the easy way or do it the right way. At the start of the summer, I decided that at every juncture, no matter what pressure I was under, I would do it the right way. It is the decision Ivan makes in *One Day in the Life of Ivan Denisovich*, when, as a prisoner of the gulag, he is called to end his bricklaying. He decides to go ahead and finish what he is doing, to get it right, even though he knows he will be punished for being late and no one will appreciate his skilled craftsmanship.

My effort: I pull the truck sharply to the left to miss the long and narrow black steel plate bolted over a drainage pipe. The plate is loose and when driven over makes a loud, irritating, double-clanging noise like the door of a prison cell door slamming shut, twice, in quick succession—jangling the humid peacefulness of the summer morning.

Love Kills Slowly

I let the truck coast down the incline, ease up in front of a compact, two-story wooden building holding the men's showers and bathroom for the backside of Pimlico. Leaving the engine running, I step out into the hazy buzz of overhead lights, feeling good, legs long and limber in the jeans, back—yes—needing stretching. I walk through the open door into a chamber of sticky, stultifying, pissy, buggy heat, take two steps to the urinal. Men quietly, slowly, walk in and out, an arm's reach away. *Buenos dias... Buenos dias senior...*

Rinsing my hands, I glance into the mirror. With no glasses on, I'm out of focus. At five foot eleven and a half, I'm taller than any of these black-haired men far from their homes in Mexico. T-shirt hangs from my shoulders, tucked, for the last time this morning, into worn and snug-fitting blue jeans with hand-sized holes rubbed through the inside of both calves. Belt, with my father's lightweight, silver buckle, is flat from hip to hip across my abdomen. I pull the belt in another notch. Not hard to keep my weight down with this schedule. Good Lord, look at that fuzzy face with the gray uncombed hair—gray, *thinning*, uncombed hair—and the sharp angular lines. How did you ever end up back here? Again? I laugh.

Rumble slowly past a couple of vans and pick-ups. See Milan—fast-moving, in his 20s, from Serbia—leaning into a heavy wheelbarrow of manure, pushing it into a walk-in dumpster. Park between Dickie's pick-up and Justine's black Mustang. Turn off the engine, look at Dickie hunched over the picnic table, glasses perched at the end of his nose, writing up the list of sets: seven

63

sets of four to go out between 5:30 and 8:00, and a set or two after the 8:00 to 8:30 break when the track is watered and harrowed.

The leather soles of my boots clack against the asphalt. His eyes focused on the legal pad, Dickie says, "Morning Pat." As I near, he turns, peers over his glasses, says in a whisper, "How're you this morning?"

"Morning Dickie. Feeling good thanks."

In my hand I have a program I've recently discovered for the fifth running of The Rochelle Tin Cup and "EIGHT OTHER INCREDIBLE RACES AT OLD BEL AIR RACE TRACK" from September 4, 1966. This was a day featuring a men's jackass race— "THE KENNEL RATIONS SERIES;" a ladies mule race— "THE FRISKY MATRON;" a small pony race—"THE EXTERMINATED HANDICAP;" culminating in the TIN CUP itself. Rules:

"1. All horses wearing protective head gear will be required to remove said head gear during the playing of the National Anthem.

"2. Under no condition will any rider dismount before mounting.

"3. In the event of a dead heat, the first horse to cross the finish line will be considered the winner.

"4. Spectators getting their kicks out of horses, ponies, mules, etc., will do so at their own risk.

"5. No jackasses will be permitted to chew gum in the paddock."

Charlie Shaw, whose father was a noted trainer of flat horses, wrote that. He and his friend Monk Forbes, both five or so years older than I, organized the race. Monk went on to have a successful career as a trainer. Charlie, who we all loved because he was so energetic and funny and took us younger kids to the movies and ice hockey games, committed suicide.

The Bel Air Track was about to close. We had our last dance on it that day. We were at the tail end of the heyday of Maryland racing. Throughout the 50s, there was a multitude of tracks functioning across the state. Since the glory years of Native Dancer, "The Gray Ghost," Maryland had been the center of the country's Thoroughbred racing and breeding. Native Dancer won the Preakness and Belmont in 1953, continued winning races, became a national hero and then one of the world's greatest sires, standing at Alfred Vanderbilt's Sagamore Farms in Glyndon, just a few miles north of Pimlico. But the center could not hold. Over a period of four decades, one by one, the tracks in Maryland have closed. Now, there is one rumor that the Preakness could be moved to another track and another that Pimlico may be closing altogether. Will the future of Pimlico Race Course meet the same fate as Bel Air Racetrack: bulldozers, asphalt, and yet another mall in America?

I can't wait to talk about the Tin Cup with Dickie—both of us had been there that day—but now is not the time. He is engrossed in figuring out the best way to get thirty-plus horses out on the track. There is an infinity of permutations and combinations when you throw eight grooms, four riders, four hot-walkers, and three dozen horses into the equation.

Dickie insists on allowing his horses to lead as natural a life as possible—oats, hay, a skilled and caring groom, a rider that won't fool with them too much, a rider that will let them run. No clipping of coats. No blankets in the winter. No hay nets. Virtually no drugs. Only one vet, who is a close friend, is ever seen on the shedrow, and that is for conversational purposes. Dickie keeps his horses happy, not forcing them to do anything unnatural or unnecessary, and allowing them to release their natural instinct to compete, to gallop fast, to race.

He models the operation of his stable after his Uncle Sidney Watters, a natural horseman—with time off to be a tail gunner in the Pacific Theater of World War II. If Sidney hadn't already had faith in the disciplined life when he went into the military, he had it by the time he'd flown over thirty-five missions in a little glassed-in bubble protruding from the tail of a B-24 bomber.

Sidney ran his barn at Saratoga or Belmont Park as precisely as his stopwatch clicked off the record-breaking fractions of his champion colts Hoist the Flag and Slew o' Gold. Everything was neat, polished, orderly, and on schedule.

Dickie runs his stable the same way. A well-oiled machine. It could, as he says, run on its own. He has one groom for every four horses. He has three green two-year-olds just up from his stable in South Carolina. Four three-year-olds that need to "breeze" three-eighths (let'em run, not quite full speed, for 3/8's of a mile). A couple of older horses that are getting lazy and need to gallop "in company." The young horses need to go to the starting gate on "gate days" when the gate crew is in. He has to balance the grooms. Can't have all four of a groom's horses going out in one set. Best to have one horse per groom going out. He has to balance the riders: José, late-thirties, rode races when younger, has been with Dickie for fifteen years, weighs in at 130, can ride anything; Britanny, eighteen, 145 pounds, has been galloping for two years and is patient and best on the finicky, quirky, unpredictable fillies, such as the tiny one by Fusaichi Pegasus. Justine, twenty, 130 pounds, long-legged, nice hands, good at getting a nervous horse to relax; and the "jumping rider," three times the girls' age, keeps the needle of the scales hovering at 155, enjoys getting nervous horses to relax, can gallop strong horses, "pullers," is good at making balky, sulky horses go forward, not allowing them to stop or wheel.

And there is the time of day: early, there are few horses on the track, the condition of the track is at its best, and it's cooler; later, more horses come out, there is more confusion, the going deepens as the surface is cut up, and it's hotter.

I walk past Dickie. His leather satchel, handsomely hand-tooled by Pedro, his senior groom, lies on the yellow top of the picnic table, condition books spewing out of it. These pamphlets list the races at different tracks across the country. Dickie will study them throughout the morning. And he'll look where some other Maryland trainers don't. He doesn't mind shipping far— Arkansas, Ohio, Illinois—for a stakes race that suits one of his horses. Back when he was training Broad Brush, he and Charles Turner would load Broad Brush up around midnight and he'd drive through the night, arrive at a track three states away in the morning and blow away the competition that afternoon. From 1985 to 1987 Broad Brush went to the post twenty-seven times at fifteen different tracks. He won fifteen of those, twelve of them stakes, earning two Maryland-bred horse of the year titles and over $2,500,000. He was a strong third in both the Kentucky Derby and the Preakness. I don't "look back" when riding down the homestretch of life, but once in a while I do regret leaving the track, leaving galloping, leaving Dickie in 1984, which coincidentally was right before he got Bob Meyerhoff's horses to train, including Broad Brush.

I step into the shedrow. *Buenos dias*—to Romano. Jet black

hair perfectly combed. Neatly dressed in a clean shirt with a collar and khakis. The four horse lengths of shedrow that his stalls open out onto is watered—to hold down the dust—and raked.

¿Cómo estás? he asks.

Bien, bien, I say, striding to the tack room.

Amy, José's thirteen-year-old daughter, is seated in Dickie's office, organizing horses' papers. "She's smart Pat," he'd told me one morning, looking me in the eye. "She'll be going to college one day." The upcoming week will be a busy one: two are running at Philadelphia Park, one at Monmouth Park in New Jersey, three at Delaware Park. Each horse will have to have his identification papers and his health certificate ready for the van driver when he's loaded up.

Because Amy is here, the list of sets to go out—four horses in each set, riders names by their mounts—on the white-board outside the tack room will be neatly written and I will actually be able to read them. When Dickie writes up the sets, and it's early, with little light in the shedrow, I depend on Milan (my "valet" from Serbia) and the other riders to decipher his shorthand. Amy is also putting together a scrapbook of the hundreds of photos and articles relating the extraordinary racing feats of Broad Brush culminating in his winning the Santa Anita Handicap. Bob Meyerhoff syndicated Broad Brush for $4 million. A decade later, Broad Brush's son Concern, trained by Dickie, won the Breeder's Cup Classic, making Broad Brush the world's leading sire in progeny earnings. Concern, the first Maryland-bred, Maryland-based Classic winner, went on to win over $3 million.

Pedro Mojarro, the senior groom who used to rub Broad Brush, is standing outside his stalls. Pedro rarely sits; his leg was broken in a horse accident, and now it doesn't bend. This is better than the fate of a trainer, my friend Bob Witham, for whom he'd once worked. Pedro speaks no English and it was difficult to explain, when he asked about Bob, that Bob had had a fall from a young horse, been paralyzed, and quickly made the decision to withdraw all life support.

Buenos dias, I say.

He looks me directly in the eye—*¿Cómo estás?* There's something special about Pedro. He is the oldest on the shedrow—the most knowledgeable—carries himself with a cheerful dignity. His daughter, who, as my Uncle Mikey Smithwick used to say, is "easy on the eyes," will arrive at 6:30 to "walk hots." Her bright and wide-awake five-year-old son will jog alongside her.

Into the tack room: instant heat and humidity and the cloying, overpowering, sticky pungency of oiled and saddle-soaped tack combined with the acrid scent of metal polish and the funky locker room odor of drying sweat from the helmets and protective vests. Two floor fans do their best, but there is no window and no fresh air. This room is locked tight every night.

"Good morning *Pa-trick*. How are you?" says José, crisply, with a clipped accent, enunciating each word, seated over by the two dozen leather bridles hanging from their racks. José has the build of a gymnast and is in a trim T-shirt, new blue jeans, and lightweight black race-riding boots with a four-inch band of red patent leather around the tops.

Britanny is leaning against the table holding the coffee machine, pulling off her flip-flops, and pulling on socks, boots and half-chaps. Fair-skinned and blonde with a long torso and short legs, she's in a pair of black skin-tight spandex riding britches and is giggling as is Justine, who is in her "dressing room"—seated behind a curtain of saddle towels hanging to dry from a clothes line stretched the length of the long, narrow room. Justine, tall, slim, with long legs and big brown eyes, did some modeling in Florida over the winter and spring—thus her deep tan—but didn't have the patience for it, and she is bent over, thick auburn hair mane over her head, gathering her hair into a pony tail, laughing and revealing a tattoo of a favorite horse—a filly of Dickie's that she gallops—racing across the nape of her long, outstretched neck.

The two girls are joking back and forth and José is seated there—his tack ready beside him, his arms crossed, taking it in, and grinning at me. I pick out a bridle I like—one with thin reins and older rubber sheaths on them so they'll slide through my hands, if needed. No nylon bridles here, no nylon reins that cut through your fingers. I pull my saddle off its rack, pick a medium-length girth out of the twenty hanging from nails, set a saddle pad, a wool pommel pad, a gray and yellow saddle cloth, a rubber non-slip pad and a gray girth cover over the saddle and ask Britanny, "What the hell's going on?" She's still giggling and I know what it must be. It has to be the tattoo. I'd been lecturing against tattoos for three weeks now. She had wanted to have a heart, festooned with ribbons, and LOVE KILLS SLOWLY emblazoned across it, and, below that, a skull and cross bones, all this tattooed on her—lower belly. I'd spent several mornings trying to talk her out of the skull, and offering up edited and revised versions of LOVE KILLS SLOWLY.

How will it look when you are pregnant and your belly's swollen? I'd asked as we jogged past the starting gate.

E-u-www.

Won't the baby be scared of it? I'd inquired as we turned, and began to gallop.

E-u-www.

Suppose your boy friend doesn't like it? I'd challenged—knowing he doesn't like tattoos—as we walked off the track, but also knowing that she had "drop kicked" this same boy friend at a party a few weeks ago, that he had shown up at her house shooting a pistol at 3:30 in the morning, and that a few hours later she had arrived at the barn with a police escort.

Too bad!

I LOVE JOSÉ—how about that for a tattoo! I'd offered.

E-u-www.

I LOVE DICKIE.

E-u-www.

LOVE IS ALL.

E-u-www.

Standing in the tack room, zipping up my protective vest, I ask, "What's so funny?" and with that, the eighteen-year-old with short blonde hair, wide shoulders, narrow waist, grabs the belt-area of her spandex britches, pulls them down, revealing a bright red strawberry tattooed on the smoothest skin of the prettiest ass you've ever seen displayed in a tack room.

There is something inexplicable about riding racehorses together. A give and take between riders of different ages and different sexes develops over mornings of walking, trotting, galloping and breezing side by side—a freedom between men and women that I've never experienced anywhere else. There is no censoring. No political correctness. *The Scarlet Letter* might as well never have been written. We know what can happen out on the track and we are not holding back. We are living life in the moment, exulting in having the freedom to talk about every facet of it. No big "A" embroidered on a dress. We have a delicious-looking tattoo inked onto an . . . aesthetically pleasing ass.

We discuss subjects we wouldn't dream of bringing up in other places—sex, drinking, fighting, drugs, jobs, love. One morning, as we ride, we discuss fake boobs and fake asses—I never knew there was a market for silicone butts!—and we analyze the figures of both men and women as they jog by us all morning. I do not relate any of this back to my associates in the development office at Gilman School, the prestigious one-hundred year old all-boys school of one thousand students, the first "country day school" in the country, and the subject of my first book, *Gilman Voices, 1897—1997*. But jogging along on a 1,200 pound animal bred for three hundred years to have the heart and lungs and muscles and desire to run as fast as the wind for a mile or two, and everyone around you on the same type of animal, many of them going extremely fast and not quite in control, it seems just fine.

Tell Me, Behind What Door Your Treasure Lies?

It's 5:20. Justine and Britanny waltz out of the tack room. In unison, they sit down on a bale of hay across from the white-board. Their saddles and bridles across their laps, they study their mounts for the morning and what they'll be doing.

Dickie walks up to them, asks if the chart for the morning is all right. He looks Brittany in the eye. "Yes," she says. Then Justine. "Looks good to me," she says. Few, if any, trainers do this. Dickie's also teaching Brittany; he knows she wants to be a trainer one day.

I step out of the tack room. Milan is suddenly there. He knows I need a head start on the others. This is why Dickie had written in his e-mail, "You'll have your own private valet." He'd remembered that I am not too speedy when it comes to tacking up. All morning, as soon as I hop off a horse, Milan is there. Well, I don't really *hop* off any of these horses. Instead of walking them out onto the asphalt where the grooms and hot walkers wait beside buckets filled with hot, sudsy water, and dismounting onto the unforgiving asphalt as the other riders do, I pull my horses up in the shedrow and lower myself onto the dirt surface, trying to keep the impact off the right knee, as well as the left foot, which is impossible.

Right knee— Tom's brother Ned's 750 Triumph had broken it: roaring into the Secor's driveway at the age of eighteen, realizing I couldn't make the sharp turn, seeing the stone wall, shooting off the driveway, the wall coming at me fast, I leaned to the right, hit the ground, somersaulted across the lawn and was knocked out as the motorcycle continued on, hit the wall, flipped, and landed in the midst of a cocktail party.

Left foot—Tom's legendary stakes winner John's Call was the cause of the tendinitis: galloping on the artificial track, speeding downhill, letting him tippy-toe along, Pocock Road to our left, a rabbit hopped out of the hedgerow and John instantly and powerfully dug in both toes and spooked to the right, my left foot taking all the pressure, and I felt something snap. Dickie jokes about getting me a trampoline to land on. I wouldn't mind.

Milan disengages the bridle and yoke from the bundle of tack across my arm, turns and walks fast down the aisle-way. A wave of relaxation flows through my body as I read, "Buttermilk Sky" up on the board. "Buttermilk"—just the word is soothing, euphonious, and then "Sky" gives it a little zip, character, a quixotic feel. "Buttermilk Sky"—now what does that mean? I try to picture it. No matter, it is unlike the name of a racehorse and perfectly attuned to this horse's personality; I'd like to take him home and turn him into a foxhunter.

Saddle over left arm, I step past Pedro. He's in the first stall knocking the dust off Take A Check—a good-sized gray mare with a body of hard-packed muscle, her conformation ideal for a race horse: a classy head with "an eye" that reflects intelligence tapering to a strong and long neck that runs back to firm withers over a chest and shoulders broader than most fillies', the chest narrowing to a high waist, and her back funneling into a strong rump, rounded over the top, yet tucked in as it descends to her prominent hips which lead to nicely shaped hind legs, the hocks strong, the cannon bones straight, the tendons clean, and to feet as perfectly shaped as a woman's toenails after a pedicure. Take A Check does her own thing. In a race, when she wants to win, she wins. When she's not in the mood to go after first place, she cruises in second or third.

Pedro has already brushed her off—her dappled coat reflects the dim light from an overhead bulb. She has her neck stretched out, her back bent low, while Pedro rubs and massages her, and she snaps at me as I walk past, pretending she'd bite me. I do take a wide path around her stall. She'll be my next horse and I look forward to riding her. I'd do it for free. I'd almost pay to ride her. Almost. Riding is so much nicer, riding is just absolutely delightful, riding is better than playing tennis, than skiing down a mountain, than canoeing down a river, than going for a run, than pedaling a bicycle, than swimming laps, when you're getting on high-class Thoroughbreds that are winning stakes races and when you're being paid well to do it.

The most spoiled horse I've ever seen in Dickie's barn is stakes winner Cozy Corner, a tall, long-backed, rangy, light-gray mare in the stall beside Take A Check. Pedro rubs her too and she is everyone's favorite. I love riding her. She has a very long neck, will stretch it out, lower her head, and pull hard and steadily. She has one of the longest strides of any horse I've ridden. I'll gallop her later, and when we return to the barn, Pedro's daughter with the dark, sultry eyes, and his grandson in a new cowboy hat, will be waiting by the steaming buckets. Cozy will be washed off. Then the grandson, beamingly proud, with mother beside him, will walk this giant mare around the shedrow—shank hanging loose from her halter—until she is dry and cooled out. It is a magazine cover shot that has never been taken, and it is the only time all morning Pedro's daughter smiles.

Every one of Dickie's grooms is from Mexico. Every one of them is an excellent horseman. Most are related. They live together in the bunk houses above the barns, they never complain, and they work all hours whether it's ninety degrees in the shade of the shedrow in August or twenty degrees in the stall in February, whether shipping back from the Meadowlands in New Jersey at 1:00 a.m. Friday or mucking out at 4:30 a.m. on Sunday.

I walk down the shedrow. There is a dust-coated light bulb high in each stall but no light outside the stall by the door—where the names of the horses are written on duct tape. At this hour, without my glasses, I can't make out the names. But I know Buttermilk. He's not hard to pick out, being almost a hand—four inches— taller than any horse in the barn. I see a big light bay standing in the back of his stall, as if he's hiding. Milan has his arm around Buttermilk's neck, roughhousing with him. Buttermilk is loving it; his entire body is loose, languid, relaxed. His phallus is out of its sheath, hanging down. He doesn't fight against Milan, lets him push him this way and that. Milan whispers in his clipped Serbian accent, "Are you going to be a racehorse Buttermilk? Are you going to win some races? Yes you are. Yes you are Buttermilk." Milan knows the eccentricities of every horse Dickie trains. He can tell you where and how they've run, how they're bred, and he's good at predicting where Dickie will run them next.

Milan knows how to work; he's hungry for the American Dream. He is an autodidact, the racetrack is his university and Dickie is his exemplar. One morning I was talking to him about the recession, the high cost of gasoline, the plummeting of real estate prices, the soaring national debt, the weakening of the dollar, the effect of the country's economic woes on so many. He was on foot, leading me on a horse with a history of misbehaving, the horse bumping and smacking into his shoulder, and he looked up at me as if I were crazy. He explained how things were at home, in Serbia, during the war, and how they are now, and I shut up. Milan first came to the States to work as a lifeguard for a company that runs a summer swimming pool operation. Like Dickie, the company was unsuccessful in recruiting Americans to do its work and began importing employees. Whereas Dickie looked to Mexico for his skilled rider and grooms, the swimming company went to Eastern Europe and Russia for its lifeguards. Milan was at the pool from 10:30 a.m. to 5:30 p.m. He picked up a gig working at a Taco Bell from eight to midnight. Then, he got a job with Dickie working from 4:30 a.m. to 8:00 a.m., doing everything from galloping horses to mucking out stalls, keeping the morning's work going forward at a brisk pace. Eventually, he found horses to exercise at a farm northeast of Pimlico during the afternoons, left Taco Bell, left the swimming pool company. He's just married his childhood sweetheart from Serbia, Sonia, who gallops horses at Pimlico for another trainer—Dickie's ex-wife, in fact.

Buttermilk stands still as Milan slides the snaffle bit into his mouth. I run my hand down Buttermilk's long and sensitive back and fling the rubber, non-slip pad up over his withers. Milan, on the other side, straightens it. Then the saddle towel, the thick saddle pad, the pommel pad over the withers. We each grip the front corner of the saddle towel, and together, fold it back. Then the saddle and the girth.

Because of Milan's assistance, I'm ahead of the other riders. I pull Buttermilk out, give him a walk—to loosen up his long back—one time around the shedrow. As we walk, each of Dickie's grooms looks up questioningly at me when we pass, and asks if I'd like a leg up. I decline, walk Buttermilk a full turn. Dickie steps out of the tack room, flings me up as if I'm light as a flat jockey, then keeping a hold of the reins—for this, the quietest horse on the track—walks us another turn.

Buttermilk ambles down the long aisle-way, stalls on the left, hip-high wall on the right with open space from the top of the wall to the ceiling. Screw-eyes are screwed into the wall-to-ceiling posts, water buckets hanging from them. There's a dug-up path running down the middle of the aisle, and to its left, there's a hard-packed path where the hot walkers walk. One groom fed all the horses at 4:00 a.m. The others have mucked out and bedded down their stalls so there's no clutter—bales of hay or straw, buckets of water, wheelbarrows, muck sacks—in the way. We're streamlined. Dickie runs a STRAC outfit—that's Skilled Tough Ready Around the Clock, like the Army's 101st 'Screaming Eagles' and the 82nd 'All Americans.' He likes his outfit to run on time, smoothly, morning after morning, almost on its own, as he and the other three men in his outfit did back in the summer of 1971 when with watches synchronized they'd jump simultaneously from C-130s into the darkness—"it's like the inside of a cow"—fall ninety seconds and land in the jungle within thirty yards of a bend in a river, a fork in a road. Precision. Repetition. Get it right.

"How's it going in Iraq?" he murmurs.

"OK," I say. "Andrew's finished his mission in Syria and he's back on the base."

"He'll be all right, Pat. Don't worry. They've finally gotten their act together over there. Andrew's well-trained and the Marines take care of their men. When's his deployment over?"

"Christmas."

"Good, it won't be long. Keep me posted."

He leads me out of the barn where the other three are waiting on the asphalt. He steps back inside, talks to a veterinarian who has just arrived. You don't see many vets around Dickie's barn. If it hadn't been for Vietnam, Dickie might've become a veterinarian. He attended the University of Pennsylvania as a pre-vet major, playing football and lacrosse, and wrestling, then transferred to the University of Delaware, graduating in the spring of 1968 with a bachelors in animal science and agricultural biochemistry. The war was on. Dickie enlisted, graduated first in his class at officer training school, qualified to train in Texas for a year on the Army's pentathlon team—running, swimming, bicycling, shooting, fencing—but signed up for Vietnam.

Dickie returns, whistling, runs his hand over the horses. He's big, horse-sized, and doesn't move around horses the way most of us do. He trusts his horses and they trust him. He walks right up to them, pats them on the rump or puts his arm around their necks. He presses against them, rubs his hand on their necks, reaches down, feels a tendon or two, moving from one horse to another. Mumbles a few expletives about the owners of Pimlico and whether he'll soon be commuting to Laurel.

"Any news about when it's going to happen?" I ask about the rumored closing of Pimlico for training.

"It's going to be soon, maybe October."

He notices something about the way Britanny's horse is standing. Picks a hoof up. Puts it between his knees. The shoe is loose. He grabs the shoe with his hand, twists it back and forth, yanks it off with his bare hands.

Years ago, Dickie pulled a colt called Valley Crossing (my horse Riderwood's sire, and as I point out to Riderwood, trying to inject a little fire into his relaxed nature, winner of over $1.5 million) out of his stall, ready for the groom to lead him to the paddock for a race. He looked at the colt's feet. Valley Crossing had "grabbed" a front shoe with a hind foot and snatched it off. No time to waste. Out of town, in a strange barn. No blacksmiths around. He found the shoe in the stall, got a hammer and some nails, nailed the shoe on and won the race.

First set. We head out in the dark. Approach the track. The little red lights are still blinking on the rail around the track. We wait. The horses stand.

José's horse fidgets. He walks the horse up the incline. Every morning, he times it perfectly. The second he steps onto the track the red lights magically stop blinking. Onto the track. Take a left. Jog. José is on a fast one. Off he goes, hugging the outside rail, ahead of Justine, Britanny and me. Justine and Britanny are discussing Virgin Fest, the upcoming concert to be held in the infield—Bob Dylan is coming. Dickie, being a Dylan fan, plans "to walk over and hear him play." The day before he recited the lyrics of Dylan's "Tell Me" to us:

Tell me, do those neon lights blind your eyes?
Tell me, behind what door your treasure lies?
Ever gone broke in a big way?
Ever done the opposite of what the experts say?

Tell me.
Tell me.

The girls jog off, heading "backwards"—clockwise—around the track. I stand in the stirrups. Buttermilk lazily breaks into a jog. Around the turn, by the 3/8's pole, cars are shooting down Northern Parkway twenty yards to our left. Then, we're on the backstretch.

The barns are coming up. They are more recently built than our old wooden barns on the grandstand side. Made of cinder blocks, they are hot in the summer, cold in the winter, and poorly kept up. Grooms—shirts off, towels over their arms—are sauntering around the second story porches of the bunkhouses, built over the barns.

We pass the outrider, comfortably seated in a western saddle, her horse's rump against the outside rail. "*Mister Smithwick*," she asks, mimicking a student, "when do classes begin?"

"Not for a couple of weeks, Sharon." Meetings for new faculty at Harford Day School start soon; I'll pass the site of the last running of the Rochelle Tin Cup, Bel Air Racetrack—now a mall—on the way to work.

Janon and Sissy Fisher are standing at the gap. Janon—with the exception of four years of service as a Marine—has been working at Pimlico since his father had stalls directly across from Bold Ruler who won the Preakness on this track in 1957 with one of the world's greatest jockeys—Eddie Arcaro—in the tack. Janon and Sissy are sending out their first horse of the morning ahead of us and in the tack is Donald, who was one of the senior riders here, along with Cliff Barrosox and Chucky Gore, when I was a teenager. At the time, one of the few black "galloping boys"—as we are called, no matter what age—Donald is the only one now. He's had one operation after another on his throat, often being forced to take a month off, and then, one day, he's back. He rides like an old-time steeplechase jockey, with "a deep seat and a long hold" (stirrups long, rear end further back than the young jocks, reins gripped at the withers instead of high up by the horse's neck)—which is why Janon has him in the tack: his mounts respond to his gentle hands and relaxed style by lowering their heads, lengthening their strides, and galloping around like classy stakes horses.

In 1984, one cold, blustery February morning after galloping a mile, I was walking up the homestretch, by the outside rail, approaching the gap by the quarter pole that leads off the track, on a horse called Epilogue. Donald was on a horse in front of me. Twenty yards to our left, up on the asphalt near the grandstand, was the ambulance, engine running. A door opened, the driver stepped out. Donald's horse ducked/wheeled to the right. Epilogue leaped toward the inside rail. I grabbed a fistful of mane, preparing for a loose horse to come tearing straight at me but to my amazement there was Donald still on the horse. His horse, shocked at the outcome, walked quietly the rest of the way down the homestretch. Donald did not lose his temper. Didn't cuss out the horse. Didn't kick and snatch the horse. That's why Janon rides Donald. Janon lives by a strict code: Semper Fidelis. Last month, Donald felt weak just standing in the shedrow—ended up having a pacemaker put in. Cancer, heart problems, weight loss, no vocal chords, no matter: Donald steps into the barn at 5:30 and Janon gives him a leg up.

* * *

Buttermilk has lengthened his stride and is up alongside Justine and Britanny, who are discussing job possibilities. Britanny has decided to pick up an evening job as a receptionist. We jog along, discuss this position for which she'd just been interviewed. It sounds all right, but she is being rather vague. "What is it?" I ask. "A receptionist at a motel?"

"Oh no," Britanny laughs, "it's good money. All you have to do is sit there on your ass and greet people."

"Who are you greeting?"

She is standing up in her stirrups, bent over low, back parallel to the horse's, looking straight ahead. "Well, you just sit there in the entrance hall. . . ."

"Sit where?"

"Sit there in the entrance hall to the strip joint."

"Strip joint!"

"Yes, it's good money. You greet the customers. You take their money and tell the ones that want to see male dancers to go through the door on the right, and the ones that want to see female dancers, the door on the left. They say you make a lot in tips."

"Now Britanny, we need to talk about this. You'll be behind

that desk for three nights and then you'll be hearing that the strippers are making a hundred an hour and so- and-so is sick tonight and couldn't you just give it a try." And yet, I felt somewhat ambivalent, for after all, hadn't William Faulkner asseverated that the best living arrangement a writer could have was to bunk in a brothel: you'd have all your needs taken care of, you'd meet all kinds of interesting people, and you'd have the mornings as free to write as a medieval monk in his scriptorium. (There's also the success story I've just learned of Theodora, whose father, a bear trainer at the Hippodrome in sixth century Constantinople, deserted the family. Looking for new income, Theodora's mother introduced her to professional dancing and disrobing, which led to becoming a child prostitute and eventually a well-paid paramour. Theodora converted to Christianity, and before you know it, she was Empress Theodora married to Emperor Justinian, who established Christianity as the religion of the Byzantine Empire.) But Britanny wasn't a writer . . . and also, there was one bit of personal history I wasn't planning on telling anyone but which later in the morning was brought up by our trainer. Back in the 80's at Fort Erie Racetrack in Canada, Tom and I (both our wives still in Maryland), and occasionally Dickie would stop by a tavern called the Grand Trunk (just off the track, right by the 5/8's pole) for lack of anywhere else to go for "brunch." It was the only game in town, and so, we supported the Grand Trunk, even though starting at 11:30 every morning, we were shocked and dismayed to find dancers—wearing, as Dickie put it, "the emperor's new clothes"—performing on the bar.

We jog past the 3/4 pole, past the church with the neon sign, past the starting gate, around the clubhouse turn. The first of the morning's many ambulance sirens goes off. Another man stabbed, shot or beaten up. Off he goes to the emergency ward at Sinai Hospital. Murderers, thugs, drug dealers, punks, thieves and gang members prefer to do their shooting and stabbing when the mercury rises about ninety. Out of the two or three murders a week committed on hot Baltimore nights, a high percentage occur just outside the wire in what was once the town of Pimlico where my father, Uncle Charlie White, Salvadore Tuminelli, Winky Cocks, Brian Hickey, Billy Turner, Dave Mitchell, Kip Elser, Tom Voss and I used to go after work in the morning without a thought of safety, headed for the Pimlico Hotel for the best bloody Mary and roast beef sandwich in town, or to the Uptown Bar for a beer, a shot of whiskey and a slice of beef jerky, and what is now a killing field. We stay inside the wire.

Dickie is leaning on the outside rail just past the finish line, studying each of our horses. We jog past him, pull up, turn around, and gallop off.

Buttermilk—unusual for a racehorse—remains calm. I squeeze with my legs, get him to take a hold of the bit, cluck to him, and he gallops around a mile and a quarter as nicely as can be.

Next set. Take a Check—who has her idiosyncrasies. Walking to the track, she'll stop, refuse to budge. Then—she'll jet forward and do a fake rear-up, a hop off the ground. She'll stop again. Nearing the gap, she'll want to race out onto the track. You have to stay relaxed on her, ignore her antics, and once she's galloping, she goes around like a brand new BMW with the smoothest automatic gearshift imaginable.

Sunlight Sparkling
on the Silver Rail

Third set: "Take Down Two—Pat." The summer before, when he was a two-year-old and hadn't been castrated, he'd been my least favorite horse. One morning, a new groom—who didn't last long; all he wanted to do was get through the morning—gave me a leg up onto Take Down and instead of holding the reins by the bit and walking me down the aisleway while I got my feet in the stirrups and tightened the girth, he let me loose. Take Down humped his back. I reached down to tighten the girth. Take Down started jigging. He was pulling so hard on the reins, with his head down and his back up, that the saddle slid up over his withers. We jigged around the turn by the tack room, my feet dangling, my left hand pulling up the girth billets and then he spooked at a groom setting up the water buckets outside the barn. He dug his toes in and reared straight up—banging my head on the overhead pipe running the length of the barn—and slapped down on packed dirt, hard. Not having been able to get my feet and weight in the stirrups, the impact bolted up, blindingly, sickenly, through my genitalia, through my pelvis and into my spine. Up he went again, twisting, bang went my head, and down again, the impact shooting up through the core of my body. It took me two months to recuperate. I could not hop onto Riderwood or Saitensohn, at home. I had to climb up on top of a fence and then lower myself down onto their backs like a broncobuster easing himself onto a wild one. If a horse spooked or tried to wheel and I had to tighten the pelvic muscles, I was zapped by a gnawing shock to the groin that shot up through my spine. Also, p.m. performances with the wife were not improved.

81

And now, here I am getting on Take Down every morning, and loving it. Take Down is a dark bay with strong shoulders and a broad chest. Although castrated over the winter, he still has the vestiges of a colt's thick and powerful neck.

We rarely breeze a horse alone but on the board is written "Take Down," a "P" beside it, and "3/8." I'd breezed—let them go almost full speed—several since coming back for the summer, and had not been pleased with my "nerve." The first time, I was on a little two-year-old colt, with Justine on my inside, José on my outside, and when we broke off at the 3/8's pole I could not believe or comprehend our speed. I got down low, the colt's legs were churning, the posts to the inside rail were ticking by, we were leaning in at much more pronounced angle than I'd remembered; we were flying around the sharp turn on our inside lead—the inside front leg coming down first; around the turn, I gave the outside rein a slight tug, shifted my weight to the outside, and he switched to the outside lead. Then we were speeding down the stretch and I felt like one of those old timers you see who is leaning back, pushing against the forward speed, rear end down low banging against the kidneys of the poor horse. I did nothing to help the little colt. I was a flopping muck sack, worrying how those thin cannon bones and delicate ankles could take all this pressure, and here this stunning model was happily zipping along on my inside, right up against the rail, stirrup banging against it, completely unfazed, and José was turning toward me, as if we were going for a walk in the park, looking me in the eye, and crisply asking, "Everything OK, Pa-trick?"

I breezed a few more. Even though I'd been riding steeplechase races over the spring, it seemed too fast, and I gave in. I adjusted my thinking: my breezing days were over. One more chink had been taken out of my riding repertoire. "Old-timer for hire. Can still gallop. Can't breeze." It had to happen some time, I supposed.

Milan lifts me—and I am in the saddle, feet in the irons, and standing up, stick in right hand. I walk Take Down out onto the entrance of the track at the 1/4 pole, take a left, jog backwards to the 3/8's pole, pull him up, walk out to the middle, turn and start cantering. Cantering slowly. Torturously slowly. On breezing days, Dickie likes them to *crawl* around to the pole. Down the stretch. Under the wire. Around the clubhouse turn. Past the chute to the starting gate. Down the backside. To the red-ringed 1/2 mile pole, eyeballing the upcoming black-ringed 3/8's pole. I haven't changed my grip or made any sort of move but Take Down has read my mind and body language and has his head a little lower than usual, is pulling, is picking up speed. We drift in towards the rail. I'd love to shorten my hold on the reins but if I make any move to change my grip he will take off. I keep the long hold, let him gradually pick up speed while lowering myself and now the pole is coming up, I put him on the rail, we near the pole and we're rocketing past it.

It's not like the earlier breezes on the two-year-olds. I'm in my tuck, balanced, pulling against Take Down. He's pulling hard, he's on the correct, inside lead, his left front foot striking the track first with each stride, and we're barreling around the turn just off the rail. We're flying but it's as if time has slowed: we're in slow motion, the posts to the aluminum rail ticking by metronome-like, the horse all business, the rider feeling like this is his purpose, nothing else exists outside this bubble of horse and rider speeding around the turn at Pimlico at 6:00 a.m. when most of the East Coast is asleep. Around the turn, I pull slightly on the inside rein while at the same time shifting my weight to the inside, and then, feeling that he has just completed a full stride on his inside lead, I tug on the outside rein, shift my weight to the outside and— *click*—he switches to the outside lead, his outside front leg striking the track first with each stride. I sit still for a few seconds, relax, feel him take a deep breath, and then gather him up, tighten my grip on the reins, squeeze with my legs, making him pull against me. We pass the quarter pole. I keep a good grip on the reins, keep him "on the bit," and am a part of the rhythm of his gallop. I push with each stride, through the wire, stand up going around the turn and ease him up. The sunlight sparkles on the silver rail. Inside the rail, the turf course is green and inviting. We turn, jog back to Dickie who is leaning towards us, hands gripping the top of the outside rail. He catches my eye, waiting for my report as if this were the first horse he's ever trained.

"Felt great," I say. "Felt really good—he's not even blowing."

"Was he trying?" he asks, staring directly, questioningly, into my eyes.

"Yes, yes, he was trying."

84 PART ONE

We walk the rest of the way down the stretch, along the outside rail, quietly victorious, the clubhouse and grandstand on our left. Between the grandstand and the rail is a half-acre of asphalt covering the area where once thousands of spectators in the midst of the Depression, the men in fedoras, the women in big floppy hats—including my mother, her school, Garrison Forest, shut down for the day—cheered on War Admiral and Sea Biscuit. Weeds are sprouting up between the cracks of the asphalt. The weeds grow tall. The cracks grow wide. Yes, the backstretch of Pimlico has gone to hell, to the weeds, or to the rats. You've never seen fatter, healthier, happier rats! They nibble and scratch and scatter and play tag all morning, in and out of stalls, back and forth across the aisleways, rats with glossy coats that look like they've been curried, brushed, and rubbed, rats that barely get out of your way when you're coming back on your first horse of the morning, rats that are bigger and stronger and healthier than any of the hordes of inbred and emaciated cats, a plague of rats.

Yet, this is one of the best *racetracks* in America. A racetrack is not an inanimate object; it is not an oval covered with a layer of dirt on it that remains the same day after day. A racetrack is like a racehorse—it is alive and breathing and in training. Consisting of layers of dirt, sand, stone, rock, the surface is painstakingly cared for by Pimlico's maintenance crew. In the heat of August, you step out onto the track when it opens at 5:30 a.m., or at 8:30 after the break: it has been watered and meticulously harrowed, the lines from the harrows straight and parallel to the inside rail. It has the same springy cushion it would have in April. Trainers from out-of-state tracks ship to Pimlico to breeze on its enviable surface.

We take a fifteen-minute break at 8:00. This time of day, Dickie revels in finding anything in the news that is humorous in a pathetic way, especially if it shows the complete lack of good sense—the item often gleaned from page five or six of the *New York Post*—of Ivory Tower liberals, office-bound racetrack administrators, crooked and hypocritical politicians, and Pentagon tacticians who have forgotten the simplest strategies of warfare, well documented since Alexander the Great! Switch the topic, get him talking about zippers, standard martingales, spurs ("I'll pull them right off a rider"), anything that inhibits a horse's free movement, "gyps" (backstretch lingo for penny-pinching horsemen who treat their horses poorly), the *New York Times* (and yet, he enjoys

The New Yorker)—and you will hear a string of original epithets woven throughout an entertaining tirade.

One minute later, a well-dressed, leggy, female guest of an owner might step into the shedrow, and there Dickie will be: speaking clearly. No cussing. Pontificating about his latest passion. For a while it was Civil War history. Then, it was photography—he rushed out and bought all the best equipment. Next, literature of the Irish War of Independence. One winter he was immersed in the lure of the Iditarod Trail Sled Race. Books on tape: he loves anything by David McCullough—especially his history of the Brooklyn Bridge.

The morning rolls on. One horse after another. Milan has to leave early. Dickie becomes my valet, helps me tack up, and explains his dreams and ambitions for his extended family of father, sister, brothers, nieces and nephews. The investment he likes to make more than any other, whether it is vet school or prep school, is in the education of his young relatives—and they spin out into such a complex spider web of relationships that I can't help but get all tangled up in it as he explains, while giving me a leg up, what one niece or young brother is doing, where he or she is in college. He grips my ankle, lifts me as if I'm a flashlight without batteries, holds me too high, hovering, hanging in the air, my left leg perpendicular to the horse as I struggle to swing the rest of my body around facing the correct direction. If he's in mid-story, he grabs a rein and walks me an extra turn around the shedrow. If he's concluded a thought, the second I snap free of his grip, the dancing, jigging horse rockets forward and Dickie is three stalls down talking to a girl jockey. He gives the worst leg ups. I realize now it is because—he has never, as an adult, been given a leg up.

The girls, José, and I gulp water out of our bottles in the tack room as we pick up fresh saddle towels and girth covers for each new set. Then, with relief, we're all off our last horses, a full day ahead of us. It's bright. It's sunny. We riders are laughing and joking about what we're going to do. I yank off my steaming helmet and sweat-drenched T-shirt, put my head under a faucet of blasting water. José and I kid the girls: why don't they do the same. They pull off their vests, revealing tight, black, athletic tank tops. They lean forward, shake out their hair, then stand straight up, lean back, raise their elbows high and push their hair back. Dickie walks around, thanks each one of us individually. He's the only trainer I've ridden for who thanks everyone in the barn at the end of the morning. He's getting ready to ship up to Monmouth Park. Justine stands straight, stretches her neck, rolling her head to the left, then back, her hair swinging behind her, to the right and forward. Dickie walks up behind her, puts his big hands on her collarbones, his thumbs between her shoulder blades, and massages her, finding the hot spot. She leans back into him. José raises his eyebrows, grins and rolls his eyes at me. Neither of us has ever received a massage. Justine, Britanny and I walk out of the shedrow, the grooms saying *mañana* and me calling back *adiós amigos* and *hasta la vista*.

Twenty minute drive to the countryside on a Sunday. Arriving home, I let my body down in the Adirondack chair looking out over the back field. Riderwood and Saitensohn are happily grazing on the other side of the stream that is flowing freely due to my early-summer digging but needs weed eating. Unlike the managers of Pimlico, I plan to get around to it this afternoon.

I look in admiration straight ahead at the new fence Ansley and I put up. To my left, no longer the ramshackle chicken house of my youth, a twenty-four by eighteen-foot leaning eyesore, which I had patched and re-patched, about to collapse. Ansley had insisted we level it. She'd rented a dumpster and hired a farmer with a bulldozer; he and I knocked the chicken house down, filled the dumpster. She hired a stonemason to lay a stone floor, and now we have a patio. He'd also laid the stone sidewalk behind me so we don't have to tip toe down a path of irregular stones, dodging the mud, on the way to the back porch, which now has four new six-foot long steps. Late one afternoon, she and her friend Betty had been standing on the porch talking to our prima donna carpenter, getting an estimate. I approached the duo, "... that's way too much. This is a simple job. We can do it ourselves." The prima donna carpenter left in a huff. I heard Ansley say, "OK now, let's get *organized*." And they did, measuring the steps, cutting the boards, tearing out the old boards, and hammering in the new.

Behind the house, and to the left of the porch, my mother had built a kennels boarded by a high fence of chicken wire. It had become overgrown. The old locust tree was half dead. Shoots had sprouted up all around it. Multiflora rose had crept in. Bushes had grown into huge, gangly creatures. The spring after Mom died, Ansley tore out everything and planted a rose garden.

I stand. Thirsty. The hell with it. I walk to the kitchen, grab a Canadian ale, pour it into a glass. The fresh taste brings back the summer of galloping for Dickie at Fort Erie—how about the afternoon I took him sailing on my twelve-foot boat and we got caught in a hail storm—the dry, bitter, forest-rapids-over-rocks, thirst-quenching Molson quaffed at the Grand Trunk, the Canadian beauties dancing on the bar. Now the father of a young daughter, I scold myself, then chuckle, "What the hell, I ain't perfect." I fill a bucket with hot water, drop in a sponge, return to my chair. It's 9:50—I am supposed to be ushering at church but luckily I'd found a replacement. At the moment, Ansley is seated in a pew looking beautiful and innocent and seductive in her Sunday finest as are many of the women seated nearby—so proper, so saintly, so pure—and the minister is giving the sermon and the streams of cobalt blue, soft magenta and incandescent yellow are filtering through the stained glass windows and the foam is subsiding in my glass, the sun is peeking around the house and lighting up the dew on the grass, setting it aglow. I take a sip, and another. I unlace my boots, pull them off. Pull off the damp leggings, the soggy and leather-stained socks. Dig my toes into the cool, wet grass. Warfield whinnies. I look behind me. He's up by the gate to the top paddock, pumping his head up and down. When he sees that he's gotten my attention, he stands perfectly still, looking me straight in the eye, pricking his ears forward. Barefoot, I walk up, open the gate. He wanders out onto the lawn, down to the thick grass by my chair, grazes. I sit. Feel Warfield's soft muzzle against the back of my neck. I hold the glass up. Warfield slurps some ale, slaps his lips together and returns to grazing, his lush strawberry tail swishing lazily across my shoulders.

I reach into the bucket of hot water, grab the sponge, squeeze it out. Pick up a boot. Rub hard against the sweat-and-salt streaked leather on the inside of the boot. Do the same to the other boot. Set them in the sunlight. Feel the relaxing onset of fatigue. Think back to the interview with Chinua Achebe, his recommendation to writers—"Go for it" and "Read." I'll read another chapter about Eleanor's stormy marriage to Henry II, and her plotting to have her son Richard take over the throne, take a snooze, swim some laps in the neighbor's pool, and "go for it": head for my writing room in the barn. In the late afternoon, I'll crank up the weed eater, and afterwards, I'll sit on the porch steps, rub polish into the creases of my dried boots, and buff the worn-thin leather until it reaches a high gloss. I like these old boots. I won't let them fall apart.

This Wayward Boy

School has begun. I've never experienced anything like this accelerator-pushed-to-the-floor pace, every single second being with the Middle School students. They are unlike any others. They do not have the early-Monday morning blues like Upper School students. They do not have a let down after lunch like adult students. They do not tire and put their heads on their desk in the late afternoon like college students. They do not care if they are hot or cold or deprived of food or sleep or coughing and sneezing and spiking a temperature. They *go go go* full tilt, all day, from 7:45 until 4:00. They are my pages becoming squires, my squires becoming knights, my knights becoming lords, my lords becoming kings and queens, presidents and prime ministers: I love them; they will rule the world. And all this at Tom's alma mater—whose headmistress, Sara Brumfield, referred to him as her "wayward boy"—the only school he ever liked, where he used to sit in the boiler room looking over racing publications with Jack Buchanan, the maintenance man, and give tips on who was going to win at nearby Delaware Park, Pimlico, Laurel, or Bowie Racetrack that afternoon. He clearly remembers showing up at school one morning with a broken finger and Ms. Cameron Minion, one of the founders of the school—and the daring, energetic, charismatic originator of the Medieval History course and program, i.e. my predecessor—immediately taking him to the hospital to have it set, and another day, arriving at school with a bad cut on his hand and Mrs. Brumfield pulling him into her office, cleaning it, wiping disinfectant on it, and bandaging the hand of her wayward boy. Sara Brumfield stood for freedom and joy and serendipity and creativity in expression. Going out on a limb. Taking a chance. Challenging authority. Sticking up for the underdog. She was open. Harford Day was open. Harford Day was an adventure. And now Head Su Harris is carrying on the tradition.

My sister Susan went to Harford Day, along with others her age from Monkton. Our parents fell in love with the school's lively, outdoorsy, free-spirited, adventuresome, field-trip-based, experiential, kinesthetic approach to every day. Harford Day was brand new at this time and some parents didn't even know its exact location. Billy Christmas, who pushed his car to the dare-devil limits of Evel Knievel, was speeding a full carpool to the school one morning and neither Tom nor any one else in the car would give him any directions. "If you don't tell me this minute, you're walking to school." No one said a word. Billy stopped the car in the middle of Bel Air; five children at the fourth and fifth grade levels hopped out; he drove off; they walked the mile to school.

I pile the homework on. I assign essays, short stories, journals. They don't blink. They pick up pen and paper and go to work. In twenty minutes they come to my desk and about their work—which a college student would spend a week on—they say, "done," and slap down a few sheets of unedited but imaginative and highly original handwritten material on my desk.

Teaching English—summer reading. Teaching Medieval History—Fall of the Roman Empire. Study hall—they don't like this; neither do I. They want to be on the move.

Recess duty: I'm playing touch football again. I'm playing glum tag. I'm playing soccer. I'm returning to the freezing, overly air-conditioned room drenched in sweat.

Advisee period—projects to plan, performances to practice, special advisee lunches to organize and schedule.

Lunch duty—my room that holds twenty comfortably is filled with forty students. As Willie Loman in *Death of a Salesman* so craved, I am popular. Watch what you wish for. You can't move in the room. They are at every desk; they are hanging off the counter; they are crammed in the corners; they are *under* my desk. Under my table.

I can't get their names straight. I have too many Kates, Kaitlins, Katy's, Katey's, Kati's, and a Catherine or is it Katherine?

We've started a poker game during lunch. It's fast. All boys so far. Five of us. Chips, cards, rule book on table. They've picked up the game immediately. They have amazing memories—can recall the cards put down. Jack cheated yesterday. This is not for real money. It's for fun. Yet, I saw him slide a card out from under the deck just like in the old westerns. Later, I pulled him aside, gently talked to him about it; he cried.

Papers to grade. Quizzes to give. Parent meetings to schedule.

Parents email me around the clock. I never once in my years at Gilman had a parent email me.

Parents buttonhole me during carpool duty. Carpool duty! Moms dressed in tennis skirts and yoga pants sit up high talking on their cell phones, windows wound up, air-conditioners running, engines thrumming, in Hummers, Sherman Tanks and Military Expedition vehicles built to climb over the mountains of Alaska; in Porsche and Mercede SUVs that can cruise at one-fifty; in jacked up Ford F650 super-trucks designed to pull six-horse vans; in Land Rovers built with periscopes and air-pipes so they'll be ready when Noah re–rigs his ark—waiting as we, the valets, the butlers, cheerfully load up their forty-pound Anne's and sixty-pound Sam's.

Upcoming meetings with psychologists and therapists of students that seem to be doing fantastic to me. Upcoming meeting with the PTA—I'm supposed to give a knock-it-out-of-the-ball-park report on the English curriculum for the entire school. Parents skewered the new science teacher who gave a report at the last meeting.

Am already having early-morning and late-afternoon meetings with parents of our angelic scholars. Am trying to keep them straight. Parents are divorced. They are remarried. Double the emails. Double the telephone calls. Double the work. (And Tom, you should see the second wives. Double the breast size. Double the boob jobs. Half the age. Double the trouble staying focused on the interview at hand while the dad is proudly showing off his new catch and the new catch is blissfully gazing back and forth from him to her hand bejeweled with the big new dazzling diamond.) Try to remember which night the student goes to which parent. Try to remember which is the biological parent, which the step-parent, and which gives a damn about the child. Then—you've been interviewing one mother/father couple, another mother/father couple, and you look up and here come two men. Here come two women. Who's who? What's what? Brian Macdonald, whom I've befriended, wants me to do a power point presentation on Riding and Writing for the entire school. When? In four days. I've shown him and one class a short documentary on Tom and me teaming up in our later years—he the trainer, I the rider—and competing in the Maryland timber races. "Your friend's an alumn? Can we get him to come up and give the talk with you?"

Time is flying, several weeks have passed, and September 19th is approaching. Tom's birthday. September 19th—the big day. Then, every year, he's a year older until I catch up on my March birthday, and we gallop through late spring and summer the same age. That's over fifty years of birthday parties. Early every September, at the end of the Saratoga Race meet, and at the start of school, we know what's coming.

In the pre-teen years it was pin-the-tail on the donkey—a game I disliked—where a parent handed you a pin with a donkey tail hanging from it, blindfolded you, spun you around, and everybody laughed as you staggered off in the wrong direction, attempting to pin the tail on a bush or tree or friend's nose. The only party-goers who were successful had to be cheating, peeking under the blindfold. Also, Tom's father, Eddie, usually started off helping out and he was just a little rough, tied the blindfold a bit too tight, spun you a touch too fast, pushed you away to find the donkey too forcefully. He never lasted long, but still. Following that was bobbing for apples, sack races, and relay races where you and a partner had your legs tied together. Last was hide and seek, and sardines—great fun. I loved it all, except pin-the-tail.

A few years later we were hooked on cops and robbers, or fox and hound—twenty of us fanning out around the house, out to the woods, down the hill to the barn. We had wild, fast chases. Our parents all knew each other—Smalls, Vosses, Secors, Igleharts, Merrymans, Smithwicks, Bosleys—and they'd be under the awning of Eddie's and Jen's (we called Tom's parents by their first name, and, now that I think of it, so did Tom) back patio having a drink, laughing and forgetting about us as we tore around outside. And Gary would be there, Gary Winants, our mutual godfather, best friend of my father, best friend of Tom's father, and the best giver of birthday presents. He never failed. For all his life, he hand-delivered his present the day before Tom's birthday and the day before my birthday.

On becoming teenagers, it was football. (In these years, Gary gave Tom a ticket, along with one extra for me, to see a Baltimore Colts game.) By this time the group had expanded, including new friends from school. Tom had a younger brother, Jack (my father's godson), and we'd allow him and a few of his cohorts to play. Carrying the ball against his hip, Tom would lead us out front, away from the parents' view, to the big field bordered by the asphalt entrance driveway to the house on one side, and a football field's width away, the gravel driveway to the barn on the other.

We knew that this was Tom's party and he had first choice when picking his team as well as when picking the position he wanted to play, which was quarterback. He could really throw. It is a skill of his that few today know about. His motion is the same as when he throws a punch, or serves a tennis ball, or splits a log: a short snappy backswing followed by a quick powerful release. The punch—will knock you off your feet. The serve—can be a blistering ace down the middle or might hit you on the foot. The pass is the best; it's a sure thing. He'd have a serious, calm, professional expression—think Johnny Unitas—while we ran around yelling, "Here, here, I'm open!" (Half of us actually hoped he didn't pass it to us. If we dropped it, we'd have to face him in the huddle: "What happened out there?" he'd hiss dismissively.) He'd eyeball one of us, position his shoulders perpendicular to his target, then pivot, change the angle and look at another; the *One-Mississippi, Two-Mississippi's* would be nearing *Five* and rush time; he'd wave with his left hand to go deep, holding his right arm, cocked back, the ball just behind his ear, ready to release, and then at *Five-Mississippi* he'd release it, and it'd spiral high, beautifully, arcing over the opponents, to a receiver way out there.

We'd try to play two-handed touch but the rules would be broken, the two-handed slaps coming down too hard, knocking players off their feet, until we were really at it, full-on tackle football, and there'd be bloody noses and boys stomping off the field and lost contact lenses and threats hurled—mayhem—more fun than you can imagine. The parents, having such a good time on the back patio, never bothered us. I do remember Gary strolling out and watching us for a quarter, and later in the day, even giving me some pointers.

Upon turning sixteen, added to the birthday parties were

girls, booze, adults, driving to and from the parties too fast, and since we were both galloping horses on the racetrack and riding a few races, Tom would invite our new racetrack friends. Plus— throw into the formula Jack and his friends, now part of the '60s counterculture, hippy movement, and you had a party that did not want to end. By this time, most people just gave silly cards for a present. Not Gary. He would give Tom a subscription to a classy equine publication and a glossy coffee table book about British steeplechasing. We'd wait six months to see if my present in March measured up.

I need to at least get the birthday boy a comical card or whimsical present or serious book, drop it off. How to check in with Mimi, see what she has planned? It's impossible to make a call from the school building. Students are at your elbow. Teachers knock on the door and then step in. The cell reception is iffy in my room.

I go outside, out on the fields, pace, push Mimi's number— and suddenly it's as if the entire Lower School has been released. I know these students from recess duty at the jungle gym when I stand on my head, hang upside down from the monkey bars, do pull ups and chase the little acrobats hand-over-hand across the horizontal ladder. They come swarming across the field, jumping up and down, all around me, informing me that I am talking on a cell phone, staring at the cell phone as if they've never seen one—why do they keep looking?—then suddenly exploding with joy, "Penguins. You have penguins on your cell phone!"—yes, the cell phone cover I bought at the beach has a hologram of penguins on the back—and then they're yanking on my tie, jumping up and down, pointing at it, "You have penguins on your tie!" looking up at me, "Mr. Smithwick, do you like penguins?" pulling my red bandana out of my rear pocket and holding it up, waving it, taunting me with it, then laughing and taking off. Running away with it. I leave a message that makes no sense. Later during history class, in the middle of Attila the Hun burning and terrorizing and ransacking his way towards Rome, Mimi calls. The students are astonished that I answer the phone. Their eyes pop and they whisper to each other about it. Nothing big like the fiftieth, Mimi says, laughing. They're just going to stay home and have meatloaf. I tell the students that this is the wife of an important alumnus, and I'll be giving a talk and doing a power point presentation on this alumnus on Friday. They gape at me for answering the phone. I ask them to say hi—"Hi Mrs. Voss," they exclaim. When I hang up, one goody-goody asks, "Mr. Voss? Is he the one in the movie you showed us?"

"Yes," I say, pleased.

"He's the one that was smoking," she continues.

"Smoking?" another girl says. Then the two of them are talking about it.

"Yes," I say, "I'm afraid he does have this one bad habit." Oh Lord, I'm sure the scene of him smoking in the movie will get back to the parents. Brian had warned me. "You can't show that here, Patrick. These students are pampered and protected—they live in an unreal world. That smoking scene will register with them like someone shooting heroin for you or me." I dive back into an analysis of the blazing speed and killing power of Attila's horse-driven war machine sweeping across Europe.

The bell rings. Students rush out. Two of my most invested medieval scholars approach my desk. Both are riders. One, Casandra, tall and thin, is a miracle. She's adopted—from Kazakhstan, and like her ancestors the Huns, she can really ride. Here she is with me, flourishing in an independent American school, riding in horse shows every weekend, leading her herd of middle class American friends, when she could just as well be living in poverty in Kazakhstan. Every Monday morning, the moment I enter the room, she grabs my attention, brings me to the white board where she has drawn a detailed map of her favorite show ring class—the pick your own course—which is judged primarily on speed and on not knocking down any rails. While I'm attempting to unpack my satchel and trying to remember just how I was going to start off my first period class, she is telling me how she jumped every fence, why she chose to turn sharply here, switching to the left lead, take four strides and jump the spread fence, switch leads in the air, land on the right lead ready to jump the next, where she could pick up speed . . . and not bothering to mention that she won the class until I ask, or to mention that she was champion of the show, until I ask and then demand she bring all the ribbons in and hang them on the white board behind my desk.

"We can't wait to hear your talk on Friday," she says. "My

mother knows Mr. Voss."

"She does. That's interesting. How does she know him?"

"The hunt came through where she boards her horses. One of her horses jumped out of the field and was running away from everyone chasing it. Mr. Voss told the others to go on, and then quietly rode up to the horse, caught him, and led him back to our barn."

"That was nice of him."

"I know Mr. Voss, too," said Leah, four feet tall, looking me seriously in the eye.

"How did you meet him?"

"I was out on the children's hunt. I had gotten up early and braided my pony's mane and tail. Mr. Voss rode up to me at the meet and said it was the prettiest braiding job he'd ever seen in his life and would I come over and braid his horses."

I got ready to say something. Some girls were at the door. "Come on!" they called. "Come on!" It was recess. Out Casandra and Leah ran.

Anointed Sovereign of Signs and Groans

This whimpled, whining, purblind wayward boy;
This senior-junior, giant-dwarf, Dan Cupid;
Regent of love-rhymes, lord of folded arms,
The anointed sovereign of sighs and groans,
Liege of all loiterers and malcontents,
Dread prince of plackets, king of codpieces, . . .
And I to be a corporal of his field,
And wear his colours like a tumbler's hoop!

— William Shakespeare, *Love's Labour's Lost*

His fiftieth: that was the most memorable of Tom's birthdays. I had been sitting at my desk, in my quiet Gilman office, editing the alumni magazine, protected and spoiled by my assistant/secretary across the hall. (Why did I ever leave a job where I had an assistant/secretary, and an excellent one at that?) All was going well. Mimi telephoned, gave me the time and day of the party, informed me she expected a toast. "Not too long, Patrick. You know how Thomas is."

"Yes … , yes, I know."

His sigh. I could hear it as she spoke. In the midst of a talk—of a toast, of a eulogy—I could pick it out. He'd slump his shoulders, look at me or whomever was speaking with the most disappointed, pained expression, eyelids drooping as if he might ease off into sleep, and release a very audible—just one—sigh.

At Oldfields School, on the stage of the David Niven Theatre, I once played the distinguished part of the bard himself in a tightly written slapstick comedy, *The Night Shakespeare Slept*, about the young William coming to London and failing at being an actor. The setting is a tavern. I, William, am the only male character. My dreams have been shattered and I am drinking my worries away, sliding off my barstool into drunkenness. Every one of my lines is a recognizable quote from a male Shakespearean character—Hamlet, Mercutio, Macbeth, Horatio, Romeo, Brutus, Robin Goodfellow, comedies, tragedies, histories all mixed together; and every line declaimed by the hostess and the barmaid is a memorable line from a notable female character—Lady MacBeth, Ophelia, Gertrude, Titania, Juliet, Katherina, Cordelia. There are wild and hilarious juxtapositions.

Tom and his top jockey, the fastidious Englishman Bob Witham in those early years, had been forced to hear me recite my lines as we galloped horses together on Atlanta Hall Farm (with his serious, no-fluff, goal-driven English education, Bob could give the play, the character's name, and in some cases, the act and scene, of every quote), and I must've told them when the play was being held. On a Thursday, the night of dress rehearsal to which only the Headmaster and a few faculty members were invited, the first time I walked out on the stage and glanced into the audience of a dozen, there Tom and Mimi were in the front row. My adrenalin shot up.

At one point in the play, I push my chair away from a table, stand, wobble—am *supposed* to be at a loss of words for a few seconds before falling straight backwards into the arms of the "barmaid" and the "waitress" with whom I'd practiced this move over and over. I am supposed to stand there, wavering, gesticulating, trying to formulate a sentence but failing to articulate a clear thought before I fall back. In that brief moment, as I looked out into the audience, I heard Tom release a painful sigh and I knew he thought I'd forgotten my line—or, was he joining the cast, steadfastly staying in character, playing his part as the "anointed sovereign of sighs and groans"?

"Fifty/ nifty." I could hear them as I sat at my desk. "In Two *Thow*-sand/ he will *Wow* them." That's how many of the toasts would begin. Where would I start?

We go back a ways. There is a photograph on my dresser of us: we're two years old, and it is the last photo where I, a bit plump, am markedly bigger than Tom, who is skinny, looking more like his younger brother Jack. Six years later, things have changed. I have a photograph—these were taken by Mom—of three of us standing by the smokehouse: Tom, in light-colored, long-sleeved shirt, sleeves rolled up, and blue jeans, bottoms folded up, in the middle—his hands on his hips, his elbows out, forcefully looking into the camera's lense. He's bigger-boned, more muscled. I, in khakis and blue polo shirt, am on one side, thinner and an inch shorter. Tom Whedbee, also in khakis and polo shirt, gawky and the tallest, is on the other.

Then, there are photographs of us riding. First, he's on the thick-coated, sturdy Rafferty and I'm on Nappy, who had a snappy show pony's conformation. Mom is taking us to the lead line class at nearby St. James. These are small ponies. A few years later, I'm on Queenie, my bay; he's on Pepper, a gray, and we're going out cub hunting. These are large ponies. Then, there we are in our early teens, on Mom's Thoroughbred show horses and hunters. I'm on Just in Time, a flashy dark bay; he's on Whimsey, a quiet, light bay you had to spur along; and his grandfather Ned Voss, then Master of the Elkridge-Harford Hunt Club, assisted by Wassie Ball (who taught Tom, now Master, most of what he knows about fox hunting) is pinning the ribbons on our horses' bridles— the pair class—at the Elkridge-Harford Hunter Trials.

It wasn't all horses. We loved canoeing immediately after, and sometimes during, a good storm. We'd race up to E. H. "Tiger" Bennett's in Madonna, toss Tiger's fiberglass canoe on top of the car, drive to Deer Creek or Gunpowder Falls and brave the rapids. This was after our apprentice years of canoeing with Tiger—outdoorsman, philanderer, drinker, farmer, carpenter, camper, skier, retired steeplechase jockey, free-spirit, Princeton almost-grad, great friend of my father—and being taught the J-stroke, how to survive on the river, how to "head for the V" when approaching tough rapids, how to drink a couple of bottles of wine on the way down.

Toes Up

All had been going well at Tom's fiftieth. I'd decided to do something different on this chilly night and was reading a sonnet on Tom—first quatrain: love of nature and horses; second quatrain: love of family; third quatrain: love of friends and loyalty: rhyming couplet: bringing it all together—friends, family, horses, and nature. At the moment I began reading the third quatrain to this congregation of friends and relatives, and to Tom's godfather, our godfather whom we shared, I looked up, expecting to have eye contact with Gary. I was standing in front of the fireplace in the living room. It was a chilly night, and the warmth of the flames on my back felt good. The two steps leading down into the room from the front hall were crowded with listeners as was the space to the right of the steps and in front of the built-in shelves filled with classic leather-bound books on racing and foxhunting. An eager audience wanting to be entertained, wanting to laugh. I made a joke about Gary, glanced around, still didn't see him. I took a step away from the fire and returned to my sonnet.

Gary had not been excited about my recent return to race-riding. In fact, he'd criticized me heavily—saying I was doing it just to be in with the "snobby, supercilious and phony mink and manure set," and to play the part of a country gentleman like the rest of the social climbers taking over the sport and I ought to "glue my ass to a chair"" every morning instead of placing "amateur derriere" in saddle. He had been relentless. "Look at what happened to his father," he told people. "He's risking everything ... for what? For a few seconds of glory. It's all about his ego." I'd been looking forward to talking to him and ironing out this

101

acrimony. For all my life, he had been a strong supporter as I ventured away from the world of horses into journalism, teaching and writing, and now this.

The day after the birthday party, I returned home early from work. The chill of the previous few days had gone and there was still some daylight left. I made a pot of tea, grabbed a handful of student-written poems, plunked down in the Adirondack chair on the lawn, and was reading, enjoying and grading the poems.

I got a call. "What're you doing?"

"Just started grading some papers."

"That can wait. Come over here and pick me up."

"Where're we going?"

"Gary's." He gave a long, low sigh. "We're going to Gary's."

"Be right there."

I pulled into his entrance, parked by the kitchen door, walked up the steps into the kitchen. He was seated at the counter, staring straight ahead, smoking. He didn't look well. He hadn't shaved, his skin was sallow; instead of gripping his cheekbones, it sagged. There was a bottle of brandy in front of him and two empty crystal glasses. He poured a generous shot into each glass. Handed one to me, took the other. We drank them down.

A fifteen-minute drive, and then we were pulling into Gary's driveway. He loved this little cottage out in the country. The real estate agent had asked him what kind of a house he wanted. "I want a house as far away as I can get from these phony nouveau riche assholes on the Manor and yet not too far from Atlanta Hall Farm, where I go to see my horses. I want to be able to step outside and take a piss in my back yard without some fucking flagburning liberal transplanted yuppie from Baltimore calling 911 and accusing me of indecent exposure. . . ."

"OK," the realtor had said.

"Lastly, I don't want to be within shooting distance of any spear-chuckers."

"Excuse me?"

"Keep me away from any ebonics-speaking rug-heads."

The agent quit. Gary found his own house.

There was his car.

"Maybe his phone is broken," I said.

"His phone is not broken."

We approached the door. It was not locked. We hesitated. "Go ahead," Tom said.

I opened the door. We walked into the kitchen. Not a sound. The air was not fresh. Everything neat as usual. "Anybody home?" I called out, to break the tension.

Into a den that had a door leading out front. A stack of *Mid-Atlantic Thoroughbred* magazines on one side table. Another of old *Maryland Horses*. There was a wide desk against the wall by a large pane-glass window that looked out over the front lawn. Bills stacked neatly on the left. Checkbook open in the middle. Statements from bank accounts and investments on the right. A legal pad and a list of To Do's in his rounded handwriting pressed hard into the paper.

Not a sound.

The air was not fresh. Windows were closed. It had been chilly but today it had warmed up. Gary liked open windows and fresh air. I was standing by the desk. "Patrick," Tom called.

I stepped into the living room with the fireplace. Here is where Gary had set up winning photographs of his horses—mainly Cookie: one with Bob Witham in the tack, winning at a point to point. One with Bill Martin—who Tom dubbed "The Slasher" because of his use of the whip in the final drive of a race—grinning and happy, in the tack at the Meadowlands; it was a night race and the background is dark; I'm the groom, holding the shank, Tom and Gary are in the shot. Another of Cookie, Bill aboard, at Belmont Park after winning the first running of the A. P. Smithwick Memorial, Tom and Gary and I there beside two of Pop's best friends and riding colleagues, Evan Jackson and Tommy Walsh, and Pop's friend and New York valet for two decades, Dick Dwyer. What a night that was.

"Patrick."

I stepped around another table full of photographs, all of them taken by Gary's brother Peter, equine writer, photographer and editor. Here was one of Tom on Suspendido— trained by Tom, at seventeen, with the assistance of Emmett Grayson and Wassie Ball—and me on Moonlore riding our first formal race together, jumping the third to the last fence of the Benjamin Murray Memorial. I remembered the moment well. It filled me with a warm feeling. I made my way toward the fireplace. Gary—in his quest to save every nickel—had installed a woodstove in front of the fireplace. The side door was open. Gary was lying in a heap by the side door, a load of wood under one arm.

"My God," Tom said, "My God."

A gush of tears burst from my eyes and a flood of memories overran my mind, wave after wave: The birthday presents, hand-delivered, and then always the sitting down with him for a few moments of eye-to-eye contact as he asked how my life was going, and listened. I saw the telescope—sixth grade at Gilman. The camera—junior in college. The book on photography—first job as editor, reporter, and photographer on a newspaper. The book on magazine journalism, *The New Journalism*—first job on a magazine.

How Pop had loved Gary, who'd had polio as a child, walked with an unnatural gate, had a tremor—his hands, his head. Pop had told me when I was a boy that Gary never held back. He went out for the football team at Gilman, with the limp, with the tremor. A tear slid down my father's face. "All his life he had this disability. It made him bitter. It did. But he never complained, never asked any special favors. He played on that football team and he could knock you on your ass."

Our godfather—he had brought us together. He was proud of us. Photos of Tom were scattered around the room. There was a copy of *Gilman Voices* on his mantle piece beside two magazines for which I had written cover stories. Beside them was a photo of Pop and Mikey, Pop in his silks having just won a stakes race on the great Neji, Mikey in a suit. It's a well-known shot—they are walking away from the trophy presentation; Mikey is leaning forward asking Pop a question. Below it, is a headline Gary had cut out of a newspaper: The Smithwick Brothers: A Winning Team.

And there Gary was: gone.

We called the police. We called Gary's brother Peter.

Sirens wailing, lights flashing, two police cars pulled into the entrance. A man from the funeral home came to take the body. He was polite, shook our hands. I learned that he had taken Tom's brother Jack away, ten years earlier; Tom's brother Ned away, twenty-five years earlier; Tom's father Eddie away, thirty-five years earlier.

The police suddenly asked Tom and I to step outside by their cars. Were we next of kin? What were we doing there? Why had we come by? How did we get in? Was the door locked? How long had we been there?

Tom and I looked at one another, realizing we were being treated as suspects.

The funeral home man took Gary's body. The police scoured the house, filled out reports. Finally, everyone left. We found the keys to the house, locked the kitchen door, and departed.

The planning of a small memorial service—we decided I would write and read a poem–out in the Meadow exactly where Cookie was buried; the spreading of Gary's ashes over Cookie's grave and around the Meadow—was ahead of us. We drove home, thinking back on the deaths we'd gone through together: first, the sudden death of Eddie, Tom's father, at 39, where we were fourteen or fifteen; then the death of my father at 47, followed quickly by the sudden death of Ned, at 30; the death of Emmett Grayson, the suicide of the fun-loving, hard-drinking, brawling Brian Hickey; the death of Tiger; the suicide of Mike White; Jack's death at 44. It continued, Mom's death—soon to come, being the toughest for me; Tom was there by my side every night for a week leading up to it. We supported one another, held each other up, gave eulogies, planned ash spreadings, tended to details, stored ashes afterwards in old silver trophies set on top of refrigerators.

Before the cell phone changed life, Tom would sometimes cut out a clip from the racing form about a horseman we'd known. Sonny Thornton—used to exercise horses for Pop and Mikey, rode some races for them, killed riding a race at Charlestown. Tiny—a non-stop talking-singing upbeat, could-drive-you crazy, hot walker for Pop, found dead in his bunkhouse at the track. Tom would drop the clip in the mail, my name and addressed scrawled fast, in a cavalier manner, as if it were an afterthought, across the envelope. If it were someone he knew I'd been close to, such as Mike White, he'd call me up, sigh, and say, "...thought you should know. There'll be an article about him in the *Racing Form*. It was suicide—but that won't be mentioned."

Upon the advent of cell phones, Tom was the first to text on an inexpensive flip top. When a fellow horseman or race-tracker we'd known in earlier years died, I would get a text.

Tommy Musser—toes up. (Tommy used to work on our farm. He was a bully; four years older than I, he would threaten me to do his work, force me into the corner of a stall and use me for a punching bag.)

Bill Riley—toes up. (Bill had raised his family in an apartment or house on Atlanta Hall, had lived and worked on the farm all his life.)

Mildred Riley—toes up. (Mildred, Bill's wife, worked for Tom's grandparents and then Tom and Mimi for decades.)

Nat Nat—toes up. (A knowledgeable and giving black man who had given me a leg up on hundreds of horses at Pimlico when he was the foreman for Katy (Merryman) Voss, and in his "retirement," old, creaky and having a hard time walking, just to "stay in the game," drove the van for Tom. His name was Nat, but since he stuttered, he was called "Nat Nat". He called me "Paddy-Paddy.")

Scotty Schulhoffer—toes up. (Scotty—Hall of Famer best friend of Pop's.)

Marvin Green—toes up. (A fun-loving, garrulous trainer Pop, Scotty, Tommy Walsh and I shared an apartment with.)

David Mitchell—toes up. Call me. (Dave had ridden races for Pop for several years, becoming a part of the family.)

Jimmy Murphy—toes up. Call me. ("Murph"—one of Pop's best friends. First, as a fellow race-rider, then as a trainer.)

Sue Powers—toes up. (Sue, extremely knowledgeable horse-woman, especially about show horses and show ponies. She attempted to teach us the fine points of dressage in Pony Club. We were terrible at the meetings, spent our time flirting with the girls.)

Timmy White—toes up. (Mike's younger brother. Suicide. Both Mike and Timmy were crushed by the pressures of the racetrack and the expectations of friends and family in the upper strata of Virginia society.)

A couple of racetrack girlfriends we'd had some good times with: *toes up.*

Earl Wiseman—toes up. No more notching. (Earl had worked for the Elkridge Harford Hunt his entire life, going all the way back to when he worked for my grandfather, Alfred J. Smithwick, who ran the hunt and was the honorary huntsman after World War I. Earl would tell me interesting stories about Alfred, who died when my father was 18. Earl had a notch in his bed "for every time I've gone to the post with the wife." Old, no longer "whipping" for the hunt, he drove the hound truck. Every time I saw him, he gave me a report on the number of the latest notch.)

Grooms, trainers, exercise riders, retired steeplechase riders, past friends of Pop's—Tom kept me up to date.

Begging for Bagels

S woop—I run, I float, legs spinning like the spokes of a bicycle wheel. The sun is out. We are out of the classroom. It has been a long flu-infested, sneezing-coughing-nose-blowing winter in the classroom followed by a wet, cold spring and now we are out on the soccer field and my legs feel good, loose and limber. The tendinitis in the left foot isn't bothering me. The old nagging crack to the right kneecap isn't acting up. Most of my students are playing some crazy form of tag—glum tag—all around the jungle gym, up and down the sliding board, across the hand-over-hand horizontal ladder, through the "pipe," dodging dashingly in and out of the flying swings, and the Frisbee is gliding, flowing, flying. I snatch it out of the air, pivot, release my arm, snap my wrist, whip it back to one of my students.

I'm out on the soccer field of Harford Day—haven't thrown a Frisbee since college, where has the time gone?—the orange flying saucer is spinning and gliding, hanging and boomeranging, my legs are eating up the ground, devouring the distances, gaining on, outsmarting the hovering, hanging, impossibly floating orange disc in a way you can't do with a football or basketball or baseball or lacrosse ball. This Frisbee is an equalizer of ages. I can keep up with these kids by anticipating its trajectory. And I can see it. Clearly, effortlessly. Unlike the lacrosse ball—white, dirty, faded, that the students bullet at me during lacrosse practice and that seems to disappear for a split second as it nears my stick.

The class had been good—with the prospect of running out of the building, out onto the green grass and under the bright sun and into the fresh air—but they hadn't been paying much attention to the *Balkanization* of the Holy Roman Empire after the death of Charlemagne. (Ha! "How Do You Like It Now Gentlemen?" How do you like that *anachronism* followed by the Lillian Ross/Hemingway *New Yorker* allusion?) The Kentucky Derby is the next day, and just three weeks earlier I'd been in Lexington, Kentucky where two other writers and I—finalists for the $10,000 Dr. Tony Ryan Book Award—had been invited to give a short talk on our books, and then to stand nervously in the room above the Castleton Lyons breeding stall as Shane Ryan, son of the late Tony Ryan, strode to the podium and announced the winner. Tom had pulled a surprise on me and was there with Mimi in the audience as my name was called out. My acceptance speech started off with thanking him, standing before me, for providing and training the horses that I rode in *Flying Change*, and for training me. We'd all flown back the next night. Student comments were due. I had my archaic—*obsolete* the students might call it—green-lined grade book on my rickety airplane fold out table, and other tools which could one day be *artifacts* (Medieval History again, on a roll)—a yellow legal pad and a blue ballpoint pen—and I was madly scrawling rough drafts and notes on students, the entire flight home.

At 5:00 the following morning I arose, typed up comments, rushed to school in the pouring rain, drove right past Ernie Nuetzel, our iconic nonstop lecturing septuagenarian history teacher, Filibuster Ernester I called him, the Polonius of our Danish castle, laughingly directing the traffic with, what was that, a riding whip? And what was that on his head, a hunting cap? Oh well, I was on a mission, paid this no attention, drove past him up to the main door, asked the eccentric, erratic, high-IQ— but attention-wandering—technology man, who roamed around the campus in a tall, bouncy hat out of Dr. Seuss's *Cat in the Hat*, to please take the two large victory-proclaiming posters I'd brought with me and the box holding the trophy. He did so. I parked the car, picked up the items, walked through the building and toward my classroom.

Where the hell was everyone? One of the biggest pain-in-the-neck students—I'd given him countless detentions, written his mother I don't know how many emails, pulled him aside and talked to him man-to-man after many a class, this very student, Jason, was suddenly standing right before me in the rain, his back perfectly straight, looking me in the eye, shaking my hand—with a good strong grip—and saying, "Congratulations Mr. Smithwick, congratulations." No one was outside playing—well, of course, it was raining. And yet, I heard no noise, no hubbub, nothing, and saw no one with the exception of one teacher, big, burly, bearded, gruff Brian, who normally paid no attention to what was going on outside of his *keep*. He was strangely standing at the one window that looked out on the walkway approaching the building. I held out the five-foot long $10,000 poster-check, pointed to it. He frowned irritably, waved urgently and pointed exasperatingly for me to go to the side door to enter the building, which I did and then walked to the first turn where the soda machine is, and truthfully, I did have a feeling they might have planned something, just an inkling—the type of feeling I've had hundreds of times before and which has almost never panned out. I've had this feeling, over and over, at Gilman and nothing had ever come of it. It was always another student, another teacher, who received the accolades, the award, the surprise, the big check, the all-expense paid sabbatical, the toasts and roasts, making me feel an also-ran, a brisk jotting of marginalia, a *drollery* (the grotesque yet whimsical figures—two parts animal, one part human—drawn in margins of medieval illuminated manuscripts, and more recently sketched in the latest first editions of my seminarians.)

I rounded the turn at the soda machine, and there was the entire Middle School. They had been quiet, obedient foot soldiers preparing for the ambush. They were lined up against the lockers of the hallway, teachers and students forming a gauntlet, and there was Filibuster Ernestus—with whip and riding cap, oh I see! Ernie announced my arrival over his megaphone as if I were a conquering Roman general at the head of his legions drawn by a four-horse chariot through the streets of Rome, the *vir triumphalis*, the *triumphator*, immortal, linked to Alexander the Great . . . and then there was a screaming, cheering, yelling, applause echoing off the metal lockers.

I announced that I was at "a loss of words." I pulled out my trophy—a scalloped, foot-high replica of a medieval round tower. How suitable for me, for my students. It was modeled on the towers monks built on the coasts of Ireland to protect themselves from marauding Vikings. I launched into a lecture. The founder of my award, Irish billionaire Dr. Tony Ryan, had had this tower built on his breeding farm, Castleton Lyons, and it was now the symbol for the farm. . . . "Loss of words, loss of words, you've never been at a loss of words," yelled out super-energetic and electrified Livia, one of my favorite students and the best writer on the campus. With its long, gradually narrowing, mottled cylindrical body and its pointed tip the trophy looked like something else, a rather magnificent something else, and every adult who had seen it had made a shocked comment, every woman had grabbed it at the tapered top and had slowly run her hand down to its thick base (Tom laughingly pointed this out at our celebratory dinner after the female owner of the restaurant bought us a round, and congratulated me, looking me in the eye while gently tracing her fingers up and down and around the trophy set directly in front of me), but not one of my students made an off-color remark for the entire day it stood on my desk.

That day, after thanking Katy Dallam, Head of the Middle School, for organizing the surprise, I promised each of my classes a party: donuts, bagels, whatever they wanted, for the next day! The next day, I didn't bring a thing. The following day: I'd been too busy the night before. One class in particular cajoled, coaxed, wheedled and whined—wanting their bagels. One girl, Caitlin (a beautiful singer whose voice tore at your soul!), urged me to write a book about the class and to call it "Begging for Bagels." "Write about us, you'll win more awards, but when are we having the bagels?" Finally, Ansley and I stopped by Donkin' Donuts on the way home from dinner, just about bought out the store, donuts of every color and type, many of them covered with pink and red and yellow sprinkles.

Next day, parties at the end of every class, teachers glaring disapprovingly at the ruckus in Room 210 as they walked by, Big Nurse, the Spanish teacher stabled a few stalls down, losing her cool, tearing out of her room like a plump spinning top, planning on whipping my door open and lambasting my troops, but, at just that moment I'd gone to the kitchen to get some plates and Livia had jokingly locked the door and Big Nurse had a hissy! When I returned with a stack of plates she was delivering a dynamic *jeremiad* (English vocabulary) on their noise, on sitting on the chair tops, on the danger of locking the door, and giving them advance notice on what their fate would be if this ever happened again: they'd be thrown out of school, never be accepted by another school, be turned down for a job at the 7-Eleven, never get into college, never get married, never have children; their lives would be absolute miserable flops, and all because they'd jokingly locked the door on Mr. Smithwick—who could not have cared less!

*　　*　　*

The air is chilled
but the sun is bright
and I am thrilled
to be on this site

playing with my students, the week to be over in minutes, and not having anything to do over the weekend—no rushing to the airport, no being frisked between my legs to see if I have three balls and if the third one might be a bomb; no being questioned by smirking security guards on what the hell was that phallic thing that showed up in the scanner while Tom, free and on the other side of the X-ray machine, laughs and makes faces at me; no searching for luggage and after finally finding it, waiting for a sniffing German Shepherd to give me the go ahead; no comments to write, talks to give, interviews to prepare for, reporters to call back, contacts to make. As on most of the first weekends in May, I'd go for a ride, mow right up to Derby time, rush into our house, out of the late afternoon heat, open a Smithwick's Ale and watch the race.

I had been scheduled to attend the Parents Association Kentucky Derby Cocktail Party and Fundraiser. The two rather demanding mothers—both psychologists, "The Dynamic Duo," we called them—who were the heads of the Parents Association had dreamed up a vague scenario which included me attending the party in racing boots, britches and silks, and hopping up on a horse which I would van over. Then each set of parents would have their pictures taken with me and the horse as if I were Ron Turcotte and the horse were Secretariat, and they were Penny Tweedy (Chenery now) and family—having just won the Derby. This was not something I was looking forward to.

I had finally stopped riding steeplechase races a few years earlier, and now, over 60, I was no longer allowed to ride races. My race-riding tack—my feather-light boots (my father's), my light saddle (my father's), my white britches, blue and light blue silks, rubber bands to wrap around the wrists of the silks, helmet, goggles, light stretch girths, light tan yoke—was all neatly polished and cleaned and washed and packed into my old leather tack bag, and stored in the attic.

After a lifetime of conflict about whether to ride or not to ride, I had just won an award for writing, not riding, and the last thing I wanted to do was put on that outfit when I was back to normal weight—the britches would feel too tight, my slight love handles would reignite that old guilt from my teenage years—and with gray hair poking out of the ear straps of the helmet, parade around a bunch of people who didn't know a thing about racing or horses, and have that mantra start back in my head: Why aren't your riding? Why didn't you ride more races? Win more races? My boots, my silks, my helmet, my britches—were real; they had dignity; they were not a costume. To get on the horse, and just to pose, like some phony, a clown, a model! Not even to walk, trot or canter across a field—I'd been told there was no such field available. To have that feeling seep into my bones of being light and airborne and free and fast and young and high up and away from the daily disturbances of lowly pedestrian life, but not be able to cut loose, gallop, school, race—ugh!

Before I'd left for Kentucky, I had called Peter Jay, who trained and boarded horses nearby. We set it up. He'd watch the Derby at home, put a horse on a trailer, and drive over. I'd watch the Derby at the party, and as soon as the horses were under the wire, Superman-like, I'd sneak off to a telephone booth, pull on my race-riding outfit, and be waiting. We'd surprise the parents. This was a highly synchronized maneuver. Top secret. Peter Jay—gifted writer, noted columnist who had been the Saigon Bureau Chief of the Washington Post during the Vietnam war—would give me a leg up and hold the horse as if he were an old-timey groom. We'd have some fun.

After we returned from Kentucky, I emailed all parties involved, and scratched. I needed a weekend off. So did Ansley. Plus, I didn't think it would work. The Parents Association Moms had told me to bring books, set up a table, sell them—but they hadn't mentioned anything about a book signing in their invitation. I'd be a sideshow. The parents would just stare at me, keep their distance, regard me as an oddity. I was delighted to be rid of this responsibility, chore, errand, irritation. What a relief!

*　*　*

Suddenly there are more students on the soccer field. Big, fast, strong ones. Eighth graders—thirteen or fourteen pour out onto the freshly mowed bright green grass. It's spirit day and they're in wild colors: orange Baltimore Orioles shirts, fluorescent lime-green and pink socks, oversize red and blue-framed sun glasses, a few purple Ravens jerseys. Su, the Head of School, is with them. Even she has let her math class out early. Seeing her, I could feel guilty about reneging on my appearance in the Winner's Circle at the Parents Association Party; after all, she had been the one to broach the concept to me months ago. But I don't feel guilty about my change of heart. I have blissfully, completely, happily, entirely forgotten about it! *Mister Smithwick! Mister Smithwick!* I spin that orange Frisbee flat and hard half way across the field. We race and laugh and catch and chase the speeding weightless disk. I hesitate for a split second; the Head of School is on the field, should I do something different? Should we throw it to her? She is up there, getting older, moving a little stiffly. Yet, she plays tennis every weekend. She plays in the faculty-student basket-ball game every year. She is at the top of her game; I've sat in on her math classes—phenomenal: she makes it fun; she makes it relative; she does statistical analysis of the odds on horses running in the Triple Crown races; she runs sharp, disciplined, clear meetings; she encourages us to experiment, to take chances, to be individualists, to conduct exciting, provocative classes. Then, I have a shock: she is actually my age and has just announced she'll be retiring next year. For a split second, I look at her, and I imagine the students looking at me with my gray mane flying, and seeing the same sort of aged educator. Oh well, I'm used to this from riding races against teenagers. I send the thought whirling up into the sky, let it float off into the clouds, refocus and run full steam ahead, keeping the wheels spinning.

One girl is on crutches—knee problems. She is the daughter of one of the Dynamic Duo. Her knees have been hurting all spring—no wonder! Over the winter she played basketball on the school team and indoor lacrosse on her "rec" team. This spring, she's been playing on the school's outdoor lacrosse team as well as a "travel" team. Meanwhile, her favorite sport is field hockey, a fall sport, and she's been practicing with her hockey team on the weekends throughout the late winter in preparation for a tournament in Florida during spring vacation. In late February, she started limping. I had asked her about it.

"Oh, just a sore knee."

Then, she began wearing these silly figure-eight patches—like large Band Aids—across both her skinny knees.

I checked with her. "Oh, my physical trainer says they're just sore."

Spring break was coming up. The tournament. "Why don't you give your knees a rest, Josephine. You can't let these coaches keep pushing you like this. You've got to learn to take care of yourself. You're still growing."

"The physical trainer says it's just temporary and to put ice on them every night."

"Josephine, that's not natural...." She flew to Florida, played in the tournament. Now, she's back, and her knees hurt so badly she's been on crutches ever since.

As I run past Josephine, she, leaning on her crutches, says to me in a lowered voice, "Mister Smithwick, why aren't you having your picture taken?" Now what the hell could that mean? I am focused on the Frisbee. I go racing by, catch up with it—I love how you can do this—snatch it out of the air. Jog back. "What'd you say?"

"Why aren't you having your picture taken?"

"What picture?"

"With the horse—at the Kentucky Derby party."

"Oh, I just couldn't do it. I could tell it wasn't going to work. It's too much trouble shipping a horse over. And I have a really busy weekend already." (Not true. 1. I'd talked Peter Jay into shipping *his* horse over; he lived just a mile from the party. 2. We had *not one* engagement or activity planned for the weekend.)

As I dash off, I hear her say to a friend, "Too much trouble? My mother's not going to be happy about that."

I pay no attention to Josephine's remark, sprint into the open field to draw a good fling of the Frisbee.

And then, I'm out. Off the campus. Outside the perimeter of the guard fence. Fences. "Good fences make...." I work in a fenced-in school—the fence to keep the neighbors or anyone else *out*. Soon, I'll be back galloping for Dickie at Pimlico Racecourse—also encircled by fences, as well as lights and guards, to keep the neighbors *out*.

I am driving away from the constant pressure, interruptions, cacophony and bells! Bells for the end of class. Bells for the beginning of class. Bells for recess. The bells are stationed in walls, in corners, above doors, everywhere all over the campus. Edgar:

> Hear the loud alarum bells—
>> Brazen bells!
> What a tale of terror, now, their turbulency tells!
>> In the startled ear of night
>> How they scream out their affright!
>> Too much horrified to speak,
>> They can only shriek, shriek, . . .

Relax for one moment in the boys' bathroom where no administrators (all women), no female teachers can venture; ah, take a break, joke with the boys, have that old feeling of we're-all-in-this-together, let the water flow, pull up the zipper, step out, *RINNNNNNGGGGG* goes the bell right by the door, eight inches above your ear. There is the fire alarm—that old-fashioned sound, no different from when I was a student. The tornado warning—a *whoop whoop ring, whoop whoop ring*. And the lock down—the worst of all. One of the alarms is in my room, on the wall directly behind where I do most of my teaching at a handsome lectern of stained pine with swirling patterns in the grain that Mr. T, a new friend and Head of Maintenance, made me. It is a bone-tingling, skin-scrawling, high-pitched military-defense, the Russians are coming!, the Chinese have landed!, *screech screech screech*—I jump half a foot off the ground—over and over ("again my friend, we're on the eve of destruction"), and we can't leave! We have to "lock down" in the room. We've had multiple meetings after the horrific December 14th murders of twenty children and six adults at Sandy Hook Elementary School in Connecticut on procedures to follow during a lockdown. We've all thought about what we would do if a crazy terrorist, a psychotic, white supremacist, Nazi-worshiping, swastika-tattooed bastard with a semi-automatic weapon—how about your mother's Bushmaster XM15-E2S rifle, now that's something for NRA hollowheads to keep around the house to use for target practice or shooting deer—crashed into our building. How brave would we be? Would we take a bullet, a barrage of bullets, to save a student? We wondered, we questioned ourselves. We've been told to lock the door, hide in a corner, to stay quiet, cower there like a hen with her chickens. I don't like that picture. I've rehearsed the scenario in my imagination, over and over. If I hear the lunatic coming down our hall, going through one room, then another, I'll lock the door with the deadbolt, push the desk and as many chairs as the students can muster up against it. Then I'll pick up a heavy chair, throw it through the window, scrape away the glass, help the students jump out, and sprint away from the campus. (The thought had occurred to keep my shotgun under the desk . . . I pictured myself up against the wall, waiting for him to enter, and then pulling the trigger, satisfyingly blowing him away just as I had the coyote leaving the barn a few weeks ago after I'd seen him snapping at our Yorkshire terrier, Alfie.)

I am wheeling away from the campus in my mother's thirty-year-old, light blue Ford 150—muffler bluttering, rear fender rattling—detaching myself from the school for the weekend, freeing, leaving, celebrating, moving fast through space and time. Windows open. Air rushing in. Leaving the town. Past the glaring neon lights of the last fast-food, fat-producing franchises, and the gas stations, stop lights, used car lots, quick oil change stations, drive-through car washes, drive-through banks, drive-through hamburger joints. Good Lord, can't Americans get out of their damn cars to step into a bank instead of sitting out there behind the steering wheel, pushing a button to lower one window, all the others closed tight, engine straining, muffler spewing out carbon monoxide creating killer smog that is dealt with by cranking up the air conditioner higher that then spews out more chlorofluorocarbons that are destroying the ozone layer, leading to more Americans developing melanoma which makes them less able to go outside and more in need of chlorofluorocarbon-produced air creating an ever-worsening, self-perpetuating suicidal cycle. . . .

Can't they get out of their cars, walk ten or twenty steps, and look a bank clerk in the eye instead of talking through a weird echoing back and forth speaker system, and sending notes and checks and cash whooshing back and forth through a pneumatic tube to a human three feet away? Can't they get out of their cars to eat? They'll soon become a new species of four-wheeled animals, human car-turtles. Why don't they just live in their cars, never walk, lose the power of their legs, become humans on wheels? But how would they procreate? They couldn't. The human race would die out.

My satchel is in the back seat stuffed with papers to grade: Medieval History students have written and designed imaginative and historically accurate journals, complete with maps and illustrations, recounting the crusades they've just completed—including one rather risqué account by Livia, "Eleanor of Aquitaine"; English students have handed in portfolios of their poems for the marking period. I look forward to the journals and the portfolios; must carve out time over the weekend. First though, I'll do a final edit of the galleys for *Young Voices*, the School's literary journal, of which I am the editor and for which students have been contributing short stories, essays, memoirs, poems and art all year. It goes to press Tuesday. Exams to write. Lesson plans to put on the website . . .

I pass the last fast-food franchise, pull away from the stop sign. The road narrows. Traffic thins. My speed picks up. Trees on either side. No traffic. Windows open, fresh air rushing through blowing my hair, blowing the images of hundreds of my lively, energetic, imaginative, indefatigable charges out of my mind.

Deer Creek

I am now on the country road headed north to see Speedy Kiniel, Speedy, who during my youth on the racetrack—Pimlico, Laurel, Timonium, Monmouth Park, Delaware Park, Saratoga Springs, Belmont Park, Aqueduct—had been the fastest man in my father and uncle's racing stable of fifty or so Thoroughbreds, could, while singing, do the work of three men, Speedy, who as a young man in the ring emulated the style of Sugar Ray Robinson. I'd seen him fight at Saratoga many a time and had never seen him lose. He was there at Monmouth Park the afternoon my father had the bad fall over a hurdle, and he was there at Belmont Park—I was fifteen—watching over me during those horrifying days after the fall when we didn't know if Pop would live. Speedy, part African-American, part Native-American—Cherokee—whose own father had died when he was young, who had gone to work at twelve, who sang gospel music at church as a youth and then went on to sing with bands that opened for Motown groups—including Marvin Gaye, the Temptations, and others—before my Uncle Mikey grabbed him away from another trainer, and away from the world of music, and never let him go. He'd rubbed all the stakes winners and had worked for the Smithwick brother team for most of its twenty-year domination of the sport of steeplechasing, and had either shipped, tacked up, ran, bandaged, ridden, cooled out all of the greats: Neji, Bonneville, The Sport, Mako, Jay Trump, Hill Tie, Inkslinger. After Pop died in 1973, Speedy continued for another twenty-five years with Mikey, living on the racing farm at Hydes, ten miles east of Prospect Farm, until Mikey died. He then helped me with my racehorses when I'd returned to riding races at the age of fifty.

In moments, I'll be with Speedy, who now has glaucoma, is almost entirely blind, and whom I am going to coax out of the room he is renting in the basement of a house, out into the sunshine, into the truck, and bring for a drive, fresh, creek-cooled air wafting through the windows.

The road follows Deer Creek to my right. The water is clear—the creek broad—the water rushing over the rocks. We are in Rocks State Park. Star-spangled points of blinking light play glum tag on the water, bright diamonds lighting up for a split second and then vanishing, thousands of bright diamonds. Then shade—the trees green and leaning toward the river—it makes me ache to get the canoe out, set it bumping and bobbing against the rocks, and point it down this river Tom and I used to navigate.

Today, I'll keep this visit to Speedy from getting too long, and I'll stop and visit Tom on the way home, tell him how I was up in this territory, "Tiger's Country." What the hell, why not talk him into going canoeing? Wouldn't that be fun? He'd be stuck in the canoe with me and he'd have to talk. We'd communicate. Besides, I need to check on the infection he got in his leg at Saratoga and then rubbed raw riding every morning. I'm sure he hasn't seen a doctor. And it's right above his bad foot, the one with the bunion that has gotten worse and worse over the last few years until the ball of his foot has twisted to the side and several toes are overlapping others. He refuses to go see the world-class foot surgeon and energetic free spirit I'd met while writing a book on Union Memorial Hospital just as he's always dug in his heels against having a physical, having a colonoscopy, going to the dentist, seeing a therapist, meeting with a marriage counselor, being put in a treatment program, or anything involving a doctor or hospital while calling those of us who do follow the dictates of the normal American's health plan, a pack of (expletive deleted) hypochondriacs. He has forged his way through life and illnesses and deaths and difficulties by calling on the power of his will, although occasionally, he gives in to Mimi's perseverance, and listens to her.

I am soaking up the sunlight. I am holding the steering wheel, looking out the open windows at the tall trees, the gushing river, the wind and water-swept rocks. Speedy can't see this. I focus on how I will describe it to him, make it come alive.

There, to my right, a rickety old iron bridge crosses the creek to a field. The iron struts and cables are thin and rusty. It looks as if it should have a "DANGER KEEP OFF" sign on it. There is nothing on the other side but a field of golden winter wheat shimmering in the sunlight, swaying in the breeze. What is the bridge doing there? Is it a private bridge? Do farmers use it? There are no barricades to keep one off. I'd love to pull off the road, cross that bridge, the wooden boards reverberating under the rubber tires in that peaceful manner, park in the grove of trees across the field, get out and walk down to the river, where it turns away from the road, sit on a rock in a spot of sunlight away from the crowds of students, the hundreds of questions, the ringing of bells, the roughhousing, noisy, about-to-hurt-themselves boys, but I cannot get away from that remark of Josephine's. Why couldn't I have gotten out of there without having heard, "My mother's not going to be happy about that"? At the end of the day, the last class, why did I have to hear that? The odds were against it. Josephine was not in my class. We'd just come together by chance out on the field. I had been on the verge of disembarking from school with no worries, an unusual, calm weekend coming up. Josephine was one of my all-time favorite students. "Love is not a feeling," she'd begun one essay. "It is an action." This was my student . . . and was that an 'untruth' I had told her? Was that a harmless 'stretcher'—as Huck calls it? Or was it a lie? A lie such as Marlow decries?

Driving out of the shade of the woods, left arm resting on the sill of the window as my father used to rest his, wind blowing the thin hairs back, sunlight warming the top of my arm and left shoulder, I slow and cross a wooden-planked, sturdily-reinforced, wrought iron bridge. It is anchored to both sides of the creek by heavy stone masonry worthy of the early Romans and the overhead struts and beams have recently been painted a dark green. Speedy would be able to hear the soothingly familiar sound of the rubber wheels first going up on the boards, then thrumming across, and feel the reverberations coming up through the chassis of the car but he wouldn't be able to see the rapids below, the fresh green paint on the overhead beams of this 19th century bridge, or the newly painted cherry-red 1960's Ford pick-up pulsating with power, heading up the slight incline to the bridge, the whole truck vibrating, taking short stutter-steps forward as the proud teenage boy behind the wheel impatiently revs the engine and rides the clutch, waiting for me to pass.

There is a fork in the road. I take it to the right, start up a steep hill and realize I've made a wrong turn. What am I doing? How many times have I made this drive? Spacing out. Thinking about that remark of Josephine's!

I turn into a driveway, back out, coast down the hill to the bridge. Begin to cross Deer Creek again. Stop. Look down at the rapids, and instantly I am in the stern of a canoe with Tom. It is late one afternoon, in the midst of a hurricane, the river three feet higher than usual, and we are sweeping around a turn, the water rough, brown, foamy, branches and trees being swept down with us. There up above us on the bridge is Tiger's red army jeep, Tiger waving—not hello, but Stop! Stop! Halt! We give our old go-to-hell hunting call, pass the take-out spot, and dart into the chute, a funnel, the canoe—an unwieldy aluminum tub we'd had to borrow, our fiberglass model under repair—seeming to go out from under us. We paddle hard, keeping our speed faster than the river's, making it around one boulder, then another. The current takes us straight into the third. The starboard side of the bow smashes against the rock—Boom! Then, it scrapes along to the left. We try to push away. We whoop and yell. We're going to make it. But we are leaning in slightly, leaning upstream into the flow of the river, and the power of the current is pushing the hull out from under us, the canoe is filling with water, and over we go. In the stern, I'm relieved as I see Tom go over into the spray, away from the rocks. Then, I too am overboard. I'm struggling under the canoe, thrown against the boulder. My head whacks against the solidity of it. The water is in my eyes, in my ears, in my mouth, pummeling me. It's roaring. I'm dizzy. Weak. The canoe, incredibly, is bending, wrapping around me, trapping me against the rock. I'm sliding downwards. It looks like this is it. I see Tiger throwing something down to Tom. I hear Tom, "Grab it! Grab the rope!" He's on a boulder upstream, throwing a line to me. I miss catching it. Miss again. And then I have it. He pulled me out, many a time.

I'm looking forward to stopping by Atlanta Hall on the way home from Speedy's. I'll check with Tom on the location of the bridge and rapids. He'll remember. All my spring pit-stops have been at Speedy's—usually after going to the grocery store, buying a big bottle of orange soda, a big bag of pork rinds and a box of Ritz crackers, then heading for Kentucky Fried Chicken and getting "a breast, two thighs, and a leg, biscuits, French fries, cold slaw. You got it? Can you remember that Sonny-boy," and, right as I'm finally leaving town, pulling into yet another 7-Eleven and pouring "a hot black-like-me coffee" for him, and, what the hell, one for me.

I look down at the rapids one last time, start to drive off the bridge and at that exact second TOM VOSS CELL pops up on the screen of my phone. Amazing. His timing. It's always like this. Still on the bridge, I stop the truck, answer the phone.

"What're you doing?" he asks.

"You won't believe it. I am driving across the bridge over the rapids on Deer Creek where I almost met my maker canoeing with you."

"That was a Day to Remember," he says, alluding to Walter Lord's *A Night to Remember*, a book and topic he loves.

"Yes," I say, "hopefully we'll have some more, but not quite like that." (I pictured us loading the canoe, bent into an V-shape, into the back of the open jeep, and then later transferring it to the top of the Corvair, and driving up to the house of its owner. "Oh shit," Rick Poole said, stepping out onto his porch. "You can keep it.")

"What're you doing up at Deer Creek?" Tom asked.

"I'm heading up to Speedy's."

"You'd better watch it. He could become a burden."

"Yes, that's true. What are you doing?"

"I'm sitting at my desk making up a chart of horses to gallop on Sunday—with no riders."

"Need a rider?"

"Yes." He sighs.

"What time?"

"Seven-thirty. I'll have one tacked up and waiting for you. You'll have four to go. Then, we'll go up to the house and have shad roe for breakfast. Don't tell any of your friends."

The shad must be running. Shad roe and champagne. We used to have it once a spring on a Sunday after work: Pop, Tiger, Mom, Tom, his mother Jen, J.B., J.B.'s mother Sara, Brian Hickey, Billy Santoro. Pull a sweating bottle of champagne out of a galvanized steel bucket of ice. Pour another round. Take a sip of

the dry fizzing bubbling cheap stuff Tiger had bought a case of for the price of galloping five horses. Crisp, salty bacon beside the roe. Squeeze the slice of lemon on the roe. The champagne, the rich salty roe with a drop of lemon, a slice of toast. The way the champagne would quench your thirst after having been up since 5:30 galloping at Pimlico, then at the farm. Tiger popping the cork on another bottle, raising his glass to toast to the future of us young race riders that spring (he called Tom "Sir Loin" and me "Sir F-a lot")—to our future in the tack with the horses in the afternoons and in particular with the fast fillies (the toast might turn bawdy) in the evenings. A laughing, sun-filled, cork-popping celebration—moments of our youth together rushed over me like the cool pounding water on hot summer days cascading from the waterfall a few miles up Deer Creek where we used to skinny dip with Tiger: life was an all-out, full-steam-ahead, damn-the-torpedoes celebration.

Every Friday after school, I'd call Tom. What were we going to do? Well, most likely the usual. We'd head for the Merryman's or the Fenwick's, over in the Worthington Valley half an hour away where all the good-looking girls and their friends were. We'd drink and celebrate on the drive over in the Corvair—accelerating before big bumps, sending it into the air. Upon arrival, we'd drink and celebrate and laugh and dance and jump out of the loft of the barn and ride horses in the dark with the Merryman sisters, toboggan all night with the Fenwick sisters—often be run off the place by an irate father—roar around to a party or two.

We worked every day of the week, including Christmas, New Year's, Fourth of July, Thanksgiving. I galloped horses for Pop at Pimlico 5:30 to 8:00 before going to Gilman. Tom had horses in training at an early age, fed, mucked out and exercised them before and after going to nearby Hereford High.

Weekends—no matter how late we'd been up the preceding night—we were working for Pop: driving to Pimlico at 5:30, then exercising the horses at our farm. Soon we were schooling horses that Pop—his stable expanding—boarded at Jen's barn. Emmett Grayson, who had worked for Tom's father Eddie, lived in a room in the barn, worked for Tom—tutoring him in the old, tested ways of racing horsemanship—eventually becoming Pop's foreman, his most trusted employee, and Tom's and my mentor on the topics of boxing, race-riding, drinking and, that great mystery: women.

Sundays, back from Pimlico, we were loading horses to go up to the Elkridge Harford Hunt Club to "breeze," starting at the bottom by the bridge beside Pocock Road, galloping up the gradual hill with the road on our right, easy, easy, turning left, and then letting them pick it up, three or four of us, head-and-head, going all out down the long the spine of the ridge. After getting the thirty horses out, Tom and I would mix up a batch of Bloody Mary's. Pop would invite some friends over. We'd have lunch and start on the next project: building new hurdles at Jen's with Tiger, burning the multiflora and weeds that had grown up over the stream, throwing bales of hay down from the loft to the stalls, backing the pickup into the barn, loading it up with hay to take to the track in the morning, laughing and joking with Pop or Emmett or Tanza or Brian Hickey or Tiny or Dave Mitchell or Salvadore Tumenelli—none of whom are still with us.

For the last years that Pop was riding races and reducing, losing thirty pounds every spring, going from his natural weight of 165 down to 133 to ride hurdle, brush and timber races and become the greatest steeplechase jockey in America—Tom and I were along, in the car, outside the jocks' room, at the barn at Delaware Park, Monmouth Park, or at the hunt meets, Middleburg in Virginia, Fair Hill in Maryland, after the races were over and everyone was moving slowly, languidly. The grooms—black and from the south, professionals, having grown up around race horses, show horses and hunters on farms in Virginia, North Carolina, South Carolina with fathers as horsemen—would be calming and soothing and bandaging the horses and Pop would have pulled out a feed tub filled with bottles of Budweiser covered in ice and the millionaire owners in their suits and long dresses—Rolls Royces and Cadillacs parked a few feet away on the dirt and chaff and droppings—would sit on upturned buckets, talk to the grooms, have a beer, Tom and I there, loving it, wanting nothing else, with the exception of that one period, thirteen to sixteen years old when we teamed up with Tom Whedbee (skilled at the statistical analysis involved in the placing of bets and then forthright in the dividing up of winnings) to gamble, asking Pop, asking Mikey, asking jockeys Bobby MacDonald and Scotty Riles and Jimmy Murphy and Tommy Walsh who was going to win. We bet safely, boringly, conservatively, "across the Board," meaning our picks could finish win, place or show. Actually, we didn't place the bets. There was a tote board and pari-mutuel betting at Fair Hill. We were too young to approach the windows. Never mind, we had sometime jockey Melvin Farrell on our team. He bet. We won. He collected the money. Pop was winning; we were winning; life was a celebration.

The racing season concluding at Thanksgiving, Pop could eat. Mom started cooking again. Roast beef. Lamb. Steaks. Hams. Potatoes! Butter on the table. And we could get away from the daily, relentless mucking out, bedding down, haying, watering, bringing in, bandaging, feeding, turning out, training, riding schedule of race trackers and horsemen—to go skiing.

Mom taught us how to ski on the big hill behind Tiger's farm—"Mount Bennett." A dozen of us would be there, including the Small twins: Sass, my sister Sue Sue's best friend, and Stephen. Sometimes their brother Dickie would make an appearance. In the Upper School at Gilman, six years older than us, strong as a horse and on the varsity football, wrestling and lacrosse teams, he was a big shot but didn't act like one and would ski all afternoon with us.

When skiing at Tiger's, we'd sip his cider. When doing much of anything at Tiger's—preparing to canoe, to ski, to school his horses, to race his old red jeep through the woods—we'd first head down to the old wood-shed housing the cider barrel. We'd taste the cider like the most sophisticated of sommeliers, and if it hadn't fully fermented, Tiger would help it out with a shot of a secret *elixir*.

Before we had our licenses, all our families would go up to Laurel Mountain, a small ski resort in Ligonier, Pennsylvania for a week-long ski trip after Christmas. The Upper Wildcat. The Lower Wildcat—the toughest slope on the planet. I can see the moguls; I can feel the moguls. I can picture every one of us: how Katy Merryman (later, Katy Voss, after marrying Tom's brother Ned) would twirl her arms around and around to warm up her hands; how Francie Merryman, no matter how cold it was, how late in the day, always had a glowing smile and looked so warm and cozy in her puffy parka, her blonde hair billowing out of her wool ski hat with the bouncing pompom, that you wanted to unzip that parka and climb in there with her; how Jack, Tom's younger brother, somehow had the magic for skiing in his bones, could laughingly spin around 360 degrees when the rest of us were perfecting our stem-Christies and soon surpassed every one of us, even my mother; how extremely long those old wooden skis of Pop's were; how Sue Sue would bundle up in so many clothes she was as wide as she was tall and she could pick up the heaviest, most ice-encrusted rope tow, grab hold of it and take it to the top of a slope without one complaint; how excited and fun Mom was every moment of the trip, how Tiger, our leader, would break away from his peers, wine skin flapping against his side, lead Tom, Tom Whedbee and I, Sue Sue, Merrymans, Fenwicks and Smalls on adventures bushwhacking and cross-country skiing through the unpacked snow in the woods, fast.

In the early spring, the most fun to possibly have on a horse could be had at Tiger's—we'd tack up a couple of his "timber" horses. Hoping for the best with our tack—frayed stirrup leathers, girth buckles attached to dry-rotted elastic strips, rubber grip completely worn off the reins—we'd follow Tiger out to his course in the woods. With no warm up, he'd give a hoop and a holler, and we'd gallop full tilt over every kind of fence imaginable, all made by Tiger and us, through the twisting, turning paths.

Tom started smoking. That was cool. Pall Malls. He always had a maroon pack of Pall Malls in his car or in a pocket of his jacket, and he took a cigarette out of the pack, squinted, lit it, the exact same way Pop did.

We both drank bourbon—Early Times or Old Grand Dad (Pop's favorites)—and couldn't understand why other teenagers went to the trouble of buying a heavy, unwieldy case of beer for the night, lugging it around, attempting to hide it from parents and the police, and then drinking one can after another, when we could just pour a couple of shots of bourbon into a glass, top it off with a splash of "branch" and be on our way.

We both had a red bandana hanging out the back right pocket—which gave us a stamp of individuality. This was a sartorial statement of Pop's. By the time he retired from race-riding, there was a whole generation of young up-and-coming riders who were galloping around tracks up and down the East Coast with red bandanas stuck in rear pockets fluttering in the breeze.

An image: there'd been a major snowstorm. Plows had pushed the snow two-stories high on the shoulders of the Jarrettsville Pike. Tom and I'd been skidding around in my Corvair. Sunny day. No school. We're standing in the middle of the Jarrettsville

Pike with house-sized piles of fresh plowed snow behind us. Our bodies facing away from Mom, we've twisted our torsos around so that we are grinningly looking into the camera, while Mom is focusing her camera on the red bandana billowing out of each of our right-rear pockets, and I am holding up a fifth of Early Times—in celebration.

The snow melted, the days grew longer and the grass greener, and our world began to spin faster and faster as it orbited around our passion for race-riding, threatening at times to go reeling off into the abyss when we began to ride races and to fight the weight. In the spring, as we learned from Pop, we cut out bread, potatoes, beer, wouldn't even think of having dessert. Best for me, after galloping at Saratoga for Pop, was to have one poached egg on whole wheat toast and a vodka and grapefruit juice for breakfast. Tom, bigger boned, and an inch taller (until Gary's horse Cookie stepped in a fox hole out hunting one day, gave Tom a cruncher, and shrunk his spine by an inch) would have a Pall Mall. At night, I'd have scotch. He'd have bourbon. Then we'd have steaks and salads. The weight would fall off, but not enough. Tom usually was making weight for a timber race—155—when his normal frame should've been 175. I could do the timber races—early on—without reducing, but Pop had some three-year-olds, which were running over hurdles (one and a half miles, *fast*) and they got in with 130, which meant I had to weigh 125.

By this time, I'd wrecked the Corvair—our WW I bi-winged, open cockpit fighter. Gray, small, a symmetrical profile, the roofed over area in dead center, front and back windows slanting down at the same angle, front hood and back trunk the same shape and dimensions so that it looked like a car you could point in either direction, which we did, we did. . . . *That last night at Saratoga, victoriously laughing and singing and driving home via sidewalks, a policeman "pulling us over," and after we told him how important to the success of the Saratoga meet we'd been, just what big shots we were, he barked, "OK, you'd better be out of town by sunup. If I see this car again, I'll lock you up." At 5:30 that morning, the Corvair was gingerly, sheepishly, quietly going through its four gears, headed down Union Avenue, and out of town.*

Next was a light-weight, black Ford Falcon with a V-8, three on the tree, and a powerful heater. I'd pull on long waffle underwear, turtle neck, corduroys, wool sweater and a rubber suit, crank the Falcon up, drive the two miles to pick up Tom. We'd cruise around drinking screwdrivers, heater blasting, stopping to visit friends, and losing five or six pounds. We spent many a night before a race sitting naked in saunas together, skin feeling as if it were being stretched tighter and tighter around our rib cages. "Tom, you've got to get out! Tom, you've got to get some fresh air," I'd say, stepping outside just before I might faint.

I left home. Tom stayed. Teaching and journalism took me away from the horse and racetrack life. First, I married the love of my teenage years when she was a freshman in college and I was a junior. That did not last. At graduate school at Hollins College, Virginia, I met and fell in love—at first sight—with Ansley Dickinson from Florida. I proposed—and before we knew it, there Tom, my best man, and Hank Slauson and I were, in the Orlando City Jail, having had too much fun at the rehearsal dinner. Tom Whedbee had fought his way out of the melee of bouncers and cops and had not been "booked." Tom, Hank and Tom Whedbee, and close friends Rob Deford, Reed Huppman, Willie Dixon, and J.B. Secor supported me through this difficult period, but some relatives and family connections thought I was headed down Disaster Highway—barely out of one marriage, diving into another.

A favorite photo: We've had that hard night, no sleep, and are stiff and sore from brawling with cops and bouncers. I'm to be married in moments. We're in our tails, standing on the cinder block steps beside the dumpster leading to the back door of the church; I'm sipping a scotch, Tom a bourbon. The photographer has been staging photographs of Ansley and her mother and the bridesmaids in the church. They've been fluttering around, looking beautiful, the center of attention. Tom and I have been neglected. The photographer steps out the back door and starts to rush importantly to the front of the church. "Hey," I say. "How about us? I'm the Groom and he's the Best Man." He stops and laughs, drops down on a knee, and snaps a quick shot of us standing tall by the dumpster.

Ansley and I moved from the Eastern Shore to Petersburg, Virginia and began our teaching careers. Tom called, told me about the hopping journalism scene in Maryland. There was a new magazine in town, *Style*, and a new weekly newspaper, *City Paper*. *Baltimore Magazine* needed good writers. Three daily papers—one morning, two afternoon. Within commuting distance, in Rockville, was a new equestrian magazine. He lured me back, offered me a house on Atlanta Hall, the rent—$50 a month.

We each had our first child, a son, early. Mimi and Tom had Sam; Tom asked me to be the godfather. Ansley and I had Paddy; I asked Tom to be the godfather. We had godson birthday parties. This was a time, our thirties, when Tom and I were misbehaving in some ways, and we'd get lectures, reprimands, from Gary—both our fathers deceased, Gary stood in for them, "put his foot down," on our behavior—and to celebrate a period in our lives as eighteen year olds when an older woman introduced the concept of the after-dinner-drink to me, we'd have a couple of stingers. We did have some fun. As F. Scott Fitzgerald wrote in *Tender is The Night*, "The drink made past happy things contemporary with the present, as if they were still going on, contemporary even with the future as if they were about to happen again. "

Tom and Mimi had Elizabeth. Ansley and I had Andrew and then Eliza. We were all busy. Tom and I kept up with each other during that hectic decade of our forties through attending Paddy's and Sam's games: soccer, ice hockey especially, and lacrosse. Gary too. Part of the glue that bound us together, he'd be there on the sidelines.

Early on, I had a hideaway, a "bolt hole," my monk's cell, a scriptorium on the third floor of the old Monkton Hotel in Monkton, a village half an hour away on my bicycle. No telephone. No frills. No technology—just a trustworthy, decades-old manual Royal typewriter. No one knew where I was.

One morning, deep into a paragraph, I heard the door three stories down open, footsteps climbing the steep wooden stairs, two sets of footsteps. All the way up to my floor. Down the hall. My door burst open. Tom took a step into the room, stopped, legs spread, hands on hips, took in the décor—writing table, typing table, typewriter, shelves lined with sheaves of notes. Someone was right behind him. Tom shook his head back and forth as if I'd just made some grievous error. "You're turning into a pale-faced introvert," he said. "Come on—we're going hunting. You're on Mickey Free. The meet's at my place."

From behind Tom, Bob Witham (Bob 'Without'em,' as Tom called him) popped out. "Good morning, Pa-Patrick. We thought you could t-take some time off from your b-book to go hunting.

It's a beautiful morning. . . ."

Tom stepped up to the table, looked at a chapter called "A Leg Up," about Pop having cancer, partially paralyzed, and asking for a leg up onto a rough horse, a "rogue," no one else can ride, then schooling him over three hurdles better than any horse in the barn had gone: Tote'm Home II. Tom had been there. That summer, Pop gave me a leg up on Tote'm at Saratoga, and I won my first hurdle race. A decade later the story had been published along with dazzling watercolors that gave the affect of speed and movement, in a glossy horse journal. Tom had handed me a published copy before I got mine from the publisher. Now I was reworking it for a book.

He and Bob were at it—detective work, sleuthing—poking around my cell, flipping through manuscripts covered with marginalia in red and blue ink. Tom picked up a block of three hundred typed pages—a myriad of sticky notes protruding from them—lifted it up and down, feeling its heft.

Bob watched. "Pa-Patrick, how long have you been working on it?" he asked.

"His whole life," Tom answered, now looking at a chapter on Emmett. Tom had read this chapter when it'd been published in a literary journal. I had mailed him one of my three free copies. "His whole life." He knew. And he didn't have to talk about it.

Hacking home from the hunt late that afternoon, Tom, Bob and I were walking across a field toward Atlanta Hall's long, lower driveway, the sun shooting its striated scarlet and yellow streaks across the "finish line field" and into the blue-gray bottomed clouds above. The main house was straight ahead. We rode up a steep, short incline, and then, three abreast, walked along the bank of a pond—its waters clear and still: it was a baseball diamond sized mirror, and looking into it, you couldn't tell the difference in reality between its reflection of trees and clouds and us three and the fence line, and the actual trees and clouds and us three and the fence line. A flock of geese circled overhead. They descended—a perfect V, in tight formation, one landed, another, another, wings walloping the air, bodies jostling the water, sending ripples out in expanding circles, a dozen widening gyres colliding with one another, the water's earlier crystalline mirror-image of the clouds and scarlet rays and flying geese now breaking up, coming alive, as if the paint of a portrait by Cousin

Frank Voss had become liquid again and begun spilling and gliding across the surface, the colors mixing and merging. It took our breath away. We continued across the bank, leaned forward, and the horses stepped up onto the asphalt driveway. We headed for the barn. There was one light on in the house, second floor, to the right, Tom's dressing room. (Later, Tom pointed out that I had left it on, raising his electricity bill.) The horses clip clopped. I let my feet out of the irons, stretched my legs. I mentioned the mystical settings in Morte d'Arthur—"Sir Thomas Malory," Bob crisply stated—and how this scene was like something out of Arthurian legend. In a hushed voice, Tom said, "Yes, but you don't have to talk about it."

Blessed Water
from Lourdes

"You know, I hate, detest, and can't bear a lie, not because I am straighter than the rest of us, but simply because it appalls me. There is a taint of death, a flavour of mortality in lies—which is exactly what I hate and detest in the world—what I want to forget. It makes me miserable and sick, like biting something rotten would do."

— Marlowe in *Heart of Darkness*

I drive across the bridge, take a right and head north. I am deep in the park—headed upriver—and now the trees give way and there is a recreational area to my left: a parking lot, and an open lawn that juts out peninsula-like with the creek flowing around its perimeter. In the center is a pavilion filled with enough picnic tables to seat two Middle School soccer teams. I glance in the rearview mirror, jam on the breaks. Wouldn't this be a great place to bring Speedy? Sunlight, the creek, open space—he could walk around, get some exercise.

I grab my cell phone. A lie; it was not an untruth; it was not a stretcher; it was a lie. I did not have to bring the horse. It would not be a lot of trouble. I had all the riding gear ready. We did not have a busy weekend. *"You know, I hate, detest, and can't bear a lie,"* Marlow tells his audience of one or two awake listeners sprawling on the deck of a yawl on the Thames, waiting for the tide to turn, as he begins his story of steering a battered steamer up "the big river" into the heart of Africa.

I call the school. The secretary won't be there but the Head will.

133

"Hi, Su?"

"Yes."

"This is Patrick. Sorry to bother you. I'm wondering if you could help me with a couple of phone numbers. . . ." Upbeat, on a mission, I apologetically explain how I had planned to dodge the Parents Association Kentucky Derby Cocktail Party but had had a change of heart and could she give me the numbers of the director of development, the hosts of the party, and of Peter Jay. I call all three, leave messages—the show is back on—feel relieved, drive out of the park and along a ridge, then swing right and head up a steep road, looking forward to springing Speedy from his *dungeon*.

The last time I'd seen him, Kitty, who also lives in the basement, had the large-screen television blasting. Speedy sat at the dinner table away from the couches and television. We tried to talk. The news was on. I was distracted and watched as chaos was filmed: sirens wailing, upset newscasters interviewed shocked, injured and bloody runners. Rumors of what was happening next were rampant. People were screaming and crying. The suspects were being chased. Two pressure cooker bombs had exploded. People had been killed; hundreds were injured; it looked like a terrorist act, Muslim extremists perverting, twisting, dishonoring, disgracing the teachings of Mohammed. It was the Boston Marathon, April 15, 2013. After leaving off Speedy's food, cleaning up his room, I had driven home in shock listening to the horrific news.

Luke's pick-up—painted a flat black and jacked up on oversize, thick-treaded, knobby tires—dominates the entrance. Between the truck and the road, Speedy's car—my Uncle Mikey's old green Subaru station wagon—the rear bumper held on by twisted coat hangers, duct tape keeping the headlights from popping out, a Mercedes ornament drilled into the hood, a St. Christopher's ornament glued to the dashboard—slouches towards Bethlehem. A woman's bare leg and foot project out the driver's window. A wispy snake of smoke spirals out. The back of the seat is set as low as it will go. I can't see whoever is in there, but it's probably Dearyl, looking for a little privacy, talking on her cell phone. I coast up past the Subaru, past the truck, park, lock the doors, walk by a barricade-like stack of open garbage cans overflowing with bulging black plastic bags and loose trash, down the hill and around back to the door leading into the basement apartment. Luke sits in the shade of his work shed—a chrome bumper, four chrome-spoked wheels, an old hood and a welder set outside the shed—talking on his cell. The tip of his cigarette glows red, dims and smoke billows out in a widening gyre. "It's wild. She's acting crazy. I'm not going in there, no way, no matter what... Everything was fine when we met at the courthouse and then as soon as she got in there the shit hit the fan...."

He's talking about Melody, the explosive matriarch. She lives upstairs, is hooked up to an oxygen tank, which she drags back and forth from living room to kitchen while she lights and extinguishes cigarettes inches away from the intake valve and cracks the whip on her extended family. Luke sets his cigarette on the edge of an oil-saturated workbench, picks up a can of beer, takes a sip, and nods at me.

I knock on the basement door, hear "come in" in a cheerful voice, open the door and step into the thick block of still, stale, chilly smoke. I push through the narrow kitchenette, into the living room. No windows. Speedy is dressed up, straw fedora perched on his head—fluffy white hair sprouting out the sides— seated at the table on my left, ready to go, tapping the cane he'd made, carving African symbols into the handle. He's wearing a handsome pair of brown herringbone wool suit pants held up by suspenders and a khaki shirt with button-down chest pockets; he's pulled his customized sunglasses through the epaulets on his left shoulder. His goatee—thin and wispy and white—has grown long, and the skin of his face, as he often tells me, is black and smooth and without a wrinkle. A thin rope, keys attached, hangs from his neck. And he has something new, a braided necklace he's made from red, white and blue strands of string; from it hangs a small, shiny purple stone.

"How you doing, young man?" he calls out cheerfully, looking in my direction.

"Good, good," I say. To my right is the over-sized television screen. The volume is up. A shirtless, bearded, heavy-set man covered in tattoos is hauling an alligator out of the water while another stands by with a big-barreled rifle ready to pull the trigger. You can hear every sound in the boat, the water splashing against the aluminum sides, the scales of the alligator being dragged over the gunwales, the men's feet shifting—the music is about to hit a crescendo—and there in the big living room chair is Kitty, Melody's daughter, Luke's girlfriend, taking a deep pull from a cigarette, a liter of Mountain Dew and a mountainous bag of chips on the table beside her. She's just back from a week's stay in the hospital, which, Speedy has told me, saved her from going to jail. She'd been having fainting spells, couldn't walk, and they'd had to call an ambulance to take her to the emergency ward.

Kitty pushes on the sides of her chair, heaves her body up out of the cushions. She glares at me—it is a scared sort of look, her eyes about to pop out, as if she's just seen a wolf prowling in the living room or a snake slithering under the couch—and begins the *ordeal* (Medieval English method of trial by water: Toss in the accused—if she floats, she is guilty, and off to be hanged, drawn and quartered, or burned at the stake; if she sinks/drowns, oh my, she is innocent—Kitty would definitely sink, making her innocent) of maneuvering her impossibly voluminous body across the room to the kitchen. ("Four hundred, I tell's you! Four hundred—not a pound under. You get under her, and you's dead!") She steers her slow thighs past me over the gray carpet, into the kitchen, and begins washing the overflowing pile of dishes. I walk through the narrow passageway to the edge of the long dining table where Speedy is sitting. Behind him is a black woodstove that is never used.

I glance at the growing assemblage of official state and county documents spread out over the table: a court summons for littering, another asking for proof of employment for 2012, a court summons for falsifying documents and illegally receiving workmen's compensation for a year, and yet another, this one for theft of jewelry. These documents are addressed to different members of the family: Melody's granddaughter had stolen jewelry from her own mother Dearyl, and Dearyl had pressed charges. The granddaughter and her boyfriend at the time were driving through the nearby town when the county police spotted them and gave chase. The granddaughter leapt from the car, sprinted through several back yards before being apprehended. She was currently serving time and Melody, Kitty, Luke and Dearyl were working to get her out so she could return to taking care of her two children, Melody's great grandsons. Meanwhile, Melody—the only one without a record but who can't function without taking a pull from her cigarette followed by another from her oxygen tank—has custody of the boys.

Then, Speedy is standing. Gracefully, no rush, he pulls his patched and customized sunglasses out of the shoulder epaulet, opens them, and using both hands, staying cool, sets them just right. He reaches up, adjusts his straw fedora that he's painted purple at a jaunty angle. He refuses my hand, and using his cane, showing off, finds his way out into the sunshine and fresh air. Soon, he's tapping around the rusty front bumper of the pickup. "You don't smell that! You got's something wrong with your nose! This truck always has that smell of burning oil. . . ."

"OK, now we're going around the front. . . ."

"I know's that! What you think I am, stupid? One day this rusted-out rattletrap jus' going to blow up on you and you be killed dead. Bam! Just like that. Your wife'll have no more husband. Your kids will have no more dad. They be picking up pieces of you all over the road, off in the ditch, up in the woods. Just like you said Andrew been doing over there in Iraq. But these won't be pieces of his buddies; they be pieces of *you*!"

"OK, step back a little so I can open the door."

His old car is parked under a tree. There is a deep dent in the driver's door. I think back on all that I've heard about that accident, including the vast sums of money he plans to get from suing the driver of the car that hit him, even though he's admitted to pulling out in front of the oncoming car.

We drive down to the park. "No, I don't want to get out."

"Come on, Speedy. It's beautiful here. We can walk across the lawn, sit at one of the picnic tables over by the creek. You need to get some exercise."

He shakes his head.

"Hear that?" We listen. There's a family sitting at a picnic table over by a swing set. Two children are swinging, the father pushing them. They have food and drinks set up on the table, a cooler by the side. I describe the scene.

"I ain't walking down to no table by a creek. Snakes are out now. They be *snakes* in the grass!"

I get out, walk around to his door, stand in the sunshine.

"I got the Icy Hot, and I got the pads. I can't massage your shoulder with the Icy Hot and put on the pads with you sitting in the truck."

He agrees to walk to the pavilion. I direct him down the cement path and pull a heavy, steel-legged picnic table out from under the shade, just able to get the bench into the sunlight. He sits on the end of the bench, pushes his suspenders off his shoulders, unbuttons his shirt, pulls it down while leaving his arms in the sleeves.

"What's this? Something new?" I ask, pushing the necklace string with the small purple stone to the left shoulder.

"That's an amest-theth you knuckle-head. It's from the mountain in Ethiopia where Moses laid out the ten commandments and where Jesus carried them."

"It's not a lapis lazuli?" I ask, joking around and thinking of one of Yeats' last great poems.

"No, it ain't got nothing to do with the Zulus. No Zulus in Ethiopia! They're down in South Africa. Lord, I hate to think what those students learning from you."

"Where'd you get it?"

"Peter Popoff. He sent it. I'll get you one. You needs it more than me—it keeps you from getting drunk but it has other powers too."

I take out the Icy Hot, put a good dollop on his right shoulder. "Maybe Peter Popoff should do some work on this shoulder."

"It's from rubbing horses," he says. "It's from years and years of rubbing horses for your Uncle Mikey." I rub it in. I massage the thick, relaxed shoulder muscles. "That feels *so* good. That feels so *good*. You ought to take this stuff and rub it on Riderwood's shoulder every day. Every day! You listening?"

I let it dry and open a package of silly and expensive pads he'd insisted I buy. I stick them on strategic spots on his back and shoulder, pull out a roll of first aid tape, tape an X over each pad. He pulls his shirt back up, re-sets the suspenders, and now, he's feeling good, he's sitting on the end of the steel bench and he's talking.

My head is becoming congested and damn if I don't feel a swelling and a soreness in my throat; students have been sneezing and blowing their noses, staggering around with their eyelids drooping, asking to go to the infirmary, and leaving early all week. I take a step out of the cool shade and stretch out in a spot of sunlight (English class: literary term—Hawthornian use of *chiaroscuro*) on the grass and listen: Uncle Mikey, Pop, horses, his family, his first wife, his second wife, his cars, my grandmother, and why he moved to New York in his twenties. . . .

"I was working at the Aberdeen Proving Ground in the kitchen. I knew Arthur Connelly—"Do You Like Soul Music"—worked with him at the mess hall at Aberdeen. I was living near Fair Hills. Yeah! Had to be at the food line at 4:00 a.m. every morning. Cooked and served food. There was one guy—all he did was put a big spoon full of gravy over the potatoes—that was at lunch. At breakfast, I shoveled chip beef onto plates. I was going out with Mary. She had identical twins. Twins there in her house every night. Shoveling on food every morning. And Mary's other daughter often stayed there. You didn't want to be around her! A man tried to rape her. She killed him with a baseball bat.

"What do you mean? Hit him . . . ?"

"I don't mean *hit* him. I mean she beat the shit out of him with a bat and *killed* that bastard! Killed him *dead*! Would *you* want to be sleeping in the same house with that woman?"

"Not particularly."

He rolls his head in exasperation, "One day I called up my brother Nut. He was in New York. I told him I had to get out. 'Be there tonight,' he said. I pack'st everything I had, hid it under the steps. Then, in the middle of the night I heard that brown Oldsmobile coming down the road. You could hear it with those glass packs on the muffler half a mile away. *Blub-blub-blub-blub.* I got out of the bed, grabbed my stuff, threw it in the car. He revved the engine—that thing was talking!—we peeled out, and I moved to New York.

"I signed on with Marvin Gaye's band—he had his covitis—looked terrible. I had processed hair—just as long and *so* pretty. He hated me. We'd go to play and they'd all call out, 'Speedy! Speedy!' And he'd sit there and stare at me.

"Then I had a band, Fat Boy and the Comets. Milly Jackson was with us—*ugly*!

"We had a pink Mercury we took on the road. Cruise easy at 100—all of us asleep but the one driving—through the night to the next club.

"Then we had the Soulations—three brothers, two cousins, Tyler Smith on the sax. We had a trombone, bass guitar, lead guitar, organ. I played the harmonica and sang—country, hillbilly,

soul, hip hop. We'd keep you hot. D.C., Philadelphia, we were on
the Dick Clark show in Philly. We had corduroy suits with silk
inside; they were *so* pretty...

"Then, we had a new band, the Red Toppers. . . ."

We drive to the 7-Eleven. He starts asking about Saitensohn.
"How's his tendon? . . . Is he eating well? . . . How often you riding him? . . . You going's ta run him again? . . . Don't ride him
this summer! The ground gets hard, too hard for that old tendon.

"How thick is his coat now? *His coat still thinks he's in Germany*!
It's cold there and that's why he gets such a thick coat! Don't you
know that? You needs to rub on him. You needs to curry and rub
on him and get all that old hair out.

"Don't gallop all over the countryside, get him all hot and
wet, then put him in the stall like that! He don't need to be in a
stall at night anyway! Let him go *out*. A horse wants to be *outside*.
They moves at night. They grazes and walks miles and miles.

"And don't'chu put any bandages on him. You's likely to
put'em on too tight and hurt his tendon. If there's any heat at all,
you call me. I'll get down there and put that bandage on!

"I love that horse. That horse's like me. We the same. We
gots' the same spirit! I might just buy that horse from you and run
him myself. Yes sir, we could make some money—how much'chu
want for him? I'd tell the jock to bust out'ta the gate and go straight
to the front."

I park in front on the door to the 7-Eleven.

"Something wrong with this truck."

"There's nothing wrong with it."

"Yes there is, I'm telling you, you'd better get it checked. I
smells it. I can *smell*. There's something burning. You remember
I told you."

"OK, OK." No point arguing. "I will remember." I'm thinking back on teaching "Oedipus Rex" at Gilman: Teiresias to
Oedipus—"I am not your servant, but Apollo's ... Listen to me.
You mock my blindness, do you? But I say that you, with both
your eyes, are blind. . . ."

I turn the engine off. "Now I wants my coffee *hot* and *black
like me*. You got that?"

"I got it."

"And I needs something to go with it. Some cookies."

I buy him a cup of coffee, some cookies. He sits beside me while I make a few more calls about the Kentucky Derby signing. He says hi to Peter Jay. I think about taking Speedy to the signing, letting him hold the horse. He starts telling me about his dreams: His brother Nut has finally been released to go to heaven. An old man with a beard had come to Speedy in the middle of the night and told him Nut had been riding motorcycles in the mountains, and that's why Nut wasn't in heaven, but now He was going to get him. Speedy was so relieved to hear this. He spoke with a deep baritone imitating the old man with the beard.

I ask Speedy how his eyes are doing. He launches into a lengthy explanation of why his left eye is no good: the operation, the Indian surgeon whom he hates and who "had no office"— leaving a stitch in his eye, that in turn infected his eye, and now he has no sight in it and he's going to sue the Indian doctor for every penny he has. I've taken Speedy to the hospital in Bel Air, to the Wilmer Eye Clinic at Johns Hopkins, to a surgeon at the Greater Baltimore Medical Center, and to his internist, an Indian woman he loves, who has her office in the basement of a small, one-story house between used car lots, and over and over he's been told by every single doctor that the one stitch which the ophthalmologist had left in—for just a week—is not the reason he'd lost sight in his eye, is not the reason for the high pressure in his eye, but "that dog don't hunt." He's getting a lawyer and he's going to sue.

"And I've been hit. It's from the boxing. You get hit. You get hit over and over again. I think it might be partially from that boxing. That's it. Yes, indeed. But God is looking out for me. He's going to give me my eyesight back. You gots'ta get that water!"

"Ah, Speedy."

"You gots' ta get it. You people"—that means you *white* people"—you have no faith. The water is from Lourdes. It's blessed water. I want that water. God's told me. I needs'ta get that water from Reverent Popoff and rub it in my eyes."

I tell him that Rev'd Popoff is the ultimate in scam artists. I explain that Ansley and I had looked up Popoff on the Internet, that he'd been prosecuted for being a phony back in the days of the Johnny Carson show, that we read about how he'd been caught: his wife, equipped with a hidden phone, would wade through the audience, listening to people talk, get their names and ailments, then communicate with her husband through a hidden phone in his ear. He'd run into the audience, call out the man or woman's name, address and specific ailment, and supposedly heal it on the spot. He'd proclaim, "The message comes from God." After being exposed as a fraud, he lost his following and went bankrupt, but now, two decades later, he's back, and living in a million-dollar mansion. He's jump-started his ministry for the African-American audience selling "Miracle Spring Water!" It is sent "free"—"Miracle Manna," providing health and healing powers. Then, he mails persuasive letters asking for donations. One search revealed the following headline "Televangelist—fundamentally evil." We saw him getting into his Porsche, refusing to talk to a reporter. We saw people interviewed who had sent him thousands of dollars and lost all their savings. I was not going to call Reverend Popoff! (What I didn't say was—how about the name? Peter Popoff. Who is going to follow an evangelist called that?)

"Well, he's back now, ain't he? God is taking care of him. Reverend Popoff! He's blessed the water. He'll send it to me. I have faith. You don't understand. I have faith and that water will heal me! I talk'st to him just the other day."

"What?"

"Yes, he called and invited me to a revival."

"No way."

"I'm trying to tell you something *and you won't listen!*"

"OK, OK. Not so loud."

"He told me to come on over to where he was doing a healing."

"What'd you say to him?"

"I couldn't get there, numbskull. I told him I couldn't get there."

"Where was he?"

"North Carolina—at a Holiday Inn in Charlotte, North Carolina."

I picture Huck following the "Duke of Bilgewater" and the "late Dauphin" (the "King") into the revival camp meeting tent, and watching amazed and bewildered as the King delivers a heart-string-pulling speech on the epiphany he's just experienced, causing his immediate transformation from sinning pirate to saintly pirate-reformer, and then, rubbing the tears from his eyes, blessing and praising the people, passing his hat, while little girls kiss and hug him, villagers invite him to stay a week, and the duped and deceived fill his hat with a total of $87.75.

I get him off that topic and focus on convincing him to make an appointment with his ophthalmologist.

"No, I ain't going back to him. He's in with that phony Indian doctor who took my sight, the one I'm going to sue. I ain't going to *neither* of them no more. I'm going to get the water from Reverend Popoff. I have faith!"

"All right, let's stay calm."

"I'm going to Lourdes one day and then I'll see again."

We sit quietly for a moment. Cars pull into the 7-Eleven. Men and women open their doors, get out, shut their doors, go into the 7-Eleven. Men and women walk out, open their doors, shut their doors, start their engines. He sips his hot coffee. I describe what each individual going in and out of the 7-Eleven doors looks like.

"I've gots' another reason this one eye," he points to his right eye, "might be a little weak. It happened when I was just a teenager." He takes his sunglasses off, rubs his eye.

"I was living at home and goin' out every night. My mother told me I had to straighten out. I just kep' on drinkin' and stayin' out all night and comin' home drunk, fallin' asleep in the bed. She talked to me. She said she'd told my father what I was doin', and if I didn't straighten myself out, he'd do it for me. I paid no attention to this silly talk. The next night I was out with some girls and could barely get the car in the driveway. I staggered up the stairs, fell in the bed. And then, there he was: on top of me. I was young and strong. I grabbed him by the chest, pushed him off, thought it had to be some sort of nightmare. He grabbed me by the neck, threw me up against the wall, punched me in the gut. I fell to the floor. He was on top of me. "You've gots'ta straighten out! You've gots'ta help your mother!' He had a beard now. I couldn't get him off. He punched me in the face—one-two, one-two. *Hard*! He slammed my head on the floor. Then he punched me one more time up by my eye and my head almost *spun around*. It took me a week to recuperate from that beating. I couldn't see for three weeks, then it gradually came back, but never all the way."

We drive on. I picture that same bearded black man that was going to save Nut, up on top of Speedy, slugging him. After a while, I slid in a question out of the blue, "What age were you when your father died?"

"Five. I was five years old."

We talk about the Derby. "Orb," he says. "Put everything you have on Orb. It came to me. Remember: Orb!"

I think back on that inspiring class of juniors. Third floor. Huge, old-fashioned, paneled windows letting in the late-afternoon light and air. The rambunctious Gilman boys (including two star lineman from the championship football team and a boy who wrote lines of lyric poetry that could dazzle and ring and sing like those by Dylan Thomas) soon mixing with the girls—they were rambunctious too, and one was both brilliant and beautiful, writing short stories and articles for magazines and usually one intellectual step ahead of me, while another was an All-American field hockey player with her photograph in the paper every other week and she was definitely one step ahead of me the day the girls challenged the boys to a field hockey game and we were crushed—from next door Roland Park Country and Bryn Mawr as we began a year of studying "The American Dream," in typical Gilman unorthodox, quixotic fashion, with *Oedipus Rex*. Teiresias, the seer who cannot see, but can:

> Enough. Go think that over.
> If later you find error in what I have said,
> You may say that I have no skill in prophecy.

The Parents Association Kentucky Derby Cocktail Party Fundraiser

After standing out on the lawn and barely being able to make out Orb crossing under the wire first on a dim and hazy screen—yes, my Teiresias was right again, on the mark, and I hadn't put down one penny on the winner; after changing into boots and britches and silks, each of these having a strong emotional significance for me, and sitting on Peter Jay's retired race horse for silly photos of parents holding up one of my father's old trophies, in fact, a large and important trophy, a trophy given the family by all his friends to start a memorial race; after surviving this exhibition of feeling like a clown, making a joke of something that is sacrosanct to me, I am awkwardly positioned in the den of our hosts' basement through which a stream of women on their way back and forth to the bathroom is passing while I'm attempting to politely, modestly, pull off my boots, britches and silks, having just been in the tack, and feeling down, feeling a tinge of sorrow for myself, an undertow pulling me out to that dark, depressing depth: I would be riding no more races. I had reached the age where the "pale-faced bastards"—as Pop called them—had decided we would ride no more; and yet, there I'd been, just like at a race meet. Peter had offered me a leg up onto Man the Shipp, a strongly built bay gelding, but the horse was jumping around, Peter had his hands full, so, showing off, I grabbed the pommel of the saddle with my left hand, the back of the saddle with my right, bounced once, and hopped up. Felt good, first time I'd been on a horse in silks for three years. Stood in the irons. Patted Man the Shipp as partygoers approached him from the wrong end; told them to step up by his shoulders.

They posed, holding up my father's old trophy. Cameras clicked. Flashes went off. Over and over, with a different set of parents, we had the photo taken as if we'd just won the Derby. What did Man the Shipp think we were doing? He'd been in the winner's circle; he'd had his picture taken—and it took one minute, then was over. First, he became fidgety. Peter jiggled the shank; I patted him; we worked to keep him still. Towards the end, his body tensed. The muscles of his neck tightened, became rigid. I squeezed with my legs to have him go up a step, but he wouldn't budge. He was losing patience. Peter looked at me, I at him, and we called it a day.

I helped load Man the Shipp into the trailer, was interested to learn that Peter had gotten him as a ten-year-old after finishing third in his ninetieth start. The horse had won over $600,000. ". . . farm manager now," Peter said, lifting up the tailgate.

"What'd you say?" I asked, standing in the trailer, rubbing the horse between his eyes.

"He's fully retired now and holds the position of Assistant Farm Manager." We had a laugh. I thanked Peter, patted Man the Shipp one last time, and headed back into the *melee*. Immediately, I was asked by parents if it'd been fun. Fun, I said, it was as if you'd gotten all geared up, ready to have a romantic time with your wife, and then, she walks off! You're left sitting there, no wife to romance, no race to ride. They say you're too old to ride a race and yet on that horse you'd felt 17, 18, 28, as if you'd never stopped, as if that was where you were supposed to be—more so than in front of a room of twenty sixth graders *pontificating* on the Plantagenets.

Leaving the basement, now in mufti, I walk to a table where Ansley has just started setting up our books. A group of parents is waiting. One, a young good-looking mother who is not in her normal carpool attire—is this Arthur's mother wearing makeup and jewelry and a skimpy dress?—takes me aside and says, "I was worried."

"About what?"

"Well, you might've had a few drinks and been out there somewhere."

"Ha—out there with my wife?" I ask, not sure exactly what she meant, as I cockily sit down, jauntily open a book and with *panache* (derived from medieval French for feather in back of helmet) began to inscribe the title page, a line forming behind her.

"No, actually, I thought you might be out behind a tree relieving yourself."

Woa-o-o-o. Hm-m-m-m.

And I keep on, continue signing—no longer the young writer caught *in flagrante delicto* (medieval Latin term, which I do not teach) with his young wife. No longer the young up-and-coming jockey, the young up-and-coming newspaperman, the young up-and-coming teacher on his way to being a college professor, the young writer on his way to penning a critically acclaimed novel, but rather an older, down-and-regressing man with a weak bladder standing in the shadow of a tree holding his limply retired member and taking an urgent leak.

It's getting dark. Ansley and I fold up shop. A student helps me carry an unsold box of books, some posters, and my tack bag out into the apple orchard to the royal blue, twenty-two-year-old Jaguar convertible XK8 Ansley's father has just given me. We return to a circular table on the lawn where Ansley is seated. I first sit down to the right of Allison, our kind and gentle science teacher, leaving a space between her and the quiet dark-skinned man with thinning black hair, a Harford Day father I presume, on her left, thinking Allison's husband Sean, from Montana, will be coming over and looking forward to talking to him about Montana and camping and hiking and bicycling but something causes me to change my seat. I get up, move my plate and drink to the empty space between Allison and the father, having no idea that this change of seats would be the catalyst enabling me to look into the soul of a man who I would soon discover was trying to reclaim his life. The quiet man's wife, two decades younger, fair-skinned, with hair thick, curly and dyed blonde, is in the midst of joking about her husband's attempts to hide his age. She holds up her fingers—they are smudged with black from a Sharpie, and we laugh. She discusses how he should at least "properly" dye the few tufts of hair he has left, and enjoy it, before he loses the rest. I chime in with how Ansley attacks me with scissors—tell of being clean-shaven, showered, and dressed up driving down the Jones Falls Expressway on the way to a black tie dinner emceed by Bob Hope and with my father's friend and riding colleague Eddie Arcaro as the guest speaker the night before the Preakness when she reached across the front seat, yanked a hair out of my nostril. I relate how I'll be dressed up, knotting my tie in front of the mirror, feeling peaceful, and suddenly, like the wild man, Cato, in *The Pink Panther* practicing his karate on Inspector Closeau, there she'll be, left hand gripping my chin, right hand with scissors moving in on my eyebrows. We're all laughing.

The mother moves on to discussing carpools and their youngest attending kindergarten at HDS, mentioning they have some older children, his from another marriage, but not being specific about how many, dodging the normal and expected giving of a specific number, with "We have so many children."

I almost make a joke out of it—"Ha, you have so many that you can't remember"—but I notice the oddness of her reply, sense something awry. After hearing an inventory of what one child in his twenties is doing and another at seven, and still another at twenty-three, Ansley asks, "How many children in all do you have?" The mother looks questioningly at the father. The father, who has an accent, murmurs something along the lines of ". . . who will always be twenty."

No one pays attention. I lean toward him. "Excuse me?"

He turns toward me. I am looking into the beautiful soft brown eyes of a man and he is saying, "We have one son who will always be twenty," his face pinched, eyebrows tightened.

I make an innocuous reply about sons today taking so long to grow up, thinking he meant his son is immature, will never grow up, and just then the parents of a student walk over to say hello. I stand, step away from the table and talk to them. When I rejoin the conversation at our table we are listening to a story about death by drowning, ". . . he was strong, a strong swimmer, a weight lifter. He had a ripped body. . . ." a story that must've occurred years ago, I assume. I remain silent. I'm hungry, need more food. Thirsty, would love a large glass of water. Cold, am itching to get up and move around. The spring dew has settled, my feet in leather loafers are wet and chilled. I sit and listen, as the father tells the story, as he pictures his son in the undertow, exhausted, giving out, but fighting, fighting with all his heart and strength while watching his two friends being rescued, *one*—the scuba diver swims out, kicking hard with his fins into the waves off the Puerto Rico beach, pulls him in, *two*—the scuba diver swims out into the undertow, kicking hard, brings the other friend in.

He treads water; he switches to stroking towards shore, trying to stay above the waves. The undertow pulls. It grabs and pulls and wrenches him downward as his father's words swirl around and around his head in the waves, "Don't go in the water there. Just stay on the beach. I know that beach. I've had to rescue swimmers on that beach. Listen to me, son, the undertow is powerful there. It can drag you out. I don't know how many times we had to take the boat out to get surfers," and he'd laughed and said over his cell phone, so confidently, so blithely, "We'll be fine, Dad. We know what we're doing." He weakens, hearing his father's words, seeing his father, seeing the image of his friends on the shore searching for him, seeing his mother, his sisters, his brothers—*why didn't I listen? why didn't I listen?*—a guilt filling him. He wants to hug his father. He wants his father to dive into the water as he'd seen him do a thousand times as a child and swim powerfully out to get him and gather him up and pull him to the shore. He wants to live. He wants to graduate from the training school and become a patrolman, then a policeman like his father and make his parents proud, some day marry and have children and his parents would come visit. . . .

The mother and father had been flying back from Los Angeles to Philadelphia and the mother had been getting all sorts of emails: "Where are you?" "We're trying to reach you?" "Why won't you answer the phone?" They'd had to endure the flight. Next day, the father was in Puerto Rico, on the same beach where before moving to the States he'd had his first job as a patrolman. He was in the same boat, with the same squadron of policemen, searching in the same way as he had years earlier, but this time he was searching for his son. He tells me this. The others are discussing the high quality of the Lower School program at Harford Day. He leans toward me and looks into my eyes and relates in a hushed voice how he rushed down the beach searching for his son in the surf, for any sign of him, even for his body, yes, knowing he was really searching for his son's body, and he got so far ahead of the rest of the officers that the patrol became worried about him and began to search for him as he searched and pleaded with God for a miracle and his eyes burned from the sun's reflections off the water but he didn't care. His story brought me back to a sunny day on New Smyrna Beach in Florida, cars driving up and down the hard-packed sand, people in swim suits, mobs of them, laughing and striding happily in and out of the ocean, rock'n roll music blaring from the cars parked shoulder to shoulder on the beach, the sticky salty air, the bikini babes greased up with sun tan oil, and son Paddy five years old—I couldn't find him: I ran, searched, sprinted looking out into the water, up into the rows of cars, knowing I appeared crazy, wild, frenzied, wanting to ask, "Have you seen a little boy...." But that seemed ridiculous, there were hundreds of "little boys, " thousands of little boys. Where was mine? I chanted to myself. I prayed to myself. And then I found him. I saw him. I saw his tan, hard-packed body, his wide-shoulders, his dark hair. He was standing in the ocean. He was looking back over his shoulder at an oncoming wave. The wave rolled in, he threw both arms forward, pushed off, propelling himself, catching the wave, and I was sprinting through the surf as he rode the wave in, the churning water at my ankles, at my knees, and then I had my hands around his chest. I picked him up as if he were a feather and spun around and around, his feet dragging in the water and sending up a spray. He was laughing and laughing, "What're you doing, Dad? What're you doing?" Another wave was approaching—I tossed him high, high, he flew, arms and legs flailing, landed in the wave. I dove into it, swimming to him.

Thirty years later, I am looking into the brown eyes of a father who will never swim to his son again, never grip his son around his rib cage, never hear his son's voice, never again marvel at his son's quick, confident athletic movements, never call out his name. And how about my son Andrew? When will I call his name? When will he call me? When will I wrap my arms around his chest again? He is back in the States. He is safe. But now—he calls me "Patrick." When he was a boy, and we were alone together, he called me "Daddy." He loved it. He said it often, looking into my eyes. Then, he graduated to "Dad," and now he rarely speaks to me. It is long distance over the telephone, and he calls me "Patrick." He is renouncing, rejecting his inheritance, everything I'd taught him, everything I'd ever done for him. He doesn't remember lying in bed, his head in my arm, tearing up as I read *Sleeping Beauty* to him. He doesn't remember the rollicking, radio-cranked, rocking-and-rolling car pool days of driving to school and soccer games and lacrosse practices and camp outs, our car filled with his friends. Nada. Nada nada nada. Every misstep he's made in his life is my fault. He would prefer never to see me again. He might change his name. Two tours in Iraq. Yes. PTSD—yes, I get it. And now the undertow is pulling Andrew away from me, away from his entire family.

The mother is telling Ansley and Allison that they have another son, the oldest, who is in the military. He's in the Air Force and is about to be deployed to Dubai. "Could it happen again?" she asks. All conversation at the table stops. Silence. Then she says, "Could it happen again? What are the odds?" The mother and father eye each other.

I tell them that sometimes I felt our son Andrew was safer when he was with the military in Iraq than back in the USA driving 100 mph down to nightclubs in Mexico and just getting back to the base at Twenty-nine Palms in time to pull on his boots and go out for "PT," and while I'm saying this, I'm picturing myself on a Sunday, a summer day, in our living room, the windows open and the fresh air flowing through. I was seated on the sofa and he'd called from his base in Iraq. "I'm going up north," he'd said. "I can't say where. I'm leaving the base and I'm going north. There's something big about to happen. You'll hear about it. I just wanted to tell you that I love you." There was a lag time. I had to wait several seconds after he spoke to speak back to him. If either of us spoke too early, the words would all come at the same time. I remember the long pauses. He was in Iraq—what the hell was my son doing in Iraq? I was in Maryland. What the hell was I doing in Maryland? Why wasn't I with my son! Why wasn't I by his side? Why wasn't he in Maryland and I in Iraq? How had Bush and Cheney and the neo-cons and Rumsfeld managed to send my son all the way to Iraq, and other sons, thousands of them to Iraq, where they were being killed? How did they sleep at night? How could they sleep with the knowledge that just one American boy had been killed, or had his legs blown off, or had his sight ruined or his psychological well-being shattered. . . . I'm drifting away, thinking of that nightmarish year, when I hear the mother ask, "How do you get over it?"

All talk stops. "How do you get over it?" she asks.

Absolute quiet—pleasing in its immediate intensity. And then Ansley says, "Time." She says it again, "Time."

I'm wrung out. I'm ready to listen. What if this had happened to Andrew in Iraq. What if we'd lost him there. He'd been in the midst of fire-fights in Iraq—had done and seen it all, and he was back in the USA. This man's son went out to go for a swim, and he's gone. What if one of those bullets that hit Andrew's Kevlar vest had been aimed higher and had hit him in the face? What if Andrew's fellow Marines had been a split second slower when that kid pulled the AK-47 on Andrew and pulled the trigger? What if that had been Andrew, and not the sergeant, in the portable toilet that was blown up by one of the hundreds of grenades launched into the compound? What if that had been Andrew, and not the kind, caring and patriotic young man, Nick:

> The time you won your town the race
> We chaired you through the market place;
> Man and boy stood cheering by,
> And home we brought you shoulder high.

who was his role model at Boys Latin School, his inspiration on the cross-country team, who had Andrew doing four hundred sit-ups, four hundred pushups, one hundred pull ups, and twenty full-field wind sprints every day after cross-country practice in preparation for completing the Navy Seal Odyssey program—a twenty-four hour test of stamina, strength and perseverance—Marine Capt. Nicholas Lee Ziolkowski, scout sniper and team leader, who was killed while leading his squad into heavy combat in Fallujah?

What if those body parts Andrew had to pick up had been parts of his body and that another Marine had to pick up. . . .

Ansley begins to describe the plane crash that changed the life of her family. It was a private single prop. Her brother Tom was in it, with his fiancé Mariane Duva and her sister Caroline, going to the Bahamas for the weekend. The pilot brought his son for the first time. As the plane neared the airport, the air traffic controller screwed up. A commercial jet flew directly over them. The small plane was caught in the vortex and sent spinning to the ground. Ansley explains the reactions of her brothers, her father, herself, the effects on the fiancé's family. She explains how the two families came together, how they are still extremely close.

And then a tutor who has a bit of flair, Lorraine, a Francophile—high heels, short skirt, low cut blouse, great smile (on an early

Monday morning, passing in the hallway, she'll make a remark about her weekend activities that is so out of the norm of typical teacher "worked on my lesson plans" remarks that you'll stop in your tracks, release a laugh and ask her to expound on that subject) walks up to me and states, "I've got to tell you something."

I stand, step away from the table.

"I've enjoyed going to bed with you," she says, "but my husband is getting tired of it."

"Really?" I say, reminding myself of the way Tom says this, stretching out the word, when you hit him with a zinger, "what are we going to do about the husband?"

She laughs and explains that she's been reading my book in bed, she can't stop reading, her husband is trying to go to sleep, and she keeps laughing and waking him up. Then she asks me insightful questions about the book. We're having a good time. I notice our table is breaking up. There has been no closure. There has been no dénouement, as I tell my English class every story has (denouer—French, to untie), while drawing on the whiteboard a line gradually descending from the climax to the resolution. I somehow wrenched my lower back hopping up on Man the Shipp; it is aching, stiffening. My feet are clammy, as if the circulation is cut off, and I'm hungry. Need something hot to drink. The caterers are packing up. I make a sandwich of barbecued pit beef. I'm disappointed that the horseradish has been put away. These guys are in a rush to get the hell out of here. The food is cold. No sauces to spice it up. Nothing nonalcoholic to drink beside water. I'm tired of water. Ansley and I walk to the bonfire, are instantly warmed, forget our conversation at the table. Ansley learns some new gardening techniques from Phil our host. I talk to Phil about the man-sized *trebuchet* he's building for launching water balloons and tennis balls during the outdoor "jousting tournament" at our upcoming Medieval Feast. We try to leave but cannot synchronize it. First, Ansley finishes her glass of wine and asks, "Are you ready?" "Yes," I say, but just at that moment Phil, standing beside me, launches into an interesting story. Then, I tug her arm. "I'm ready," she says— but at that moment a polite Harford Day parent hands her a fresh glass of red wine and inquires about the typical schedule of a day-student at Oldfields, and would she recommend Oldfields for her daughter.

Finally, we're in the Jaguar, heater warming our feet, driving home fast in the dark, my back aching, my clarity of vision on the progression of my life blurred—that feel, the feel of the horse between my legs had come right back to me, and I had craved, yearned for it to continue—my throat sore, glands swelling and head stuffed up. I'm focusing on the actual driving, the car steady, taking the turns smoothly, without any swaying or lag time; the steering crisply responding to my hands on the wheel; the clutch and gears and engine instantaneously responding to my feet and my hand on the stick shift. I'm asking Ansley questions because I do not feel like talking. Her words wash over me. Like a wave it returns, the father from Puerto Rico and his son's drowning. We're quiet. There're pauses between our remarks. I wonder how many years ago it had occurred. She knows. The wife had told them when I'd stepped away to talk to the parents. They'd found the body just seven weeks ago. Seven weeks. About the time I was out skiing with Paddy in Colorado, where he's opened up his own practice of pediatric dentistry.

I slow it down. I'm driving through the dark, down the narrow country road, through time and pain, trees close on either side, looking straight ahead, and I hear her say that when they had gotten up from the table to leave, tears were dripping from the father's face and he had walked away, to the edge of the lawn, to the apple orchard, to wipe the tears from his eyes. Gripping the steering wheel tightly, I focus intently on the road ahead as my vision blurs.

That Monday at school I didn't tell anyone about Josephine's remark—how it had caused me to change my mind. I made a point of asking Josephine if her mother had gotten a photo of herself with Peter, Man the Shipp and me. Yes, she had. I didn't thank Josephine. I could have. I could have explained it all to her, made a moral of the story out of it. Instead, I savored it. Savored this change—this one little catalyst, a tiny shift of weight, this one prod that could've been missed: suppose Su had not allowed her class out; suppose the Frisbee had not flown over in Josephine's direction and I hadn't run past her and heard her remark; suppose the afternoon hadn't been beautiful, the first in ages, and the students hadn't asked me to take them outside. Then, I never would have been touched by the beauty of this father, those deep brown eyes—the son swimming, kicking, stroking, fighting the undertow, all of us fighting this undertow, this force trying to pull us under: thousands of veterans of Korea, Vietnam, Afghanistan, Iraq every morning upon awakening considering the option, the total release from the phantoms and nightmares, from their paranoid obsessions—it is about to happen again, they are being followed, chased, spied on, relentlessly pursued and tracked—and why not end it all? There is no one they can trust. Their lives have no meaning. Why not just bail out, today, this morning, end the pain, end the perception they have of not being wanted, appreciated, needed, loved? Crazed Muslim extremists hack to death a young British soldier in London, blow up innocent marathoners in Boston; young American men gone mad force their way into schools shooting innocent children and adults; glaucoma takes a the eyesight of a poor black man who for most of his life had no medical insurance; innocent black Christians are taken to the cleaners by an evil television evangelist, and soon, innocent Bible-reading black Christians at a prayer meeting are massacred by a hate-obsessed, psychopathic, white supremacist. The undertow grips, pulls, wrenches us. "...The blood-dimmed tide is loosed, and everywhere/ The ceremony of innocence is drowned;..."

It is on the news every night. Somewhere on the globe something terrible has happened. CNN, ABC, NBC, PBS, Al Jazeera America, the BBC reports on it. We become numb to it. Sitting on our couches, we push the remote button, change the station, watch football or basketball. The son dies, drowns; the son leaves. The father does not want to live; he wants to give up. He fights against it. He raises his children. He sets his alarm, gets up in the dark and goes to work.

For God So Loved
the World

Monday morning at school, trying to get to know my soft-spoken advisee Rosemary Gillam, I ask how her mother Ginny, a veterinarian who had in former years galloped and worked for Uncle Mikey, and her father Jeremy, a trainer from England, are doing. Then, thinking of my Pimlico-based exercise-rider colleague José who after finishing at Dickie's drives out to Jeremy's farm to exercise horses, I ask, "How's José? Do you ever see José?"

Her face changes. "He's not doing so well."

I picture José in the tack room at 5:15 a.m. His grin, then, "Good morning, Pa-trick," he'd say. "How are you?" Galloping horse after horse. Joking and talking in his clear, clipped English as we rode back to the barn. "What happened?" I ask her.

"He had a bad fall, and now he can't move from the waist down."

One time, a horse goes down. I email Rosemary's father and mother to get José's number. I email Dickie. He answers immediately. "Terrible, terrible situation." This from a man who has discovered he has cancer all through his body, is undergoing an intense simultaneous treatment of chemotherapy and radiation, and was told by the doctors he had six months to live and he'd better send his horses to another trainer because once the treatment started he'd be too weak and too sick to go to work. What's Dickie do? Gets up at 3:15 the next morning, goes online, checks the racing results, searches for races with conditions that fit his horses, steps into his truck and is marching up and down the

156

aisle of his barn at Pimlico at 5:00 a.m. saying good morning to his loyal crew from Mexico.

During my first free period, I call José. "Pa-trick," José says in that clipped, clean, crisp way, with a slight Spanish accent. "I don't know what happened. We were breezing. My horse was going fine. We were going down the stretch, and suddenly he collapsed. He fell. . . ."

"Did he break something?"

"No, he just fell."

He fell and José's life, and his family's life, and the life of the racetrack has changed.

Tuesday—arise at 4:30, drive Ansley to the airport to visit her weakening father in Florida, teach all day, visit José at the hospital, ride Riderwood and Saitensohn, clean up the house, grade a few papers, the night getting later and later, the last hot night of fall, swatting at the damn stink bugs buzzing all around the light as I study the Battle of Hastings, alone in the bed, can't get to sleep, up late, missing Ansley, I've overdone it again.

Wednesday—"Speedy Kiniel New" vibrates and rings its way across my desk. I'm across the room at the lectern. Arthur, my most polite and considerate student, asks, "Want me to answer it? Want me to answer it, Mister Smithwick?"

Patrolling the fields while on recess duty after class, I retrieve the message: "Patrick, where've you been. I have some things I've got's to talk to you about." He was speaking in a low, calm voice, a gentle conspiratorial whisper. I pictured him in the hovel, head bent down low to his flip phone so Melody, in her living room directly above, can't eavesdrop. "Listen," he says into the only spot on the phone not wrapped with black electrical tape, come on by on your way home from work. Here's what I need, you ready? A bottle of orange soda. A bag of pork grinds. Some Ritz crackers. Peanut butter. Three oranges. You can get that at the grocery store on your way up. Then, stop by Royal Farms and pick up some chicken. Two legs, two wings, some French fries and a biscuit. I'll see you soon. Thank you, buddy. I appreciate it."

After work, I don't go. It's just too much. I'm selfish. The teaching has drained me. Ansley's absence has weakened my zest for life and work. I'm still thinking about the visit with José. I'm flat.

Thursday morning—up early by myself. In pajamas and robe, I feed and hay the horses, muck out the shed, rush up to the loft to throw down some hay and straw. On the way in, and on the way out, I walk right past a spot of bright early morning sunlight illuminating the initials "J. S. K." carved into the cement Speedy and I had laid two summers ago. We'd mixed and carried and lugged the cement up the bank by the big sliding doors of the barn on a hot summer morning. There was a narrow trench, caused by years of erosion, running alongside the sliding doors where water was draining into the stalls below. We'd started pouring the cement at 10:00, the trough to fill becoming wider and wider as we reached the end of the twenty-foot barn door where the hill dropped off, down to the driveway. We poured another entire wheelbarrow of cement. Added one layer after another. He was giving me orders. I had no idea how to mix or set cement. Finally, victoriously, we smoothed it out so that it looked natural, like a waterfall we thought. We got the job done. It was noon. No shade. The sunlight baked the concrete; it reflected off the side of the barn. We were in the hottest place on the farm at this time of day and we were delighted to be finished.

Ansley came out to look at it. "Awful," she said. "It looks awful. You can't have it like that. It has to have edges. That's a mess! It has to come down in steps."

All the energy drained from me. I wanted to quit. This was ridiculous. "Get the sledgehammer," he said. I didn't move. "Get me the sledgehammer!" I got it. He swung it with crushing power. Beads of sweat flew from his face. He broke up the hard-set cement. I carted off the pieces, filled potholes in the driveway with them.

We mixed up a new wheelbarrow of cement. Poured it. Used boards to flatten the top and keep the sides vertical. We stepped it down. I was seeing stars. I'd be bending over, smoothing the cement, buttressing a board with a rock, and when I stood up a thousand fireflies, an explosion of blinking amoebas would fill my line of vision. He carved his initials in the cement. "J. S. K." He made that extra effort to carve them.

Driving to work, I call Speedy.
"Where you been?"
"Had to see a friend of mine at the hospital."

"Who's that, Tom?"

"No, why'd you think it was Tom?"

"Cause last time I saw him he looked terrible, worn out. And smoking—every time I go to Royal Farms he's there buying a pack of cigarettes, Pall Malls, just like your daddy smoked. He's getting too old to train those horses. Just like Mikey; he'll kill himself workin' on that farm. Well, who was you visitin'? Wha'chu doin'—keeping it a secret?"

"José—I used to gallop with him for Dickie?"

"What happened to him, break his leg?"

"No. A horse fell with him while breezing. He can't move from the waist down."

"Live by the sword, die by the sword. I'll pray for him, and you remember, your daddy was paralyzed. First they said he'd die. Then they said he'd never walk again, and he sure as hell would never ride a horse again. But what'd he do? He proved'em wrong. I'll pray for José and he'll prove'em wrong too. When you coming up?"

"After school."

"All right. I'll be at the table."

"How ya doing?" he calls out as I enter the dark basement.

"Good, good."

"Here," he hands me the keys to his room. He holds one finger up to his lips and blows on it. "Now you got the stuff, just don't say anything. Keep quiet. Put it on my bed and lock the door when you come out."

On the table is a frayed white plastic bag wrapped tightly around something. Its ends are neatly tied in a bow. A book, a large book, I think. An old large book which he wants me to sell, like the guitar pick he claimed was Jimi Hendrix's. What a fight we'd had about that. He'd researched and found the biggest pawnshop in the world, out by L.A., and while I was out there one summer doing book signings, he'd wanted me to stop by and get $5,000 to $10,000 for it.

I walk across the basement, on my left the black wood stove, to my right a large couch and chair set up around the gigantic television screen. I poke the little key into the padlock of his door. It snaps open. The stale smell of the windowless room—the sharp ammonia scent of urine—sweeps over me. I set the bag of food on the bed, take a step back towards the door, hesitate. I glance down at the tall white bucket with the plastic top on it. I should check it out, and if it is full, carry it to the *garderobe* on the other side of the kitchen, open the top, and poor the contents into the toilet. Then I remember. A wave of relief sweeps through me. He is paying Luke to do that now. I back out, lock the door.

He stands, puts a couple of fingers through the loop of plastic. I can now see that it is an oversize book. "My Bible," he says. "There's something I want you to read."

We walk out. He gently grips my bent arm at the elbow, and we go step by step up the lawn, over the lip of asphalt, through the tight spot between the front bumper of the pickup and the big bush, down the length of the pickup, and take a left at the front of the pickup.

He stops. "Why you keep bringing this old thing up here. I can smell it a mile away."

"I bring it because it's easier for you to get in and out of." I chuckle to myself, amazed at his perspicacity. Ungrateful so and so, I think, laughing at the two of us, *The Odd Couple.*

We take a right, walk alongside the truck. I have Speedy stand back, as I open the door. I put his right hand on the top of the door, have him step forward, and remind him where the grip above the window is.

"I know, I know. What you think, I've lost my memory?"

Get him in. Lean over in front of him, my belly against his belly, to stretch the seat belt across his bulk. "This Meals on Wheels is putting too much weight on you. We need to get out and go for a walk."

"I'm fine. I be getting plenty of exercise. You just get this truck going. I don't want to be a skinny-looking rake like you. The girls like me like this. Look at my face. Look at my skin. It looks younger than yours—you getting all wrinkled from all your rushin' around and worryin' and workin'. . . . You worries too much. You need to hand it over, put your life into the hands of the Lord. You tearin' around that farm, mowin' and weedeatin' and fixin' fences and runnin' that tractor. You've gots'ta stop. Early grave, that's what you're looking at, an early grave. . . ."

We're a couple of Sunday drivers, headed for the 7-Eleven. He's into full lecture mode. Could've been a great minister—except for the drinking and the women and who ever heard of a "boxing" minister? Well, there is George Foreman. . . .

"God is hope. Peter Popoff's got it. I saw him in a vi-shin. He came to me. He said, 'You've got's it. *Two...! Hundred...! Thousand...! Dollar...!* Your debt is *paid.*' I'm a Christian. I been serving God a long time. You didn't believe me. Now I'm gwyne have a bran-new apartment with a *dishwasher,*" he says. "Anybody ain't got no dishwasher ain't got *nothin'*! I'm gwyne have no glass. Just plastic. Plastic cups and plates so they won't break. I'm gwyne have a *fob* to get in the door. It's a little round thing—you press it up 'gainst the door and *BWHANG*—the door opens. *You* can't get in. Nobody can't get in unless I *lets* them in. Then there's gwyne be a nice lobby. *Big!* I'll have people over and they can sit in the lobby. I might just get married again. . . ."

I think about that. Did he ever got divorced from his second, or is it his third wife?

". . . to some old money," he laughs. "*Oooold* money. I'm so happy I don't know what to do. It's gwyne have a big bathroom, a kitchen, a dining room. You didn't believe me. You didn't believe it would happen. *God* told Jesus what to do. *Jesus* said, if anything, '*I'll do it.*'

"Wo-a," I motion with my hand, raising it up and stepping it down, realizing that this motion does no good but doing it anyway. "Not so loud. Please, I'm right here."

"*Jesus* is here. He's here right now. Ain't no doctor can heal your cancer. Jesus came through, just like Nut in the Grand Canyon riding motorcycles. My brother Nut's in heaven now. . . . And my sister's boy, my nephew, he's is a prophet—he prayed for me and his prayers were answered."

I park the truck in front of the 7-Eleven.

"Oh yes, get me a cup of hot black coffee—ha, remember, *black like me.*" He grins. He leans back. "And I'd like a cookie, a good cookie—something like an oatmeal cookie."

"All right. All right," I say, getting out. I step around to his side of the truck, "Anything else, sir?" I was going to joke, "How about a chocolate milkshake and a cheeseburger with fries," but there was no place that could serve up such an order within miles and I was concerned that if I mentioned such a meal, he'd want it, he'd demand it, he'd have to have it, I'd receive a scolding about being selfish and too skinny and working too hard and not enjoying life, and off we'd go on another three-hour adventure.

"No, that's good. A hot coffee, *black like me*," he says, lowering his voice. "And a cookie, a good cookie. Can you remember that or should I write it down?"

I go in. A man in a rumpled black suit, knot of his tie pulled away from his neck, is standing at the counter opening up a new pack of cigarettes, waiting. The clerk is away from the cash register, over by the lottery ticket machine punching in numbers and printing out tickets. I walk up and down the meager shelves, see every single kind of granola and candy and energy bar made in America, but not one cookie, then finally—ah—a bag of cookies. I dance outside to the truck. "There's a bag of chocolate chip cookies that looks pretty good. . . ."

"No."

I step through the doors back into the 7-Eleven. There are now two unshaven, middle-aged men in worn and dirty T-shirts at the counter buying cigarettes, lottery tickets, and an oversize bottle of beer each. I stride fast up and down the shelves again. Come back out. Walk up to his side of the cab. "Fig Newtons—Fig Newtons are looking good. . . ." I do happen to like Fig Newtons and wouldn't mind one myself.

"Nope."

Return, open the door. The two men finish folding their lottery tickets into their wallets. Hold the door open for them and they walk out. Step in, and there, right beside the lottery machine, is a stack of the biggest damn cookies you've ever seen. They look like they could be oatmeal. I pick one up, turn it over. Above the list of two dozen ingredients making up this delicacy is the word, *Oatmeal*. Happens to be my favorite. There's also a yellow sticker with $2.35 written on it. I sigh. Buy it, and a hot black coffee, $1.75. Head out.

"Oatmeal," I say.

"Yes, yes, that's good."

I get in the cab, hand him his coffee. Pick at the plastic wrapping around the cookie, trying to find an edge, a corner.

"What're you doing?"

"I am *trying* to unwrap this cookie."

"Here, give it to me."

"I got it, I got it."

"Good Lord, what the hell you teach those kids every day

when you can't even *unwrap a cookie?*"

Pull the plastic off. Hand him the cookie. Unknot the perfectly tied yellow bow of the plastic bag. Pull out a large, handsome, soft-covered Bible.

He's set up: cup of hot coffee in one hand, crumbling oatmeal cookie in the other.

"A good-looking book."

"Large type," he says. "Go to John 3:16."

Suddenly a racket is approaching, cacophony, dissonance, a loud high-pitched engine and rap "music." It gets nearer and nearer. A man in his early thirties in a little Japanese pickup, rusted below the doors—it's been customized, has a sleek purple, plastic cover over the back, is about three inches off the ground, and has been outfitted with superchargers—pulls up, parks, leaving one space between us, and sits there with his window open, the engine racing, listening to the racket. I think about moving our truck.

"John 3:16—*can you find it?*"

"Yes," I return my focus to the Bible in my lap. I flip through it. It has all kinds of cool charts, diagrams, illustrations. In the middle of the book, there's a chart - left page, of the Old Testament, right page of the New Testament—of the books, subject matter, length of the material, time periods, themes. I could have used this last fall when my Medieval History class was studying the birth of Christianity, which I had inserted into the course because few of the students attended Sunday School or church and none knew anything about Jesus's life and teachings, with the exception of a girl who is Greek Orthodox, a high IQ boy who is Catholic and at twelve-years-of-age knows the New Testament much better than I, and a go-getter, will-get-the-job-done, will-one-day-be-president girl, who is Jewish.

"Do you an' Angie go to church?"

The rap shuts off in the pickup. The driver revs the engine higher and higher, then turns it off. Tenseness eases out of my body. I glance over at him, notice the smeared tattooes running down his neck, the studs in his ear, and a ring through his nose. I'm grateful for the quiet. I adjust. Then another "song" kicks in, this one almost all bass, a pounding, throbbing bass, the tin pickup not much more than a big speaker for the *boom boom boom* accompanied by menacing lyrics.

"We used to go a lot, but we haven't been going much this year."

"Well, you should read the Bible. One day—*ziiiip!*—you're going to be *gone*! You work and you rush around. You need to read the Bible and the Lord will take care of you."

"All right. Yes, I'd like to read the Bible some more."

"And pray. If I was *you*, I'd *really* pray. And if I was you, I'd ask Angie to pray for me. You needs all the praying you can get." He takes a bite of his cookie, a sip of his coffee.

"I pray every day. I talk to the Lord. You've gots 'ta talk to him if you want him to take care of you. He'll take care of you but you've gots 'ta *ask* him. You people think you know everything but you don't. Look at Mikey. *Ohhhhh*, I hates 'ta think where he is now. What *comes* around *goes* around. He thought about one person: *Mikey*! He'd screw a snake if that's all there was, and he'd screw his mother or brother out of their last dollar, as you know. What *comes* around *goes* around. You see what happened to Mikey don't you—Parkinsonians Disease. Eats you up from the inside. Well, you just like Mikey. I don't know if there's even any hope for you. You might just *die* and go *straight to hell.*'"

The cacophony emanating from the pickup beside us continues. I'm trying to ignore it. Why the hell does that bastard have to pull his truck up ten feet away, turn it off, then leave the window open and play that racket? "John...." I'm saying, flipping through the pages. "John 1, John 2, John 3. . . ."

Speedy is uncharacteristically quiet.

John 3:16 is half way down the right hand column on the left page. I decide to start early. I scan the page, pick it up where Jesus answers Nicodemus the Pharisee, "Very truly, I tell you, no one can see the kingdom of God without being born from above."

The rap from the pickup cuts off. I continue reading. It is quiet in the parking lot now. Speedy's window is wide open. I am well aware that everything I'm reading is being heard by the man with the shaved head, tattooed neck and multiple face piercings in the driver's seat one space away.

Verse 13: "No one has ascended into heaven except the one who descended from heaven, the Son of Man. And just as Moses lifted up the serpent in the wilderness, so must the Son of Man be lifted up, that whosoever believes in him may have eternal life."

"Yes, yes, go on," Speedy says.

"OK," I say, focused now, "Here's verse 16: 'For God so loved the world that he gave his only Son, so that everyone who believes in him may not perish but may have eternal life.' "

Speedy shifts in his seat. He concentrates, he stares straight ahead. "That's it," he says. "Now read it slowly."

" 'For God so loved the world that he gave his only Son.' "

"For God so loved the world that he gave his only Son," Speedy repeats.

" 'so that everyone who believes in him may not perish,' " I read.

"so that everyone who believes in him may not perish."

" 'but may have eternal life.' "

"but may have eternal life."

The young man beside us is leaning back in his seat, eyes closed. We go through it two more times. Then Speedy has it. We finish. The young man quietly gets out of the pickup, shuts his door and walks into the 7-Eleven.

I turn the key, we head back. "You been baptized?" Speedy asks.

"Yes, yes I was—I've seen the pictures and the baptism book."

"What! You mean the preacher held you above a little font an' sprinkled some drops on your head?"

"Yes, that's what he did."

"That's not being baptized. It says in the Bible you got to go *under* th'water. The preacher needs'ta hold your *whole body* under th'water, then you come back up and you're *re*-born. He's gots' ta just about *drown* you and you come back up out of that water reborn as a *Chris*tian—you know what that means?"

"Yes."

"No you don't. You think that sprinkling of water on your head baptizes you. Well, when you come back up out'ta the water and you been baptized like in the Bible, then you are sittin' beside the father, the son and the *Holy Ghost*. Everything is in three's. Did'ja know that?"

"That's interesting."

"You'd better believe it's interesting, you damn fool. What's a cross—it has three points, right? You know, if you have an injury, if you fall and hurt yourself, all you have to do is make a cross "— he outlines a cross on his chest—"like this, and it will heal."

I drive. I see myself—ten years ago, exhausted, fifteen pounds under my normal weight, having had a fall in a timber race that day. I'm sitting on the footlocker in our barn. When the horse went down, I'd sat back, ridden him to the ground, and then been catapulted to my right. I'd had my stick in my right hand and had broken the impact with that hand, which had been whacked backwards. Sitting on the footlocker, I looked at it, hoping it wasn't broken. It throbbed. Swollen—it looked like an old-time baseball glove. Speedy sat down beside me, placed my hand on his knee. He poured rubbing alcohol on the hand, closed his eyes, made a cross and massaged the hand. He prayed. Silently. The swelling drained out and the throbbing ceased.

"Do you understand the whole point of being baptized?" he asks.

"What is it?"

"You damn fool, it's so you can go to heaven. If you haven't been baptized, you can't go to heaven. You get hung up in perga-*tu-or-y* and you just stay there forever *in lim-bo*."

I try to change the subject, ask how the search for his apartment is coming along. Maybe we should make some calls, contact some more people, check on his status.

"I'm not worried about that. *You have gots'ta go to the Lord*! You can't just wait for him to come to you. Why, you could be standin' there, and he could walk right pas' chu."

I'm listening.

"*Patrick*!" He looks over at me. "You've just gots' ta reach out for the Lord. You know what I mean?"

"Yes, yes I do."

At home, I feed the pups and go straight to my writing room with a satchel weighed down by essays to grade. I knock out three or four good ones, wanting to make a start before Ansley gets home, but my focus is waning. Warfield is standing four feet away, outside my writing room, looking in at me staring out at him. I have forgotten to feed the horses. He is licking his chops. Riderwood and Saitensohn are out of sight; they must be in the top field. I open the door—what used to be the entrance to what was a milking parlor—walk back around to the feed room, get a half dipper of sweet feed. Warfield ambles into the shed. I duck under the rail, step into the shed, toss the feed in a feed tub, rub Warfield on the star between his eyes, run my hand down his neck. He finishes the feed, turns, places his forehead against my hip and rubs against me, nudging me, pushing me into the wall. Laughing, I grab a brush and rub rag off the wall. Starting at his ears, I pull his chestnut mane over, on the wrong side, the "near" or left side, and brush it down. I've given up trying to have it lay on the far side. Mom had brushed it, braided it, tried to train it to go to the "correct" side for years, and it always swung back. I pull his long, gleaming mane over, and brush it down, getting all the knots and tangles out. I move to his thick tail, pull out the briars, brush out the hairs matted together with dirt. I pull the rub rag out of my back pocket, lean into him, and rub his neck, shoulders, back, rump until he's ready to jog into the ring at Madison Square Garden.

Nothing Gold Can Stay

Nature's first green is gold,
Her hardest hue to hold.
Her early leaf's a flower;
But only so an hour.
The leaf subsides to leaf.
So Eden sank to grief,
So dawn goes down to day.
Nothing gold can stay.

— Robert Frost,
"Nothing Gold Can Stay"

1

Right there—four horse lengths from where I sit, he lay down for the last time. Yesterday. Saturday. I'd been walking him. Ansley had rushed out to the end of the entrance to flag down the vet. I was pulling on him, talking to him, keeping him on his feet. He was sweating, hot, wanting to lie down. Finally, he stopped, directly in front of this writing room, and he lay down for the last time. I sat on the ground, picked his head up and gently set it on my lap. Patted him. Rubbed the white star between his eyes. Looked into his brown eyes. Talked to him.

He knew I was there with him. He could see me, feel me, smell me, hear me. He tried to get back up. He had lain down with his feet pointing up the incline—towards this room. Below us was the stream. I got under his withers and pushed with all my strength; he heaved himself, attempted to will himself up. He swung his four legs high to gain momentum, brought them back down preparing to lift up, and I saw him rolling and rolling here where the load of sand had been dumped ten years ago. *He had dug, pawed, gone down onto his front knees, lowered his glowing-chestnut body, given that wonderful moan of joy and satisfaction and relaxation, rolled, stretched out the entire length of his body, rubbed his neck and head against the sand, then suddenly, joyfully—pulling his body together, making it compact—pushed off and rolled up, up, all four legs in the air for a split second, the softness of his belly vulnerable, exposed, and then over onto the other side, stretched his body out, moaned in delight, brushed his head and neck against the sand, pushed off—all four feet suddenly in the air—and all the way over again. Riderwood was standing by and there was no way in heaven or hell he could roll over, back and forth, like this. Saitensohn approached, put his nose to Warfield's rump, pushed, and with incredible power Warfield flowed up, poured up off the sand in one surging motion, and then, continued up, up, onto two legs, straight up, pawing the air. He came down on all four, took a few yearling-like leaps, kicking up high behind, then rose straight up again, pawing the air—the stream below him, the big field spreading out behind the stream, Riderwood and Saitensohn now goofily galloping around in circles—came down and took off bucking and farting. Approaching the rocky stream crossing, he stood off, made a twelve-foot broad jump, landed and continued galloping up the hill, stopped at the knoll that overlooked the farm, put his head down and started to graze.*

2

It is on this spot four horse lengths from my desk in this one-time milking parlor, on the old sand roll, now grown over with lush green grass, where you can see the outline of his body, the grass smoothed and flattened and soothing to look at (usually coming across such an impression in a field has the same affect as walking out through the snow to monitor morning recess, taking a few steps onto the soccer field, and seeing the imprint of a child's snow angel from the day before)—that Warfield lay down for the last time. I was stroking his face, looking into his eye, talking to him, and his eye was looking out at this man with tears running down his face, this man whom he had known and grown to trust over a twenty-five-year period *but first there was the woman with the wonderful, gentle hands and the smooth commands who rode him cross country and fed him and held him for the blacksmith and pulled his mane and brushed it every day trying to get it to lay on the "correct" side and then this man had come along, always with the dog Sawyer who had a chestnut coat like his own, and they had started going for long rides, fast gallops, jumping all sorts of fences, and then, the boys on the ponies—it was the man on his back, the chestnut retriever Sawyer by his side, the iron-gray pony Nappy with the dark-haired boy Paddy in the tack, and later the pony Blossom with the blonde-haired, cap-gun shooting, cow-boy-hat-wearing boy Andrew in the irons. It was usually in the winter and they rode out the big back field through thousands of acres of countryside and freedom and laughter and conversation. Then, there was the winter and spring of giving a lead to that thick-necked and stubborn little pony Chim Chim with the little girl Eliza in the man's childhood saddle with the box stirrups, and the following summer of going cross-country through the wet grass and cool woods of the early morning with Poppy, the old, gentle and wise Shetland, the little girl Eliza laughing and talking and feeling safe on this kind pony.*

The boys and girl grew too large for ponies. They drifted off to other sports, to college, to war, to dental school, to graduate school. And then there was the young woman with assertive legs riding him in another way, Adrienne who rode him every second she was on his back, while the man was now on a green horse, that big, lazy, lanky, long-striding, huge-jumping, happy-go-lucky bay Riderwood and then that wild-as-the-wind, wants-to-jump-everything-at-top-speed Saitensohn, soon to be given the barn name Charley by that older singing, fast-talking, fast-moving, soft-handed man Speedy. Adrienne rode him like a show horse, her calves and heels pushing him up into the bridle and her hands holding those cumbersome double reins of the double bridle as no one else could so that he didn't amble along, neck low and outstretched and pulling on the bit. Instead, he looked like a dressage horse, his neck arched, his body compactly taut between Adrienne's legs. At this time, there was also the boy who had become a man, the boy/man whom he trusted, the boy/man Paddy who could hop on him and get him to relax, who never rode him in a double bridle with that cursed curb chain around his chin but instead used a simple twisted steel snaffle. He knew there was no point trying to wear down Paddy by relentlessly pulling, as he did other riders. There was no point going sideways or flinging his head or acting as if he were going to take off, as he did with other riders. He knew that the boy/man had no fear and was strong. If he had to, the boy/man could always lean back, pull on the reins and hold him, and so he trusted the boy/man Paddy and Paddy rode him with a loose rein, like no other. He liked the boy/man—how about that time in the dusk when Paddy released his hold on the reins and let him school fast, by himself, over three four-foot hurdles on the race course down the hill from the indoor track that was a half-hour hack away, right after the boy/man's father had told the son to stand there and watch. To stand and watch as the father schooled the new horse the father seemed to think was so fast when in fact he knew, he could feel it deep within his Thoroughbred desire for speed, for competition, that if he were allowed to put his head down, stretch out his neck, and lengthen his stride, he could go head-and-head with that new German show-off any day of the week. If the man/boy pointed him towards the hurdle and loosened his hold on the reins and leaned forward, he'd fly straight as a hawk diving at its prey—without wasting energy as the new horse did snapping his head back into the rider's face, jumping up and down in one place, lunging and leaping forward trying to yank the reins out of the rider's hands—and that December evening in the gloaming after the hack over to the farm with all the race horses, immediately after the German horse had schooled, the man/boy had lined him up, pointed him at the first hurdle, dropped his head and let him gallop full tilt over those hurdles, the man/boy—not a man, not a boy, not a son, a rider now, a rider, sitting back with a deep seat and a long hold, something that cannot be taught, it was in his blood—as his father had ridden for forty years, and his father's father for another forty—letting him run and jump and show that new German horse just how to do it.

What does a horse know? Within a five-mile radius of this farm, Warfield knew which direction was home and how to get there. A few times, far away, hacking home in the dark, I stopped steering Warfield, set the buckle of the reins on the pummel of the saddle and let him take me home. He wanted to get home. For all his life on the farm he was the leader of the herd. He was always smaller than the next new horse but that made no difference. It was the size of his heart that counted; it was his assurance, his natural dominance, and any new horse sensed this immediately upon arrival.

He knew me.

Early in the morning, when I stepped out of the house with the pups—Alfie, our youthful Yorkshire terrier, and Tidbit, our senior dachshund—to feed, he would pick his head up from the grass, watch me walk toward the barn, and start ambling in, the others following. At the end of a day's teaching, I'd drive into the entrance, get out, take two steps, look up, and wherever Warfield was in the fields surrounding the house, he'd have his head up and he'd be following me with his eyes. In the late spring when we had the windows of the bedroom wide open, and the pollen count was high, how I loved awakening to him grazing outside, twenty yards away. He'd *chomp*, take four or five bites, sigh, blow air out his nose; *chomp*, take three bites, sigh and blow air over loose, *bluttering* nostrils. On a winter evening, if I strode into the barn to check on the horses, maybe throw blankets on them, and slowing down now, being on their time now and not on human time, I felt the need to relieve myself, I'd watch Warfield stretch out, arch his back, relax, drop his penis out of its sheath, then Riderwood, then Saitensohn—soon to be given the stable name Charley—and we'd all be going together. I'd wonder at the magic of it, this boyish across-species communication. I'd wonder if I could ever explain it to anyone. Maybe not. With one exception—Tom.

Yawning was the same. When I had the two bays in work for racing over the winter, I'd come out at 10:00 p.m. to give them a pat, a scoop of feed, check them over and top off the water buckets. Warfield would have the big shed, that the stalls opened into, all to himself, while the bays were ensconced in their stalls. One of us would yawn, then another, and another and we'd all be yawning simultaneously. It'd been a long day.

3

Five lengths away is the blanket of matted grass where he made his last attempt to be on his feet, to be moving through space and time and the farm that he loved, to be up, beside Charley, galloping beside Charley, grazing beside Charley, swishing his tail across Charley. The man was stroking his face, looking into his eye, talking soothingly to him, and his eye was looking at this man who had tears running down his face. He was not going to give up. He lifted his head, he groaned, he lifted his head high. The man stood halfway up. Knees bent, the man gripped the lower shoulder with his left hand, the lower neck with the right, and keeping his arms bent at a forty-five degree angle, pushed up with the strongest muscles he had, those in his legs, pushed with all the strength a human his size can summon.

Warfield swung his weight and got one foot underneath himself, then the other, and tried to push up. *Struggled to push up.* Looking into the man's eyes, the man holding the weight of his head and neck, a shock, a heave, a blow went through his body, his spirit left him, and the man was standing there holding his head, carefully, gently, lowering it, pulling a bandana out of his pocket and setting his head down on it.

Thursday—I'd taught my full schedule, and used every recess and free period to jot notes on my students and prepare for the back-to-school parent conferences that night. I drove home, called the horses in for dinner. They jogged to the shed, filed into their stalls. I cleaned up, giving them time to relax and eat and play around with their feed in our old dark blue/light blue galvanized steel feed tubs with the inner rim to keep the feed from spilling out. Then, I'd gone down the line: first, unsnapped the runner— a rubber-coated chain stretched across the opening of the stall door snapped to screw eyes at both ends—patted Riderwood's big shoulder, gave him a love slap on the rear end, and he'd moseyed out of his stall. Then, unsnapped Saitensohn's runner, held my hand out, and out he came, fast, on tip toes, his chest bending away from me, his back absorbing my sweeping hand, lithely, gracefully slinking away from my hand as our wild barn-cats do every morning. Holding my hand still, the tips of my fingers running across his shoulders, down his ribs, across his rump as if they were going down the keyboard, *pianissimo*, of our piano, it eased me, quieted me, calmed me. Warfield was leaning hard against his runner and an old racetrack webbing—a strong nylon mesh with three snaps on each side—pawing with one foot and seesawing his head up and down. I put my hand on his nose, leaned my weight into him, pushed him back, ducked under the runner and webbing. He needed both. If you just had a runner, he would put his neck under it, march forward, ripping the screw eyes out of the wall, and merrily jog out to his knoll at the top of the big field.

I rubbed Warfield's face, talked to him, ran my hand down his long neck, thought how now that summer was over and the flies were gone, I should pull his mane. I patted him across his strong back and his full rump. He pushed against the runner and webbing as I looked over his legs. I put my hand on his nose again, pulled him back, unsnapped the runner/webbing and out of the stall he burst. This was the horse that the vet charged me an extra $75 for giving a "physical," which consisted of running her hand over his legs, taking his temperature, and listening to his heart with a stethoscope—"Heart murmur, he has a heart murmur. Are you still riding him?"

"Yes, I school him cross-country."

"Does he show any signs of getting fatigued?"

"No, none at all."

"Well, he's getting older and with this heart murmur, you never know. I'd be careful."

That was five years ago. I'd been careful for a few months. Didn't ride him much. Then discussed it with Tom.

"That's ridiculous. Half the horses you ride probably have heart murmurs. You probably have one yourself."

Alfie, Tidbit and I followed the three horses into the big field. They were up on the knoll. Between them and the pond was a flock of geese devouring the horses' grass. *Goose goose goose*, I called out, low, so as not to disturb the horses, but loud enough for Alfie to hear, and he took off—ran into the midst of the waddling, honking, taking-flight, upwards-spiraling confusion of aggravated geese. Returning to me, he barked and yapped and snapped at the horses' heels, Charley kicking out—flying hooves too close to Alfie—and prancing away, Warfield snorting and galloping up the hill, Riderwood following at a jog. I took a fast forty-five minute walk with Alfie and Tidbit, showered, and drove back to school where I went all-out meeting with parents until 9:30.

The next morning, Friday morning, the alarm went off and I did not. My body rose up out of the sheets but my brain and energy, all my zip, remained in the bed. All morning at work, meeting the last of the parents, I was groggy. Finally, after jump roping with the third graders, I came to life.

That afternoon—the faculty party. I was antsy, wanted to get home. Wanted to crank up the 1959 Farmall and mow the fields. It was a sunny day. I knew Ansley planned to work straight through this Friday afternoon and then give a report at the trustee dinner. Also, I kept thinking of the poor dogs locked in the house. But it wasn't just the need to mow, the need to let the dogs out; something was pulling me back. Then, I was out of the faculty party, made my escape, drove home, was on the tractor, the big wheels spinning around on either side of me, going at a good pace, getting the job done, the thrumming of the engine and the wheeling-slashing blades of the belly-mower coming up through the chassis of the tractor and through my body, *mowing, mowing*—a perfect time to check how the horses are doing, watch them move around, ensure that they are sound, to look for freshly dug groundhog holes near posts, limbs fallen on top rails, beer cans thrown into the field by late-night, beer-swilling ignoramuses. I saw Riderwood, but no Saitensohn, no Warfield. Didn't think much of it.

I was mowing on the west side of the barn and couldn't see the stream on the east side. The power and roar of the tractor was vibrating through my body. Around and around the front field I was going, on a mission, when I suddenly pulled out of the circuit, roared behind the barn and into the big field—for what reason I cannot remember, for no reason. I just had a feeling I'd better do it, and the tractor took me, carried me through the gate, behind the barn, where at first I saw something strange: a bay, a tall elegantly built bay standing like a sentinel on a hummock and a few feet below him, near the stream, in a low area, I saw a splash of chestnut, *down, lying down*, in the thick grass by the stream close to where it flowed into the pond—*not moving*. I roared over, jumped off. Ran my hand down his neck. Alive, alive! He was hot, sweating. He was breathing but not moving. Seemingly peaceful but down.

I raced the tractor back to the garage. Grabbed pad, pen and rub rag from the barn, cell phone from the house, ran back to Warfield. Charley was standing directly over Warfield, nudging his rump, trying to get him up. Warfield wasn't moving. He wasn't flicking his skin to get rid of the flies. His stomach was bloated. I kept flicking the flies away with the rub rag. This—that he wasn't twitching the skin anywhere on his body when the flies kept pestering him—was shocking. His eye—so gentle, so beautiful, so deep, the brown, the depth—did he see me? Flies congealed at the corner of his eye. He didn't shake his head or blink to get rid of them. I brushed them away. His head was heavily positioned on the grass, his other eye down hard in the wet grass. This was a stoic horse. When injured, he always cooperated. He had rarely been injured. This was a smart horse. Warfield was the most intelligent horse I'd ever known. He was breathing weakly, as if he were about to stop. The heart murmur—had it finally led to a heart attack? Should I tear my shirt off, hold it over his nostrils, and quicken his end, let him leave us, stop this suffering? Barely breathing. How long had he been there?

I called our vet. No answer. I called his assistant. No answer. Ansley drove in the driveway, saw me in the field. She had changed her mind, decided to come home for a short break before assuming her evening duties at Oldfields. "Call Tom! Call Tom!" she hollered. I hadn't seen Tom since Saratoga. He never answers his telephone—what's the point? I called. He immediately answered, no joking, all business, sensing something, asking quick questions, giving crisp orders. "No, he hasn't had a heart attack. Get him up," he said. "Get him up." He asked more questions. I gave the best answers I could. "I'd come over but I'm too far away. I'm downtown. I'll call Gary. He'll be right there."

Ansley was there beside me. Thankful, I was so thankful. She didn't hesitate. She called school, "Yes, I know it's the trustee dinner. I'm in an emergency on the farm and I cannot make it."

Gary Murray, Tom's son-in-law, arrived in minutes. Instinctive Irish horsemanship. Young. Positive. Calmed us. Gave Warfield a shot. Ten seconds after the needle went in, Warfield was up. Could it have just been the prick of the needle that did it? Did the medication work that fast? Was it just a coincidence? Ansley was with me. And then she was walking Warfield to the barn and Charley wouldn't leave his side. Charley crowded Ansley. He pushed against her, shouldering up to Warfield. He almost stepped on Ansley's feet. I was worried he'd clip her heels. She laughed, "Go on, Charley!" Just like an old-time horseman. She waved him off. He dropped back a step and put his shoulder against Warfield's hindquarters, his head over his rump, and he pushed and nudged Warfield, kept him walking. Around and around a circle, Ansley walked them both.

All's well. A fluke. An aberration. A stomachache that has passed.

4

Saturday morning, I am at my desk looking out over the big field, keeping an eye on Warfield. He is standing by himself up in the top left corner. Facing away from me, facing the fence. Not grazing but looks OK. Riderwood and Charley are off to the right and over on the knoll in the middle of the field where the three of them usually graze together. Earlier, at dawn, I had banged the metal bucket with a steel dipper, called them in, given Warfield a close look, fed each a scoop of sweet feed, and let them out. Gary had checked in via cell phone. "All's well," I'd told him.

Nevertheless, though I am attempting to not allow myself to notice it, I do feel uneasy. Why is Warfield standing up in that left corner by himself, facing the fence, and not grazing? He's fine. I worry too much. It's time to get to work, to focus, to apply ink to paper, to stop procrastinating. . . .

Now what? He rears up. He gallops towards the stream, looks like he's going to jump the stream at his usual takeoff spot. He stops. Stops suddenly, joltingly, and puts his head down. He doesn't jump the stream. His head down low, he walks slowly across the stream, heading this way, for the barn. Charley, above and in the middle of the field—head raised, ears pricked forward—is watching.

Warfield is walking towards me. He must be retreating from the flies. That's it. He is getting away from some big-assed horse fly. He's lost the fly and has slowed to a walk. Since he's over this way anyway, he's ambling up towards the barn, to go in the cool shed and take a break from the bugs.

He's down. He's thrown himself down.

5

And now, Sunday morning, the sun rising, I look out the window, over the stream and up the hill at a mound of fresh dirt. For twenty-five years I've seen you stand there on the knoll, grazing, lift your head and survey the farm, your domain, your kingdom. Now, all that energy and beauty and strength and endurance and power, all that experience we've shared, all the horses and ponies we've known together that have come and gone since you've been here: Silver Charm and Eloquence—Mom's chubby champion-bred Welsh ponies. Guber—the retired seventeen-hand show horse, a wonderful boarder. Kaput, Tom, Jefferson. Riverdance, the mistreated quarter horse we rescued—mischievous, youthful, unpredictable. Nappy, the small iron-gray pony with the spirit of a wild mustang—Paddy, his main jock, and I buried him near where you now lie. Blossom, the only horse or pony, besides you, who died on her own from old age. Chim Chim, who we sold and, incredibly, became a champion 4-H pony. And recently, Riderwood and Charley—our relationship with them, past and present, severed, our partnership as horse and rider wiped out. How can it be? I cannot imagine not being able to rattle a bucket of oats, call you in, tack you up, hop onto you strong back—*you never flinched or sagged when I hopped on*—and feel your powerful stride surging beneath me, taking me, like a wave gathering momentum, breaking into that long-striding jog, toes barely touching the ground, floating through space, flying through space and time as you carried me, as I rode you, as we journeyed together through our lives.

6

There'd been a storm, high winds, heavy rains, tornado warnings, and we'd been let out of school early.

Driving home, the truck's windshield wipers shut down. I was barely able to see the road. Pulling in the driveway, the downpour turned to drizzle. By the time I was in the house feeding the dogs, it had stopped altogether.

Perfect.

I changed into my favorite blue jeans, T-shirt and work shirt, made a mug of steaming-strong Irish tea, pulled the rubber Muck Boots Tom had given me one birthday (actually knock-offs, the cheapskate) and headed out with Alfie and Tidbit.

In the barn, I opened a wooden footlocker from Pop's training days half a century ago—light blue with a dark blue cross on the front. Speedy used to bring it, neatly packed with our supplies, to the races. Ah yes, there it was: a cumbersome half bag of grass seed, Kentucky fescue. Tossed it and a bucket in a wheelbarrow.

Alfie barked at the cats, chased them out of the feed room. Tidbit sniffed and scrounged in the stalls under the feed tubs for spilled oats. I pushed the wheelbarrow outside, opened the door to the hay and straw stall.

Threw three bales of straw in the barrow, stabbed a pitchfork into a bale. Found Tidbit beneath a feed tub, picked her up—firm, compact, like a football—carried her to the house.

Grabbed the smooth wooden shafts, lifted up in the age-old way farm hands—we'd studied the invention of the wheelbarrow in medieval history—have done for thousands of years, and bending my back, keeping the handles low so the front bale won't fall off, headed away from the barn and this writing room, Alfie jogging alongside, down the hill toward the stream crossing, reaching up to grip the pitchfork handle to steady the top-front bale as the wheel of the barrow dipped into an indentation, *the old rolling spot where I had sat with him, rubbing and smoothing his neck, rubbing and patting his flanks, looking into his eye, talking to him, Charley standing above us watching, the vet on her way, the vet finally arriving, a young, cute vet, opening the gate, holding a bucket of needles and medications, and—"He's gone," I'd told her. "He's gone," I said, in disbelief, and yet, in relief. She examined him. "Could've been a lipoma on a stalk," she'd said. "A tumor. Has the effect of tying the gut into a knot. Everything backs up and then suddenly it bursts, and the bacteria travels into the bloodstream."* I pushed the barrow back out of the indentation up over the lower lip, and it rolled freely down to the new stream crossing I'd put in that summer, a pipe laid in the stream, water flowing through. The ground leveled out and on the stone dust over the pipe the barrow was steady and easy to push. I took my eyes off the path ahead, glanced to the left, to the splashing/swimming hole the horses had dug in the stream, and further up to a series of deep hoof prints in the bank, from which, ever since I put in the stone dust and gravel crossing over the pipe, Warfield would launch himself over the stream and then canter up to the barn.

Feeling the weight of the bales, I leaned forward. The wheel slowed as it rolled into the thick wet grass. Using short choppy steps, I leaned into the handles, pushing up the hill to the rectangle of clay four horse lengths long and two wide. All along, I managed to hold a mug of hot tea, a not very marketable skill I have developed over years of experience in the pushing of wheelbarrows.

I set the mug of steaming tea on the top bale of straw, pulled the bucket out of the wheelbarrow, stepped onto the slippery, gummy, red clay lying there without its grass cloak, naked, exposed to the air and rain—and for a second I thought of Warfield beneath all this dirt, and though my mind will sometimes seize on an idea, especially a negative one, and nag and needle, rub and scratch it like a mosquito bite, making it worse and worse until blood is drawn, in this case, I immediately, instantaneously, forcefully, clicked off this image, zapped it from the screen.

Bend knees, bend back, pluck a handful of stones out of the gluey clay, straighten legs, straighten back, drop stones in the bucket. The old galvanized steel bucket. Dented and scratched, paint chipped off. *Traps.* Our traps. On the racetrack, that's what we called the gear we shipped with the horses. Pop filled this bucket with water thousands of times. Emmett carried it, hung it from a screw eye in the stall at Saratoga, Belmont Park, Delaware Park, Monmouth Park, Pimlico, here on the farm, thousands of times. Jack the Indian, Salvadore Tumenelli, David Mitchell, (Dave, you left us too early), and Brian Hickey, (Brian, so did you), and even Bob Witham (Bob—you were in such great physical shape. I can see you galloping your horse under the wire at Pimlico just a few years ago) carried this bucket. Mom filled it, cleaned it, hung it in stalls for forty years after Pop died, and Tom filled it many a time, setting it up inside walking rings for horses to "water off." All but Tom are gone now. I have to find the time to explain this thought to him, share the emotion with him.

The bucket rings every time I drop a stone in it. I lean down, pry and push a rock projecting out of the earth. Set the bucket down—the protruding steel rim of its bottom biting into the clay—and grab the rock with both hands. Push and pry and pull it. Get on my knees, finger through the muck, grip the bottom of the rock. Straighten my legs, bringing it up out of the mud. Pressing it against the cupped area between my hip and my groin, I sidestep—boots blobbed with clay, heavy with clay, widened with clay—in choppy steps to the wheelbarrow, drop it in.

Take a few steps, bend over, pick up a stone, a rock, another, another. Drop them into the bucket. Snatch the bales of straw out of the wheelbarrow, set the bag of grass seed on a bale. Wipe hands off on clean, wet grass. Take a few sips of tea. Irish tea. Hot. Strong. With milk and a touch of honey.

Trudge through the clay in fat clay boots. Pick up another bucket of stones. Unload into wheelbarrow. Not rushing. Not concerned about finishing this job and moving on to the next.

Drizzle. It doesn't seem the drizzle is falling from the sky. The molecules in the air are so charged, so heavy with H2O, they are congealing into drops.

Grab burlap bag of seed, hug it to my chest and start spreading—tossing handfuls, arcing the grass-seed so that it disperses through the air and lands in a large looping C-pattern, over and over, pleasing, reminding me of something. Reminding me of doing this motion here before? This same free tossing in a large C-pattern? Right here? On this hill, overlooking the farm, on this spot around which Mom had the show ring fences set up for years, on this very spot where she had the "spread fence"—three four-and-a-half foot standards on one side, three on the other, and across the first standards, eight-foot rails set a foot high, across the second standards, rails set two and a half feet, across the third, rails set three and a half feet, making a fence with a five-foot spread over which Warfield had flown late one afternoon, Thanksgiving, after the rider had had a couple glasses of red wine and the rider's mother had set the third rail up so that it was teetering four feet on top of the standard, set it there, laughingly daring her son, daring Warfield, and Warfield and rider had jogged down to the stream, turned, cantered, galloped into the spread fence and up and over—*That feeling. Nothing like it. To fly—without touching the rail. Warfield, you took my breath away*—I focus on the rhythm and the sweep of throwing the seed and it comes to me: Here, not long ago, I'd stood tall with Ansley, Paddy, Andrew and Eliza, and sisters Susan and Sallie, beside me—the horses watching—and had spread Mom's ashes, reaching into the urn, fingering through the ashes that were not ashes, not soft and fluffy and something that would float in the air and flutter to the ground, but rather something grainy, gravelly that fell like pellets—this was where we had spread Mom's ashes, and way back, Pop's, and most recently, some of Mikey's, with this same swinging, life-giving motion of spreading seed. Over and over, going from one end of the site to the other, I spread the seed.

I dig my fingers between the tight baling twine and the hard-packed straw of a bale, set the bale on the ground, wrestle one wrap of twine off. I lift the bale, let the side with the remaining twine drop onto my knee, cracking the bale open. Whip the twine into a loop, tie it in a knot, toss it in the wheelbarrow. Break the second bale open. The third. Pull old pitchfork—bottom half of shaft light blue, top half dark blue—out of the barrow. Its tines are spread: someone had gripped the outside tines of the fork and pulled them outwards, widening their reach: Emmett

Grayson—loyal to Pop and then to Tom until his dying day.

Shove the fork into a flake of bright yellow straw, lift it up over the raw clay, shake the fork, breaking up the flake and letting the clean strands of straw fall. Sweep the head of the fork back and forth, back and forth, while shaking it. Another flake. Another flake.

I wonder how I will get all the straw spread without having to stomp over the dirt, disturbing the grass seed, but, having been working on the farm for all my life, I know to just keep going, keep moving. It will come to me, don't stop and think, and it did. So simple: spread a wide swath of straw, step forward onto it, spread another wide swath, step onto it.

The bales go quickly. I push the wheelbarrow back to the barn where I dump the stones and rocks onto the stony entrance I'm building in front of my writing room, throw in a bale of straw, and start back, bumping down into the indentation, pushing across where he'd lain in his last moments, where he used to love to roll—all the way over, and back, all the way over, and back. I could see the cute underside of his belly, his coat thinner there, the swirl of the white hairs of his cowlick visible, his legs sweeping high and straight up as with confidence he went all the way up onto his withers and spine, hovered, and then over.

The rain I want to think of as a drizzle is no longer a drizzle except in my mind. It is raining hard. I lean into the shafts of the wheelbarrow and push through the wet grass up the hill I had ridden Warfield across thousands of times headed for the hand gate at the top, his head down low, his stride long and powerful, the age-old rhythm of his walk settling me, bringing me into the moment, there with my mother, and later, my sons, and then my daughter, and a confidence and strength would come to me, a feeling of being pleased with where I was and what I was doing would overcome me, and the worries of bills to pay and work to do and remarks people have made would be gone. They didn't "leave" or "vanish." When I threw my leg over Warfield and settled down on his back, it was as if they had never existed.

Set the wheelbarrow down beside the bare clay. No pitchfork. Damn. Walk back to the barn to get it? I like the feel of shaking out flakes of straw with a pitchfork. Many old timers like the more hands-on approach, and I turn to it, picking up a flake, walking it out, shaking and breaking it up. Picking up a few flakes, walking them out, shaking and breaking them up. A nice rhythm. Rivulets cascade from the brim of my cap. I'm wearing my oldest blue jeans, ripped at one knee. The insides of both calves are worn out. They have rubbed against Warfield's sides for hundreds of miles and now they are splotched with clay-mud, splattered with it, the denim clinging to my legs as I work twenty yards below where I remember and gradually visualize digging the graves for our golden retriever Sawyer, for Nappy, for Willie, a Labrador retriever Mom had rescued, for Minou, Eliza's kitten, for Tiger-Lilly, my cat, and though I didn't know it then, over the upcoming winter, in the dark, on a cold night, after going to the vet's with Eliza to have the pup of her childhood put down—I would gently lower Tidbit's warm body into the grave I'd dug earlier in the week, and cover her with God's soil.

Shaking the straw, I envision Warfield beneath me in the long cut-out. It'd been dug by J.C.—a lithe, hard-working, country-boy jack-of-all trades—with a skid loader. J.C. had lowered the bucket, put the skid loader into forward gear, dug into the earth, filling the bucket, backed it out, dumped the dirt by the side. He'd driven it back down, sometimes continuing straight out the other side so that the end result was a trench twelve feet long, six feet wide, with a curved bottom and vertical sides. J.C. had picked Warfield's body up with the bucket, gently lowered him into his resting place and begun covering Warfield's hindquarters with the soothing dirt. I had stood by Warfield's head, shoveling scoop after scoop onto him so that gradually I'd covered his shoulder, his neck, working my way up until I'd reached his head, and finally covered his eye, and his ear, and I had walked away, back to the barn.

7

There's just one area in the upper rounded corner, a curving swath three feet wide and six feet long, that is still bare. I take excess straw from the covered area, spread it over the upper corner. It's OK, but spread thin.

Clothes clinging, rain falling, I stand on the knoll and look across the stream, at the big red barn, and then going downstream, to my left, at the red corn crib, the brown-shingled smoke house, the big brown-shingled barn-garage, our brown-shingled house, a paddock, the pond. Not a soul in sight. The rain falls. The clothes are doing no good. What is their purpose? The jeans, which are tight as I like them for riding, grab at my thighs, constricting every step. The red-checkered work shirt feels suctioned to my skin. I pull the shirt over my head, feel the freedom of the rain pelting my back, glance behind the house at Ansley's rose garden where the old locust tree once stood. Having no shower as a teenager, I used to take a bar of soap out back during rainstorms, and scrub and enjoy the miracle of the rain pellets striking me until one afternoon a bolt of lightning struck the locust tree beside me, exploding its trunk and blowing off a thick and heavy limb that struck at my feet. I stand for a moment. Another time. . . .

There was still another time when I'd had this feeling. It was at Tom's—at Atlanta Hall; we'd been hunting all morning in the rain and sleet. Tom wanted me to breeze a horse, Welterweight. I jogged to the truck, wrestled my way out of my sodden wool hunting jacket and clammy under layers, feeling the bee-bees of frigid rain beating on my shoulders and back, feeling alive, wonderfully alive, before I pulled on a dry turtle neck and thick Irish sweater, got a leg up on Welterweight, met Tom in his truck at the track, and had one of the most memorable "works"—a two-minute-lick fast gallop—of my life.

I push the barrow back to the barn, looking forward to a hot shower, arrive at the straw stall. There is one last bale. I lean back, preparing to push the wheelbarrow forward into the stall. Instead, I step into the stall, lift the bale, toss it into the wheelbarrow, celebrating the freedom of movement that comes from having a bare torso, feeling alive and fit and doing the right thing and at that moment thunder crackles over the farm, cold rain pours, and a lightning bolt sizzles through the sky. I should go in. This is crazy. Look, even Riderwood and Charley are galloping in. Where's Alfie? He also has better sense.

Thunder booming, I kick off the boots, step out of the jeans, pull boots back on, am out on the site in boxers and boots splitting open one last bale over my bare knee, shaking the straw until it is spread evenly over the entire site.

Returning to the barn, I find a rub rag, duck under the runner into Riderwood's stall. I rub and massage and talk to him.

Out of his stall, under the runner and into Charley's stall. Rub and massage and talk to him. The rub rag snaps and cracks—bringing me back to the days of holding a horse for Emmett outside in the late morning shade at Belmont Park, the morning's work almost over, Emmett laughing and brashly telling me stories—what it was like being a black man in a white army, and why he learned to box—explaining his plans: what he will do with all his money when he wins the Number's game. Or holding a horse for our top groom Tanza, rubbing not quite as hard, his thin black arms rubbing gently, as he quietly relates to me—but almost as if he were talking to himself—how far the horse he's working on, Curator, is going to win next time out if Dave Mitchell will just listen to what my father tells him, how much money he is going to win on him, and how he's going to spend that money. I'm in another world, I'm in the rhythm of it, I'm looking forward to the next horse, and my body automatically, without thinking, swings around to the third stall in the row, ducks low under the runner and webbing—and the stall is howlingly silent, shockingly still: four walls, a window and an achingly wide-open space devoid of energy, life.

No chestnut horse looking me in the eye, furiously pawing. No reason to scold, "Stop it! Stop it, Warfield!" and to rush to him before he digs to China. No reason to grab a clean rub rag and gently wipe away the sleepy-stuff from the corner of his eyes, then massage the small white star between his eyes where his coat is thinning, knowing that at any second he'd suddenly lift his head—*Enough of this*!—lean against the runner-webbing, paw forcefully and I'd push him back so I could unsnap the runner and webbing, let them drop, and at twenty-eight years of age he'd barge out of there, break into a canter, leap over the stream, sprint to the top of the hill, prance and jog and snort as he waited for Charley, then Riderwood, to join him, and then put his head down to graze, the three of them on the knoll together, Charley shouldering up to Warfield, laying his head and neck across his rump, pushing him a few steps forward to where the straw is now spread, the seed is planted.

Hallelujah!

B ob—"Bob House New"—calls during my afternoon study hall. Bob is a retired businessman married to Mikey's former accountant. He's a detail man. He understands the system—bureaucracies. He's been contacting all sorts of social service organizations. He's gotten the apartment. He has actually gotten the apartment. And he has the specific day we'll be moving in: this Sunday, November 24, 2013, a week before Thanksgiving, and one year after he'd begun the search process. Hallelujah!

Speedy calls me at school, leaves a message—makes an order, just as if I'm in delivery service at the grocery store. I listen to it while I'm walking around the fields doing my recess patrol duty. I listen but take no notes. It includes a new item or two, mouthwash and floss, as well as more Icy Hot and patches. After school, I drive to the grocery store, pick up the usual and head up to Rocks State Park.

Open the basement door. The stench of stale tobacco smoke billows out. Wish I could leave the door open as I did over the summer. Watch my step so won't trip over the orange electrical cord that runs out the door, through a mud puddle, to Luke's shop. Walk into the living room. The huge television screen is flashing colors. It's some sort of talent show with buzzers going off and applause and laughter and then another would-be star steps out onto the stage to try to dazzle the judges. Kitty is seated in her chair, oversized bottle of Mountain Dew by her side, sucking on a cigarette, staring at the screen. She looks up at me—her eyes are dagger-like. I don't know if they are scared daggers, or hating daggers, or frightened daggers, but they have a knife-like look. She strains, pushes herself out of the chair.

"Hi Kitty."

She stands, sets those wild eyes on me. "Hi Patrick." She steps over into the narrow kitchenette, turns on the faucet, starts washing the pile of dishes in the sink. I walk through the basement.

Halfway to Speedy's bedroom door, I stop. This is something new: there is a bed up against the far wall. Luke sits up in the bed but doesn't swing his legs around. He's in his pajamas. "Hi Patrick."

"Hey Luke, getting any better?" He'd gotten a job building fences for a man Speedy and I knew well, whose family had worked for the Smithwick Racing Stable for generations, but he'd hurt his back.

"No, I go to the doctor, he gives me pills. I take them for a few days, run out, and then the pain comes back worse than ever."

I knock on Speedy's door.

"All right. All right. Be right there." I hear his feet sliding towards the door. Then I hear his fingers lightly tracing their way across the surface of the door towards the knob. He opens it.

It's dark inside. "Go on, turn on the light," he says. I flip on the wall switch.

Inside. Cramped. Big bed takes up most of the room. Chest of drawers on the right and to the left of the doorway, an aluminum upright with hats, fedoras perched on the top, and a large white hanging bag stuffed with clothes bending the main horizontal pole. Half-filled black garbage bags are piled up against the rack. Straight ahead, a high stool, an office chair, more half-filled garbage bags. In the back, a radio on an African-American religious station. All across the floor, crumpled up paper towels and tissue.

"Come on in. Shut the door and come on in."

I step in, swing the door behind me three-quarters shut, hoping he doesn't notice. I want some more air, even if it is the smoky air from the living room.

The bed is covered with neat stacks of shirts and pants. How did he do it? He could organize anything. I think back on our garage. It had become a storage area, a dumping ground; it was overflowing with tools and axes and broken lawn mowers; fence boards and posts, bicycles, the tractor, the wagon; it was summer and the sleds hadn't been put away; the bags of salt and the snow shovels were blocking the entrance; everything was a mess. Speedy arrived at 9:00 sharp on a Sunday morning. When was this? A year ago? Two years ago? "Everything out! We's goin' to take everything out!" Soon we were building racks, hanging tools, organizing axes and hammers and mauls. We cleared out a space for the tractor. We threw out old junk. I climbed up into the vast loft of the garage, and he lifted the sleds and toboggans and skis up to me. Leaning down through the big trap door—as he lectured me on not falling, on not killing myself and why the hell did I take such risks—I was thinking of turning the loft into an apartment, a place for Speedy to live. Ansley had thought it a good idea. Walking by the garage, day after day, I envisioned him being up there in the loft and imagined what it would be like. We didn't have the money to do it. I never told him about that.

"Here's the coffee," I say, clearing off a spot on the top of the chest of drawers. "I'll put the soda and pork rinds here, and now, where do you want the chicken? This isn't Royal Farms, this is Kentucky Fried."

"*Shhhhh*! You damn fool. Is that door shut? I tole' chu to keep your mouth *shut*. If you jus' keep your big mouth shut and not go blabbing away."

"All right. Calm down. What difference does it make?"

"*Shhhhhh*—they can hear everything you say in here," he says, pointing first to the far wall, then to the ceiling. "I'm not suppose to have any food in here."

Oh Lord, it's been over a year now they've seen me walking in with plastic bags from Klein's Supermarket.

"Where's the mouthwash and Icy Hot?"

"Oh Lord," I sigh. "I forgot it."

"You forget an awful lot. What's wrong with you? You losing your mind? Do you forget to grade your students' papers? Do you forget to feed your horses? Do you forget your wife's birthday?"

"OK, OK, you are not my wife."

I chuckle to myself, thinking of Tom. I'd hooked the old 1958 Rice trailer up to the pickup and driven Riderwood over to Atlanta Hall for his first school over hurdles. I'd wanted Tom there to watch. I knew I'd ride well and Riderwood would jump well if Tom were there; Tom empowers me. Riderwood went well, although instead of brushing through the hurdles, he jumped a foot over each. "That's all right," Tom said. "That's good; you want to make a timber horse out of him, don't you?" Afterwards, when Tom and I were loading him up, Riderwood balked, refusing to go up the ramp. I was in the trailer, pulling on the shank, Tom at the rear end. "Give him a little tap on the ass," I'd said, and added, "please." Tom gave him a swat, Riderwood walked up the ramp, and Tom said, "You don't have to say 'please,' I'm not your wife."

"Now," I say to Speedy, "Do you want me to get this chicken ready to eat. It's in a box. There's cole slaw too. . . ."

"No, set it on the chest of drawers and I'll eat it later on tonight."

There is barely room for the two of us to stand. The open door is letting some air in but along with it the screeching from the television. And now blasting from Speedy's radio is rip-roaring Gospel music.

I ask him if we can turn off his radio.

"Oh, you're too much. You're jus' too damn much."

I think about volunteering to turn it off but I don't want to wade through the tissues and paper towels and junk on the floor, to get to the radio. I let him head over. He clicks it off, turns around, maneuvers his bulk back through the narrow space between the bed and the shelves up against the wall. Sits down on the end-corner of the bed but he's not far enough into the bed, the corner gives way, collapses, and down he crashes into the narrow space between the bed and the shelves. He laughs. It's the first time in ages I've seen him laugh like this. His whole face lights up and he laughs and laughs, his body shaking with each chuckle. I reach down to help pull him up, but it's no use. I can't budge his bulk. He slides and inches his body out of the narrow space, up to the foot of the bed, turns himself around, still chuckling, so that he is on all fours, and pushes himself up.

We start in on the clothes. I pick up a shirt. He asks me to describe it. I do, and then I put it in the correct pile. He's already packed one bag of clothes to be cleaned. Here's an old quilt given to him by Kurt Rosenthal, who rode for Mikey most of his life, who lived on Atlanta Hall Farm, and was the only "galloping boy" in the history of horse racing whose true calling was being an interior designer modeled after Billy Baldwin. Speedy definitely wants to keep the quilt. Here's a blanket—it's worth a lot of money. We sort through all the clothes. He pulls me close to him, whispers: he has three envelopes Bob made up for him, each with a name on it, and cash, along with a receipt, in it. On the day of the move, Sunday, I would be in charge of handing one to Luke—for carrying out his bucket of urine each day and for helping me pack the truck; one to Kitty—for cleaning out his room after he leaves; and one to Melody—for the month's rent. None should be opened. I was to hand over the envelope to the right person, who would then fill out a receipt, hand me the receipt, which he would take and give to Bob.

I've got to get going. I tell him I'll be back on Sunday at 10:00 or 10:30, we'll pack up and leave. "It's getting dark. I've got to feed and hay the horses."

"I tole' chu the Lord would take care of me, didn't I?"

"Yes."

"All your plannin' and worryin' me and askin' questions, I tole' chu he was watchin' over me and now I'm goin' to have my own apartment. *Ohhhh* so nice. A clean kitchen. A living room. A bedroom. You're going to be jealous. You're goin' ta wish you had such a nice place. You just keep on working yourself to death on that farm. You should listen to me. I tole' chu about Riderwood. Didn't I tell you?"

"Yes, you did."

"Didn't I tell you he came right up beside me out there in the livin' room. Came right up to me and tole' me something was wrong. And I called 'chu up and tole' 'chu you'd better go check on him, something was wrong, and it was, wasn't it? Riderwood was *talkin'* to me."

He had called early one morning last summer, frantic, told me to immediately go out in the field and check on Riderwood. I hadn't paid much attention. That afternoon I was mowing, preparing to go on a trip to visit Paddy. I'd just had a massage so my back and shoulders would be good and loosened up, and I could whip up on Paddy on the tennis court. I noticed Riderwood was acting strange, kept shaking his head. I got off the tractor, called him into the barn. The cribbing strap—a tight strap around his neck to keep him from gnawing on the top boards of our fences and sucking air—had slipped around to an uncomfortable position. I struggled to loosen it, to unbuckle it, finally got it off. I brought it into the kitchen, cleaned it with hot water, rubbed it with saddle soap and Lexol, returned to Riderwood, reached up to put it back on. In a horrifying explosion of violence, Riderwood reared up, smashing his head on an overhead beam and whipping his head towards me, throwing me across the stall and into the stone wall, knocking me out for a few seconds and mashing my left shoulder so that it ached horribly, I couldn't use it for two months, and I soon lost two straight sets to Paddy. Luckily, fifty years earlier, when Pop was outfitting the barn for racehorses, Emmett Grayson had nailed a thick sheet of plywood across that stonewall, or I might not have made it.

"You see, I can communicate with the spirits. You people just don't know. You don't believe. You've gots' ta believe in the Lord Thy God. *Who's Jesus?*"

"The son of God."

"Yes, he's the son of God and you come to God through Jesus. And prayer, you've gots 'ta pray. You and Angie started going to church again?"

"Not this year, I've been so busy." Here comes a lecture. And the irony of it—where was I on many a Sunday? When was the last time I had talked to my son Andrew? When was the last time I had seen Tom? When was I going to get around to bringing Dickie a hot, spicy Indian dinner to help knock that cancer out of his body? When was the last time I had taken a walk with Ansley?

"Too busy to come to the House of the Lord? Too busy to pray? You just keep workin' yourself down to the bone. That's all you think of. You're just like your Uncle Mikey. All he thought about was work and those horses. He'd stab anyone in the back, kill his best friend, just to get a good horse. Horses and women. Ha!" —he started to laugh—"How that man would chase the young fillies! Nothing could stop him. How about that time they put the thing in his car, what's it called, you know the thing you turn on and it copies your voice?"

"The time Nancy put the tape recorder under the seat."

"Yes and Mikey took off, flying, with that young girl in his car. . . ." Off he goes, on a bawdy story.

We laugh. "All right, I better get going.

"You better *watch out!*" Speedy suddenly says, throwing out those last two words as if each were a slap to the face.

"What do you mean?"

"I'm telling you! You better listen! Wasn't I right that time about Riderwood?"

"Yes, you were."

"He was hurtin'! His neck was hurtin'! You lucky he didn't kill you."

"You're right."

"Of course I'm right. Well listen to me this time, listen to me carefully: you're goin 'ta have 'ta kill Charley before he kills you."

"What in the world are you talking about?"

"I'm tellin' you." He looked up at me, his eyes huge. He put his hand to his head as if it were a pistol, pulled the trigger. "*POWWWW!* You going to have to *kill* him or he's goin' to kill you!"

"Speedy, Charley is not going to kill me. He's doing fine. Just a couple of weeks ago my students were standing outside his stall patting him."

"He's *jealous.* I've seen it. He's jealous of Riderwood and one day when you're out there with Riderwood he's going to come at you, knock you down, kick you in the head. Angie is going to find you out in the field with your head split wide open and your brains spilling out."

"Speedy—what has gotten into you?"

"You get on Riderwood and go out, and Charley don't want you to leave, right?"

I see. He's backtracking. Something in his mind has clicked back to couple of months ago. For years, I've had at least the three horses, Riderwood, Charley, and Warfield, so that whenever I went out riding on either Riderwood or Saitensohn, Warfield was there with the other. But after Warfield died, I got on Riderwood one day, rode him out to the back gate; Saitensohn followed alongside, rubbing his shoulder against Riderwood, and when we got to the hand gate, Saitensohn stood in front of it, blocked it. I turned away, jogged Riderwood around the big field. Saitensohn went along with us. When we were at the bottom of the hill and attempting to canter up it toward the gate, he crossed over in front of us and kicked up both hind feet at us, stopping us, and would not let us pass. Finally, I got Riderwood through the gate and outside the perimeter of the fence. I rode up and down the fence line, acclimating Saitensohn to being in the paddock by himself. He jogged along with us, every step. Each day I rode a little further away from our farm, but kept close enough so I could hear and see what Saitensohn was doing—which was galloping all around the paddock. Day after day we had worked on it.

"Oh," I say, remembering I'd asked Speedy what to do about this. "Saitensohn's OK about that now. . . ."

"You get an old rope shank, put a chain on the end of it, tie the chain around Charley's nose and onto his halter. You jus' let it hang there, and when he runs all around—*WHAM!*—he'll step on that shank and it'll snatch the hell out of him..."

"All right..."

"You better just kill that horse. He's jealous. Kill him! You hear me!"

"I've got to go. See you Sunday."

"You won't listen. You're just like Mikey—you're too stubborn and look where he is today. That horse will kill you!"

"All right, I'm going out the door. I'll turn the light off."

"Don't forget the mouthwash."

Driving home. Dark. Depressing. Dreary. Why did he have to ruin the visit with that crazy outburst: Kill Charley. Your wife will find you with your head split open.

Home. Dark. The cold goes right through my teaching clothes. I let the dogs out, load and unload logs using the wheelbarow, fire up the woodstove, throw down the hay, feed and hay the horses, rub and pat Charley and Riderwood, return to the house, feeling grumpy. Tell Ansley what Speedy had said.

"Well, Charley is a little crazy," she says. "*Does* he follow Riderwood? *Is* he jealous? Don't I remember you telling me something about that?"

Oh Christ!

"Why does it bother you?" she asks. "Just don't pay any attention to what he says."

PART TWO

---

*He (the boy) watched it for the next two years from that moment
when Boon touched Lion's head, and then knelt beside him,
feeling the bones and muscles, the power. It was as if Lion
were a woman—or perhaps Boon was the woman. That was
more like it—the big, grave, sleepy-seeming dog which, as Sam
Fathers said, cared about no man and no thing; and the violent,
insensitive, hard-faced man with his touch of remote Indian
blood and the mind almost of a child. He watched Boon take over
Lion's feeding. . . .*

— William Faulkner, *The Bear*

One More Horse

Excerpt, Racing Journal
31 August 2006

I was sitting here in my writing room in the old milking parlor getting ready to go to a book signing at a Baltimore bookstore when the phone rang. "Patrick, do you want another horse?" It was James, a young trainer leasing a farm a few miles away.

Good Lord. What an opening. We had just moved to the farm. *Racing My Father* had come out in the spring. Andrew was in Iraq, I was still having book signings and presentations from Pennsylvania to Virginia to Kentucky to California—and dedicating every one of them to Lance Corporal Andrew Smithwick of the United States Marine Corps.

We had Warfield. I'd smuggled Riderwood onto the farm the fall before without telling Ansley and had been running him in some timber races—he finished second in five straight races; Tom told me he was "the best timber horse in the country"—some friends had given us a lively part-Thoroughbred, part-quarter horse whom we'd named Riverdance, and I'd finally, after breaking them, after teaching them to jump, after training the little fat rascals how to go cross country, after schooling and showing them to one possessed Welsh pony aficionado after another, I'd given up on selling the two cutest Welsh ponies of Mom's, Loafer's Lodge Silver Charm and Loafer's Lodge Eloquence, (both impeccably well bred and registered with The Welsh Pony and Cob Society of America, Inc.) and had given them to Amy, a wonderful riding teacher. I was working part time at Gilman, we had three new boarders on the farm that Speedy had gotten for us: Nashua, Citation and Tom Rolfe we called them. They were galloping around in the front paddocks, tearing up the turf, wearing a deep path all along the fence where Nashua nervously paced, and eating the grass right down to the roots. Their owner, a high-powered Intensive Care Unit nurse at Johns Hopkins, was a former Mikey groupie. $18 a day per horse. $378 a week. We cut a deal: made it $300 a week. Like clockwork, she drove her old BMW M-3—the racing engine perfectly purring—in the entrance every Friday late afternoon and handed me three crisp one hundred dollar bills. In her early forties, shapely, the thickest brown hair—she'd often stop by at feed time looking for me to go for a ride with her in the gloaming. After riding, she had a habit of following me up into the dark haymow, helping me throw down the bales, and well, being very available. She could get Riderwood, a gelding, to completely relax by rhythmically rubbing him down after we'd ridden, to the point where he'd groan, drop his phallus out of its sheath and even have it banging against his stomach. "Look at Riderwood," she said, laughing, one cold winter evening. I glanced in the stall. "How about you?" she asked. "You said your back was a little sore. Would you like a massage?"

I had fences to patch, fields to mow, horses to feed, and had just picked up an evening writing class to teach at the University of Baltimore. I was galloping every morning at Pimlico for Dickie. No, we really did not need another horse. We did not need another horse to feed, another horse to eat more of the grass on our ten acres, another horse to shoe, another horse for the vet to treat.

"Well, I might."

"If you want him, you've got to come over and get him right now."

"Why, what'd he do?"

"If you want him, you've got to come over now. I'll load him onto the trailer and bring him over."

"How do his legs look?"

"Good, you'll see; he's bowed once, and he might've been nerved."

"Nerved?" This was a form of surgery I hadn't heard mentioned in years. It consisted of taking the nerves out of a specific area of the foot if the horse is experiencing pain there, and it could, since the horse wouldn't have any feeling in the nerved area, make riding the horse dangerous.

"Oh, never mind about that."

"How long have you had him?"

"A day. Listen, this horse is really well bred. He won at Cheltenham over hurdles. An American saw the race and bought him for a quarter of a million. I'll give you his papers."

"I can't come right now. I've got to go to a book signing. Could I stop by afterwards?"

"All right. What time can you be here?"

"Four o'clock. I'll see you at four."

"OK. He's got to be off the farm by the end of the day."

I drove in the entrance, up by the bank barn where a long gooseneck trailer was hooked up to a pickup, around the barn, and there was James waving me towards him. It had gotten hot and he was standing there by the gate, on the other side of which was a dark bay horse. I hopped out of the truck, walked closer. It was a *gaunt* dark bay horse. The flies were buzzing around his head. He was stamping his feet. He was a dark bay horse of a good height, sixteen two or so, and his hip bones were sticking out, you could count his ribs, and he was stamping his feet to get the flies off. On his right front leg, he had one hell of a "bow"— the most important tendon in the leg, extending from the back of his knee to above his ankle, was bowed outward where it should be straight. Also, just above his hoof on this foot, there was a small scar, marked by a two-inch line of white hair, perhaps the incision from when he was nerved.

He had a classy, Arabian-shaped head with a small star, and as I neared he held his head up high and looked me straight in the eye and I looked him in the eye and I knew I'd take him. He had a long neck, high withers. You could see the outline of his spine leading to a rump that was surprisingly well-rounded, considering the state of the rest of his body. He didn't eye me as if he were a skinny, sun-burned, bowed, past-his-prime horse being kicked off a nice farm for doing something ornery. He looked me in the eye as an aristocrat, as a horse of presence, as a winner.

"I'll take him."

We loaded him up. I drove home fast, called Riderwood, Warfield and Riverdance in from the big back field—put them in stalls. I got a bucket of feed and lured the Wild Bunch—Nashua, Citation and Tom Rolfe—out of the front paddock, near where we'd be unloading, and into a side paddock. James pulled his long, low rig up at the end of our entrance, led the horse down a short ramp. I walked out to meet him with a leather shank. We unsnapped his rope shank, snapped my shank to the halter. "Good luck," he said. "You can have the halter."

"What's his name?"

"Oh, I've got to give you his papers." He stepped toward the cab of the truck.

The horse was spinning around me. I held the shank loose. He scrambled and pivoted in a circle as if he were practicing a new dressage move. I laughed at the absurdity of the whole situation. I was crazy to do this. He started whinnying, his head held high, his eyes pricked forward, his eyes flashing one direction then another. I kept the shank loose, like letting a fish run with your line. I could hear my three horses whinnying in the barn. I heard the three boarders galloping around in the paddock—ripping up more grass. Then, Warfield was galloping through the front field headed for us. Must've broken through the runner of his stall. I should've closed his stall door. He was wildly whinnying and his tail was up and he was headed our way at a full gallop. I was trying to do all this quietly. Ansley's car was in the garage. She was most likely up in the bedroom, decompressing after work, reading her latest detective novel. Could, hopefully, have fallen asleep. Warfield skidded to a stop, banging up against the boards of the fence. James stepped towards me, handed me an envelope thick with papers. "Good luck," he said. "I've got to go."

"What's his name?" I asked again.

"He's German. It's a German name. Saitensohn," he said, pronouncing it "Satan-son," and then looking away.

It was rush hour. Cars were whipping past us on Manor Road. He walked around the front of the truck to get in. Saitensohn was pulling to the right towards Warfield. Warfield was acting like a three-year-old colt, stamping his feet and snorting. Saitensohn's neck went up like a stallion's. He arched his back. He reared up three feet off the ground, pawed at Warfield. Warfield did the same. They came down and thrust their noses together. I tightened my grip on the shank, Saitensohn on my right. They snorted and pushed and pawed and then each let out a loud, high-pitched

squeal. Saitensohn went straight *up, up, up*, pawing and squealing, and I thought, this is enough. I let him come back down.
He was tight against the fence. Warfield took off, tail high, galloping away from us. Saitensohn's left shoulder was up against
the fence, the top board bending into the field, and he was facing
away from me. I pulled on the shank. He didn't budge. The
shank was fully extended to my right and I was looking at his
rump. I pulled again.

He did not back up a step or two and then turn towards me,
as any other horse would have done. He calmly, smoothly, raised
himself up on his two hind legs, hovered for a second, swung
himself towards the fence, his front feet sweeping over the top
board, continued around, and then landed, gracefully, facing me.
I'd never seen a horse do this; I would learn that this was his cho-
sen method of turning around when he was up against a fence or
even a wall.

I walked Saitensohn, dancing and jigging, up the driveway—
his feet *crunch/crunch/crunching* too loudly on the crusher run,
pulled him over onto the lawn as we went under the bedroom
window, and then led him to the barn. Nashua was bucking
and careening around circles in the bottom paddock, trying to
stir Tom Rolfe and Citation up, but by this time they had their
heads down and were sweeping across the paddock like mowing machines, their teeth set on *low* and *fast*. Riverdance and
Riderwood were banging around in their stalls. Warfield galloped out of the top field, around the barn and down and into the
big back field. Saitensohn was jerking me off my feet. The hell
with it. On reaching the barn, I opened the gate and turned him
loose with Warfield. They bucked and galloped, and then suddenly, side-by-side, they put their heads down and started grazing. Friends for life.

That night, I told a white lie. "What was all that commotion
at the end of the driveway?" Ansley asked.

"What commotion?" I asked, staring straight at my beer. I
stood up. "Come on pups—want to go out."

"I heard whinnying and a horse galloping around," Ansley
continued.

"That was Warfield acting like a wild stallion," I said, opening the door. "Come on pups, let's go."

Ansley was standing by the stove, stirring a big pan of shrimp creole, a favorite of mine. "What had him so upset?"

Sawyer, our golden retriever, and Tidbit tore out the door, scrambled across the porch and flew down the steps. Standing by the open door, trying to follow Sawyer and Tidbit, I said, "I took Riderwood out to graze on the lawn. Warfield's getting so herd-bound that he busted out of his stall and galloped over to us."

"Do you think that's the right way to do it? What do other people do about their herd-bound horses? Maybe you should ask Tom."

I knew what to do. I didn't need to ask Tom. But I wasn't going to retort. Good Lord, I'd just made this up. And besides, in actuality, Warfield was my only horse who was *not* herd bound. He was independent. He was the alpha male. "Sawyer! Tidbit!" I called, stepped outside, shut the door behind me, took the dogs for a short walk, then headed for the tack room.

I looked over Saitensohn's papers. They were long. Son of Monsun—the leading sire of Germany—he was born in Germany, ran multiple times in Germany, then in the Slovak Republic, then in France. He ended up in England, where he brought his total number of European wins to seven, his last being at Cheltenham, in front the whole way. The American bought him, shipped him to the States, where he placed second or third in seven races, including graded stakes such as the Temple Gwathmey. In '04, he bowed badly, running on the hard ground at Saratoga in the A.P. Smithwick Memorial, and had to be vanned off the course. He was turned out for the 2005 season, then came back in '06, finishing in the money half a dozen times, but he never got his fire back after breaking down in the A.P. Smithwick. By the time of his final two races, he'd gone completely sour, finishing last in one, pulling up in the other. He'd been retired, turned out in a thirty-acre field, when James talked Saitensohn's trainer into letting him take him, and try him out as a point-to-point horse and hunter. My Black Beauty.

Excerpt, Racing Journal
First Ride

The next day, I galloped for Dickie, showered at Gilman's faculty locker room, and worked in the development office writing a magazine story. Drove home. Pulled on boots and blue jeans. Fed the Wild Bunch out in the field. Called my horses in and fed them. While Saitensohn was eating, I stood beside him, patted him and talked to him. I got a set of tack, ducked under the runner, reached for his halter. He wheeled away from me. Facing me was his rump and two powerful hind legs. I knew I shouldn't be doing this alone, but I also knew it was one of those times when I was going to go ahead and do it. It was like going canoeing with the boys in a hurricane; it was like cutting the skis loose at the top of a double black diamond; it was like having Pop give me a leg up onto yet another rogue, and then stepping away. I gently placed my hand on his rump, stepped to the near side, his left. *Wo-a boy. Wo-a-a-a-a boy.* Patted him. Ran my hand upwards, along his back. Just when I was by his neck, he spun again.

I got a bucket of feed. Stood in front of his stall jingling the feed scoop against the side of the bucket until he gingerly stepped towards the bucket and I slid one hand away from the bucket to his halter.

Tacked him up, led him around the field with a loose rein. Walked him along the fence outside my writing room. Stood him there, stepped up onto the first board, then the second. The tough moment was the split second when I would not be on the fence and I would not be on him; I'd be suspended between the two and he could do as he pleased. I climbed up on the fence, placed my hands on the pommel of the saddle, and, like a rodeo rider, lowered—eased—myself onto his back. Once in the saddle, feet in the stirrups, I felt good. I was ready. There was no explosion.

We ambled down to the stream crossing. I was riding long, heels down, and with a "deep seat"—butt towards the back of the saddle, thinking how nicely everything was going. He stopped dead. Put his nose down low, stared at the crossing, and froze. I pulled on the right rein. Pulled on the left. Squeezed and urged him on. Couldn't get him to budge. Walked him up and down in front of the stream. Pushed. Shoved. Squeezed.

Rode back to the barn, put him in his stall. Let Warfield out. Passing the tack room, I grabbed Pop's old race-riding stick off the top of the bridle rack. I pulled on a pair of spurs. Led Saitensohn out to the fence, got back on. At first, Warfield hung by our side, sniffing us, placing his shoulder against Saitensohn's rump. I kept scooting him away. Rode down near the stream. Finally,

Warfield crossed the stream to go up the hill to the good grass and with that I reached back and cracked Saitensohn with Pop's old stick while simultaneously squeezing with the spurs. He took off, jumping twenty feet over the stream.

I jogged him slowly in a circle, going to the left. What a mover. He glided. He floated. I didn't have to make myself post, *up/down, up/down, up/down,* feeling it in my back, as I did on Riderwood. His flowing movement pushed me naturally up out of the saddle. He fought against the bit. I kept my hands down. He pulled harder against the bit. I pulled him up to a walk.

Turned around, started jogging to the right. Not so good. He was popping his head straight back at me. He hated it when I pulled the right rein. Every time I had to pull on the reins—*bam*—his head would come back at me, just missing my face. I heard a loud snap. He'd broken the martingale—the taut strip of leather that was attached to the girth between his legs and ran up to his chin where it was snapped onto the noseband. He started jumping up and down, slapping his head back, going sideways, the broken leather strap whipping against his neck, all his weight on his hindquarters. There was no way I could lean forward without getting my face whacked so I reached back and cracked him with the stick. He jumped in place, jumped in place, finally put his head down and took off across the field headed straight for the wire fence and thick hedgerow of multiflora rose and it looked like I was a gonner. Four lengths from the fence, I got strong, he got some sense, and we pulled up.

I started riding him cross-country. After he ducked and wheeled to the left, dropping me on the hard ground—twice, I must admit—I learned that he always spooked or wheeled to the left. Soon, I was prepared, heels down and ready for him to spook or duck to the left. He never did it again. I never gave him the chance. As soon as I was on his back, I focused, anticipated every move, as I had learned to do on Pop's rogues as a teenager.

When I tried to canter him or gallop him slowly in a circle, his head whipped back too close to my face. He broke another martingale. I kept picturing the French bridle with the ropes and pulleys hanging unused in Tom's tack room. Finally, I drove over, asked Tom if I could borrow it.

This bridle had a thin rope that went from the bit, up to a set of pulleys at the upper jaw, and then back down to connect to the yoke at his chest. The pulleys at the jaw were attached to a strip of leather behind his ears and over his "poll," the horn-like bone right between his ears. When he threw his head, the force would cause the rope to tighten the strip of leather across the poll.

Saitensohn fought it. Sometimes when it tightened on him he'd stop dead, refusing to move. Other times he'd shake his head, trying to get it off. One day Janon Fisher, Pop's great friend, called to ask how "the new horse" was going. I told him I was using a French bridle with ropes and pulleys and was having a difficult time. There was a pause on the line. Then Janon said, "What about your hands, Patrick? Have you forgotten about your hands." I returned the bridle to Tom the next day.

Speedy Meets Saitensohn

Excerpt, Racing Journal
Early October

I was going out fox hunting—really, it is fox chasing, we virtually never "catch" a fox—on Riderwood, getting him in shape for the races in the spring. One day, the "meet" was only a mile from our farm. I'd been out on Riderwood, took him home, tacked up Saitensohn, hacked him to the meet, and waited for the huntsman and whippers-in to return with the pack of hounds to their van and the hound truck.

I was sitting on Saitensohn, relaxed, riding long like a cowboy. Waiting around the trailers and vans. Many foxhunters had already come in. Some had put their horses in the trailers and were seated in fold up chairs, laughing and having a drink. It had been the children's hunt, and there were lots of girls holding cute plump Shetland and Welsh ponies with pink shanks. Grandparents, relatives and friends had come. This was a perfect introduction. I walked Saitensohn around, letting him sniff people and ponies.

Speedy was there. Leaning on the cane in his left hand, he patted Saitensohn, talked to him, ran his hand down his neck, down his shoulder, felt the thickness of the old bow. It was the first time I'd seen Speedy with a cane. This was Speedy, the fastest man on the shedrow, and now he had to use a cane. Mikey had died a few years earlier, and Speedy, in his early-sixties, had moved off the farm for the first time in thirty years. Ansley found him a position grooming horses at Oldfields. It seemed ideal. The head of the riding program got along well with Speedy, and the facilities were top notch—a new state-of-the-art indoor riding arena, beautiful barns, lots of turn-out paddocks like at Mikey's, a nice schooling course—and Oldfields is one of the few schools on the East Coast with hundreds of contiguous acres for cross country riding and with girls who are interested in every discipline of riding. The school is located within a short van trip of two of the best hunt clubs in the country, the Green Spring Hounds and the Elkridge Harford. Speedy was in his element. But one afternoon, out in a field bringing a horse in for the night, the horse spooked and stepped on his foot. After working all his life with the wildest Thoroughbreds on the track, a big old "warm blood" had put him out of commission. He'd had an operation, the surgeon had screwed pins into the delicate foot bones, and he was now on disability.

"What's his name?" Speedy asked.

"Saitensohn," I said, pronouncing it "SITE –en—zon," as the Germans I'd asked told me to say it.

"SATAN-son," he said. This was something I was trying to get away from. Over and over, if I were riding cross-country and Saitensohn was acting up, didn't exactly look like a lady's hunter, might be jigging and snapping his head back and flinging a gob of sweat/foam towards the polite questioner on a calm, platter-footed hunter we'd come across, I'd give his name and the inquirer would then slowly enunciate, "SATAN-son," eying me as if I were crazy to get on a horse with *Satan* in his name. "Son of Satan," he'd state, frowning at me. Even Tom told me, "One day you reach an age when you stop getting on that kind of horse."

"This is nothin'," Speedy said, gripping his cane half way down its staff in his right hand, leaning down low, and gently running his left hand over the old bow. "I can tighten this right up." Saitensohn put his head down and pushed against Speedy. Speedy stepped in front of him. Saitensohn rubbed his head against Speedy's side, pushing him with some force. This would have knocked any other man back a few steps, and the man would have been embarrassed, might have wanted to step forward and snatch the rein or pop the horse in the mouth. It didn't budge Speedy's broad-shouldered, six foot two, 250-pound frame. He laughed.

"What's his name again?" Speedy asked.

"SITE-en-zon."

"SHITE—zen—on."

"No, it's SITE-en-zon."

Speedy rubbed the small star between Saitensohn's eyes. Saitensohn rubbed his forehead against Speedy's side. Speedy laughed. "Charley!" Speedy exclaimed, rubbing the horse between his eyes, stressing the *CH* sound. "We'll call him *CH*-arley." He ran his hand down Saitensohn's neck. "Charley, you look raggedy-ass wi' this old thick coat. *Patrick!*"

"Yes."

"I'll be by ten o'clock Sunday morning ta'clip him."

"I don't know. That might be easier said than done."

"Don't you worry. It has been said, and it will be done. Right Charley?" Saitensohn put his head down low at Speedy's stomach, rubbed against him. Speedy laughed.

A graduate of the Kiniel School of Life and Horsemanship from the Mikey days—hair in a pony tail swinging between her shoulder blades, tight black jeans and a pink wool turtle neck—sauntered over, started talking to him. Then, my BMW-driving nurse was there. And she was in neither her usual turtleneck and jeans nor her nursing scrubs. She was wearing tight slacks and a light blue cashmere sweater. That's it. The cashmere sweater was a low cut V-neck—a rather stunning décolletage for out here in the hunting field, where most of us were wearing boots, britches and black, 18th Century English-styled, wool riding coats complete with white stocks wrapped high around our necks, a gold pin at the Adam's apple. She rushed over to Speedy, hugged him, as he stood up straight, leaned away, gently pushed against her, and laughed. Saitensohn and I meandered off.

I was deep in this imbroglio of kids and ponies and grandparents and bourbon/port and beer-sipping foxhunters when I heard them coming. It was a timeless moment out of a Sir Alfred James Munnings' print. There was the huntsman in his Pink coat (Pink being the name of the original tailor of this thigh-length, waist-tightened, red coat with gold buttons), the pack of two dozen hounds behind him flanked by Pink-coated whipper-ins, walking fast towards us. That lasted one fifth of a second. Suddenly, we were a clip out of a VCR tape, a student had accidentally hit the *fast backward* switch, and everything was going the wrong direction. Or, we were a moment out of John H. Morris's poem "Running It Backward"—the projector of an old home movie suddenly spins the film, and a life, backward—which I had my students act out. He started backing up faster than I knew a horse could go, knocking over buckets, careening too close to ponies, causing grandmothers to drop their drinks, mothers in their new light-wool riding jackets and stretch britches that showed off their fit haunches spilling their bloody Mary's, horses to jump and stomp around in their trailers, little girls to shriek, until we were out of the parking area, over by the woods, and I pulled on a rein, spun him one hundred and eighty degrees so we were at least going forwards, and steered him onto a path in the woods away from the meet and towards home.

Excerpt, Racing Journal
October 8

Speedy pulled in the driveway fifteen minutes early. Parked Mikey's old Subaru in front of the white sliding door to the aisle way. Got his cane out, then his clippers and a can of oil. Using the cane, and grimacing once or twice as he limped into the barn, he set the clippers and can of oil on a footlocker. Returned to the car, picked up a mane comb and another pair of small, quieter clippers, for the ears and head, set them on the footlocker.

I was calling Saitensohn. Oh Lord—he had found the one soft spot down by the stream and had rolled and rolled in it. This would not go over well.

Leaning on the gate, watching Saitensohn galloping around the field, Speedy said, "You go'in ta get him in, or we go'in ta stand here and watch him all day."

"Come on, boys! Come on, boys!" I called out, banging the metal bucket with the aluminum scooper, whisking the scooper around the feed in the bucket.

Warfield stopped, pricked his ears forward, then took off for the stream crossing, jumped it and jogged toward the barn. Riderwood watched, then jogged over the stream crossing. Saitensohn stood, neck arched, tail high, in the middle of the big field, reared, flew across the field, stopped, looked around, and was shocked to see no one in the field. He put his head down, pinned his ears back, bucked and galloped to the stream crossing, jumped three feet over it, landed and jogged to the barn.

Saitensohn fussed around. Using the bucket of feed, I lured him into a stall. We leaned on the wall outside the stall watching him nervously eat—he'd take a few bites, then throw his head up, look all around. He was stamping a front foot and kicking out with his right rear.

Speedy ducked under the runner, stepping into the stall before I could tell him I'd had some problems doing just that. *"Charrrrrley!"* Speedy called out, as the horse turned his rump directly at Speedy "Ah *Char—ley,"* he said, putting his hand high on the rump, giving it a pat. Walking up alongside the horse, he ran his hand up his spine to his withers, patted him on the neck and talked non-stop, "How ya doing Charley? You go'in ta cart this old man around some racecourses? You go'in ta win me some money, Charley? Yes you is. Ah, Charley," he said, reaching his head, "You just like me. You a little jumpy. And you're fast." The tension flowed out of the horse, his body relaxed, his head dropped. Speedy patted him between his eyes, leaned forward, ran his hand gently down one leg, gently down the other, then back to the first—"I can take care of this old bow. There's no heat in it and I can tighten it up. Next spring Charley, next spring. . . ."

Stepping out of the stall, eying me, Speedy's tone changed: "You know's I can't clip a horse that's dirtier than a pig in a pigsty! You know's it. Why didn't you keep him in last night. I tole's you I was coming this morning. *Where's that old vacuum cleaner your father used to have?"*

"No way you're going to be able to use that on him."

"I ain't clipping him until he's clean and he won't be clean until I vacuum him."

"I haven't used it in years."

"Just show me where it is."

We dug it out of a cob-webbed corner of the feed room. A heavy, rusted, steel box—three feet long, one foot wide, and one foot in height—held two and a half feet off the ground by four steel legs. It had a thick hose protruding from one end with some cracks in it. Over forty years ago, Emmett Grayson had painted the top half of the box dark blue, the bottom half light-blue.

"Take this," Speedy said, handing me his cane. I leaned it against the tack room door. He knocked the dust and cobwebs off the old machine with a brush. "Where's your duct tape?" I jogged to the house, found Ansley's duct tape. He taped the holes in the hose. We dragged the heavy apparatus out into the aisle-way, plugged it in, turned it on. It blasted away, loudly, just as it had forty years ago. Speedy flicked the switch forward, it blew old dust and hair out. He flicked it backward, it sucked air in. "I need's a coat hanger." I stood there. He looked up, into my eyes, as if I were so pathetic, couldn't I do just something to help out. "Can you get me a wire coat hanger?" I jogged into the house, up the stairs, grabbed one out of Ansley's closet.

When I returned, he had disconnected the hose from the machine. He took the coat hanger, unwound the wire below the hook, flattened the curlicues, bent the hook so that it would fit in the hose, stuck the non-hook end through the nozzle and pulled it through the hose, the hooked end catching clumps of decades-old hair and dirt. Charley was doing his imitation of a merry-go-round with the speed stuck on fast.

"Who's he friends with, Riderwood or Waldo?"

"Warfield. His name is Warfield, not Waldo."

"OK—Warfield."

"Well, he bosses Riderwood around. I'd say he's more friends with Warfield."

"Get Waldo in and put him in the stall next to Charley."

I caught Warfield, put him in the stall. Riderwood stood outside the stall for a moment, then charged out of the barn. "Get Riderwood, put him in the other stall."

Speedy was turning the vacuum cleaner on and off, acclimating the horses to it. I stepped into Charley's stall to catch him. He wheeled away from me and I ended up facing his rump.

"Lord, please save me," Speedy sighed, watching us. "Didn't your daddy teach you anything?" He unbuckled the runner, let it flop against the post, leaving the stall door wide open. He stepped into the stall. Charley was eying Speedy. *"Charley,"* Speedy asserted, lowering his voice to a deep, gravelly tone. *"Stand up here.* You know better than that." Speedy walked up alongside him, gave him a pat on the neck, snapped the shank onto his halter, led him out into the aisle, handed me the shank.

Without further ado, he flicked on the switch to the vacuum cleaner, flicked it off, flicked it back on. He put the suction cup on his hand, took it off, put it on his overalls, yanked it off, put it on his shirt, pulled it off, held it up and showed it to Charley, then gently touched him with it. Charley threw his head up and jumped away. "You goin' ta get me killed!" Speedy said to me. "What's wrong w'chu. Andrew knew how to hold a horse. Why don't chu. Give me that shank." He grabbed the shank. "Now stand up here, Charley," he said, looking Charley in the eye. He gave the shank one good snatch. I went to take it back from him.

"No, you go on and ride Riderwood. I'll tend to Charley."

Big Diamond Jim

Thinking of Andrew, I headed for the Hunter Trials course—the hundred-acre field on Sidney Watter's Dunmore Farm where for decades the Elkridge Harford Hunt had its fall horse show. I was riding from one farm, originally owned by my mother, and by my father—inducted into the Hall of Fame in 1973—directly to another farm, now owned by a Hall of Fame member, inducted in 2005. How many riders can do this?

On the course, I stayed in my best form—spurring Riderwood through a herd of cattle and around four of Dickie's yearlings; Sidney might be watching from the kitchen window. It seemed just a few years ago Andrew and I would stop by on our Sunday ride, Andrew on his 30-year-old pony Blossom, and I on Warfield. Happy, Sidney's overly-protective German Shepherd would ferociously pound and leap at the kitchen door. We'd see Sidney's form, all six feet of him—tall, neatly dressed, hair perfectly parted—through the windows of the door as he batted down Happy. He'd open the door and out Happy would race, Sidney, looking like Cary Grant, right behind. He'd walk up to a jigging, spooking Warfield with full confidence, and soothingly chant in his mellifluous voice, "Wo-a now, wo-a boy, that's a boy," while running his hand down Warfield's neck.

"This is a nice-looking horse. Beautiful coat. How much you want for him?" he'd ask, gently resetting the forelock under the brow band and smoothing any misbehaving swatches of mane over to the correct side.

"Fifty thousand," I'd say.

"Put him in the barn," he'd say. "I'll take him. Check's in the mail."

214 PART TWO

One weekend, I'd taken Andrew, then twelve, to see the movie *Memphis Belle*—about a B-17 Bomber made famous in WW II.

"Sidney," I said, "you flew in a bomber like that during the war, didn't you?"

"Oh yeah, I might have."

Andrew was sitting bolt upright on Blossom, a holster with "six shooter" on each hip.

I knew Sidney had flown over 35 missions in the Pacific Theatre.

"How many missions?"

"Oh, I don't know." He cleared the air with an embarrassed laugh. "Enough, I suppose."

"Where were you in the plane?"

"It's not important," he said.

Andrew's posture sagged, going from that of Braulio Baeza on Buckpasser in a post parade to that of Bill Hartack after losing a race.

"Wait a minute," Sidney said. He strode back into the house where he'd been raised. We could see lights flicking on upstairs. We heard him trotting down the steps. And then he was out holding up a large plastic model of a B-24 Bomber. He pointed toward a little glassed-in bubble in the tail of the plane. "I was right there."

Andrew was mesmerized. We asked Sidney about the bombing missions. All he said was, "You do what you have to do." He walked up to Blossom, gave her a pat, put his hand on Andrew's knee, looked Andrew in the eye and said, "Now those are some good-looking chaps. And where'd you get those cowboy boots? I had a pair like those when I was your age."

Two summers ago, I stepped into Sidney's kitchen. In his late 80's and somewhat frail, operating at a slower pace now that he had a touch of Alzheimer's. He stood up, "Haven't been doing much work today. I was out in the barn for a while this morning and now I'm finished up until feed time. Come on in, have a seat." A couple of visitors, also wanting to congratulate Sidney on his induction, arrived. There was some confusion. He caught my eye, "Let's check on Jim."

Big Diamond Jim is a large-boned, eighteen-hand, gray Thoroughbred with a mark shaped like a diamond on his rump.

Sidney named him after an apocryphal fish. When Sidney was a boy, his father took him in a horse-drawn buggy to watch Loch Raven Reservoir fill. As the water rose, Watters Senior told Watters Junior there was a fish swimming in those waters called Big Diamond Jim; the fish had a diamond in his lip, and whoever caught the fish could keep the diamond. Now Watters Junior had the "fish" and the "diamond."

Sidney and I strolled to the barn. Jim, in a paddock, picked his head up from the grass, spotted Sidney, jogged up the hill, stepped into the coolness of his stall. Huge. Big-boned. Sidney stood beside him and I was worried Jim might knock him down. Sidney gave him a pat on the neck and Jim rubbed his head against Sidney's chest. "Looks well, don't you think?" Sidney asked. "Yes," I said, eying his big belly, having learned from a laughing Dickie that Sidney was feeding Jim more often than needed. ("What can you do?" Dickie had asked, spreading his arms wide, and looking straight at me with wide-opened eyes, "It keeps him busy, gives him a purpose.") Sidney spotted some droppings in the straw. He walked down the aisleway, got a pitchfork, returned.

Staring at Jim's massive shoulders and his big front feet with the oversize steel shoes, I said, "Hold on," taking the pitchfork. Sidney let me pick up the droppings, carry them out. When I returned, there he was standing in the stall, holding a dipper of oats, beside Jim. He gave Jim a couple of pats, poured the oats into the feed tub, and with one hand tracing a line along the length of Jim's spine, high-stepped back through the deep straw, ducked under the webbing and was out of the stall.

* * *

I pulled Riderwood up, headed for Sidney's house. Dickie's pick-up was parked by the kitchen door. Riding across the checkered-pattern cut of the lawn, I pictured Sidney mowing as a boy—walking behind a hand mower that was too heavy for him, so he'd hooked it up to his pony. Or, I chuckled, was this story a Sidney-stretcher, just like one of Dickie's? Had I been gullible?

I gave myself a check over, remembering the snowy winter afternoon Sidney had stood just outside the door at dusk. I'd been on the driveway, twenty yards away. The wind was picking up, the snow was coming down, Warfield was spooking, and Sidney said something I couldn't decipher about my stirrup leather. I'd asked him to repeat it. He'd walked out in his shirt sleeves, and in one graceful motion, pulled my stirrup out from under my foot while looking me in the eye and saying, "Your stirrup leather's twisted the wrong way," and then setting my foot back in correctly.

The stirrup leather wouldn't be twisted on this day. I was ready for inspection. The door opened. Happy burst out, not as ferocious as in her youth, followed by Dickie. "Hey Pat!" he said, slapping on his old-fashioned floppy wool cap. "Hold on." He stepped back in. Then, adjusting the visor of an old-fashioned floppy wool cap, out came Sidney.

On The Light Rail

Mid-November

Dear Andrew,

Just got your letter. I'm excited your buddies are enjoying reading *Racing My Father*. Also, I'm very pleased that the book has helped you understand me better. Thank you so much for your compliments.

I've been thinking of you a great deal. Just the other day, hacking over to see Sidney, I was reminded of the long rides we used to take. Remember the time Sidney brought the model of the B-24 out for you to see?

All's well here: teaching, riding and training the horses. New horse behaves better each day. Speedy's started working for me. He asks about you often. I've started on a new book. In a week or so I'll send you a chapter. I hope you get a kick out of it.

You can relate to your buddies that you've recently learned that a few mornings ago, while you were fighting in Iraq, your dad was on the Light Rail going into Baltimore, on the way to a teachers' conference when this big man in old Marine camouflage fatigues stepped aboard. I was wary the moment I spotted him; you've told me how the Corps does not want its soldiers out in the public wearing their fatigues or uniforms. He started talking to the young female teachers from Oldfields a few seats back, and your dad knew what he was up to as he talked and stalked, preparing to ask for money, to beg, this young, healthy-looking man going on and on about how wonderful the Ravens and Orioles were, and then how terrible the war was, and I was trying not

218

to listen. Then he said he'd been a Marine and had gone AWOL. Had no money and could they spare . . . and he started pressuring them, intimidating them. At this point, I was thinking of you in Iraq and here this big begging AWOL bastard was disgracing everything being a Marine stood for. I stayed calm. I texted Paddy—couldn't text you in the desert—told him I was shaking, trembling. I knew your Mom would tell me to disregard him but a fury was building up inside me about to burst. (Complicating the issue was that he was black, one of the young teachers was black, and if I did something it could be misinterpreted by her, and also by anyone else, that I was being politically incorrect and even racist. I wasn't. He was a man, that's all. Didn't matter to me if he were white, black or brown, just that he was "yellow.") I pictured you up on your heavily armored truck, fingers on the trigger, driving through the desert in Iraq. I pictured you going room to room, sweeping a house, a village in Iraq. And here was this man: AWOL. Disgracing the Marines. I didn't think to do it—it was as if I were in another body—I saw myself get up, walk down the aisle to this man the size of a Ravens tackle. Feeling the blood and adrenalin surging through my body, I heard myself say, "My son is a Marine fighting in Iraq. You are a disgrace to the Corps. You'd better leave these women alone and get off at the next stop. If my son were here," (I pictured you standing beside me in your uniform, neat, trim, perfectly fitted. I didn't *imagine* you there. I *saw* you there. I *felt* your presence. I felt your strength flowing into me) he'd throw you off at this second. He's not here. I am."

He got off. I received a resounding applause from everyone in the car.

Chapters from the new book on the way soon. Meanwhile, take care of yourself. Stay safe. I'm very very proud of you.

Love,
Dad

Training Charley

December 11

I'm excited. After several evening consultations with Tom, I have sold half of Riderwood to John Egan, a Kentucky-bred classmate of mine at Johns Hopkins who has now, with the encouragement of his youthful and highly energetic wife Lynn—a passionate, lifelong show-ring rider—taken up an interest in fox-hunting and steeplechase racing. I offered half of Saitensohn to John, who passed the opportunity on to his wonderful mother-in-law, Winky, Mrs. John H. O'Keefe, who used to own hurdle horses years ago, and in fact owned Ballet Master, a horse I galloped every morning for two years, and schooled many a time, when I worked for Jill and Bobby Davis a few years back (1975), and a horse I came to love. Winky and John will be paying half the training bills. Riderwood will continue to run in my name and in our old family colors, light blue with a dark blue cross. I have the same set I wore when I won my first race on Crag at the age of thirteen. Saitensohn will run in Winky's name and colors. I couldn't have a better pair of owners.

Saitensohn and Riderwood compliment each other well, having opposite temperaments. At the moment I am looking out my writing room window at Riderwood attempting to stand still in the field and graze while Saitensohn is approaching from behind, forcing Riderwood to walk a few paces, so that Saitensohn can have that valuable patch of ground to himself. Thus, they progress across the field, much like many of us do through life, having a good bite of grass, wanting to settle in one spot, but then being forced by the vicissitudes of nature to lift up their heads and move on to that next spot, where the sun is warmer on the back and the turf is greener to the eye and the grass tastes just a little bit sweeter.

December 12
Dear John and Winky,

Saitensohn was on his toes as soon as I hopped on his back. It was dusk. He was looking at this, looking at that, as we walked out on the tractor path. He holds his head higher than Riderwood and he walks up on his toes, ready to spook at any second. Staying in the saddle, I leaned forward, opened the handgate to the Hunter Trials Course. We walked out into the field and he suddenly stopped dead. I was used to this. We would be going cross-country, he would stop. I'd pull the right rein, pull the left, squeeze with the spurs, tap him with the stick. No matter. He would not budge. One evening, I thought, I'll get him. I just sat there. I let him stand. I did not fight him. I relaxed and acted like I was enjoying the moment. He got bored after a minute or so, and moved on. I was learning. He was learning. We were learning together.

It was dark out. It was cold. I'd had a long day of teaching. I relaxed for a few seconds. He was staring at something. What the hell could it be? We were up on a hill, out in the middle of a hundred-acre field where I'd been exercising him for a month now. And then I saw it. A mile away I could make out a green light. It was the new light, green at this moment, at the corner of Manor Road and the Jarrettsville Pike. It had just been put up.

I leaned over, looked at his face. I could feel his heart beating hard between my legs. His eyes were wide open, staring at the little dot of glowing green a mile away. He was breathing in and out, harder and harder, his nostrils flaring wider and wider. A breeze picked up from the west. I wondered, what was going through his mind? What was he thinking? The light changed to red. He continued to stare. Why did it make his heart beat fast? Did it remind him of something years ago, a green light at an intersection in Czechoslovakia, the twirling red lights of an ambulance in France, the brake lights of a fast-stopping van in England?

I poked him with the spurs, tapped him with the stick, and on we went—but he was riled up for the rest of the ride.

His feet are getting long and the right-front shoe is loose! I've got to call the blacksmith.

Yours truly,
Your trainer/rider

P. S. Bill for the month enclosed.

January 6
Dear Winky and John,

Had a great day of hunting last Saturday.

Hacked to the meet and actually got there ten minutes early! A record. A record that was not in the least by my doing. Speedy Kiniel has started coming by in the afternoons and on hunting mornings to help me get the horses out.

Riderwood was feeling sharp. We took off over a coop, then the whole field galloped down into a post-and-rail, up over another coop, and the run was on—we were running and jumping. Someone stopped and there was a jam up, people going every which way. I kicked Riderwood on, and we galloped right through the ruckus and over the log jump. Riderwood got to jump alongside other horses and had a great work out.

After the run, Riderwood and I snuck away from the field—back to the farm. I rubbed Riderwood down, turned him out, tacked Charley up. I have neglected to tell you that Speedy has fallen in love with everything about Saitensohn except his name and has given him the stable name of "Charley." I hopped on, rode out and joined the hunt as they hacked back to the meet. Charley calmed down after a while. There was an outside "tea" set up. The riders were off their horses eating and drinking everything except tea. I rode Charley around, right up to the tea table. People gave the both of us slices of apple. A former trainer and a former jockey of Charley's were there and they looked on in amazement.

Charley was offered a glass of port, turned it down, so I had it. He grazed and relaxed, and then, when the port hit, and egged on by Joe Davies, I schooled Charley around the place over some log jumps and a small post-and-rail. He felt so good, so powerful. My job: hold him back, try to get his head down, and nearing the fence, keep my hands low . . . , release . . . , and up and over we fly! Returned. Let Charley join the tea and have some broccoli and carrots. Cute girls came out and patted him. He licked the dark foamy head off the top of a Smithwick's Ale, took a few sips, and let me have the rest. He loved the attention. I, of course, did not even notice it.

Hacking home, I was pleased with the day. Saitensohn is a fast, strong walker, and he cruised home, on the bit, wanting to break into a jog, then a canter, then a gallop, while the sun was setting and the geese were wheeling in circles, honking and landing in ponds, and I was feeling more and more relaxed and at one with my two race horses. I could've used a scotch "neat," a hot bath, and a nap on arriving home. Instead: *rub and rub and rub*— Speedy has trace-clipped Charley, but his coat running down his neck, over his back and around his rump is the thickest you've ever seen, and I had to rub the dried sweat off him.

Put Charley in a stall, let Riderwood out, fed, hayed, picked up, rush, rush, getting late, showered and raced to a Barnes and Noble book signing where my first customer was a tiny woman whose son has quit college to be a jockey. She directed me in the writing of an inscription that became an epistle, a treatise on why—the ironies of life, of all inscriptions for this book!—he should immediately stop "reducing," let his weight go back up, return to his studies, and forget about pursuing the life of a jockey.

Yours truly,
Patrick

January 13
Dear John and Winky,

Meet at Sycamore, Joey's new farm. Had the best day. Hunted Riderwood.

We had a good run. Galloping into a coop, Sebastian Cromwell, back for a week from Ireland where he is hunting and riding amateur races, is in front on an old, experienced timber horse. He gallops over it, then slows and props approaching a little board fence, his horse twisting as he pops over it. Riderwood stands off and flies over the coop. He keeps going straight and jumps the board fence. Riderwood wants to go! I drop his head and we come up alongside Sebastian at an open gallop, heading for a post-and-rail. Sebastian eases up, doesn't want to jump it head-and-head. I let Riderwood gallop on into the post-and-rail. He feels strong, his stride eating up the ground. Up and over we sail.

We're about a mile from the farm, and there's a lull in the run. We leave the field and jog back here, only to see that the hunt has picked up another scent and is headed fast this way. In fact, they sweep right across my back field, causing Charley to put his tail up and tear around like a two-year-old. I get a bucket of feed, catch Warfield, put him in a stall, acting like it's feed time. Lure Charley into his stall, give him a scoop of feed, dust him off with a rub rag, throw on his tack, head out. By the time we catch up with the hounds, they have quit hunting for the day and are hacking back to the meet.

Back at Sycamore. Compliments on Charley's behavior— from J.B. Secor. Pop Charley over a few. Joe Davies gives me a glass of port. Ride around the tent. The owner of The Wild Bunch pulls in to the tea in her red BMW, steps out, wearing a long, tight, baby-blue cashmere dress, and not much else. She carries a bottle of champagne to the tent, pops the cork, tip-toes in her high heel boots over to me holding high a glass filled to the brim. Charley sniffs and licks around the fizzing bubbles. She reaches up towards me, pulls me down and gives me a kiss and a hug. I decline the champagne. She downs it, returns to the bar and brings me a glass of port. We discuss the latest shenanigans of The Wild Bunch. I finish the port, hand her the glass. Feeling the warmth and glow from the port, and a confidence combined with a what-the-hell, let's-do-it attitude swelling up in me, returning to me (that feeling Tom and I lived and breathed as kids schooling Tiger's horses through his woods after having a glass or two of his cider, and later as teenagers hacking home on rank race horses after a couple hours of fox hunting, the sun going down, having a pull of port/bourbon out of a silver flask—the sweet silvery-tasting elixir cold to the lips, then hot going down—breaking the rules we'd been taught by my grandmother Suzanne White Whitman, by Wassie Ball, by Pony Club founder Mrs. Erskin Bedford, and jumping head-and-head over everything we could find the whole way back to Atlanta Hall), I give Charley a squeeze, jog down to the board fence with bushes in front of it. Walk him up to it, give him a look. Turn, jump—stands off, lands. Turn… and we canter, then gallop over four or five fences, ease him up to a canter, a trot. Walk back into the tea area.

Blythe, Joey's wife, tells me I am the first to jump the new inset—three panels of the fence that were built half a foot lower than the rest of the line fence. Saitensohn puts his head down and relaxes.

Ride home, slowly, pleasingly.

At home. Open a bottle of Boordy Vineyard port made and given to us by Rob and Julie Deford. Stir the embers of the wood stove, toss in a couple of logs. Sit by wood stove, call friend and supporter of my writing as well as riding, Hank Slauson. Tell him about the day—I want to convey the exhilaration of it to Hank. Call Janon Fisher. Thank him for pointing out, after I told him about the French bridle, "How about your hands?" Janon laughs and says Pop would be proud of me.

Get a bit tipsy. Call you both. Having fun. Muck out, push wheelbarrow, do off horses, sweep barn, clean tack.

Yours truly,
Trainer/rider

Bill enclosed.

Late-January email
John,

Friday, I was despairing. How could I continue to train? The snow is turning to ice. I haven't been able to push the wheelbarrow out to the manure pile so I've been piling the manure outside the shed. Hope it's not this bad in Kentucky. Ice is forming all over the entrance to the shed. I'm worried they'll fall trying to get up the incline. I'm worried about Saitensohn's tendon, his old bow, in this ice, about slipping and straining it. I could jog them on the road . . . but on Saitensohn, that could be dangerous. What to do?

In rumbles Mikey's old Subaru. Out steps Speedy in his heavy canvas coveralls. "Hi there sonny-boy, how ya doing!"

I tell him my training has ground to a halt. Show him the mountain of manure outside the shed and the icy entrance.

"You need a *straw ring*!" Speedy calls out to the world. "Like

Mikey'd have—a manure track. You need to *make one.*"

"How am I going to do that?"

"All right. You got's some money?"

"Yes, I do.

He's walking towards the barn, carefully picking his way across the iced-over driveway, examining every spot where he plants the cane. In the barn, he stops. "Fire up that tractor of yours that belonged to your great-granddaddy, hook it up to the wagon and bring it right here. *With my brains and your brawn, we can do anything.*"

Two hours later, we have shoveled six loads of manure onto the wagon, driven the tractor and wagon out to the field, and shoveled it off in a big oval.

First, we tack up Warfield. Test it out on him. Good.

We untack Warfield. Speedy rubs him off. I tack up Riderwood. Jog around our new track.

Return. We untack Riderwood. "No," Speedy says when I head for Saitensohn's stall. "You just get me the right tack and I'll put it on."

I rub down Riderwood. Speedy walks into the next door stall. "Who-a Charley. That'a boy Charley." He pats him, talks to him. Charley gets up on his toes preparing to spin away from him. "Charley!" Speedy calls out, deepening his voice. "Stand up here!" He stands there like a pony while Speedy tacks him up. I jog Charley, around and around, return.

Riderwood is lying down—I'm worried as hell. Twisted gut? Get him up, walk him around. "He's fine," Speedy says. "He just wants to rest in this stall that I've bedded down *so nice*—not like the way you do it—I wouldn't mind lying down in it myself with that nice young woman you was talking to at the meet the other day. . . ."

"OK, OK."

"What's wrong? We's just two men. Can't we talk about what two young men think about? I remember a time when you was younger and that's all you thought about. Remember that summer you had that dark-skinned girl?"

"That was her tan. She was tan."

"Well, she was just about as tan as me. And I remember you taking her up to Saratoga and . . ."

"That's enough."

"It don't mean nothing against Angie. She knows you was young and wild like your Uncle Mikey."

Speedy rubs Charley down, feels his legs. "There's a little heat in that old tendon," he says. He gets out a bottle of rubbing alcohol, splashes it onto his hands, and rubs it, with both hands, on one leg, then the other. Then, he wraps the prettiest bandages around both legs and pins them perfectly. When he stands up, I have my checkbook out. We haggle a bit, but I'm faking it. I know I'm going to give him whatever he wants. "You worse than Mikey!" I cut him a good check.

—APS

February 15
Dear Winky and John,

The deer carcass.

First day, I'm hacking Riderwood over to the Hunter Trials course for a gallop. We're on the tractor path with a thick hedge-row and trees to our left. The path turns sharply to the left. We break into an easy jog and suddenly there's a full deer carcass, with flesh torn off the shoulders and rump, and guts spread out onto the tractor path. Riderwood spooks, shoots out to the right, away from me, into the cut corn field. I'm hanging, my right foot up in the air, all the weight in my left stirrup and on the right rein—I have an image of him galloping off across the fields—but I hang on and he swings back under me.

Next horse, Charley. I'm prepared. I let him see the carcass from afar—as we walk closer and closer to it. He snorts and spooks and we sidestep by.

Next day, the carcass has moved to the edge of turn, closer to the hedgerow. Foxes. Hopefully not coyotes. Next day, not much left, just the flesh on the bones. Big black turkey buzzards stalk the scene. Later, coming home on Charley, I yell—trying to get the buzzards to fly off. They stare at me, remaining perched on the carcass—protecting their meal. Charley is getting mixed messages. I keep my heels down, squeeze with my legs, ready for them to flap.

Two weeks later, the carcass is gone. The skeleton is in the woods and is not visible. Riderwood passes this spot and doesn't blink. Not so with Saitensohn. As he comes around the turn, he gets up on his toes, starts jigging and dancing. Rounding the turn, he lowers his head, sniffs and snorts, looks where the carcass was and spooks to the right, out into the cut cornfield. He forgets nothing, remembers everything.

Yesterday, I was thinking about the moments one has riding: living in the present, in the quiet, especially over the winter. All alone out there. Seeing a big red fox trotting across the white crust of the snow. The deer. The beautiful bird with the white under its wings, and the blue tips—some kind of hawk? The *crunch-crunch* of the snow beneath our feet. It is the peace, the everlastingness, the eternity, the wiping away of all cares and worries, the being alone, out like on a sail boat—yes, like the winter of dredging for oysters under sail on a Chesapeake Bay skipjack—on a horse, just as man did 1,000 years ago.

Riding Charley on the Hunter Trials Course in the late afternoon, we were jogging when the two eaglets flew over, soaring and cruising and hunting. He stopped dead, looked up, and watched. I didn't fight him. I let him relax watching the eaglets dive and play, then rode to the bottom of a hill, turned, dropped his head and let him gallop full tilt up the short part with the good going. That cleared the brain out.

Feeding him that night, he gave me a big nudge, and another, and rubbed his head against my chest. He pushed me, laughing, up against the wall of the stall; he was telling me, *Everything is going to be all right.*

Thankfully yours,
Riderwood and Charley

Speedy and Charley Team Up

March 3, email

John,

I'm up for this day. I've arranged for Billy Santoro to come over and help me with schooling Saitensohn. I awake in the morning thinking about it: which configuration of horses should I have go out? Billy on Riderwood, me on Saitensohn? Billy on Warfield, me on Riderwood? Around and around.

Billy arrives. We go out. First set: Billy on Warfield, me on Riderwood. Have a good school, considering the greasy and, in places, icy conditions. We return. Billy stays on Warfield. I hop off Riderwood and tack up Saitensohn.

Billy gives me a lead around the Griswold's course. Charley is throwing his head and misbehaving. We circle around the "hog fence," or as Mikey called it, the "tight fence"—rails set one on top of the other between two half posts on one side and two half posts on the other, the posts then wired together—jumping it again and again, trying to settle him down. He hits it one time, which is good for him. I had planned to gallop over a few fences with my stirrups jacked up. Change plan. Lengthen irons. Canter over log, around, over log, around. Then, do the same with coop.

We head for the Hunter Trials course. Billy gives me a lead over a few, but it's sketchy for Warfield; he's barefoot and he's slipping around. I ask Billy to pull up, and I let Saitensohn pick up the pace until he's not throwing his head. He's pulling hard and going a little faster than I want. We loop around the course, jumping half a dozen fences well, but not exactly in control.

Afterwards, Billy and I have steaming-hot Irish tea by the woodstove. Decide both horses are ready to run in timber races in a few weeks. I finish in the barn. I'm ecstatic. Energetic. Crank up the tractor, hook up the wagon, drive it to the woodpile, load it up with split logs, drive it to the back porch, unload. Stoke the wood stove, toss in locust logs. Clean out the fireplace, lay newspaper, kindling, and a mix of maple and ash logs. Hear the wheels of Ansley's car crunching on the crusher run. Help her bring in the groceries. Take shower.

Standing by the fire, drying off and rubbing myself down, feeling the heat of the flames on my bare skin, looking forward to Tom and Mimi coming over for dinner, I yell up to Ansley, "I feel perfect. I feel perfectly wonderful." And I did. I did.

—APS

P.S. Before dinner, I was talking about teaching Robert Frost's "Out, Out –" and Tom, sitting at our counter in the kitchen, took a sip of his Coors Light, a puff of his Pall Mall, and recited flawlessly all four verses of "Stopping by the Woods on a Snowy Evening," which he learned in the fourth grade at Harford Day School. A showstopper—the wives were impressed.

March 28

I'm hunting Charley. Meet's at 11:00. Two classes at Talmudical Academy, a Jewish orthodox school in Pikesville, on the other side of Pimlico, starting at 2:00—picked up this gig in December. Forty minute drive. A tight squeeze.

Arose early, wrote for an hour, fed, hayed, mucked out. Rode Riderwood. Cleaned tack. Pulled on hunting clothes. Back out: Saitensohn has busted out of his stall and he has rolled. I bring him in. The mud is drying up. Turning hard—like hand-sized fish scales. The meet is at Paul and Suzie Bozman's—just a football field away and it looks like I'm going to be late. I'm out in barn, rushing, despairing—how did this happen?—and Speedy rumbles in. Talking and working and currying and vacuuming. I make the meet on time.

Up on Saitensohn, I see a fence, and I feel like giving him a squeeze and heading into it and flying over—a very good sign. Return, wrung out, sweaty. Need to cool him out, water him off, rub him down, and then get ready to go teach my afternoon classes. Time has flown. Good Lord, how can I make it to class?

Speedy drives in. "This horse needs bandages!" He stands Charley in aisle way. "You go teach. This is my horse and I'll take care of him," he says, sitting on a bucket, gently rubbing Bigel Oil onto Charley's tendon.

Shower. Chilly out—tear through closet looking for a pair of corduroys. Give up. Pull on khakis, shirt, jacket, hop in the Ford-150, and I'm on my way. Get caught in huge traffic jam on the Beltway. Ambulances and police cars with sirens wailing and lights blinking wedge their way through the gridlock. Time for the start of my first class is approaching. Call Shimmy, the Head, and tell him I can't make it. Finally, fly down the shoulder, get off Beltway. Stop at Office Depot—this is becoming a sunny spring day— get paper and ink cartridge for my printer. Am preparing to print Part I of memoir I'm writing, *Flying Change*.

Back. Relax. Put feet up, begin reading what I'll be teaching the next day, *A Connecticut Yankee in King Arthur's Court*. Doze off. Cell phone rings. Mark Simon: My memoir *Racing My Father* is a semifinalist for the Castleton Lyons-Thoroughbred Times Annual Book Award. The purse: $10,000. I take Esmerelda off the winter rollers, pull her out into the fresh air and go for a bike ride I'll never forget.

Back at house, things don't go so well. This often happens when I'm excited about something. When will I learn? Ansley seems grumpy—or am I impatient, energetic, ready to roll? Yes, I want the world to be happy, celebratory, like me. We argue about where the corduroys are. Who gives a shit. That leads to Ansley criticizing the mess I'd made in the bedroom: jodhpurs, turtle neck and sweater from hunting tossed on the bed, dirty blue jeans and turtle neck in a pile on the floor, drawers and closet door left open, wet towel hanging from door handle. Then, dinner. I'm trying to celebrate—drink some wine. Ansley and Eliza get in an argument about modeling and about us paying $2,500 for Eliza to take a modeling course. Cocky, arrogant, the all-time know-it-all, I confidently step into the fray, thinking I am being impartial and objective and will iron out the acrimony. Disaster. Ansley laces into me for siding with Eliza, and there goes my evening.

Just goes to show—that saying I learned from Alan Watts' *The Way of Zen*:

Before: Chop wood
mow grass
carry water.

After: Chop wood
mow grass
carry water.

March 29, email to John Egan
Hey man,

Rode Saitensohn in inaugural running of Sycamore Steeplechase—a school over at Joe Davies. Joe has been a big help with Saitensohn, offering me his whole place to school around and making me feel comfortable there. At least, I thought it was going to be an easy school.

I'd decided to hack over. Had just gotten back from teaching at the Talmudical Academy and was running late. Joe's is two miles away. I didn't want to have to rush over and then also have Charley do a three-mile school. I'm not in heavy wool britches; I'm not in my grandfather's solid, knee-high black hunting boots; I'm not in the heavy black hunting coat Tom gave me. Am wearing my old jodhpurs, the same ones I wore at the age of eighteen— the moleskin loose and comfortable at my thighs and rump, and snug, so you don't get rubbed, around my calves; the fabric pulled perfectly over the top of my ankle-high, light-weight, lace-up galloping boots. I feel comfortable, light, springy, quick. I feel eighteen. Speedy drives in. "The trailer, the trailer, numbskull. You've gots' ta use the trailer."

"I can't get him on the trailer. I've tried and he won't go on."

"Leave that to me. Jus' back the truck up to the trailer and hook it up."

"I'm telling you, I couldn't get him to put one foot on the ramp..."

"Hook it up! What'chu try'n do? Break Charley down! Jog all the way over there, run in a race, and then hack home?"

He steps into the stall. "Charley, Charley," he chants, running his hand down his long neck. He tacks him up. I prepare to pull him out of the stall.

"Timber shins—Charley's got to have his timber shins! You go'in ruin this horse."

I pull out two old hardened foam pads, each five inches by ten. Speedy spits on his hands, rubs the spit onto Charley's right hind shin, slaps the pads onto the shin and wraps elastic vet wrap around and around his leg. He does the same with the other. No one can put on a better "timber shin." If it's too loose, it can flop around, the wrap can come loose, the horse can step on the bandage, injure the leg. If it's too tight, the wrap can cut off the circulation, damaging the tendon.

I pull a halter over Charley's bridle, snap a shank onto to the halter, preparing to lead Charley out of the stall. "Give me that shank," Speedy says.

I hand him the shank.

"Now," he says, eying his cane leaning against the wall. I grab his cane, hand it to him.

He leads Charley out of the barn and towards the trailer, shank in one hand, cane in the other. "You stay behind me and put the ramp up." Charley follows Speedy into the trailer without the slightest hesitation. I push the ramp up, set the clamps.

We arrive to see the top field overflowing with big new diesel pickups pulling six-horse goosenecks, several old-time, six-horse Imperatores, and all the latest hot shot amateur timber riders from Pennyslvania dressed to the nines. We back Charley off our 1958 Rice trailer. I reset the saddle. Speedy gives me a leg up. The young jocks have their stirrups jacked up high as if they're at the track. I hadn't been able to walk the course, didn't have time, and I look out at a very "trappy" looking set of fences: flags up here and there, post-and-rails, board fences, coops, logs. We're filing down to the start. There's the winner of last year's Hunt Cup beside me.

We're at the start. There're some professional riders here too. They're looking cocky. Charley is nervous. He's lunging forward, and then, when I pull back to stop him from leaping, he freezes and starts shaking all over. I keep him moving. Louis Bosley—J.B.'s first cousin—is the starter. Tall and commanding, he's raising his flag. "All right riders! Are you ready riders?" Instead of walking forward, towards Louis, the riders are looping their horses back, down the hill, near the woods. No one wants to go first. I certainly don't want to go first. I want a lead. I want to park myself behind an older horse, gallop around and have a good school. I don't want Charley to see "daylight," meaning no one is in front of him; this causes a rank horse to want to take off full speed.

I'm now stuck at the front of the pack. I have to keep moving, going forward, or he might "freeze." Louis asks, "You OK, Patrick." "Yes," I say continuing forward. He drops the flag. The riders just sit there. I've never seen anything like it. The hell with it—I nudge Charley, and off we go, in the lead, faster than planned.

We're going uphill, all Charley's weight on his hindquarters. He's holding his head high and "climbing"—he's not galloping along in long smooth strides, he's raising his knees high, expending more energy going up and down than forward. I can't touch his mouth. Can't pull on the reins or his head will go even higher. Have to keep my hands low and let him go, faster, faster. We hurdle, up and over the first—hit it behind, but we have the timber shins on—up a hill, and soar high up and over the second, another three-and-a half-foot post-and-rail. Turn sharp to left, head into log. Up and over, through the chute of people, down steep hill, still in front. Over the little three-foot board fence with bushes planted in front. Going too fast, we over-shoot the next, which is sharp left. We swing wide and have to almost ease up to make turn. Up and over, then open gallop to board fence. He finally has his head down, someone alongside us now. He's pulling hard to the left, and my right hand and arm, holding the stick, is shot. I slide the stick into my mouth. Up and over, then, we have a choice: big post-and-rail, or, to the side, a smaller, solid log jump. Go for smaller log and lose ground, which is what I want. Would like to get in behind some other horses! *Wasn't this supposed to be a school?* Last year's Maryland Hunt Cup winner jumps the big one and passes us.

And now here comes a damn in-and-out. We're flying, can't get straight at it. Jump the first, the "in," on an angle, land, barely touching the ground before we take off over the "out." Gallop full speed up steep hill, horses around us now, through open gate. "Wo-a boy, wo-a boy." Someone is right "off my hocks"—not a good place to be: his shoulder is by the rump of my horse, and when my horse takes off, his will also want to take off—as we gallop into a post-and-rail. Up and over, nice. Over the mulch crossing on the driveway and then nicely over another small post-and-rail. Across lawn, galloping into brush jump—*whoosh*—hurdles perfectly through it. I drop his head, let him run-and-jump over the next three.

Heading up hill, we take sharp left and finish over the last, a bunch of us close together. It's trappy. Saitensohn puts in a short one—takes an extra half-stride, forcing him to pop up over the fence, which is OK by me; I want him to learn how to do this. We gallop down the stretch to the finish behind two professionals whipping and driving, Saitensohn not tired, pulling steadily.

After the "school" the recently-retired amateur rider Sebastian Cromwell, from Pennsylvania, nattily dressed in polished English paddock shoes, British Warm, cigarette dangling from a lip, and fedora perched at a jaunty angle, approaches us while Speedy is down on a knee pulling off the timber shins. I know Sebastian has returned from Ireland where he rode "Bumper races"—flat races for amateur riders—over the winter before deciding to hang up his tack. His face is full; he's put on a few pounds, might even be developing a paunch.

"That'a boy Charley," Speedy is chanting. "That'a boy. You a winner Charley, you a winner."

Sebastian takes a pull of his cigarette, looks at me. "Would you like one, Young-blood?" he asks, parroting Mikey.

"No thanks, I don't smoke."

He pulls a silver flask from his inside pocket, offers it to me. Speedy has glanced up but hasn't said a word.

"No thanks," I say.

He takes a sip, asks Speedy. "Want a shot?"

"Sebastian, you knows perfectly well I don't drink no more. And you should probably do the same."

"Young-blood," he says, again tainting Mikey's expression, "You should get rid of that horse," he proclaims. "I saw him pull up in the A. P. Smithwick at Saratoga a year or so ago. And today, why the hell didn't he win that heat? He doesn't have any guts."

Speedy and I both know he didn't "pull up" that day; he bowed so badly he couldn't walk and had to be vanned off the course. Speedy stands up, takes a step toward Sebastian. He's got a different look in his eye. It's not menacing; it's not angry. It's cool. It's being ready. He stands about a head over Sebastian, hands by his sides.

Sebastian walks away.

"That chicken shit ought'a go back to Ireland or England and stay there," Speedy says. "What does he know about guts. Charley has more guts, more heart than that sonovabitch can imagine and if he ever comes near Charley, I'll pull out my shank" –in one motion he reaches into his right pocket, pulls out his switchblade, snaps his wrist, the long, shiny blade flips out, and he makes a jabbing motion, "And his time will be up! Patrick, he's just jealous. He's got to knock somebody. Makes him feel big. Don't you pay any attention to him. That'a boy Charley. That'd a boy," he says, closing his knife, putting it in his pocket, leaning down and gently feeling Charley's legs.

"Now, this horse done enough! Let's load him up. Imagine: you wanted to hack him two miles back after going for this school. That wasn't no school. That was a race. What'ch doing going so fast on him, taking the lead?"

"That wasn't my plan."

"Your plan! If you want to be a trainer, you gotta to know what the hell you getting my horse into. Come on Charley."

He walks Charley around a few times, female groupies from the Mikey days coming up, "Speedy! Speedy! Who's that horse?" Speedy stops, lets them pat Charley, tells them he's going to win the Hunt Cup.

I hear, "A.P., A.P.,' turn and see J.B. Secor approaching with a big grin. He's in his work blue jeans, a gray-patch of Bowie mud on one knee, a pair of old, but shined, Kroops zip-up paddock boots, and he's pulled a classic, light suede jacket over his turtle neck with the frayed edges. J.B. doesn't have the height of some, but what he lacks in height, he makes up in presence and forthrightness.

He looks up from under the brim of his Irish wool cap, into my eyes, "A.P., how about that start?" He laughs. "Those young jocks weren't about to help you out, were they, A.P.? Not like the old days, is it? I liked the way he went. You didn't need to be out front like that but what the hell could you do?" I relax for a moment. The announcer is calling for the runners in the next race. Jocks are getting leg ups. J.B. pats Charley. "You've done a good job schooling this horse, A.P." He turns toward Speedy. "Don't you think he has, Speedy?"

"What I think is we got to load up and get this horse home. Charley's done enough for one day. You old-timey jumpin'-rider-turned-trainers standing around shooting off your mouths while this horse is wringing wet and needs to be cooled out and rubbed off."

Charley's First Win

Excerpt, Racing Journal
March 31

Hop on Riderwood in the morning. Hack over to the Griswolds and gallop around Nancy's half-mile straw track. Start rushing. It takes me forever to get all the stuff ready: foot locker, bandages, pins, cooler, foot pick, bridle, halter, shank, hay net filled with hay, five-gallon containers of water—not to mention that I was up late last night running around finding my britches and silks, polishing my boots, cleaning my spurs, getting rubber bands to wrap around the wrists of my silks, finding thin socks so I can slide into Pop's old boots, cleaning my racing saddle, checking and cleaning the girths, finding and testing out my goggles. I need a valet. A valet and a groom and a trainer.

This is the day. Saitensohn in a timber race

Speedy arrives. He's not going with me. It takes two hours to get there, two hours to get back, and we'll be there for three or so hours. It'd be too costly. He wants $25 an hour. Anyway, Morgan, the van driver, can run Saitensohn. I take a quick shower. Drive out as Morgan pulls in. Speedy will help Morgan load up the horse and the traps.

Wanting a cup of fresh coffee, I stop by a bagel shop I used to frequent on the way to Gilman. At first, it brings back good memories. I order the coffee. The television is on. The news. There are a dozen people in the shop. No one is listening or looking. I look up. There is a strong-shouldered young man on crutches with two artificial legs taking his first steps. There is a young man in a hospital bed with no right arm. He is being interviewed. Then, it shows him a few weeks later, lifting a cup of coffee with his artificial hand. A picture flashes onto the screen. Five or six men from the same platoon. They had all been in the same Humvee. The one with the artificial hand is the only survivor. Switch—to Dover Air Force Base. Shots of body bags. My body begins to tremble. Customers walk in and out, paying no attention to the news. Do they know we are at war? I get my coffee and bagel, set my money on the counter, do not wait for change, walk to the car. I'm shaking. Hyperventilating. I drink the coffee. Eat the bagel. Tears pour. The world swirls. I want to get out, grab a sledge-hammer, smash all the cars in the lot. Break the large sidewalk windows to the café. Turn on the pickup. Rev the engine. Crash it into one car after another. Not the best way to prepare to ride a race.

I pull myself together, focus on the act of driving, think about the upcoming race.

Arrive: look at fences. Like what I see. Wish I'd brought Riderwood. All are new, three-and-a-half-foot straight up and down "tight" fences and definitely not big. I check out the start. Realize we jump the first fence on the crest of the hill, then dip down, turning sharply to the left, go up and over another on the crest of a hill, and down a longish hill into the third. It will be difficult not to have him take off.

Return to the start and check the flags for the first three fences. Want to know their exact location in case I'm in front.

Weigh in. Pretty young woman at scales. I make 163. Weight in the program is 160.

Saitensohn is calm as Morgan puts on timber shins. Fool with bridle. Morgan wants the cross of the figure eight lower on his nose than I. Get tongue tie on. That is—grab tongue, wrap two-inch wide strip of bandage around it once, then pull strips down around his chin, and tie them like a shoelace. This is to keep him from getting his "tongue over the bit." Calm as we lead him over. Calm in the paddock.

Saitensohn and I are settled as we jog and canter to the start. It's away from the crowds. I tell the starter I can't stand still. He asks me to go to the head of the group and lead the horses in a circle. We file out onto the course. The starter drops his flag and hollers, "Go." Saitensohn puts head up, I lean slightly forward—and whack, he flips his head right back into my face, into my nose. I wonder if I've broken it. Raise my hand and feel it. Damn, I look at my hand: blood. OK you bastard, you've done it now. I drop the reins, let him roar into that first fence, we jet over it, up and over, down the hill, to the left, and now, good Lord, we are flying down the hill. *Whoosh*, over another, and on the flat now, trying to steady him. He flips his head up into my face. It's this wire bit—a severe bit consisting of two narrow strands of twisted steel. Years ago, when I was in the sixth grade at Gilman, Pop put it on Crag's bridle when I won my first race. It was supposed to keep him from running off with me. Well, this was a different horse. It was a last-minute decision to use it, and it is not working worth a damn! He hates it. I wish to hell I'd just left the smooth, rounded snaffle on him, something he could grab onto and pull against. Over the three in the bottom, fine, then up the hill. I look back. They are still at the bottom, on the flat, two fences back! A quarter of a mile back!

I ease him up, let him take a breather. It doesn't last long. He sees the next fence—and accelerates. He does this with every fence. Once the fence is within range, he starts increasing the length and speed of his stride.

Around we go.

I try to slow him, but when I do, we get in too close and he hits the fence. They're way back. We go past the start again. Jump the one at the top on the crest and barrel on down into the third to last. I don't send him into it. I sit still. He doesn't make any adjustments. He gets in close. I take a deep seat and a long hold and he wallops it behind.

After the fence, I gather my reins back up. He feels like he's hurting, not moving right behind. I have a sickening feeling. His natural, flowing movement is all off. He's moving jerkily, as if limping at a full gallop. Then, one stride, another, another, he pulls himself together and now he's pulling hard going into the last and I say the hell with trying to slow him down. I ask for a big one and he takes off a stride early, rocketing over it. I hear a round of cheers and applause from the spectators. I can't help but let him run through the stretch. We cross under the wire, I'm laughing to myself—go to pull him up and can barely do it.

Ease up. Feel like letting loose and crying. Want to let it out.

I am so proud of Saitensohn. Deep inside, it comes back to me: all the work since that first hot August day—how gaunt and shabby and unhappy he looked. How he wheeled. How I couldn't ride him across the field. How I couldn't jog him around a circle going to the right.

Pull him up, jog back. Douglas Lees, the top steeplechase photographer in the country, is there, and another photographer, clicking away. A reporter is there. Interviews me, asks all about Saitensohn. Receive a big silver trophy. Norman Fraley presents the trophy. Good Lord, this trophy is in honor of a Greenhaugh. It must be a relative of my former Oldfields' student, Sarah. I think of Sarah. I see her approaching me in the classroom, yet another handwritten twenty-page "short" story in her hands, two days late, but here it is, and you'd better believe it'll be a good one, a wild and adventurous and suspenseful one. I see her skiing down a steep hill, long, blonde hair flying, on an Oldfields field trip I organized. And I see her as an adult, camera with telephoto lense in hand, taking some of the best photographs on the steeple-chase circuit.

Dozens of people pat me on the back and shake my hand as I walk back up the hill to the van. The steward in charge of entries approaches me grinning, shakes my hand, "Only a Smithwick could've gotten that horse around that course. Only a Smithwick." I feel part of a tradition, part of something larger than myself. I'm representing the family.

Ellen Horner, with whom I'd galloped thousands of horses for Dickie Small two decades ago, is grinning and laughing and congratulating me. "A quarter of a mile, Patrick! Wait till I tell Dickie. He's going to want you back on his horses this summer."

All I want to do is call Ansley. I desperately want to call Ansley. I wish she were there with me.

Back at Prospect in the late afternoon: Morgan is giving me all kinds of orders. Wants to run Saitensohn in a $7,500 claimer over hurdles. Where does he get these ideas? We put Charley in ice. Each foot in a bucket of ice, but I don't have enough ice. Morgan is telling me how to pick up this foot, put this one down. Charley keeps stepping out of the ice bucket. It's his knee I'm worried about. Hitting that second to the last with his knee. Morgan leaves. I call Speedy—hoping to get him to stop by the next day,

Sunday. He's at Royal Farms near Hess Road. He drives over immediately. Without me asking, he's brought two bags of ice.

The Pro. The Master Groom. The Leg Man of all Leg Men. He pulls up by the barn in the old Subaru. The back seat is down and the entire back is filled with stuff—notebooks of his art work, paint brushes, fishing poles and tackle boxes, his horse clippers, tool box, buckets, a fold-up movie director's chair, and, a box containing what he swears is Jimi Hendrix's guitar pick. He grabs his cane, walks, putting weight on the cane with each step, to Saitensohn. Carefully takes each foot out of the bucket. The bucket is too shallow. The ice doesn't go up to his knee. He says to graze Charley. I let him "pick" the clover he loves up by the big sliding doors of the barn. A big diesel truck rumbles in the driveway. J.B. steps down out of the cab, asks about the race, pats Charley. "My Aunt Betty would love this horse, A.P. She'd loved this sort of mover. Phlegmatic—she called it. Phlegmatic. You've really done a good job."

"Fluid, a fluid mover, maybe that's what she called it," I said.

"That's it, fluid."

I tell him I'm still looking for the right bit and that the twisted wire snaffle had definitely not been a good choice. He listens intently, and says, "A.P., I got just the right thing for you." He climbs up into the truck, rumbles out the driveway.

Speedy opens the back of his station wagon, pushes aside a couple of horse blankets, pulls out two black, four-foot long wraps with flapping Velcro attachments. I wonder what they are.

"Bring Charley down here."

I lead Charley down to the bottom barn door. Speedy takes the shank. Leaning into his cane with each stride, he leads him into the aisle-way, turns him around and stands him up as only he can do. I'm worrying. That one knee is puffed up, swollen, has heat in it. I know that's the one that hit the third to last.

"Don't you worry. I'll take that right out!" Speedy says.

He sets each foam pad down on the cement floor in front of Charley and fills the interior pockets with cubes of ice, letting Charley see what he's doing. Then, he stands the boot up, gently wraps it around Charley's leg, pulls the Velcro straps across. Wraps the other leg. "Sonny-boy," he says to me, "from now on, every afternoon this week, after you let him out or ride him, I want Charley to stand in the stall for an hour with these on. Got that?"

"Yes."

J.B. drives in, leaves the truck running, steps out. "Here A.P., try this. It should work." And it did. I used J.B.'s "ring bit"—a light snaffle combined with a simple metal ring that goes through the horse's mouth and around his chin—for the rest of Charley's racing career. "I got to get back to the barn. An owner just stopped by. See you A.P. Hey Speedy, take care of that horse's legs!" He rumbles out.

Speedy and I clean out the stalls. I cut the strings on a bale of hay with the axe handle that has a triangular blade from an old mower bolted into the end—a Speedy invention. I grab two flakes, each about four inches thick, toss them into Charley's stall, two flakes into Riderwood's stall, two into the hay rack for Warfield.

"You needs hay nets. That way you know just how much they've ate." Using his cane, he walks fast to the Subaru, pulls three hay nets out of an old feed bag. "You got some screw eyes?"

"Yes, yes, but the drill is broken. It won't take a charge."

"I don't need no damn drill. Get me a hammer and a screw driver and some screw eyes." He's breaking into a sweat.

He steps into Charley's stall, holds a screw eye up high in the corner and hammers it with smashing force into the steel-hard chestnut beam, then sticks the screw driver through the eye and twists it around. He does the same in Riderwood's stall. Then, he collects the hay I'd tossed in. He opens wide the mouth of a hay net, stuffs in the flakes. He does the same with the other. He grabs his cane, limps fast to his car, returns with an old-fashioned hanging scale with a hook on it. "These are Mikey's old scales," he says, "Mikey Power!" He gets the hammer, smashes a screw-eye into the chestnut beam by the feed room, sticks a long screwdriver into the loop of the screw-eye. He inhales and then exhales loudly—twisting the screw eye one full turn. Inhales, then exhales loudly—twisting the screw eye one full turn. Does it one last time. Snaps the rusted scales to the screw eye.

"I been meaning to tell you to put up these hay nets and this set of scales. But I might just as well do it myself 'cause you ain't never go'in ta get around to it."

He holds up a net full of hay, sets the loop of the cord into the hook, lets it loose. "OK, that's fifteen pounds." I'm sweeping up.

"You hear me?"

"Yes. Yes."

"Now, every night when you fill these nets up you know exactly how much you giving each horse. And you won't be wasting hay. The horses won't be dragging it all across the stall. We go'in ta win some races, we need to be exact—like your Uncle Mikey."

He walks into each stall, draws the cord to the feed bag up through the screw eye, pulls down hard—jerking the hay net up high—and then ties a slip knot.

"And one more thing: from now on, when Charley runs, I go with him. "

"All right. All right."

"You tole' Andrew about this horse?"

"A little."

"Well, you can send him one of those E-Z mails now, or write him a note. Can you do that?"

"Yes, I can."

"You tell him not to worry, you was jus' about to break this poor horses leg and put yourself in Shock Trauma but now you got Speedy working on him, and everything's goin' be all right. We'z goin' ta win some races."

"All right. All right."

"Now, take those leg braces off Charley and clean out the ice."

He rifles through my old footlocker. "This foot's killing me. That damn doctor put the pins in all wrong. I been back and he says he may have to take'em out. I'm going to sue'im for every penny he has and then we going to buy our own van and *I'll* be driving Charley to the races." Finds a plastic container of "Bowie mud," and a set of bandages.

"Get me a bucket of hot water."

He sets two thick rolls of cotton, two sets of bandages and an overturned bucket in the aisle. I bring the bucket of hot water back from the house. He pours some into another bucket, pours in the dried Bowie Mud, stirs it.

He goes to his car, pulls out a wide piece of cloth, about a foot and a half long. He reaches in his right-hand pocket, pulls out his "shank," changes his mind, puts it back in and pulls a Swiss Army knife out of the chest pocket of his overalls. Opens the scissors, cuts a dozen thin eighteen-inch strips on one side, a dozen thin eighteen-inch strips on the other.

I lead Charley out, stand him up. Speedy puts a dab of

Furacin on the cut/nick on tendon, the wet cloying Bowie Mud—or poultice—on both legs, down low over the ankles, and over the sore knee while talking one-hundred words per minute about Bonneville, the speed hurdle horse Pop used to ride who shattered race track records and is now in the Hall of Fame, and this horse and that, and Von Csadek, the eventual Hunt Cup and two-time Gold Cup winner: when he first came from Charlestown no one could handle him. Speedy put him in a stall with a wooden floor. He was jumping all around, misbehaving, fell on his ass, all the way down. Mikey said, "Oh, is he all right? Oh, you'd better get him up!" Speedy said, "No, just leave him there!" Speedy stepped into the stall, the horse stood up, and he was as quiet as could be from then on. Doug and Margaret Worrall got the horse, trained him and went on to win over twenty timber races with their son Patrick, just a kid in high school, in the tack.

He wraps two cotton bandages around the sore leg, one below the knee, one over the knee. Then, he takes the cloth with the strips, wraps it around the front of the knee, and ties each strip behind his knee—creating a "spider-web bandage."

All's well. I have a swig of Irish whiskey right out of the bottle, and some more. "You better stop drinking all that whiskey! What are you, an alcy-holic? You've got to stay straight to ride Charley next week!"

"Next week!"

"Well, he'll need more time than that. I say he be ready to run again in three weeks."

He stands up slowly, unraveling the knots. Looks at his cane leaning against the tack room door. I get the cane, hand it to him. He shifts his weight to the cane in his right hand, reaches up, pats Charley on the shoulder. "Now listen, you leave these bandages on! You turn Charley out tomorrow with these on, bring him in, leave'em on. I'll stop by at feed time and take'em off—see how the knee and the tendon're doing. Don't you touch'em!"

"Yes, yes."

"They stay on for two days. Then we go back to the ice."

"Think we should give him some Bute?"

"No! Charley don't need no more Bute! That Morgan already gave'im too much after the race. Don't you give him that Butezolidan—it just masks the problem. And it's bad for his bones. Don't you know that? Bad for his intestines. You keep

Morgan away from this horse."

I invite Speedy in. He sits at the kitchen counter. Talks in a low voice now. Polite. Ansley has dinner ready. We three sit down and have a victorious meal. Speedy kids and cajoles me in front of Ansley: "Patrick has no business taking Charley down to Virginia and running him in that race so soon. No business. When I was at Royal Farms everyone was talking about it. They said Charley was wild—looked wild going around that course. I told them, I said, "He looked wild, you're right about that, and he's going to look wilder still when Patrick cuts him lose in the Hunt Cup and opens up a fence on the field...."

Ansley is being quiet. I hear her murmur, "The Hunt Cup?"

"Yes sir, Charley can run. He's a born racehorse. We'll cut him loose the end of April. Patrick!"

"Yes."

"You send Andrew an E-Z mail and tell him."

I'm laughing and feel "high as a kite," as Mom used to say.

Points to remember:

I don't like that standing at the start business, waiting for someone to go. When the starter drops the flag, I'm going to let him roll. As Pop always said, "A length at the start is a length at the finish."

Ride your own race. No matter what people tell you to do, when you get to the post, clear your head and do your own thing. Isn't that what Pop taught me about riding as well as life: listen to the vets, listen to the trainers, listen to the owners, listen to all the so-called experts, but then, when you lower yourself into the saddle, when you put your feet in the stirrups and grab a hold of the reins and ride out of the paddock onto the track, do what in your bones you know is right.

Heart

May 13—Mother's Day
Dear Wink and John,

Sunday. Mother's Day—up early. Rained overnight. On Riderwood. Out on Hunter Trials Course. Grass is *green green green*. Sun is *bright bright bright*. Fox is *red red red* as it goes leaping across our path, into the woods. We jog down to the bottom. Grass is tall and wet. The ground is softened. Reach the bottom, and let him gallop up and around, a strong steady gallop, and I am judging him, watching him, feeling him—thinking: Should I have run him today? We ease up, jog back down to the bottom, and this time I drop his head and let him dig in. Riderwood tosses his head with his thick powerful neck, cocks his jaw to the right, and up the hill we go, devouring the ground, eating it up, the green wet grass flying by beneath us, the sun's rays reflecting off the eastern-facing side of each blade of grass. We pull up and he's hardly blowing. Perfect, maybe he would have run great today, but this breeze, three quarters of a mile, is exactly what he needed. This is what is best for *him*.

I hop off Riderwood, cool him out. Speedy arrives. I am starting to rush. Post time for Saitensohn's race is 2:00. Speedy takes over. I take a shower, looking out the window, hoping to see the van pull in. Showered, tack in the cab of the pickup, I'm set. Ansley cooks me two "eggs in the middle." I wolf them down. Had gotten too light. This is a hurdle race; that trip at Blue Ridge, and the one before at Sycamore—both over "timber," post-and-rail and board fences—were a bit on the wild and risky side. I've taken him off timber. All Saitensohn's races in Europe had been over hurdles. In this country, each hurdle is four feet high, consisting of a three-foot high, thick, heavy foam "roll (behind which is a steel cage) and a foot of "brush"—plastic shoots painted green. Galloping into one of these, the horse hurdles fast over the roll and brushes through the top eight inches of brush. Charley is a born hurdler.

The race is for amateurs only, and thus, to accommodate the amateur rider, and to encourage him or her to ride, the weights are higher than for professionals. Charley has to carry a ridiculous amount, so I'd been putting on a couple of pounds. Was now at 152.6. Will be using Pop's old lead pad.

Check with Speedy. Ask if Morgan, our van driver, has called. "No, he'll be here. Don't you worry." Hop in pickup. It's 10:30. I'd told Morgan to have the van at our place at ten on the dot. I'd made this very clear.

Head up the road. Call Speedy. "Is Morgan there yet?"

"No," he'll be here soon. Don't you worry. He'll get here right at 11:30 when I have to give the horse the Lasix.

I call Morgan. No answer. I never should have trusted him. I drive on. 11:00. I call Ansley. Still no Morgan. I keep driving. I know this drive up Route 1. It should be a nice, relaxing drive. I'd been looking forward to it, to settling down and coasting up through the countryside and across the Susquehanna at the Conowingo Dam.

11:30. Call Speedy. Call Ansley. Still no Morgan. My fault. Speedy told me not to allow him near Charley. Speedy told me we needed to get our own rig. Morgan had done this once before; in fact, that time, he never showed up at all!

11:45—I call Tom, have to call one barn, then his cell, then another barn. Finally get him. He makes plans to take us. I push him. He has it set up. His van will pick up Charley and Speedy. I pull into Willowdale. 12:00—Ansley calls and says Morgan has just pulled into the farm. I call Tom back, cancel going with him. Hectic. I'm fried.

Weigh in on scales below the stewards' stand. Walk back out to van area at 1:20. Ansley has surprised me; she's driven up in the van with Morgan and Speedy! They must've been flying, bouncing Saitensohn around in the back. We tack up in the van.

Charley is relaxed. Walk to the paddock. Speedy leads Charley over, but his foot is hurting too much.. I take the horse and give him a turn around the paddock and then, it's *"Riders Up!"* Speedy throws me up on the horse.

We file in at the start, going to the left. Charley tosses his head and goes sideways. I have to push him forward so we don't bump into the other horses. We cross in front of three horses. The starter thinks I am trying "to steal the start" and chews me out. I tell him I can't let my horse stand still: "He'll freeze."

We file in again. We start to move forward. Charley gets his head up. There are a couple of horses ahead of us. The starter drops his flag. Charley has his head up for a few strides. I keep my hands down on the withers. His head goes down, the reins tense, the reins are taut, and we shoot out of the pocket, go to the front, approach the first hurdle and whoosh through the top brush. I pull on the right rein upon landing, and he is pulling now, really pulling to the left. We go down through the bottom, wet and soggy, approach a white flag. We're going to have to turn sharply to the right. Leaving my right hand on the right rein, I cross my left hand over, and grip the right rein with it so that I am now galloping into the second hurdle with both hands on the right rein . . . we head into it . . . approaching it on a surprisingly sharp angle... *whoosh*, up and over. We barrel down the hill, turning to the right, whoosh over the hurdle. Galloping through the flat in front of the stewards' stand, I slide my left hand back to the left rein. Over the hurdle, and now another right turn. My right hand and arm are tightening. A horse is approaching on my inside. I pull Charley over, tighten it up, and the thrusting-horse can't come through.

We straighten out, pull away from the thrusting-horse as we head up the hill into a hurdle. I steady him, steady him, trying to get him to take a breather, and we get in a little close, pop over it. Charley lands, gathers himself together and starts pulling again, but now he's more manageable.

I sense—whether it's the sound, my peripheral vision, or a feeling, I don't know—I feel the thrusting-horse trying to come up on my inside again. We pull over slightly so he can't come through, and head into what was the first hurdle... *whoosh through the top brush* and and turn sharply again.

I steady Charley. Up and over a few, we loop around and then we barrel down the hill again feeling the horses crowding up behind us, through the bottom, over the hurdle in front of the stewards' stand, and here they come, up from behind us. Well, good, let them come. We let three or four pass us. I "park" Charley behind one, to get him to relax.

The jocks are starting to pump and push. I sit still, saving every ounce of our energy. We jump what was the first hurdle again, for the third and last time. I feel Charley tiring beneath me—his stride isn't as strong, he's no longer pulling against me. We head down the hill for the finish.

Going into the second to the last, I twirl my stick around and give him a good wake-up crack. We jump the hurdle on the inside, shoot past a group of horses, and come up on the inside of the frontrunner. We hook up. Down the hill, turning to the right, we fly, head-and-head. The other jock—it's James Slater, often rides for Tom, knows what he's doing, and he's on Russia, the favorite—and I are both steadying our horses, knowing we have a long stretch drive coming up.

Around the turn, it flattens out, and we speed into the last hurdle. Charley shows incredible guts. I crack him once across his rump and he stands off, hurdles it. We land head-and-head with Russia and for a few seconds Russia, on our left, starts to pull away. I whack Charley across the rump and push him and he is alongside Russia, and then Russia starts to pull away again and Charley is feeling wobbly beneath me. I think this is it, he can't do any more. I hesitate. The other horse has stopped pulling away, and here comes Charley again. He puts his head down and he *digs in, digs in*. He's running on all heart now, nothing but heart now. I am pushing him but I just cannot, absolutely cannot hit him again. I am hand-riding him, waving the stick along his neck, and we are gaining now, gaining on the other horse, we are passing him, passing him, there's a pole our left, a tall pole by the rail. I stop pushing for a split second then I realize it is not the finish pole! I'm back pushing. We pass the actual finish pole. And then, we are easing up, pulling up, head and head, close together, and James asks, "Did you get it?" He is so polite. For a jockey in these circumstances, he is being uncharacteristically polite; he is being positive about the possibility of me winning. I can't get over it. "Did you win it?" he asks. He clearly thinks we've won it.

"I hope so," I reply, honestly and straightforward. "I hope so." And I think we did.

I hop off. The stewards are taking a few minutes to review the video. Speedy holds Saitensohn. I duck under his chest, unbuckle the overgirth. I reach up, push up the flap of the saddle, push up on the saddle's billet so I can unbuckle the undergirth. Charley takes a sidestep. He staggers. He's going to fall down! Speedy rushes to his other side, pushes against him, helping him stay up. Charley's chest is heaving in and out. What have I done? He's given me everything. Everything. I pull the saddle off. "Walk him around a circle," I say. "Get him walking." He breathes in and out, in and out, walks. His lungs fill with air. He lightens. He starts to walk normally. We're waiting. Listening. Hoping. James is standing by his horse. If only that damn Morgan had come on time. Then, I could have driven up in a relaxed manner. Charley could have driven up in a relaxed manner! Charley had no time to relax after the drive. We had to tack him right up and rush him to the paddock. If Morgan had been on time, if I could've been relaxed, if Charley hadn't been thrown all around in the back of that fucking van rushing to get here on time—all that was worth, one length, two lengths, three, four or five lengths. Charley had to overcome all these obstacles that I should've taken care of. The stewards take another minute. They are looking at the video. It is a "photo finish." Then I hear it:

The winner, Russia, in the well-known white colors with a broad green horizontal stripe of Augustin Stable, the international powerhouse of the Strawbridge family. Russia, a seven-year-old grandson of Seattle Slew. That's Seattle Slew, trained by my family's great friend, Billy Turner, and the only undefeated horse to ever win the Triple Crown. Seattle Slew—multiple Grade I stakes winner. One of the greatest horses in racing history.

Saitensohn, son of Monsun, second.

Yours truly,
Patrick

P.S. Bill for the month is enclosed. Expenses for Morgan will be the last. They include the shipping up and back.

May 14

OK, just put letter in the mail to Winky and John. And this is more: after the race, back at the van washing off Charley: Speedy says, "You miss-judged the finish." Tom: all he says: "So, what happened out there?" I have had this incredible race, and that's all he says. ("So, what happened out there"—it is familiar, but in a different setting. I can't quite retrieve it. Then I have it: on returning to the huddle decades ago, if one of us missed his pass, those would be his words.)

I have seen myself getting a little meaner, tougher, more competitive. After that remark of Tom's, when his horse ran in the next race—that's Motel Affair who he put me on to gallop and settle down every single morning all winter and all spring, and who I've schooled many times, and schooled going *fast*—I actually did not want him to win. This is not an attractive trait. I'd better watch out for it.

I hike back to the van and Speedy has told Ansley that I misjudged the finish. She says maybe that is what Tom is talking about. "Anyway," she says, "when has Tom ever given anyone a compliment."

Well, my Aunt Dot, Mikey's widow, jogged up to me, grabbed both my hands, looked me in the eye and said, "That was a hell of a race, Patrick. You rode one hell of a good race. You would've won it if you hadn't had all those vanning problems. I'll call you in a few days about getting a van." Billy Meister, Mr. Tough Guy, put his hands up with two inches between them, showing me how much I lost by, and sent me positive vibes. Paddy Neilson and Johnny Fisher, both the top amateur riders of their time, congratulated me, complimenting me on my tactics and the improvement of Saitensohn's manners. And all Tom said was, "What happened out there?"

The important thing: I know that for me, and for this horse, we did something amazing. We pushed ourselves past our potential. We operated at 110 percent, 125 percent. Jumping several of the early hurdles with both hands on one rein! We excelled. We soared, and for this, I am happy. Positive. And though when living through the above I was irritated and shocked that anyone would say I misjudged the finish, I do at this moment realize and admit that I did stop my all-out finishing drive for a split second when out of my peripheral vision I saw the tall narrow post to my left, just the type that usually has a wire strung from it over the course to a pole on the other side. We still had another twenty yards to go and I had to pick it back up. Guilt, or is it shame? It is both, guilt in letting Saitensohn down after he carried an intolerable weight of 177 pounds around a three-mile course that was soggy in places. And so much *shame* that I can barely make my hand trace these letters across this page, and about this topic I cannot write another word, except to say that I suddenly had a flashback: I see Pop sitting in our living room one fall Sunday afternoon with Mom and a group of friends. I'm eight years old and we're preparing to go to Ireland, to take the great Neji to Ireland to train and to run so he can get away from the impossibly heavy weights the handicappers are giving him in America. My sister Sue Sue, Mom, Pop and I are going to spend the winter in Ireland. I see tears dripping from Pop's face. He's describing Neji's last race a few weeks earlier when he had to carry high weight of 170. Pop describes how he got to the front going down the long stretch at Belmont Park and he eased up a touch, not wanting to overstrain Neji, and another horse caught them at the wire. Neji was beat. Pop placed all the blame on himself. He got up and left the room. I get up and leave this room.

A Good School
Over Hurdles

January 6
Wink,

I had finished having a great Saturday hunt on Riderwood. I had rubbed him down, turned him out, and was preparing to ride Charley. In came Ansley's car. Out stepped Paddy—straight from a bus back from New York, where he is doing his residency in pediatric dentistry. I looked down the barn aisleway, and spied him walking towards the house.

"Paddy!" I yelled out.

"Hey dad!"

"Get your boots on."

"I got'em on. Be right there."

I tacked up Saitensohn and Warfield. Out Paddy came. It was getting late, and the sun was low. We hopped on and headed out.

We popped over a few logs. Crossed Hess Road. Over some bigger logs. Over a three-and-a-half foot post-and-rail. Over a triple log. I was in front, and Charley wanted to go, and the hill and field ahead of us was vast and beckoning and I dropped his head, and we took off. I eased him up, and we galloped into a double-log with a rail on top, going into the woods—sailed over it. I turned around. Paddy was right behind us. "Dad, did you do that on purpose? Were you going that fast on purpose?" On we jogged, over a log, then out of the woods and over a tight-fence. Saitensohn was getting older, even though he didn't act it, and I'd been working on slowing him down all fall, popping him over timber fences, preparing him to run in the longer and thus slower timber races in the spring.

We slowed, walked through the bottom, talked. Jogged up along a long hedgerow. Paddy went to the front. Over a series of big logs at a trot. Walked along a corn field, talking. Over to the Whitings. Pete, tall, vigorous, from Maine and a Chesapeake Bay guide, came out. Warfield and Saitensohn relaxed and we asked about Pete's sons. Pete stuck a hundred dollar bill in my pocket and told me to drop off three inscribed copies of *Racing My Father*. (The book sells for $24.) He'd heard "great things" about it.

We swung down across Hutchins Mill Road. I was preparing to do the loop I used to do with Paddy as a boy on Nappy. We really should start heading back on this loop now. . . . We came to a fork in the path in the woods, and to the right was home, and to the left . . . that would take us over to the Atlanta Hall. It was getting dark.

"Dad, which one would take us to Tom's?"

"Well, that one," I point to the left, "but it's getting late."

Pad's in front and he takes a left, jogs down a steep slope, under a low hanging tree limb. An old coop is coming up. We have to duck awkwardly under the limb and then goose our horses, heading for the three-foot coop; they respond with more acceleration than we had intended, and we both pick up speed, stand off, sail over, and land galloping right along, laughing.

We head for the broad, sandy crossing of the Little Gunpowder. Jog across "The Meadow," (site of the painting by Frank Voss), jog up along the edge of a cornfield to the lawn and right up to the kitchen door of the house. Mimi opens the door, walks out onto the steps . We've just missed Tom and daughter Elizabeth. They've driven off. Mimi laughs and rolls her eyes—they are two of a kind and she has no idea of where they've gone. "Would you like some port?" she asks.

"No thanks, that's all right," is my Puritanical knee-jerk reaction.

"Da-ad."

I look over at Pad. "O.K., that'd be nice."

Mimi goes in, comes out a minute later, with two crystal glasses of the nicest tasting port you've ever had sitting on a horse. It's smooth and sweet. We finish it off in two or three swallows, each going down with a warming-expanding glow. "Like another?" she asks.

Charley and Warfield are becoming impatient. They're

jigging around, stirring up the pea gravel on the driveway. "No thanks," I laugh. Mimi takes our glasses.

It's darkening. I see Tom's three hurdles, green and inviting, set up in the "Finish Line Field."

We head up the driveway toward the indoor track, Paddy repeatedly asking me what I am doing.

Then we are in the field. I canter into a hurdle with Paddy following five lengths behind. I canter over another hurdle, giving him a lead again. I pull up, think that's it for Pad and Warfield. He gallops past us into the hurdle at the top of the field, long hold on the reins, down low, sitting still, squeezing his legs, Warfield taking those long strides. They meet it just right and sail over—that's *high over* and not *brushing through*—the entire four-foot hurdle.

OK, that's enough for Warfield. I tell Pad to be our audience. Charley and I jog down to the first hurdle. Charley is acting spooky, looking at this, looking at that. He gallops calmly toward the first hurdle, we're inside the wings, and he brushes through the top portion of the hurdle, lands, and picks up the speed. I am amazed that after jumping all these coops and logs and "timber" fences, he immediately knows these are "hurdles" and does not waste any energy going high over them, as many horses would do, but brushes low through the brush. Calm, and galloping "in hand," he heads into the second hurdle. Up and over. I let the reins out a notch, he opens up his stride, we near the third hurdle, I give him some encouragement; we rocket over. That's it for debating whether he'll run over hurdles or timber in the spring. Hurdles it will be.

I ease up, circle around, preparing to canter over to Pad and Warfield but where the hell are they? What are they doing? Then I see them. They're at the bottom of the hill; they're heading up the hill; they're picking up speed. Paddy hasn't listened to me. They're picking up speed and Pad is down low, riding with a long hold and Warfield doesn't slow approaching the hurdle; they're inside the wings and Warfield stands off a little too far, jumping too high. They land, picking up speed, and I hold my breath. Paddy steadies Warfield, leans back against him, gets him under control and they fly over the second hurdle, brushing through the top few inches. They land and Warfield tries to take off but Paddy leans back against him again. They gallop into the last, Paddy sitting still, looking exactly like his grandfather in the hundreds of photos we have, Warfield's stride fully extended. Warfield gets in just right, hurdles fast and efficiently through the top "brush" like a seasoned hurdle horse.

I attempt to chew Paddy out for doing this but my heart isn't in it and Paddy is grinning and laughing, not paying any attention to my scolding, and Warfield is jigging and tossing his head, which is causing Saitensohn to dance around. We walk and jog them home in the dark, laughing and philosophizing.

In the barn, we rub them down, throw on their blankets. Feed, hay and water our three—Riderwood, Saitensohn, Warfield—in their stalls. We feed and hay The Wild Bunch out in their paddock. Inside, Paddy and I build a big fire in the fireplace, and sit down with a couple of Smithwick's Ales, some cheese and crackers.

Cheers,
Patrick

February 14
Sidney died today, Valentine's Day—perfect timing for the lady's man

Galloping on the Hunter Trials is not the same, though I see Diamond Jim is back in his paddock. What was it, one or two years ago, there'd been a family disagreement over who exactly owned and could best care for Jim. Jim had been taken off the farm. One week later, two war veterans in mufti went out on a mission. A gray and yellow six-horse van was seen pulling up outside a paddock miles away from Dunmore. The driver, a large man in a floppy Irish cap, stepped out, called a big gray horse, loaded him up, and returned him to his rightful owner, who, in his late-eighties, nattily dressed and wearing a full Irish cap, suffering from Alzheimer's but fully aware of what was happening at the moment, was sitting in the cab. No one interfered.

Late February

It's an extremely cold Sunday afternoon, the sky white with snow, two and three-foot drifts making our driveway impassable, no cars at all on Manor Road—a perfect day for writing. I'm in my barn/writing room. Ansley is by the fire in the house. Suddenly, there is a huge form peering through the window panes of my door, the form is knocking on the door, and the face is grinning, the door opens, a blast of cold air shoots through the room and there is Dickie stamping his feet and brushing the snow off his coat, taking off his Irish wool cap and slapping it against his side. He steps into the room. "Hi Pat," he says, as if this is a perfectly normal day to be visiting. He has a battered leather briefcase under his arm. I welcome him in, ask how he got here. He gives me that look of his, as if I've just gone off my rocker. "Walked," he says. "I was over at Sidney's checking on the horses, and thought I'd walk over." I look out the window, and there are his tracks, crossing the back field. He sits on the hard wooden chair that looks too small for him. Asks how my writing is going, what I'm working on, have I heard from Andrew. Then he starts talking about Ann Wolf, his girl friend of decades ago, back in the Broad Brush days.

Looking into my eyes, leaning toward me, three feet away, he says with intensity, "Pat, it was a day like this. Exactly like this. They closed the track at Pimlico. Broad Brush was jumping out of his skin. I had to get a work in, a strong work. He was entered in a stake in a week . . ." He lashed a set of chains on his van's back tires, loaded up his "pony" for him to ride, then Broad Brush, drove out to Strathmore, his family's farm, through the blizzard, and Ann breezed Broad Brush through two feet of snow up the long steep hill off Jarrettsville Pike, the one we used to ski down. "Two times, Pat. Two times, and that's what made his career."

He rummages through the briefcase. Pulls out a notebook. Pulls out a pack of color photographs. There is clear, neat handwriting in the notebook; it is not Dickie's. I flip through a few pages describing the day. "That's Ann's journal. She always wanted to do a book on Broad Brush, and it would begin with this day." He is crying now. Dickie Small—a man who could out-cuss and out-fight, and back in the day, out-drink the toughest stevedore on the docks, a man who turned down the opportunity to be a star on the Army's pentathlon team and instead volunteered to jump out of C-130s at 15,000 feet and land in the Viet Cong infested jungle of Vietnam—is in my writing room, looking at these photographs, and tears are dripping off his face. It is an anniversary of some sort. Something has brought all this back. Could it be this storm? He is thinking of Ann. He wonders if I could do a little book on her and Broad Brush. "Leave me out," he says. "It could be an inspirational book. Maybe for kids. You know, *The Little Engine That Could.*"

He hands me a photo of a grinning Ann, bundled in wool scarf, wool hat and heavy ski parka, circling Broad Brush at the top of the hill. "Ann let him run, hard, fast, two times up that long hill, and that's what made his career Pat. It all started that day." That work set Broad Brush up perfectly for his next race, and that race for the one after, and on they went criss-crossing the country and winning races, and then he isn't talking about Broad Brush. He is talking about Ann—how he might not have been as attentive as he could have been, he was so focused on the horse—it is then I realize she is no longer with us, and the emotion in his eyes, his wishing he could go back and be more attentive, his tears, his feeling for her—I later learned she had taken her life—is beautiful to see.

Win of a Lifetime

April 6
Dear John and Winky,

We have our own van now. Speedy had been telling me we needed a van. Dot had seen what had happened at Willowdale, and she flat out gave me her old 1979 six-horse box van. An Imperatore. It is like something out of *Star Wars*: the Millennium Falcon. Ansley drove me down to Middleburg to pick it up at Dot's. Driving it back, I felt like I was driving a barn. It has ten forward gears, a loud engine, a smallish cab—and in the back six stalls and more space than we'll ever need.

As soon as we got it to the farm, Speedy was there. I complained about having to press so hard on the brakes. Speedy climbed up into the high cab, pressed down on the brakes. "Why, you lucky you made it home from Virginia. You lucky you didn't run over some nice little old lady at a stop light. Ain't you got no sense at all. . . ." We opened the hood. He pulled the brake fluid stick out, cleaned it off on a rag, stuck it back in and pulled it out. "Woo-ey, you's a lucky man," he said, holding it up in the sunlight. Right at the bottom, the bottom one tenth of the dipper, there was a slight darkening. "OK, you got's ta go to the auto store and gets some brake fluid before we drive this thing one more foot." We had the van parked going up the hill to the barn, and he kept saying he smelled gasoline. He walked around the van, sniffing, struggled to get under the cab, and discovered a small leak near the top of the auxiliary gas tank. The tires needed air, badly. It needed radiator fluid. There was a leak in the roof just behind the cab, and the dripping water had created a rotten spot in the stall right behind the driver—that would be our space for storing all our "traps." The cumbersome and heavy ramp didn't work right. He knew how to fix that. Also, driving up, I'd been on a country road, had pulled over so I could get out, stretch my legs, "water the chickens," and take a break from the roaring engine, then climbed back in, revved the engine, moved forward in first and heard a terrible crunching noise. I had run the top of the trailer into a thick low-hanging branch of an oak and smashed the corner in, breaking a top light and ripping out an electric wire.

Speedy made some calls. We left the van off at a friend of his, whose father had worked for Pop and Mikey all of his life. In one week, he fixed it up for practically nothing; we drove it back to the farm and Speedy outfitted it for our first trip. He got a big plastic barrel, tied it tight in the storage stall. Day of the race, we'd fill it with water. Speedy liked being self-sufficient. He didn't want to have to trudge half a mile to an old dry-rotted hose lying in a puddle by a barn to wash the horse off after the race and to get a bucket or two of drinking water. The front and back stalls had been divided into thirds, so you could fit six horses. We took out one of the 150-pound stall dividers in the front, one in the back, manhandled them off the van, and placed the remaining dividers in the middle so we had two spacious stalls in front, two in the back.

Speedy got some paint remover and old-fashioned stencils out of the back of his car. He took the name of Dot's racing stable, Sunny Bank Farm, off the doors. With his stencils, he painted in A. P. Smithwick Stables as neat as can be.

By the end of the week, Speedy had a wall box in the van filled with bandages, needles, tongue ties, medicines, anything we might need. We threw a hay net in the back, which we'd hang up on the way home after the race. He swept all the old hay, straw and manure out, made me buy expensive bales of sawdust. He spread the clean, fresh-smelling, fluffy wooden curly-cues neatly in both rear stalls.

Early Saturday morning, Speedy was in the barn. As always, he was half an hour early. I moved the huge van so that it was at the top of the driveway alongside the bank. It took both of us to pull out the massive, heavy ramp.

Something was on my mind. I was off a beat. I was missing

this or that: not backing the van up just right the first time, forgetting the best way to pull the ramp out, not tying the sideboards as Speedy insisted they be tied.

Nevertheless, all was going smoothly. After moving the van to Speedy's preferred loading site, I left the engine running, as he insisted. All eight cylinders were firing in a good consistent rhythm. Charley strode up the ramp as if he couldn't wait to see his new set up. Speedy tied him up, attaching the chain snaps to the halter's circular metal fittings high up Charley's cheeks. There was a thick, heavy metal bar we could drop into slots so that it would run across the front of the two stalls, just in front of Charley's shoulders. "No! You crazy! Charley don't need that thing."

I jumped in the passenger seat, Speedy got behind the wheel and off we went for a two-hour drive to Virginia.

Speedy was in his element. Down the Jarrettsville Pike we went, the engine roaring even though we were just going forty-five miles per hour. He was telling me about his patents. He holds several—one for a long, specially designed foam pad with Velcro straps to wrap around a horse's shins before a timber race—and was telling me he was working on another one. Would I help him with the paper work involved in getting the patent. Yet, when I asked what the patent was: "I ain't no dummy. I ain't goin'ta tell you and have you steal the idea. I'll get my lawyer to do it. My lawsuit lawyer—the same one who's suing the foot doctor for putting the steel plates in my foot all wrong." Across the Loch Raven Bridge, onto Dulaney Valley Road, and onto the Baltimore Beltway, new, modern, streamlined cars—hybrids, small and compact—and boxy, top-heavy SUVs zipping by us on either side, as we gradually picked up speed. Around the Beltway, past The Talmudical Academy in Pikesville up on the left, where I was no longer teaching, then onto Interstate 95. We were out of a different time period. We were two generations earlier, the engine constantly thrumming faster and louder, growling and booming as if we needed to shift up another gear, and Speedy now telling stories about Mikey that pulsed with his respect for Mikey's horsemanship, his admiration of and amazement at how Mikey conducted his love life, and his awe at Mikey's energy and stoicism—never giving in to the extreme and rare form of Parkinson's, riding and training and living his life to the fullest right down to the last minute. Then, we segued to Speedy's sex life.

I'd never heard such stories. They made anything from *Tropic of Cancer*, from *Tropic of Capricorn*, from *Sexus*, *Nexus*, or *Plexus*—a few of Henry Miller's free-form biographical novels of love, lust, sex and ambition—seem tame, prudish. On and on he went. I tried to stop him a couple of times, but he did have me laughing, and he couldn't stop. He told me about putting it to women having very recognizable Social Register names, who are now aging millionairesses but were then young and dashing heiresses to robber baron fortunes, up on trunks in tack rooms in the late afternoons at the farm, down in the wood shavings in the back of this very van at hunt teas; he told of rolling around with galloping girls in the hay loft in the early mornings, driving home late at night from hunt meets with a star girl jockey in the back of a van watching the nervous stakes horse, pulling off onto a country road, laying blankets out in the dewy grass, listening to the stakes horse that Mikey was so worried about sleepily munching hay and shifting his weight from one front foot to the other while he and the star girl jockey enjoyed themselves under the stars. He related a rollicking, incredible stretcher about going to it with three at one time at the Elkridge Harford Club the night he had his band there for a big birthday party—the same night I'd gotten into a fight and he'd pulled the attacker, who was yelling as he pounded me, "You're not like your father! You're not like your father!" off me—and knew the bartender whom he ordered to spike all the drinks of the wildest, best-looking women . . . on and on. I was having *so much* fun, as he'd say, and was believing a tenth of it, and was chuckling, my feet crossed, up on the dashboard, our dashboard—unlike in our cars where I caught hell for doing this, I could put my feet there all I wanted!—but I did have one distraction, one needling thought pattern that had thrown me off earlier when packing.

I was still working at my part-time jobs. My steadiest job and best income was from working, now part-time, in the development office at Gilman, writing stories about inspiring alumni, faculty members, and teachers. I was teaching college courses in writing at Hopkins and Goucher, making good cash from The Wild Bunch, and finishing a final draft of my second memoir. But Ansley wanted benefits. And my main aim at Gilman for the past two years had been to segue out of the development office and into a full-time teaching spot. Such a spot was now open for next fall. I was interviewing for it. Even though I was an alumnus, even though I had written a successful history of the school, even though I had directed the public relations and the publications of the school through its centennial and had gotten the school an incredible amount of good press, they were not giving me any breaks! They wanted to know if I could coach—listen to this: they asked (Don't you think they knew the answer?) if I had any experience coaching *water polo*. And the head of the Upper School— who never did pay me for teaching a month of classes for a faculty member on maternity leave—kept looking at me strangely, asking about my riding: "Isn't that dangerous? How do you find the time to do it?" In the heat of the interview, not thinking clearly, acting as if I were talking to a new friend at the local pub, I explained to her how time consuming it was: the training of myself, the training of the horses, the vanning to the races, and finally, the riding of the races. Then, the new headmaster—on whom I'd just written a sparkling-positive profile for the alumni magazine—asked me about my writing. Like a dummy, I took the bait. I told him that I wrote early in the mornings and on the weekends, that I was finishing another book. I blabbed on, thinking this was good stuff—here I was, a writer, different from the other English teachers. Students could follow the next book through the whole publishing process. The new head stared at me in bewilderment. It wasn't until I was driving home that I realized he was worried about these other interests of mine: writing and riding. He was thinking there was no way I'd be able to devote myself one hundred and twenty-five percent, in the Gilman teacher/coach/ mentor model—ironically, that same model that had been a major theme in my history of Gilman—to my students. Nevertheless, I thought, if I pushed, really hard, I should be able to get this teaching position, and as we got off Interstate 95, roared and bounced onto the D.C. Beltway, I knew that if I got it, this would all have to come to an end.

No more galloping at Pimlico for Dickie in the mornings. I'd have to be at Gilman at 7:45 sharp. The rush hour traffic was terrible now; I'd have to leave the farm at 6:50. I'd be coaching in the afternoons until 5:30. And then, the commute home at that time of day would take an hour or even longer. In the winter, I wouldn't have time to exercise the horses before it was dark.

No more race-riding on the weekends. No more van trips with Speedy.

We stopped on the shoulder of the D.C. Beltway to give Charley a shot of Lasix. Sleek tractor-trailers streaked by just a few feet away from us. Speedy climbed up into the back of the van, pulled out his needle, found the vein, and gave Charley a shot of Lasix—an over-used medication in racing, a diuretic, that prevents internal bleeding of race horses—exactly two hours before post time. Speedy could give a shot better than any trainer, doctor or nurse. In his twenties, he'd been a nurse for a few years.

Here Charley was strong and wild and fit as his German ancestors, on the side of the Washington, D.C. Beltway of all places to be in this world, with this 21st century rushing past us.

Standing by the doors to the trailer, the scent of the sawdust and hay and droppings in my nostrils, looking up at Charley looking down at me, I thought: I love this. It was like being back working on the water, on a skipjack, a "dredgeboat," on the Chesapeake Bay, being in a different time period, a throwback to an earlier century, being with Speedy and with Charley and with our great old green Millennium Falcon heading down to Virginia to cut Charley loose!

We arrive at the hunt meet late. A flat race is underway. Our race is coming up. Speedy parks up on a knoll overlooking the course. I hop out, head for the paddock and the stewards table. An older official approaches me, shakes my hand vigorously, welcomes me to the races, shows me where to check in with the stewards, the clerk of scales, the vet. "We always like it when a Smithwick van rolls in," he says. "We know you didn't come all the way down here for a school."

I make the rounds, look at my watch. I don't have time to walk the course but I'm feeling good, I'm feeling confident, I'm feeling like I'm where I'm supposed to be. I'm one hundred percent here, in the moment, and am not thinking of Gilman School or anything else. I see Sebastian Cromwell walking by in boots and britches. Good Lord, he's lost that winter weight yet again and has given up on retiring; he must have found one more good horse to ride. "Hey Sebastian," I say, and shake his hand. I point to the course below us. "Can you tell me how the hurdle course goes?"

He takes the cigarette out of his mouth, holding it the European way with two fingers and a thumb. "Don't you worry about where the course goes, Young-blood. You just follow me. I'll be in front the entire way." He throws down the cigarette and walks off. "Young-blood"—mimicking Mikey again.

Back at the van, Speedy is wiping the dust off Charley's face, rhythmically running the rub rag down his neck, humming, singing a soothing spiritual. I repeat what Sebastian said. Speedy continues humming and rubbing. When I finish, he stops. Stops rubbing, stops singing. Looks me in the eye. "You let that asshole beat Charley in this race, and you're walking home. You won't be coming back in the van with Charley and me."

Hmmm.

I take Charley off the van—always a tricky proposition. We have a sheepskin loading rug running down the length of the steep ramp. It's slippery under leather soles—I'm wearing my racing boots—but good for the aluminum shoes Charley is wearing. We jog down the ramp together. I hand the shank to Speedy. Charley is pulling him this way and that, as they start to head over. Speedy's limping badly. It's a half-mile walk.

Pretty girls are driving around in golf carts, picking up riders with their tack and delivering them to the paddock. One zips by. Speedy waves hello. Good Lord, it's being driven by one of his old mentees at Mikey's. She waves and calls out, "Speedy!" as she pulls up in front of me. I hand her my tack, but don't get in. I tell her to bring Speedy and my tack to the paddock. I jog up to Speedy, take Charley. The girl zooms over, picks Speedy up. He climbs in, all smiles. I walk the jigging Charley to the paddock, and then around the paddock a few times. Speedy's there when I arrive and has found a Virginia trainer we know, to help tack up. It's Timmy, the brother of my great, late, friend, Mike White. He's upbeat, positive. This is like old times with Mike. I hand the shank to Speedy. Speedy gives the shank a crisp snatch. "Charley," Speedy growls in a low voice. "Charley." Charley immediately starts to behave. Timmy and I tack him up.

Timmy gives me a leg up. "Win this one for Mike," he says. I'm in the tack. My legs are around Charley. My hands are on the reins. I get both feet in the stirrups and a finger through the yoke. Speedy walks Charley forward, his right hand on the shank that is snapped to the bit, his left on his cane. He grimaces as he takes a misstep. I stand up in the stirrups. They feel the right length. I shift my weight from the right stirrup to the left, back and forth. The saddle is positioned just right. I sit down. "OK, you can turn him loose."

"You all set race-rider?"

"I'm set."

"See you in the winner's circle."

I ride out onto the course, and then along a rail with the spectators drinking and calling out, some kids playing Frisbee, some lacrosse, long tables set up with bottles of champagne and all kinds of hors d'oeuvres, a vintage Rolls Royce with its trunk open, and then we trot away, over towards the start, "far from the madding crowd." Charley is calmer than usual. We line up, but then the damn starter tries to back us up—and there the woods are right behind us. I remain loose and relaxed in the saddle, knowing that any little thing could set Charley off and we'd be backing out of control into the trees. The riders—all but Sebastian—are yelling at each other and the starter. I remain quiet, my eyes on Sebastian. The starter drops the flag, Sebastian shoots off, and I let Charley tuck in behind him. Sebastian is tippy-toeing right along. We gallop into the first hurdle, meet it perfectly, brush through it, gaining a couple of lengths on Sebastian who flies down the hill and into the next.

I can feel three or four coming up behind me. I stay relaxed on Charley, riding with a long hold, talking to him. "Wo-a Charley, that-a-boy Charley," and the foursome go bumping and yelling and grinding past us, shooting down the steep hill and over the hurdle, a couple of them jumping it too deeply, pieces of brush shooting into the air.

They catch Sebastian and fly over the next four hurdles, around to the start, and up through the stretch, past what would be the finish the next time around. Charley has never jumped better. We are meeting them just right, and hurdling them, gaining ground on those in front with every hurdle. I keep him relaxed galloping down the steep hill again, the going deep in the bottom. They fly through the deep bottom, divots and clumps of turf and mud shooting up all around them. Then comes the last long hill—with the good firm going.

For a few seconds, back five lengths from the pack, seven

lengths from Sebastian, I have a sinking feeling, thinking we'd let them get too far ahead of us and now it's too late to do anything about it. But heading up the gradual hill, on the firm going that Charley prefers, we reel them in. Coming up on the outside of the foursome, I send Charley into the hurdle. We stand off, gaining a couple of lengths on both Sebastian in front and the foursome in a pack to our inside. We pass the pack, tuck in behind Sebastian. Rounding the last turn, turning to the left, keeping our momentum, coming up on Sebastian's outside, we jump the second-to-the-last three lengths off the lead.

We land and I let Charley go. We gallop up alongside Sebastian. He looks over at me with a shocked expression. Another horse, a gray, is making a move and is coming up on my outside. I squeeze with my legs, letting Charley pick up speed, wanting to drag this other horse into the hurdle. He drops back a stride, just off our hocks. We head into the last head-and-head with Sebastian on our left, the other to our right, a stride behind, not a good place to be. I want to get the hell away from him in case he turns ass-over-tin-cups. I whack Charley once heading into the hurdle, whack him as we take off—we jet over it—land running full tilt. Sebastian gets down low and starts doing his imitation of the way a weak English jockey rides a finish—which is by flinging his arms and reins forward on each stride while bobbing up and down with his ass too far back and his legs going back and forth, scrubbing the horse's sides, while beneath him the horse is trying to maintain his balance and speed. I stay low and steady, holding Charley together. I'm in my tuck, pushing with each stride, a part of Charley, in synchronization with his smooth, flowing movement, each stride long and strong, my body and mind, his body and mind, one now, one flying-racing-entity forged by thousands of hours of teamwork as we go all out in one final sprint, increasing the distance between us and Sebastian with each stride—his horse's head at Charley's neck, his horse's head at Charley's shoulder, his horse's head at my foot, at Charley's rump, and then Sebastian and his horse are out of our peripheral vision. I ride strong and steady through the finish, past the pole.

Pulling Charley up, I feel it all come together. It is one of the most gratifying moments of my life. All the work and trust and effort and planning and patience has paid off. I pat Charley on one side of his neck, switch hands, pat him on the other. He had been in control, saving his energy and speed in the early part. He hadn't insisted on increasing the length of his stride and surging into every fence. He had jumped every fence well. He had done everything I asked of him. Yes, I love him.

Speedy is waiting at the winner's circle. He is joking and patting Charley and posing for pictures. After the trophy presentation, choking up a bit, I tell Speedy "I wish Mikey'd been here."

"He *is*, Patrick!" It has power, and I love it, the way, just once in a blue moon, he says *Patrick*. "Mikey is here *now*, Patrick. Don't you know it? Can't you feel it? It's *Mikey Power*."

Then, for a second, my thoughts drift to my father and riding a race much like this thirty-five years ago on a horse called Wild Amber, at Saratoga. A current of hot-emotion surges through my body. I wish Pop was there with us, and I imagine how he would congratulate me on the training of the horse, on the settling him down, and on the using my hands—*wait till I tell Janon*—and getting him to relax in the race, riding with a deep seat and a long hold, catching the front-runner and passing him, riding strong and steadily without any wasted energy to the wire.

"Your *daddy's* here too," Speedy suddenly asserts, looking me in the eye. "Your daddy's here too, just as real, just as powerful as the day you was just a kid and won on Wild Amber at Saratoga."

How does he know? How does he know what I'm thinking? How the hell does he remember that day?

"I bet on you that day. I knew your daddy didn't come all the way to Saratoga to finish second with that horse. And you didn't neither. Wild Amber! You caught'em at the last fence and then *took off* down the stretch!"

I reach for the shank, preparing to walk Charley back to the van. "What'chu doing?" Speedy asks, the pitch of his voice rising high.

"I'm walking Charley back."

"No you *ain't*. This is *my stake horse* and I'll be walking him back. Hand me that cane." He points to the cane lying across my tack. I jog over, pick it up, hand it to him.

"See you at the van," and off he goes, using the cane with one hand, holding the shank with the other, leaning into Charley's shoulder, Mikey disciples descending on him and Charley until he is walking along with a pack of admiring young men and women, and talking non-stop.

I hear a woman's voice, "Patrick, Patrick." It's my Aunt Dot.

She approaches with a big smile. "That horse's legs are beautiful. It's amazing. You can't even tell he'd ever bowed."

"They're looking good aren't they. We can thank Speedy for that."

"Patrick." She looks me in the eye—what was she, 80 by now, still going to all these hunt meets, getting up at 4:30 every morning to work on her stable of race horses and then her 2,500 acre farm. "Patrick, that horse was completely different. He galloped around there like an old hunter before you asked him to run. You've done a wonderful job on him."

"Thanks Dot, thanks, that means a lot to me." Dot's a bit stiff sometimes, not the warmest, most cuddly aunt. Without even thinking, I give her a big kiss and a hug. I take a few steps, stop, turn around, "Dot, thanks for the van! It made all the difference today!"

"Good, good. Keep riding, Patrick. Keep riding."

At the van, I see Forrest Boyce—with whom I'd galloped many a horse for Dickie at Pimlico. She's riding races now, and winning them, a hot shot on the Maryland tracks. At Pimlico in the early mornings, I am an anomaly: the grooms and riders regard me as a curiosity, an old-timer, past his prime, a friend of Dickie's there to make a few bucks galloping horses, and furthermore, a little crazy—getting on wild, rearing and bucking two-year-olds, busting them out of the gate, whipping and driving them down the stretch, when there are gray hairs poking out of the ear flaps of my helmet. Forrest walks over, her face glowing, gives me a nice kiss and congratulates me on the win and my tactics. "I'll be telling Dickie about this," she sings out. "Maybe you can lose a few more pounds and ride some of ours on the flat."

"No, he ain't going to be getting busted up riding no flat races," Speedy says, holding Charley. "And he'd better get the hell over here, stop kissing the girl jockeys before I tell Angie, and hold this horse while I give him a rub."

I take the shank. Speedy has half a dozen groupies around him. He's rubbing Charley like he's trying to peel the skin off him. The corners of the rub rag snap and pop. Charley shifts his weight from one foot to the other, bends his back one way then the other, away from Speedy's strong arm. His coat becomes brighter and brighter. It glows. Dapples are popping up on his rump.

There is not one nick or cut on him.

The groupies drift away. Suddenly my red BMW M-3 owner of The Wild Bunch is there. Dressed like a Middleburg socialite in a long, flowing skirt and a loose silk blouse, she's crying. Tears are running down her face. She's hugging Speedy. She's hugging me. She's hugging Charley. "Beautiful race, Charley, beautiful race." She jogs to her bright red car, returns. "I'm late. I'm late with this," she says, handing me a clump of cash. Six one hundred-dollar bills. Then, she's gone—the best owner of boarders I've ever had.

There Speedy and I are, up on the knoll, overlooking the course, with Charley. The sun is setting. We laugh, look at each other. I peel off three one-hundred dollar bills, hand them to Speedy.

Speedy folds the bills, sticks them in the chest pocket of his overalls, looks at me. "Where we going next?"

Monday morning at Pimlico, I'm at the starting gate on a two-year-old of Dickie's. You never feel more secure on a horse in or near the gate than when Dickie was there. I'm kicking and pushing this thick-necked colt, tapping him with my stick. He's got his head inside the gate but is bracing his front legs, refusing to more forward. Last time we were at the gate, he'd reared with Justine and had almost gone over backwards. I'm running the bit back and forth through his mouth, turning his head side to side. Dickie, standing directly behind me, joking with his buddies on the gate crew, locks his hand with the hand of a twenty-five-year-old, and—not taking a breath or even breaking the line of his conversation—effortlessly lifts the rump of the colt up off the ground so that this misbehaving adolescent finds himself neatly stuffed into the stall. José is in the slot on my left. Forrest and Justine are on my right. We're all in now. Members of the gate crew are climbing around the stalls, crouching over us, helping us settle our horses, then ducking out, under the back doors, tight against our the rumps of our colts and fillies.

"OK, Pat?" Dickie asks. "OK, Forrest?" "Justine, you ready?" "Yes," and "Looking good," and "We're ready," are called out, each of us crouched forward, looking up. These girls are going to be competitive. Get left at the gate—and guess what, you'll be galloping the whole way around the track to the wire, three-quarters of a mile, with dirt and grit blasting back into your mouth and eyes, shooting into your two-year-old's face, shocking him so you have to push harder. José might steady his horse, let you catch up. Not so with these girls! It'll be all out. You want to come out on top, or at least even.

I love the gate. I've always loved the gate. The way you hold a horse together coming out of the gate is much the way you hold a horse together going into a fence. Ready. Ready for the bell to ring and the doors to fly open and the possibility your two-year-old might balk, might spook at the banging doors, the possibility the filly beside you might try to cross over in front of you, or smack right into you. Ready ... Ready ... Legs relaxed and yet squeezing. Sitting slightly forward ...

The bell goes off, there's a whamming-clacking sound as the doors burst open. We're growling and yelling. We're bumping and accelerating out of the gate, picking up speed, all four of us together, Forrest looking like she might take the lead, José staying steady, and I love it.

I take a deep breath, squeeze with my legs, tap my colt on the shoulder, get him pulling against me, we pick up speed and now we're all four head-and-head, flying past the half-mile pole, headed for the three-eighths pole, and then the turn, where two of us will drop back behind the other two, and this is living in the present, this is riding, and I love it.

At Gilman a few hours later, I tell the head of the English department about the win on Charley. In a few days, I give him a DVD of the race. I tone down my enthusiasm and desire for the English teaching spot. It is noticeable. To get it I'd have to go all out. I don't. That is, I don't go all out, and I don't get the teaching spot.

Yours truly,
Rider/Trainer

Are We Finished?

Excerpt, Training Journal
January 25

Had a glorious day yesterday. Got up early, came out to work in the milking parlor. Chilly. Spent most of time paying bills and counting up money made from a talk I gave at the Roland Park Woman's Club (which I originally counted wrong, shortchanging myself by $100) Packed and mailed a dozen signed copies of *Racing My Father* to readers in Louisiana, Florida, South Carolina, Virginia, Kentucky, California, Washington State, New Mexico, Texas and New Hampshire, plus a box of books to England and another box to Ireland.

Back from the post office. Lots of work with the horses to do. Blustery. Wind picking up. Then, little white flakes, not many, billowing, parachuting, drifting. I'd been down on the whole horse business the night before. Despondent. Low energy. It'd been cold as hell and the ground was frozen. Tough to train on. Riderwood had been a little "off" the past few days; seemed sore in his right shoulder from when that idiot owner-rider jockey had T-boned us going into the last fence last spring. I'd called J.B., told him I was almost out of hay, my hay man said he couldn't make a delivery for a week, and meanwhile a blizzard was on its way. "Let me look into it," J.B. said. I didn't hear back from him.

Speedy rumbles in. Steps out of Mikey's old Subaru wearing his full-body Carhartt, walks towards the barn with a big smile. "How ya doin' sonny-boy? Let's get these horses out!"

I hear a diesel truck pull in the entrance. I groan. Who the hell is that? The pickup lumbers in, goes up the hill towards the top barn entrance, then backs down to the bottom white sliding door to the aisle where Speedy and I are standing. It is loaded with hay. The driver's door opens; we expect a big farmer to step out. J.B., short-legged and bulbous in a puffy down jacket and an Irish cap, climbs down the steps. "I'm in a hurry, A.P. Got to get down to Pimlico. Give me a hand." We unload and stack the bales. J.B. takes off.

Speedy and I call the horses in. Start tacking up. Speedy's talking a mile a minute. Gives me hell for not having the van running. I step outside. It's blowing now and the air is filled with snowflakes. They're no longer parachuting, billowing. They are firing down. They stab at my face. They prick my eyes. I climb up into the cab, crank up the engine, let it run for a minute, then push in the heavy clutch, put it in first gear, rev the old engine one more time and prepare to move to the usual spot for loading.

"No! Leave it right there. More leverage," Speedy calls out. He "knocks off" both horses. We tack up Charley. He fixes the throatlatch—something I'd been meaning to do for months. Pulls it through so the buckle is in the right place. I start to pull out the ramp. He makes me stop, attach a rope shank to the chain as he has told me over and over to do, and he's right, it's much easier to pull out. He's ordering me around. "Get those nails. Get a board. Get a crow bar." Fast, he works *fast*. We nail the top of the rug to a two-by-four, and set the two-by-our on the floor across the doorway, so that the rug won't slide down the ramp when we load and unload.

Speedy loads Charley. I load Riderwood, plop down in driver's seat. He's going to give me a driving lesson. Out the driveway we go. But first, he pulls the red button; we hear a *clankety-clank*. He's put it in low gear. He explains why we need it in low for when we come up the hill on Manor Road and take the left onto the Jarrettsville Pike. "You gots' ta do it *now*, before you gets to the hill. You gots' ta think *ahead* when you driving this old rig. What'd you learn at college? Didn't they teach you anything?" Van running great. Engine purring—no, that's a stretch—engine *roaring* steadily. "I knows this van as well as the back of my ass!" He's right—it climbs up the hill easily and smoothly. On the Pike—I push in the clutch, he pushes the red button down, I let out the clutch, *clankety-clank*, and it's in high gear. Works smoothly. Not what happens when I try to change the axle setting on my own.

At Tom's. Park on the leeward side of the indoor track. Unload. Charley is a handful but goes well. When galloping to the left, counterclockwise, he raises hell every time we pass the open door. Riderwood is whinnying the entire time. Charley switches leads like a Lipizzan. I can't get over it. Every time, as we approach the sharp turn, he clicks into the inside lead, leans in and accelerates. We whip around the turn. Coming out, he straightens, clicks into the outside lead. Around and around. The wind rattling the glass window panes. The snow pecking at the windows, piling up in little rows along the splintered mullions. Pull up. Not blowing.

Fingers are numb. Charley had been pulling and it was cold as hell in there. My circulation is cut off. Can't unbuckle the girth. Can't untie the knot in the reins. All I can do is slide, stiffly, off. "I got him. I got Charley. You warm those hands up."

I stand beside Riderwood in the van. Speedy takes Charley out of Riderwood's sight and Riderwood starts pawing and pushing at me. I stand beside him, put my back against his shoulder, pull my gloves off and stick both hands deep into my pants, a tactic I'd learned as a kid. The feeling returns. I lead Riderwood down the ramp, hop up on him.

Riderwood—after so much worrying about him, after letting it put me in a terrible mood, after waking up worrying—is perfectly sound! A van pulls in. Soon I'm jogging along with trainer Jazz Napravnik in the tack beside me. Cantering with Jazz behind me.

Cool off Riderwood by walking him around the track a few times. Load up. Stop at Royal Farms, Speedy at the wheel. Fill right, passenger tank. Speedy goes into the store to see if any of his buddies are hanging around. I follow, get us each a cup of steaming "black like me" coffee and a blueberry muffin. Hop up behind the steering wheel. The hot coffee and the mealy muffin could not taste better. We have to pull out, to the left, wheel around 300 degrees. Use the lower convex mirrors for first time. He's right, you can see everything up close with them.

Back. Wrestle with ramp. Discuss improving ramp. Unload. In barn, Speedy fixes feed tub Ridewood tore out of the corner of the stall. Takes out unnecessary screw eye. Nails in screw eyes for two water buckets in the shed—something we usually don't need but the stream is frozen solid. Gives me hell for using old flimsy plastic paint buckets. Fixes up runner across corner stall. Hammers and screws in screw eyes and sets two nice runners across end stall. I'm running back and forth getting him snaps and runners. "Are we finished?" he asks.

I pull out Pop's old full-size racing trunk. We clean it out and Speedy gives a talk—"Write it down! Get a pad and write it down like your Daddy used to do. You know, he kept all the records by hand, neat as can be, in a black accounting book. He wrote all the checks. . ."—on what we need. "Are we finished?" he asks.

We cut open feedbags. I have just bought three glistening galvanized steel garbage cans. I start to set them up in the back, on the clay floor of the stall beside the tack room. We're turning this small stall into the feed room. "You can'st just put them on that old damp floor. I don't care what you say. They'll rust! The feed in the bottom'll get damp and moldy. Charley's too smart to eat it but Riderwood—he's such a hog—he'll wolf it down, get a stomach ache, get a twisted gut and," he holds his hand up as if it's a pistol, "*Pow!* No more Riderwood." Out I go to the corncrib to find some boards and two-by-fours, a hammer and saw. Bring it all back. In ten minutes, we've built a sturdy platform four inches off the ground. We set the three garbage cans on the platform, open the heavy bags, pour the feed into the cans.

He sits, pulls out his "shank," plucks the mud and manure out of his boots.... "Are we finished?"

We sling our feet through the foot of snow out to the van, take the saddles, bridles, coolers out. We push in the ramp—his way: I climb up into van, lean back and pull the rope shank attached to chain at the end of the ramp, and *vwhaaam,* in it slams. "Are we finished?"

Yes. Sit in his car. Dust billows up from the seat. He turns on engine. Dust blows out. I have sneezing fit. Heater barely working. Get lecture on health. He goes on and on about me pulling Riderwood up, taking off my jacket, handing it to him, and then continuing to gallop. "You should have left it on. You has gots' ta listen! Look at me, I'm in my full-body suit. I don't take it on and off. You should have left it on. And then *after you gallop*, when you're cooling out and you off the horse and walking around, *then* you unzip it and let the body cool off *gradually*. You trying to catch pneumonia? Didn't your daddy teach you anything?"

Then, a talk on drinking, and that I probably have cirrhosis of the liver and he doesn't. He suddenly stops, looks at his watch. "Five hours," he says. "Whatever you think. You a *cheap-scape*. Just like your Uncle Mikey. And look what happened to him. What comes around goes around. Go ahead, whatever you think." We both know he owes me over $400 for accumulated loans, but I've been attempting to put that behind us. Still, just to start off the upcoming bidding war, I begin at $75. "Nooooo. *Twenty dol-lar* an hour," he says, staring straight ahead, knowing he was stepping down from the $25 an hour he had been insisting on. "That's one . . . hundred . . . *dol-lar!*"

It seems so much. I give him three twenties and a ten. Feel guilty about it. Wait for his reaction. He shakes his head. "What goes around comes around. You as cheap as your uncle."

I take the ten back, replace it with two twenties, making it $100.

15 February 2009

Early in the day, a Friday, I rushed through work with the horses, and still in my long underwear and layers of work clothes was immediately driving down 95, on the way to Perring Parkway and the indoor soccer arena. And I started thinking about it. The last game of Eliza's high school career. The last game of the long road from teams at St. James Academy to the high-spirited Hereford Hot Shots travel team to this indoor team at Garrison Forest School. And the last game for me. Paddy—soccer, ice-hockey, baseball/lacrosse, year around; Andrew—soccer/cross country, basketball, lacrosse, year around; Eliza—outdoor soccer, indoor soccer, lacrosse, three seasons. I thought back on on all the trips—to Stone Harbor, Cape May, Gettysburg, all the games at St. James, at Garrison, at Hereford Middle. Most Valuable Player. Captain. The injuries. The sprained ankles. The torn ACL this year in the last game of the outdoor season and her fight to come back and play in the last few games of the indoor season. Her magnificent final, game-winning goal at Cape May—in the sudden death. It was ending.

And then, I'm up at 4:15 the next morning, Saturday. Racetrack hours. Driving Eliza to the airport. She tells me exactly where to go, where to park. Carrying her bag, I follow her into the vast building. She shows me how to get the ticket out of a machine instead of waiting in the long line. She files down the roped-off chute, waves once . . . walks away, turns and waves again . . . and I am left alone. She is gone, gone off to Rollins College in Winter Park, Florida, where's she's been accepted, for a four-day visit. A double hit: one night—her last game; next morning—off to college.

Once off the beltway, I pulled the Jaguar over, pushed the "top down" button, waited patiently while the top rose higher and higher, and then dipped down into its well. I stepped out, reached in the back, pulled on a jacket, a cap, gloves. Hopped back in and drove the rest of the way north on Dulaney Valley Road, across Loch Raven, onto the Jarrettsville Pike. The wind had a bite to it, buffeting my face. The frost glistened on lawns of suburban homes—no one out, the road, the lawns, the driveways empty.

At home, I'm listless. I think about making a pot of coffee but don't. Ansley is the "administrator on duty" all weekend at Oldfields. She's seated at the kitchen counter, on her cell phone, giving advice to a teacher. She pulls the phone away from her ear, looks at me, squeezes her shoulders together and rubs her arms. Walks away, talking on her cell, up the stairs and into our bedroom. I step out into the cold—no energy, no zip—pick up a couple of logs, listlessly carry them to the wood stove. Open the door to the wood stove. Set the logs on the coals, leave the door open and watch, crouching, hands on knees, as flames lick up around the sides of the logs.

Ring! Vrrrrmmmm! My phone, in the pocket of my most baggy corduroys, has wandered over near the private parts. It is set—not by me, by Eliza—to ring loud and to vibrate at the same time. I jump half a foot off the floor. Oh no, not Speedy. Not that high energy. Not that whole other world. He's talking and talking. Not Speedy on this of all days.

He stops, "You OK sonny-boy? What's wrong?"

I tell him.

He listens. Asks about coming over to work on Sunday. "No," I say. I can hear the disappointment in his voice. I don't want to spend the money. He wants to make the money. Furthermore, I want to write on Sunday morning. I look at the clock. It is 9:00 a.m. "It would be a help if you could come today."

"When?"

"By ten."

"OK, see you."

Hang up. Instantly, miraculously, my energy is back. I jog out to the barn, carry my hunting tack for Riderwood back into the house, fire up some strong, gritty, hot "black-like-me" coffee, quick-fry three eggs, burn some toast—no matter, just scrape off the black stuff. Wolf it all down. I clean the tack. Bring it back out. Dig up hunting clothes. I'm back. I'm moving forward. Speedy arrives half an hour early. I catch Riderwood, bring him in, pull off his blanket. Not too dirty. "No vacuum cleaner," I say. "No vacuum cleaner today." We'd had some trouble with the vacuum cleaner and Riderwood. "You just like a girl the way you treat these horses," he says. "A little girl with her dolls." I go back to the house, take a fast firey-hot, then ice-cold shower, dress. Stoke up the wood stove for Ansley, shut the stove doors and tighten the baffles.

We load up. He follows the van to the meet at Hanlon House. What a relief. He pulls that leaden ramp out as if it's made of Styrofoam. We unload Riderwood. He holds Riderwood while I pull on my spurs, get my helmet. He gives me a leg up and—we've timed it perfectly. The second I hit the saddle, off the hounds go and we're right up in the front with Tom. We have a good "run." Jump all kinds of coops and board fences.

At one point, we're over by Atlanta Hall, actually on Andor Farm, and suddenly we're on another run, the hounds have caught the scent of a fox and are baying and slicing through the woods. Tom's not in his Pink coat and he's not the Field Master today. We're behind a dozen others twisting and turning and switching leads at a full gallop on a narrow path in the woods. The hounds are baying and thrashing through the woods ahead of us. We fly out of the woods behind the others, over a coop, swing out into a vast field, turn, and sprint across the field straight at a "line fence," that divides the hundred-acre field. There is no inset, or lower series of panels. There is no coop or set of logs. Liz McKnight, our Field Master, is heading full-tilt straight at this big four-foot fence covered in brush, daring the rest to follow. The horses in front start to slow and spread out. A few come up from behind and pass us. Tom and I keep going the same pace; we're in the midst of twenty horses. The riders are aiming at a section about five panels long where the fence is on flat ground before it goes up the hill. Liz flies up—and then she's out of sight. One or two more take off—we can't see what has happened to them on the other side. A horse ahead of us and to our right stops and the rider goes over the horse's neck and crashes into the fence. The loose horse crosses in front of us. Another horse runs out to the left, the rider just barely hanging on, her weight and momentum pulling her to the right, out away from the horse. Tom gives out a yell; I know he's down to business. We're side by side. We gallop into the fence passing others propping and slowing. We take off together, head-and-head, going up high, higher than usual out hunting—it's like jumping a Hunt Cup fence. We're close together, stirrups almost clanking, then we're coming down, coming down steeply, leaning back. On landing, we get low in the saddle, duck in and out of the fallen riders and loose horses, and open gallop across the field. Goddamn, Riderwood can really jump.

Riderwood's had enough. Eileen Poole nicely points out a place and time where I can leave, ride away from the field and back to the van without attracting notice.

Driving home, I'm not looking forward to pulling out that ramp. Into the driveway, pull up by the bank, turn the engine off, hear the crunching of the crusher run and the familiar, slightly offbeat—does it need a new muffler?—engine of Mikey's Subaru rumbling in behind me.

I climb down out of the high cab. Stiff! I'm bent over, my back and legs wanting to stay in the same position as they were behind the steering wheel. Chilly too. Not much of a heater in the old van. No heater, in fact, just heat coming off the engine. Feet numb, I hobble around.

Speedy's out of his car. "Sonny boy, you getting too old for this. Look at you!" I'm walking around a circle, trying to loosen up, and I have to laugh as I watch him, moving fast, limping towards the van using his hand-carved cane. "Wha'd I tell you, hunting this poor horse in the cold. He needs a rest. You needs a rest. You just won't listen. You just like Mikey. Go on in the house and warm up those old bones. Go on, I'll take care of this." He opens the doors to the van, grabs the chain to the leaden ramp exactly as he told me not to do, gives it a powerful jerk, and pulls it out in one smooth motion. "Go on in and get Angie to fix you something hot. I'll take care of Riderwood."

I crab-walk towards the house.

"You ridden Charley yet?"

"No."

"He be tacked up when you come out."

Tea with Sweetheart by the woodstove. Hot tea. Smoking hot tea. Toss locust logs I'd cut and split into woodstove, leave door open, let it roar—cleaning the creosote out of the chimney. Close the door, watch the flames through the glass front shoot up into the baffles, circle and whirl back around and up into the baffles again. Feel the waves of heat pumping off the stove. Pull off hunting boots and clammy socks. Pull on thick dry wool socks and insulated riding boots. Back out to barn.

Speedy gives me a leg up. "I gots 'ta go now," he says as I come down in the saddle and he releases my ankle. "Need any help tomorrow? These stalls got to be mucked out right, and you'd better get some more manure out there on the straw track. Ground be freezing up again soon."

I think about it. Need to write early. "That'd be great. How about ten o'clock."

"I'll be here, God willing."

"Lot's to do," I say.

"Don't you worry, Sonny-Boy, with my brains and your brawn, we can do anything."

Out to the Hunter Trials Course. Dusk now. On the course. Charley freezes. We're not far enough out in the field for him to see the green light on the Jarrettsville Pike. I relax, look around, trying to find what he sees. There's a rustling sound to our left. I look in the woods. Trees. Brush. What else? Moving trees? Something moving. Right on the edge of the woods, a head rises up: a magnificent head with a full six-point rack. He's confident. He's not worried. He stares at Charley. Charley is perfectly still, his ears pricked, at attention, staring back. I can feel his heart pounding between my legs, banging at his ribs. The stag turns, bounds forward—all I see now is the bright white of his tail—and instantly there are five, ten, fifteen bright white tails bounding through the woods, away from us. We jog down to the pond. Great blue heron. Two ducks. Give Charley three good half-mile gallops up the hill. Hacking home—sky is streaked with scarlet and purple wisps. Flock of geese circling around and around above us, lead bird deciding whether to land for the night on our pond or to fly down to the Hunter Trials pond. Opening gate—my friend the red-shouldered hawk swoops out of my old tree-house maple, soars down the length of the stream, lands on the fence by the pond. I untack, grateful, at peace, in the zone. Hay, feed, and head inside ready to stoke the wood stove, *To Build a Fire* in the fire place, and have a warm night with the Sweetheart.

PART THREE

What happens to a dream deferred?
Does it dry up
Like a raisin in the sun?
Or fester like a sore—
And then run?
Does it stink like rotten meat
Or crust and sugar over—
Like a syrupy sweet?

Maybe it just sags
Like a heavy load.

Or does it explode?

— Langston Hughes,
    "Harlem: A Dream Deferred"

The Move

---

24 November 2013
Sunday

Up early. Cold out. A winter morning. Bracing. Today is the day: we are moving Speedy out. He has been patient. He has been praying. He has been trying to contact that quack, phony, "Pardoners Tale" scam artist Peter Popoff.

We're finally going to get him out of that hovel.

This may, and will hopefully, be my last visit to Melody's—it could be the last time I see Kitty and Luke. Speedy—who helped me clean out this very writing room, eyes sharp; Speedy, who two years ago stood outside with my pellet gun and said he could hit the goose fifty yards away in the head, kill him, and eat him that night; Speedy, who last year cleaned out the cab of the pickup right in front of the barn, used his knife to dig down into the cracks and crevices, pried every little piece of gunk out, Speedy is now about to be liberated.

We've got the three checks, and he wants receipts for them.

I call at 10:10

"Where are you?"

"I've just gotten the truck ready and we're coming up right now."

"You're late."

"Late? It's just 10:10."

"You said you'd be here at 10:00. I've been sitting here waiting."

"Hang on, we'll be there shortly."

Ansley is wrapping newspaper around a nice set of cups and

saucers, and setting them neatly in a box. I'd found them up in the barn and had used them a week ago when I had a dozen students come out to the farm for a day of Riding/Writing/Acting/Dining. The last part, the dining, was a high tea. I wanted to hold onto them and use them again next year. She was on a mission, jettisoning what we don't need. "Ask him if he'd like these cups and saucers."

"No, he's not going to want them."

"Just ask him," she said.

I ask.

"No, I don't want anything made of glass. Nothing! I already told you that. You losing your memory?"

"All right, all right." I shake my head at Ansley, who looks disappointed.

"Don't forget the coffee," he says gently. "Hot! And black like me. Can you remember that?"

"Yes, yes."

"Then, come on!"

I fill my coffee mug, walk outside. A heavy frost. Fire up truck. Muck it out. Find ropes and bungee cords for lashing everything down. Get some extra baling twine.

We drive up, fresh, early, coffee steaming. We cruise along the rushing waters of Deer Creek. Then, there's a pool and the water is still and sunlight glitters off shards of ice.

I relax, imagine the three of us rumbling down a long, tree-lined driveway, pulling up in front of a low-slung, natural wood colored and pine-paneled building. We'd walk in the door and there'd be a good-sized dining room, a spacious "great" room with a high-timbered, gabled ceiling and a couple of long tables. Grandparent-like residents would be seated at these tables and a friendly middle-aged woman would greet us, fuss all over Speedy, seat us, and serve up generous portions of hot turkey and mashed potatoes and mixed vegetables.

There'd be tall glass pitchers of ice tea. Speedy would be laughing as the other retired members of the community would chat with him, tell him they heard he could sing. They'd heard he was a horse whisperer. Could he give a talk about racing before the Preakness? Could he sing in the choir? Could he sing something right now at Sunday lunch? A couple of the young black women who worked there would laugh at his flirtatious remarks, tell him he'd better cut it out, get him laughing. He'd be eating enormous portions, trying to be so neat and not spill anything, and he'd be thinking, "I'm blessed. I'm so blessed. Thank you, Jesus. Thank you, God. Thank you, Reverend Popoff." The women would start to sing a gospel hymn, Speedy would join in; they'd harmonize, their voices going higher and higher.

At Melody's. I drive onto the lawn, around the house and down the hill to the back. Park outside the entrance to the basement.

Garbage bag after garbage bag of clothes, blankets, sheets, towels into the truck. Luke was supposed to help. He doesn't do a thing.

Tie chairs down. Fingers numb with cold but can't tie the knots with gloves on. The wind is coming from the northwest, sweeping across this high ridge. Sparkling light. We're out. We're getting out! Ansley is back in the room with Speedy. I'm purposely, selfishly, staying out of there.

Finally, truck is packed. We hand out envelopes. Speedy demands the receipts. Kitty and Luke are filling out receipts. Then, we're walking out. "Bye Melody," I holler up the stairs.

"Bye," she says.

And we're outside. We're in the fresh air—we're out of the fetid, dank, smoky, miasmic effluvium and we're never going back. Can't believe it. Walk Speedy around the truck. I'm upbeat, positive. This is it! "When you goin' ta get this engine checked? I'm telling you, it's burning oil. You're going to be driving down the road one day and *BWHAM*, the engine is going to seize up and you're going to go right through the windshield. Suppose if Angie is with you when it happens. . . ."

We're packed into the cab—Ansley's in the middle, her legs banging against the unwieldy gear shift—driving along the spar-kling waters of Deer Creek. We're out of the cold wind. We're warm. But now Speedy, by the heater under the glove compart-ment, is getting hot. He won't take his coat off. He's sweating. Ansley is cold. She's seated directly over a small but growing, rusted-out hole in the floor, which I've covered with a mat, and which I haven't told her about. A double-bind situation such as I teach my Medieval History students. Over and over in *Morte d'Arthur* Sir Thomas Malory puts Arthur's knights in predicaments that challenge the core principles of chivalry: does the knight obey his lord, which puts the damsel he loves in danger, or does he gallop straight to the damsel, saving her and breaking his oath to his lord? Sir Lancelot lives in an on-going double-bind: he is Arthur's best knight, and yet, he is in love with Arthur's wife, Guinevere, and she with him.

"What's going on with Luke?" I ask. "I thought he was going to load up."

"He can't go outside! He's got a telephone hooked up to him."

"What do you mean?"

"When they went to court, they put a band on Luke's leg. Gave him three months house arrest. After he serves three months he's got 'ta go to jail for forty-five days. And they took his license. He was drunk. Drunk when he was drivin'. Got a DUI. Took his license in Pennsylvania. He might not ever get it back."

"I wonder why he had a Pennsylvania license."

"Oh! They took his *Maryland* license in *Pennsylvania*. You know Maryland and Pennsylvania in ka-hoots now. They can do that. They can chase you through North Carolina to South Carolina right down to Florida."

"God, I don't know why he lives in that house. . . ."

"He ain't got *no money*!"

"All right, all right, not so loud," I say, making a futile tamping down motion with my right hand that I imagine Ansley observing.

"What *man* is going to take out my urine? He's one of those hillbillies. He's a common bastard, but he's so sweet and kind. . . ."

Ansley says her feet and legs are cold. "Is there a draft?"

Sweat is coming down Speedy's forehead, under his fedora. I slow down, bend forward, reach across Ansley, and try to direct the heat vents away from Speedy and towards Ansley.

"This thing is raggedy!"

"I just cleaned it out."

"I ain't talking about that. It ain't putting out like it's supposed to!"

I downshift, mash down hard on the accelerator.

"You keep doin' that we won't have nothin' to ride in. Just keep racin' that motor. Something's wrong with that motor."

"I thought you meant the engine."

"No, I mean the heat. The motor for the heat. She needs the

heat. A woman needs the heat. You've gots'ta . . ."

I interrupt, "Bob told me you gave up pork rinds."

"I did."

I look over at him.

"But you gave that last bag to me, I might as well eat'em."

"You need to lose some weight. All that weight is tough on your heart." I picture the old stationary bicycle in his room. I had imagined lifting it up—it'd be heavy—tying it to the roof rack. "What happened to the bicycle?"

"That hillbilly stole it and sold it."

Good Lord. Desperate.

"Did you all get me the-aramarella's?"

"The-aramarella's?"

"Yes, knuckle-head—the *ar-a-mar-ellas*!"

"Your what?"

"Umbrellas," Ansley says.

"Yes, yes—I got the umbrellas."

"Lucky Angie's with us. You losin' your hearin' . . ."

"I am *not* losing my hearing."

"Yes you is, but nevermin'. I'm happy to be leaving that place. I tole' Luke I was getting' *out-ta* jail—six years!—and he's getting' *in-ta* jail—life!

"She started calling me names. She'd cuss at me. She'd call me the N-word. That's all right, I tole' her. That's all right, you keep right on cussin' at me and I'm going to call social services and before you knows it this place will be mine and *you'll* be paying *me* rent. I tole' her I could *sue* her until the night turns *blue*. No window in my room. No way ta 'scape if there's a fire. No fresh air. Nothin' in that basement is up to code. And there she is cussin' at *me* and callin' *me* the N-word and tryin' to kick *me* out."

We drive along quietly for a minute.

"You never thought I'd get this apartment. You didn't have *faith*. You didn't believe Christ the Lord was watching over me. I knew. I knew it would happen. I see things. I can see things— *vish-ons*, what you call them?

"Visions."

"Yes *vish-ons*. God sends them to me. God's been sending me *vish-ons* about my brother that was down in the Grand Canyon mountains. *Blwrrrrrr.... Blwrrrrrrr....* He's riding that motorcycle. That's where he was living at. He out'ta there now.

"I was walking there and my sister Laureen was in a big building that they have there and she was sittin' there with her legs open and had all these children and she was feedin' them and I was walkin' and all of a sudden there was my brother Nut. *Blwrrrrr....* It was my brother Nut, *Blat-blat-blat-blabrrrrr,* he pulled up on that motorcycle and he said, 'Speedy—I need *a hundred* dol-lar. It's the only way I can get Kirby into this college.'

"I said, 'I ain't got no money.' So I called Bay—my sister Bay. She was sittin' beside a building feeding people. I crawled between Bay's legs and I said—'Nut's out there in the Grand Canyon mountains and needs a hundred dol-lar so he can get Kirby into this college.' So she did. She wrote me a check for a hundred dol-lar and gave it to me. I went back out there and gave it to Nut and he jumped on that dirt bike *brrrr-blat-blat-blat-brrrrrr . . .* and went off with a bunch of others on motorcycles. There was a big ole' high fence and the others went up a board leanin' 'gainst it and over the big old high fence and when they see Nut comin' they kicked it down and Nut, Nut went straight into the thing and when he hit it *his head flew off!*"

"What flew off?" Ansley asks.

"His *head*! His *head* flew off and this man that was standin' on the other side of the, you know, the fence, He was big as the world and He grabbed Nut and put his head back on and when this man stood up, it was *Gaw-d.*"

"What was gone?"

"It was *GAWD.* G....O...D, Himself. When I looked up it was *Gawd.* When Gawd grabbed him and snatched him up, his head come back on."

"This was a dream?" Ansley said from the back seat.

"A *vish-on.* I have *vish-ons.* He throw him on this big thing, I don't know what it was, a big ship, and when I looked up it was *Gawd* ! He was taller than the Empire State Building. His robe was *white* and on each sleeve was, was ... like dark *w....i....n.....e"*—he says stretching out the word—"And he had this long black hair and when he turned his head and was lookin' down at those boys his eyes was on fire. Fire! His eyes were burnin' and then all of a sudden he disappeared, vanquished."

"What disappeared? God?"

"The whole thing. I saw Nut one last time—I still got my check for four hundred."

"The check so he could go to college?"

"NO! That was for *Kirby*—the check for one hundred dol-lar was for my nephew, Kirby, Nut's son. So *he* could go to college. The check for four hundred dol-lar is for *me*. From Catholic Charities. Moving expenses."

Moving expenses, I thought to myself, driving along in a truck into which I'd just finishing loading all his belongings.

"I talked to Kirby on the phone a month ago—he's the prophet—and he said, 'You been prayin' for the wrong thing.' He said, 'You goin 'ta get a new home, bran-new.' He's the prophet. He said, 'You been sendin' your tithing to the wrong place. You should've been sendin' it to me.'

"So I said, 'Well, I ask'st the Lord for his forgiveness.'

"And he said he was goin' to pray for me, and he got to prayin', and said, 'You goin' ta get a new home, all furnished, new—new.' This is it! He don't lie. Whatever the Lord tell you, is coming to pass.

"So I got my new home and new furniture, a check from Catholic Charities for four hundred dol-lar and he said, 'I can see money comin' to you, lots of zeros—zero, zero, zero.' That's what he tole' me: God goin' to give it to me."

"Does that mean," I ask, "you're going to start playing the lottery?"

"I don't need to play *no lottery*! Who gave me my house? *Gawd*! And how did he do it? Through *Jesus*. I seen Jesus in a field meditatin'. He's Ethiopian. I seen him with my real eyes. He's Ethiopian—Gawd sent him there to a mountain in Ethiopia with an AK-47. Gawd raised one child to guard the Holy Grail. That's where Moses's tablet is. Jesus carried it with gold posts up into the mountains. I *seen* it. It's *Gawd Power*! People think you're crazy but I ain't crazy. I got good sense. I know what I'm talkin' about. Nobody can take it away from you. If you're a good person, he'll show you—he'll take care of you. *You got to go through Jesus to get to God*."

We pull up in front of the Catholic Charities building. At that second Bob steps out. From hearing his booming voice over the phone, I expected a tall, barrel-chested man. Out comes a trim, fit, compact man, partially bald, with that same strong, assertive voice.

We walk into the building. It's lunchtime. A dozen women

with white and gray hair are seated at different tables in the dining room. The walls are a faded okra-green. The drop ceiling is low and the panels are also green. The women are pale, small, bent over. They are wearing dresses. Their skin looks thin, brittle. A few have their hair dyed blonde.

We park Speedy—big, in his denim overalls, sitting up straight—at a table. His skin is black, not a wrinkle. He takes his purple straw fedora off—revealing a full head of cottony white hair—and puts on a friendly smile. He leaves his sunglasses on. The sunglasses suddenly look wild. They're oversized—Elton John style—and he'd repaired both of the corners with glue and painted silvery designs, tiny horse heads, over the corners.

Ansley makes Speedy a plate of food, sets it in front of him. He forks into it, takes one small bite, then another small bite, pushes the plate away. The women watch. As I walk back out to the truck, no one has said a word to Speedy. They stare at him. I will do anything for him at this point. If I have to, I'll pick up all those tables, all those chairs, put them outside, then pick up those old biddies one by one, set them outside at the tables, and then sit down beside Speedy—just the two of us in this vast room.

The pickup is parked in a pullover area in front of the double doors to the building. This newly constructed building, twenty horse lengths long, five stories high, a light gray color, is in a valley and the northwest wind is barreling down through the valley. The five-story building is catching the wind and funneling it past, and in that funnel is our truck. I'm in the back, climbing around, untying my waterman knots. My hands are freezing. This is the first cold day of the year. I have to set Speedy's wheeled office chairs on their backs so they don't blow away.

Bob is returning with a baggage carrier. You've never met anyone more efficient. We fill the carrier with bulging black plastic bags. At the top by the handle, I set a nice leather-and-canvas L. L. Bean satchel that had once been Paddy's. It is stuffed to the exploding point with Speedy's papers. Beside it, I set a heavy, black Naugahyde brief case, which we'd given Speedy for a birthday present a few years ago. He especially likes it because the snaps can be locked. There are three dials. The combination we'd set was 7-2-5. When closed and locked, it was to always be set on 0-0-0 so he could turn the dials, hear the correct number of clicks, and open it. "Handle with care," I say, slapping the satchel and the brief case. "I know," Bob says in that amazingly resonant voice. "Believe me I know."

We get all the stuff into his room, not *room*, into his *apartment*. Speedy had described it to me in great detail, and from that description I had thought it'd be larger. But it is nice! Clean. Fresh air. Well lit. No tobacco smoke.

Stuffed garbage bags are strewn across the living room floor, plus a small suitcase on wheels, the black briefcase, and Paddy's old L. L. Bean satchel. Ansley is pulling the clothes out of the bags; they reek of smoke. Not just of smoke, but of a marinated smoke. An aged tetchy, sweaty, pissy, stale smoke. I'm pulling comforters and blankets out of a bag.

"Is it a quilt? Is it made of squares? Wine-colored?"

"Yes. Yes. Yes."

"Kurt gave me that, Kurt. I've got to keep that."

A white comforter. "Throw that away."

A green woolen blanket. "Keep that. Keep that, it's worth a lot of money." A "rich owner" of Mikey's had given it to him.

I've got one black hanging bag filled with hangers, an old quilt, shoes and clothes. I'm trying to pick it up. Bob grabs the bottom and we carry it to the clothes closet.

Bob is doing everything Speedy wants. He has "stocked" the kitchen cabinets—and he has included bags of pork skins!

Speedy wants to keep this hanging bag. A little motor goes off. No one but Speedy and I know what it is: one of his plastic motorcycles, engine running, wheels spinning.

We pull the clothes out of the hanging bag, hang them on the pole, extract the shoes from the bottom of the bag. We're setting up his shoe rack, hanging his jackets, opening old duct-taped boxes. Speedy's asking for this, asking for that. I place two garbage bags filled with stuff to be thrown away out in the hall and three bags with clothes to take home to wash by the door. Space is appearing. Light is coming in. The air is fresh.

Bob is showing Speedy around, giving him detailed directions in his extremely clear baritone. "OK Speedy, you walk in, take one step, and the closet is on your left. Keep going. Then the bathroom."

Speedy walks along, feeling the wall. "I know. I know."

He stops. "Now," Bob says. "Five steps straight ahead is the wall. You'll walk to it, then take a right and go two steps. . . ."

I'm quiet. Bob has taken over. Ansley is doing much of the work. This is different. So much help. I'm not the only one. I'm in the background, not quite myself. Did the unstrapping, untying of the chairs in the freezing wind suck the energy out of me? Is this warm air making me sleepy, loopy? Thought we'd have a big welcoming lunch on our arrival. I'm weak, blood sugar on zip, hollowed out, feel a little sick to my stomach, running on coffee fumes.

Speedy needs pillows, groceries, tape, plastic plates that you can put in the microwave. I insist we go out while Bob helps show Speedy around the apartment.

It's getting late. IKEA—huge lunch of Swedish meatballs and mashed potatoes. Buy pillows. Buy plates. Get a large plate of spare ribs and French fries to go. Driving back, it's dark. Where has the time gone?

Set the food down at his table. Pour an orange soda. He wants a coffee too. Oh Lord, does he want me to go out and get a coffee? I remember the small jar of instant coffee. "I can make a cup of coffee."

Up, prepare to heat up some water on the stove, but can't locate a pot. Find a mug high up in a cabinet, fill it with water. "Now listen," he says, "I only want a little bit of coffee. Get a spoon and just put a touch of coffee on the tip of the spoon. It would've been better if you'd put the coffee in the water first, and then heated it up."

Hand him the cup of coffee.

"This isn't enough. Why didn't you fill it up like I ask'st you, and what mug is this. This isn't the big mug Bob gave me."

Set a place at the table. Ribs—"OK, but not much meat on them," he says.

French fries, "I never eat'em. Tell me, as long as you've known me, you ever seen me eat a French fry?"

Orange soda, "You don't know nothin'! When will you learn? I don't drink my soda out of a *glass*—which could spill all over the place. I wants it in the bottle, this being a one liter bottle."

"OK, had enough?"

"No, this is not enough. What am I going to do? I'm still hungry."

At this point, I'm thinking: Too bad, you've got to lose some weight anyway. Too bad, you'll be fine.

"Look in the closet. Look for some tomato soup, tomato bisque."

I find a large can of soup.

"OK, now, open it up and pour it. Hold it. Take this coffee, pour it in that other mug, and then use this mug for the soup."

We get him set up. Work on his phone. He calls his sister Bay. Lords it over her, tells her what a great apartment he has, he's living like a king. Says he's going to get married again.

"___"

"Ta mow money."

"??"

He laughs. "I said 'ta 'MOW MONEY'!"

"___"

"I'm going to get married again to," and he spells out, " M… O….R… E…M….O….N….E….Y."

We drive home in the dark. I feed the horses in the dark, hay them in the dark. Push the wheelbarrow out to the wood pile, load it up, push it back to the house, unload it. Fire up the woodstove, sit by the stove, stare into the flames, and though I've stopped drinking again, have two of the best Smithwick Ales I've ever had in my life.

Ansley's doing Speedy's wash—comforters, blankets, heavy denim coveralls. We've been doing his wash for a year now. "Are we missing a bag?" she asks.

I go out and check the truck bed. No more bags.

Back in. "Where's the quilt Kurt gave Speedy?"

Oh Lord, could it be possible it was thrown out. We call Bob. I joke about having the Ale. He's already had two bourbons. I ask if he's sure he threw out just two bags of garbage. Yes he is.

"Don't worry about it, Patrick. I wouldn't worry. When I left there, and I looked at Speedy in that apartment, all neat and clean, I had the best feeling. We've done a good job, Patrick. Don't worry about that one quilt or anything else. Speedy should be very grateful for all we've done for him."

The Lion is Waking

25 November—Monday
Harford Day School

Running late for school. Jog back into the kitchen from starting the pickup. Cold night—engine didn't want to turn over. Had to crank and crank it. Worrying about starting it up to come home in late afternoon. Must remember to drive it around at lunch, warm the engine, charge the battery.

I'm buttering toast, sticking a banana in pocket, pouring a mug of coffee. Ansley is asking me questions: "Is there something wrong with the furnace? Doesn't it smell like kerosene in the house? Do you think you should check it?"

Jog back outside, hop in truck and off I go, coffee spilling, toast crumbling.

Third period, English: *Raisin in the Sun*. Students hand in reaction papers on Langston Hughes' poem, "A Dream Deferred."

Act II, Scene 1—Walter is going wild.

First, his younger sister Beneatha, wearing a Nigerian outfit, yells out "OCOMOGOSIAY!" and begins dancing and singing along with a Nigerian melody. Walter, whose been drinking heavily, enters, raises his fists to the ceiling and screams: "YEA . . . AND ETHIOPIA STRETCH FORTH HER HANDS AGAIN! . . ."

His wife Ruth interrupts, and he yells: "Shut up! . . . I'm digging them drums . . . them drums move me! . . . In my heart of hearts . . . I am much warrior!"

Then, he's "in possession of an imaginary spear and

actively spearing enemies all over the room." He yells out "OCOMOGOSIAY . . ."

Beneatha encourages him.

"THE LION IS WAKING . . . OWIMOWEH!" he yells. He "pulls his shirt open and leaps up on the table and gestures with his spear."

The students are acting it out. They're getting into the spirit of it. The room is electrified. Just when I tell Marc, "You're supposed to *jump* up onto a table, not just stand there!" my cell phone makes its funny ring. All acting stops. I don't usually have the phone in my pocket but I hadn't gotten around to taking it out and setting it on a far corner of my desk where I usually ignore it.

The damn thing is ringing and vibrating in my pocket. I pull it out. Look at the screen. "Speedy Kiniel New."

First reaction: Will get it later.

Then, I picture him in his new apartment; something could have gone wrong, he can't see! It could be an emergency.

We're about to walk over to the theater, which I had reserved for this day, so they can rehearse the plays they've written—sequels to *Raisin in the Sun*—which they would be performing on Friday. *Sequels about a black family moving into a white neighborhood.* And calling me now was *a blind black man* who has just moved into a *white retirement community.* I pick it up.

"What'd you do with my brief case? Did you go in my brief case?"

"No, I didn't go in your brief case."

"Yes you did. I remember, you did! "

"No, I didn't. I did not go in your ..." (and how I wanted to say *f-ing!*, how I wanted to say, *I did not touch your f-ing brief case,* but there I was with my students,) "brief case." The class is perfectly still, quiet, watching and listening.

I would like to cuss but I am hampered, hog-tied, halted. Good thing.

"Yes you did. You went in my brief case and took my *hundred dol-lar bill.* You the only one knows the combination."

"I did not *open* your brief case, I did not *fool* with the combination, and I certainly did not *take* any hundred dollar bill."

"Yes you did. I want it back. And where are my clothes? I don't have any clothes."

"We've been washing them."

"I need my clothes. Wha'chu think I have to wear?"

"I've got to go. I'm in the middle of a class. I'll call back later."

Then, to the class: "I wouldn't have answered that call but I was worried it might be an emergency. And I thought, here we are reading a play about a poor black family in the south side of Chicago half a century ago, and here is a poor black man calling me *now*." I explain about his glaucoma—how he'd never had the correct medical treatment and annual visits to the optometrists we all take for granted. As a boy, he never went to the dentist. It was tie one end of a piece of string to a bad tooth, the other to door knob, and slam the door. Shots, physicals, check-ups—never had them. I briefly describe the hovel he'd been living in and how we'd just moved him—into an almost all-white retirement home. This was real. It was happening today.

We return to acting out the play. Inside I am furious. It is my turn to rage. This was the last straw—particularly as it came so soon after the "you-have-to-kill Charley" episode.

Visit at Catholic Charities

27 November—Wednesday
Catholic Charities

"I met a—what'chu call him? A preacher?"

"A minister? A priest?"

"Yes—I met a priest, and he said he'd baptize me. On Sunday he's goin' to bring me up to his chapel and baptize me. I'm so happy. I'm just so happy. I can't wait 'ta be baptized. . . ."

By the time I'm ready to leave I'm thinking: Is it possible I am slightly down because he is now more independent, not so dependent on me? If so, this is surely nothing to be proud of.

I study him as he *soliloquizes* (V-*Romeo and Juliet*), making Mercutio look like a tongue-tied adolescent who is short of words. Ansley is on the couch patiently listening. On he goes with the monologue, white hair straight up, afire, hasn't put his teeth in, belly hanging out, bare black feet, mouth toothless. He suddenly looks different. He suddenly does not seem like the same Speedy. It feels as if there is a distance between us. He's on his own. He's going to prosper and have a good life and I don't feel he is grateful for what I've done. This is weak of me. This is not good. The feeling will go away.

Tomorrow's Thanksgiving. He's not coming to our place. I will not be driving over to pick him up. He is having Thanksgiving here in the dining room of the retirement home.

He's on his own now? We'll see what happens.

Ansley and I drive home. We're quiet. We walk into the house. Feels chilly. I stoke the wood stove, walk out of the kitchen to the front hall. Cold. Look at the thermostat: 47! Listen: no furnace running. Smell: kerosene scent in the air. Walk down the rickety steps into the cellar. Yes, Ansley was right. I should have checked it earlier. The furnace is off, tomorrow is Thanksgiving, the first cold front has hit, we have a slew of relatives arriving early for the dinner on Thursday, a family reunion on Saturday, and we have no heat.

A Pair of Sheepskin Shoes

It's the week before Christmas and I haven't seen Dickie for a month. Loyal friends have been driving him the hour to Laurel Racetrack every morning (Pimlico, much closer, is closed for the winter), and then back to his place in Reistertown, where he collapses back on his bed. He's been beating the odds. Was supposed to leave us six months, nine months, even a year ago, but I've heard he's gotten weaker. I've been trying to organize driving over with Tom, but it just hasn't happened.

I decide to make it a priority. I drive over one afternoon, radio off.

Headed down the Jarrettsville Pike, I picture myself a fourth grader, sitting beside Dickie in the early morning as we head for Gilman School. Kind and thoughtful, he chats with me on the way in, and when we arrive, takes me up into the mighty Upper School, showing me around, introducing me to his towering friends on the football team. At Gilman, this hard-hitting football player, this country boy who could throw bales of hay all day without tiring, has gotten a few classmates together and formed the non-self perpetuating Art Club, supporting such projects as "Eat Jello with Humility Week" and "Garver Yo-Yo Industries." They're all joking about it. The club president, as printed along with a photograph thirty-five years later in *Gilman Voices*, the Centennial history of Gilman School: "Mumbling Dick Small." That mumbling didn't change much over the years. And neither did Dickie's teenage fondness for profanity.

I see him that winter: Tall and endowed with an unusual natural strength, having the kick, the power of a young colt, he's just concluded an undefeated season on the varsity football season, a true big shot, and he's laughing and skiing with Mom, and us younger ones.

In his thirties, he's back from Vietnam. Early one morning, the sun not having risen above the three-quarter pole at Pimlico, he's chewing tobacco, leading my horse back along the outside rail, relating a Vietnam story, when another horse of his throws its rider, sprints off, jumps the inside rail, crashes through the infield, jumps back out, cuts herself all up. "Pat," he says, riding along as calmly as can be, both of us watching outrider Bruce Gill skillfully catch the filly, "after what I've seen in Vietnam, I just don't get all worked up about every little crisis any more," and continues his Vietnam story, a rather high-flying one about finishing a classified mission in Vietnam a week early, not telling anyone up the chain of command, and instead hiking into Saigon, and commandeering a house of ill repute for his squad.

I'm making the exact same drive I used to make going to Pimlico in the quiet of 4:30 a.m. to gallop for Dickie. Near Café Spice, I think about stopping and ordering him a full meal of Indian curry, and then surprising him with it. But I feel as if I am on a mission; I don't want anything to block or slow my passage; I feel he is there at home now and I want to be there.

Dickie loves to surprise, even shock you. Two decades ago, I wrote a magazine story on the novelist Anne Tyler, who lived, the story pointed out, in Homeland, not far from Roland Park. That Christmas I saw Dickie at Tom and Mimi's party, and he started talking about the novels of Anne Tyler. These are poetically written, intricately woven literary novels set in Baltimore about eccentric families, deeply moving love relationships, and much more. First he talked about reading *The Accidental Tourist*, then *Morgan's Passing*, then *Dinner at the Homesick Restaurant*. I couldn't believe it. Finally I asked, what was up.

"I read your story," he chuckled. "I realized I live two houses down from her." Then he leaned into me and looked in disbelief into my eyes. "I see her just about every day!"

That was in the 80s, when Broad Brush's fifteen wins, along with his firey and unpredictable temperament, put Dickie on the front pages of sports sections across the country. Before Broad Brush, Caesar's Wish won the Black-Eyed Susan at home at Pimlico, then shipped to Belmont where she won the Mother Goose, broke Ruffian's record, and became Dickie's favorite. For thirty-nine straight years, Dickie has won a Maryland stakes race every year, except one.

I think about his early training days when he was winning Grade I stakes and being written up as the wonder boy in his thirties. He'd arrive at the barn, muck out five stalls alongside his help, toss each sixty-pound muck sack onto his back as if it were a ten-pound, blue Gilman book bag, and at the end of the morning, when the track closed, unload a tractor trailer of hay. I think about him now, in his sixties, weakened by cancer—no matter, he is at the barn living the life he loves, plotting his training strategies, cracking jokes, planning what will happen to his loyal brigade of horsemen and horsewomen: grooms, hot walkers, riders, tack cleaners, van drivers, two-year-old breakers, forewomen (as opposed to foremen)—some of whom have worked with him for decades.

I pull in his short driveway; his truck is parked by the back door. It's a little clapboard house in a woody area. I step out, pull my heavy flannel shirt tight around my torso and knock on his open kitchen door. No answer. I walk in. Look around. His house looks just like the infamous "Red Brick Inn" in the '70s when he was working on the gate at Delaware Park and living with Brian Hickey, Josh Gill, Billy "Turnpike" Turner and Winky Cocks. It looks like the crash pad of a couple of fraternity boys who have gotten their first jobs on the track and are finishing up a long summer. Old racing programs, old *Racing Forms*, overnights and newspaper clips pertaining to races won are set in piles throughout the living room, which has one piece of furniture in it—Dickie's Lay-Z-Boy "nap chair" which he never uses.

"Anyone home?" I call out in a low voice. I tip-toe up the steep stairs. He's in the bed with a big comforter pulled up over his shoulders. He sits up. "Pat!" He grabs a pillow, places it behind his back, leans against it as if he's going to stay there. "It's great to see you," he says, "Sorry I'm in bed. I was just worn out."

"That's all right. Why don't I make some coffee or tea and bring it up."

"Tea. I can't drink coffee anymore. Oh hell, I'll come down to the kitchen with you." In pajamas and robe, he lumbers out of the bed, musters his forces, stands, walks across the room and very uncharacteristically, throws his arms around me and gives me a big hug, calling, "Ah Pat."

In the kitchen, he brews a pot of tea. The door is still ajar and a steady draft of chilly air wafts through the room. He makes two mugs of tea, sits at a little table an arm's reach from me and begins to tell me a story about his dog. He relates how he carefully researched just the type of hunting dog he wanted, located the dog out in South Dakota, had the dog shipped to Maryland, trained him, grew to love him, and then he tears up as he describes the dog's recent accidental death and the cremation he had to organize.

There's a stack of old-fashioned Irish wool caps a foot high on a table by the door, and beside it four or fives fedoras set atop one another. I comment on them.

"Got to wear them, Pat. I so much as go out to get the mail and walk back without my cap on, I catch a cold."

He explains that Liz McKnight is driving him to work most mornings, and he has another driver or two. I know he'd bought this house years ago because it was fifteen minutes from Pimlico. "I heard Pimlico will open up for training this spring."

He looks me straight in the eye, "Yeah," he chuckles, "it'll probably open the day after I die."

He talks about finishing his most recent round of treatments at the VA.

"So, the doctor checked me over, looked at my blood tests, told me I could leave. 'Set up your next monthly appointment with the receptionist,' he said. I stood up to walk out. He continued to study my chart.

" 'Oh,' he said, as I got to the door, "on second thought, don't bother.' "

Dickie thinks this is hilarious. He laughs hard while looking me in the eye.

Analyzing his illness, he explains it has to be Agent Orange that has taken away his health. He's been strong as a horse all his life, never missed a day's work, and suddenly he has this cancer shooting through his body. "We'd parachute into what had been a thick jungle and there wouldn't be a leaf on a tree. For days we'd be crawling through the dirt, hiding in it," he says. "My case fits the exact profile of other Vietnam vets who've gotten cancer late in life."

I ask about using the VA and the expense of the treatments and doctors' appointments. "The VA has been all right. Some people have said: "Why not file a lawsuit? You'd be sure to win." I don't want to do that, Pat. I'm not going to make an issue of it. It'd just make me bitter."

His energy is sagging. I stand, reach over to a coat rack, pull on a down parka. I finish my tea. He hasn't touched his. I eye a pair of ankle-high sheepskin shoes. "I'll bet they're warm."

"They'll fit you, Pat, take 'em. Jane gave them to me but they're too small."

Driving home in the dark, radio off, it starts to sleet. The roads are clogged. Traffic is barely moving. The windshield wiper sweeps back, and forth, then hesitates, back and forth, then hesitates. *Come on windshield wiper, don't let me down now.* I'm thinking about a few Christmas presents I need to buy. I'm at a loss on how and where to get the presents, then I remember Eliza will be home the next day and I can go out with her. I chuckle to myself, remembering how for years Tom and I used to do our Christmas shopping. We'd wait until the last minute, then head out for a day and evening of driving to stores and malls, spending most of our time stopping by pubs and taverns and dives talking first to bartenders, then barmaids, and one time some dancers about what we should buy our wives for Christmas.

Something rings—I jump up out of my seat before realizing its my phone. I fumble around, look: "Tom Voss Cell." Pick it up.

"Want to go Christmas shopping?" he jokes.

He's thinking about the exact same thing I'm thinking, and at the exact same time. It's as if we're on the same wavelength of energy bands whipping around the East Coast.

"Yeah, love to," I say. "Let's meet at the Fairgrounds." The Fairgrounds, across from Timonium Fairgrounds and Racetrack, was where we'd begin. We'd have a drink there, then walk across Timonium Road to the car dealership where our good friend Randy Lewis worked as a salesman. We'd drag him out, to another pub, and later return him to work before heading to a few clothes stores and jewelry stores recommended by bartenders and barmaids, making pit stops along the way.

"I was just at Sam's Club," he says, (he loves Sam's Club, the discount store) "and on the way home saw a Corvair for sale."

"Really, where was it?"

"It's right on Jarrettsville Pike, at the end of a driveway just before Allison Road. "Five hundred bucks. I thought you might want to know."

"Ha, I'll give it a look."

"If you want to get it, I'll go in on it with you."

"Well thanks. That'd be fun. I'll check it out on the way home."

"What're you doing?"

"Driving back from visiting Dickie."

"Why didn't you tell me you were going?"

"I did. I tried to line up a trip with you. Don't you remember? Anyway, I was over in that area, and stopped by."

"How's he doing?"

"Well, when I arrived there he was in bed. Then he got up and we had a cup of tea together in the kitchen. He put on a good show, but he's definitely getting weak."

A long sigh. "I'm going to get Mimi to have some spicy Indian food delivered to him."

"That's exactly what I've been meaning to do," I said. "In fact, I almost stopped and got some on the way today. How'd you know about that?"

"Liz told me. She said the curries and spices are supposed to be good for fighting the cancer."

"Yes. You know what he was most upset about?"

"What?"

"The death of his dog."

"That fits. What happened?"

"He'd gotten a new hunting dog. He was training him to stay on his property, and then one afternoon, the dog took off after a squirrel, chased it across the road, and was hit by a car."

A long sigh. "Well, it doesn't look like he's going to be here with us much longer, does it?"

"No, it doesn't."

"OK, remember to check on that Corvair."

"I will."

You Can't Make
Old Friends

---

12 January 2014
Sunday

"Good morning brother, what 'chu doing?"

"In my office, writing."

"How was Christmas?"

"Good, good we just got back from visiting Paddy in Denver."

"Oh yeah, who went?"

"The whole family. Eliza flew in from Florida."

"So nice. That's so nice. And how about Andrew?"

"Yeah, he flew in from California."

"How's he doin'?"

"Good, good," I lied. We'd had a difficult time, and now he wasn't returning our calls. "He's working security in L.A., but I don't think he likes it much. You know, he went to all the trouble to get his truck driving license, and even drove for six months or so, but he quit that."

"He'll be all right. You don't know what he's seen over there in that war. Where was it?"

"Iraq."

"You don't know what he saw. Blowing up those crazy Arabs. He probably couldn't sleep at night worrying one of those Arabs sneak into his camp and slit his throat. He just needs a little time. You his daddy and you got'ta stick with him."

"You're right."

"Course I'm right! I know Andrew inside and out. Didn't I work a year with him at Mikey's before he joined the Marines?"

"Yes, you did."

"Don't chu worry, Andrew'll come around. He just asserting himself, showing you he's his own man has his own life to live. Didn't you do the same when you was his age?

"No."

" 'No?' Well didn't your daddy want you to be a steeplechase jockey like him— instead of goin' off and workin' on a newspaper? Wasn't there all that pressure when you broke away and went off 'ta work on that newspaper?"

"Yes, I suppose so."

"Your son's no different. He's jus' like you was: he's strong-willed and wants to get his way and ain't go'in ta'listen ta'nobody. That's why he went off and joined the Marines. Ha! Andrew! We had some fun—driving the tractor out into the big field in the blizzard with him hoopin' and hollerin' sitting up on ten bales of hay in the bucket and I'd be raisin' the bucket up and down as we flew through the snow. And then—when he started riding Bronze Angle and wanted to be a jockey like his daddy. You remember that? He'd get on that horse in the barn. Mikey'd tell him to take him up on the top hill—it'd be cold as hell up there, the north wind blasting across the top of it—and jog him for forty-five minutes. Mikey'd do that to him just like he did it to your father. But Andrew wouldn't listen. I'd take the tractor up there with a few bales of hay, acts likes' I was doin' something, and I'd see Andrew jog that horse for five minutes around and around the ring, getting colder and colder up there, and then I'd see him kick ole Bronze Angle in the sides, bend down low, and let him gallop the *whole* way around the field, around the logs, around the hurdles, and when he got to that long stretch along the ridge, Andrew'd get down low like he seen his daddy do, like a *jockey*, and let that horse *open up!*

"Where'd chu say you jus' was?"

"Denver—Paddy lives in Denver and we . . . ."

"Denver. I know's all about Denver. I have a religious station on—keep it on all the time—from Denver and there's a boy out there that read the Bible in ninety days. He's only fifteen years old. He read ten pages at a time. When I get back to seeing, I'm going to do the same thing. Every day I go to mass . . . . Bob is a Catholic . . . . His wife Nancy is laid up—hurt her knee and it's infected . . . . What you being so quiet about?"

"I just found out the infection in Tom's foot has gotten a lot worse." I thought about telling him the whole story—how Tom had a vet, yes, a veterinarian, look at it back in August at Saratoga. How the vet sent a sample off to Cornell to be tested. It was returned and the vet put Tom on a program of strong antibiotics. Tom was getting weaker and weaker, didn't tell anyone, and then he was excreting blood, still didn't tell anyone until he collapsed twice in one day. Mimi immediately took him to the hospital where she learned he had diverticulitis and had lost a third of the blood in his body. Those Vosses! Why hadn't they told me? He was now at home convalescing. Had his foot propped up and was on his good behavior. The foot was bandaged but had to be treated every few days—and the treatment very painful.

"He was in the hospital for a week."

"You tell him that's the Lord's way of gettin' back at him. Tell him I said that's a fact. He use'd to kick people in the butt with that foot. His eyes look like a woman's titties on his face. You know why—tell him it's from looking at all those butts."

"The what?"

"All those *butts*. That foot—that's Bob Witham getting back at him. Don't you remember the night at Pierce's Plantation he knocked Bob's teeth out!"

"No, I don't remember that." Never happened, I think.

"Well, you remember the night my band played at your cousin Speedy's birthday party and he used you for a punchin' bag?"

"He did not 'use me for a punching bag.'"

"Yes he did. I saw's it. I had to step down from the stage and break it up! You didn't do a thing—jus' stood there and took it."

"That was a crazy night, and he was all worked up about something."

(The party was outside. Speedy's band was playing. Ansley and I had just gotten married and we were up from the Eastern Shore where I had quit my nice job as a feature writer and photographer on a newspaper and was "working on the water" as an oysterman. Suddenly Tom was attacking me, punching me, trying to knock me down, knocking me down. Speedy and others grabbed him. He kept coming at me, struggling to free himself from their arms, throwing punches. Mimi took him home. Decades later, she told me, "Patrick, you know why he did that? He didn't think you were doing enough with yourself. He didn't think you were pushing hard enough to reach your true potential.")

" 'All worked up' is one thing. Using you for a human punching bag is another. I knows' friends have differences. I knows' he's your best friend. You tell him I said to lay up in that house, stay out of the cold, and get strong before he comes back outside.

"Tell him to let Mimi *take care of him*! He's likely to go out there on that ice, fall down, and get an infection in his other foot. Another thing. He needs to stay away from those horses. He's just like Mikey—he'll be crawling down to the barn to check on those old flea-bitten hunters in the middle of the night and one's just as likely to kick'im in the head. Or he's likely to climb up in that old tractor of his with the diesel fuels coming in the cab and the heat on and no fresh air and smoking his Pall Malls and *plow*! He loves to *plow*! I's seen him plowing many a day I been there to clip his horses. You tell him to stay away from the horses and the tractor and keep his ass on the couch by the fire!

"I've gots' good friends, too. Like for me, it's Annie. We're tight as Dick's hat band. And there's Laurie—if she's loyal to you, she'll die for you. And when we had the band, man we looked out for each other. I stopped carrying a pistol when I came north, but I always had a shank, a big shank. I've made a smaller one now. Gots' it in my right pocket—*ready*! I can reach in without you's seeing, "draw it" faster than Billy the Kid, and instead of a bullet the blade whips out. Then, Sonny-boy, I can carve you up like a baby lamb for dinner.

"Now what you going to do if a big man grabs *you*, throws *you* down on the grounds, puts his foot on *your* neck. You're all alone now. All your chickens flown off and gots' as far away from you as they can. You get in that old excuse for a truck alone in the dark every the morning. You drive home at the same time every night and gets out of the truck alone, tired and worn-out in the dark. You go out to the barn alone to feed. What you going to do? You need to take a course in self's defense!

"That big man gets you down, and he's mashing your face into your gravel driveway, you get your hand in your pocket, pull out your shank and you *cut*. Cut him all across the ass. You got to work on him, slice that ass like a loaf of bread. He'll be squealing like a pig. My shank—worser than a razor. Don't you worry 'bout nothing. I'll make you one. You train yourself to put your thumb on it to open the blade. *Practice*! Put your hand in your pocket and open it real easy. Then go to work. He won't be able to sit down for a month. Or, he gets his face close to yours, *bite* him! *Chew* him! Bite his face, rip it open, bite his nose. He'll be squealing like a pig.

"Now you, you got that big, long head. If he grabs you from behind you bang him hard as you can with that big head, break his nose, get it bleeding. They scared of blood, that blood will be gushing—get him down and kick him, kick him everywhere, *kick him in the head.*

"You've gots 'ta take a self's defense course. You's so skinny and tall they think, 'He don't know what to do.'

"Now you come up on *me*, I can smell'z you. I can smell'z you five feet 'way. I lunge at you. I'm goin' to put that shank in you. But you, with that big long head, you hit the dude with the back of your head and when he goes down, if you see a brick, pick it up and *hit* him with it.

"I've got God and Jesus Christ around me. I'm actually enjoying myself. Julie's here today. She's cleaning house right now, and," he directs his voice away from the phone, "she does a good job, don't you Julie?"

"Yes, I do a good job for you, Speedy," a young woman replies.

"Had chicken for breakfast. I eat chicken any time. You don't eat enough. You look like a bag of skin with a flag flying over your head."

I'm waiting for him to ask me to come pick him up, bring him to the doctor's or do some errands. The request doesn't come.

My Tiresias says he already knows who's going to win the Derby. He goes through a list of the favorites, explains why each one is not going to make it to the winner's circle. Then, he gets to "California something. California *Chrome!*" He ticks off every feat the horse has accomplished out west as a two-year-old, tells me all about his trainer—who used to be the galloping boy for the great Nashua—"Now that poor horse, he was trained by the meanest sonovabitch that ever trained a horse, I can't remember his name and I hope I never do"—and that this trainer who used to gallop Nashua is one of the old boys—"I bet's he knew your *daddy*"—and knows what the hell he's doing and what he's doing is he's going to come East and whip every one's *ass.*

"Put's your own money on him, Patrick, everythin' you got, and then's you can hire someone to help you with the farm and the horses. That's what you ough'ta do. Tom too. He needs an assistant trainer, like he used to have. And a farm manager. You two's too much alike and both goin'ta kill yourselfs working on your farms. I knows your daddy and his daddy were good friends. I knows you've ridden horses and wrecked cars and chased pussy together and worked hard all your lives, but you ain't getting no younger. You hear me! You ain't getting no younger. You's both of you had better stop thinking you're eighteen 'cause you ain't eighteen no more. Those farms will be there long after we's all gone. Just remember, you can't make old friends."

PART FOUR

"But man is not made for defeat," he said. "A man can be destroyed but not defeated."

— Santiago in *The Old Man and the Sea*

Dear Tom

---

22 January 2014

"**O**ut, out brief candle . . . " Out the tractor path smoothed over with snow. "It can't be!" I call out, punching the air. "Life's but a walking shadow, a poor player who struts and frets his hour upon the stage. . . ." Feet crunching through the crust into the soft, fluffy powder, the crust-surface on either side of the beaten path rumpled and rippled by the broken and cracked corn stalks beneath but before me flattened smoothly with two century-old parallel indentations worn by the wheels of wagons and then trucks and tractors. "And then is heard no more. . . ." I march on the rounded hump between the wheel ruts. "It can't be! It can't be!" I call out. It is all I can do. "It is a tale told by an idiot, . . . signifying nothing."

I had stood up in my writing room in the barn a few weeks ago and seen Tom in black coat, standing in the stirrups, racetrack style, not posting, jogging down this beaten tractor path along the edge of our farm, leaning to his left to keep the weight off the knee he'd injured sledding at the Igleharts five decades ago. He was in front, leading the field of two dozen black-coated foxhunters on bays and grays and chestnuts. His eyes were looking at these same trees, across this same field. "It can't be! It can't be!" His eyes were looking at our brown-shingled house with smoke from the locust I had cut and split spiraling out of the kitchen chimney, then the big brown-shingled garage, the small brown-shingled smoke house, the red corncrib, the big red barn, and finally at its lower stone-walled corner to the door and windows behind which I sat at my desk. I was writing and editing. He was riding and training.

Now, three-quarters of a mile away from the farm, after having been awoken at dawn by Jay Young, president of the Elkridge-Harford Hunt Club, wanting to verify that Tom had died, after returning from a morning visit to Atlanta Hall where I had my last look and touch of Tom's body, I climb the post and rail to the Hunter Trials course. *It was yesterday,* "Tomorrow and tomorrow and tomorrow creeps in this petty pace . . . to the last syllable of recorded time. . . ." *a sunny fall day, before we had our drivers' licenses, the grass green, Tom on Whimsey, me on Just in Time, both young fillies of Mom's that we rode in the pair class over post-and-rails, board fences, chicken coops, tight fences, and afterwards, beaming, Mr. Voss, Tom's grandfather, and Wassie Ball, Tom's mentor, snapped blue ribbons onto our bridles and we were grinning and laughing.* I march—"It can't be!"—cotton ball puffs, on a three-count, coming out of my mouth, hitting the frigid air, each then loosening, losing its form, dissipating, before the next three-count—across the spot near the chicken coop where Mr. Voss had pinned the ribbons, and then down the hill, going into the in-and-out. Climb over one board fence, take several steps that would be two horse strides, and then climb the next board fence.

Yesterday, it seems yesterday *we jumped these two, me in front, and as soon as we landed he galloped up beside me, Just in Time started to take off, Tom had to push Whimsey to go along with Time, and we were winging it faster than we'd planned into the log fence at the peak of the hill, met it a little far out, both had to ask for a big one, and over we sailed, more race-riding style than show ring.*

"It can't be!" I try to pull out of this nightmare. It has to be a nightmare. I must have imagined that early morning phone call. The early morning visit to Atlanta Hall. Standing in the kitchen, godson Sam suddenly gripping me strongly at my right elbow, and without saying a word, walking me into the downstairs guest room where Tom's body lay on the bed.

I am marching. One step at a time. One crunch. Another crunch in my forty-year-old, leather-topped, rubber-bottomed L.L.Bean boots in which I've galloped thousands of Tom's horses. The air is fresh, energizing, ice-cold and I am feeling no fatigue. Down the valley. Up the hill. Up to the highest point. Out hunting one day, the ground was frozen solid, there was no scent, but

Tom just had to go. I was on Iron Fist, the world's most nervous hunter. He was jigging and dancing, snatching the reins out of my hands. We were standing on the crest of this hill, the wind whipping across the stark, harvested corn field; we were surrounded by proper ladies and gentlemen on well-behaved horses and for some reason J.B. started to tell the story of how he lost his maiden at a youthful age to his mother's housekeeper. This was no quick summary. It had a beginning, a build up, a climax, a resolution, a denouement—the whole works. And, it was so funny, so hilarious, so incredibly ridiculous to be relating such a tale out here where the whole "field" of riders could hear it, that Tom and I almost fell off our horses.

I halt my trek. I look north across the valley below, over the creek, over the mile of hills rising up on the far side of Hess Road to the yellow barns, then house, and at the top of the hill, the yellow indoor track with no Tom in it directing his riders to do something impossible.

It's a cold, miserable, windy day in December. A few owners are coming. He wants to show them something. Celeste and I jog and canter around the indoor track. The wind bangs against the northwest wall of windows. Tom and Robert Cutler, who "rubs" the seven horses stabled in the new stalls inside the perimeter of the track, start wrestling with the twelve-foot tree limbs that lie in the dirt alongside the inside wall. They pull the limbs out and set them across, inserting the ends into the ladder of two-by-four slots in the walls. Two feet. We are on young horses. We jog around, jumping them. Three feet. We turn, go the other way, canter over them. The owners and Tom are standing up against the inside wall between two of the jumps. Tom enlists the help of one owner, who is no help, in setting the limbs apart from one another, forming a three-foot wide spread fence, and bringing the top limbs up to four feet. These are limbs six inches in diameter that do not break slid into slots made of two-by-fours hammered into the main support posts of the walls. Make a mistake and you're out of luck.

The indoor does not have a high ceiling. On its front side, running along the driveway and facing the "finish line field," the original builder made two sections in the roof beneath which fences could be set up. In those sections, the rafters do not go straight across from the top of the inside wall to the outside wall. Instead, two A-frames were built into the ceiling creating an extra three feet of overhead space so that your horse can jump high without tearing your head off. However, a decade ago, the back side had collapsed in a storm, and when it was rebuilt, no A-frame spaces were constructed. The two-by-six rafters go straight across. In short, I ride a little tall in the saddle, and as the fences went up, I did worry about my forehead catching a well buttressed two-by-six at a gallop, which could've been the end of me, but I didn't bring this up.

"Patrick," Tom says. "You go this direction." He points to the right. "Celeste, you go the opposite, and I want you both to time it so you meet here at this fence and jump it at the same time." I stare at him as if he is crazy. Does he really mean it? Yes, he does. And there my potential owner stands beside him. He owns the timber horse I want to ride in the spring. Celeste notices my hesitation. "What's the matter, Patrick? You scared?" Her favorite means of relaxation on Sundays is to jump out of airplanes. Tom takes a pull of his Pall Mall. He is training me. He is showing this owner what I, an old timer, can do. He has confidence in me. He takes another pull. Hands on hips, keeping his face directed toward the fences, squinting his eyes, he looks up at me, directly into my eyes, and holds it for a second.

I did it. First at a canter. Then at a gallop. On a young, but athletic, horse. Celeste was not even fazed. It took my breath away. Day after day, he pushed me beyond what I wanted to do, what I thought I could do, whether it was breezing horses, schooling over hurdles—fast!—or following him down the row of a just-cut corn field at a full gallop out hunting, sprinting up a steep hill, and then jumping out over a four and a half foot board fence.

Tom is no longer standing inside the big sliding doors of the indoor track watching us boomerang around and around. He is no longer walking down the aisle of the old bank barn, exercise saddle with pads and bridle draped across it over one arm, and unsnapping the webbing to a stall to tack up a horse—*the same bank barn where on a rainy day we heard John Lennon had been murdered, and after every set we couldn't cool them out by walking them. We put them in the stalls, grabbed a fist full of clean straw, twisted it into a bundle, and rubbed and rubbed while we listened to a rock'n roll station play Lennon songs all morning. Godfather Gary Winants rubbed his horse Cookie so long that Tom had to chase him out of the stall. Jack "Chubby" Ball, thin as a rake, was rubbing Mickey Free. Bob Witham was wrapping bandages on a flat horse. Bill Riley bustled around, neatening up. And John Lennon was there with us.*

From the hilltop, a breeze picking up, scooping the top dusting of snow off the crust and blowing it into my eyes, making me squint, I can see the yellow house, the old sprawling farm house, the living room with its wall of leather-bound equestrian books, its open space in the middle where Mimi had set a New Year's table for four a year ago and we'd had the most magical dinner by the fire. Tom had a hundred-year-old book of his grandparents' on the table, with a slip of paper marking a page. He opened it, asked me to read a passage before dinner: a beautiful poem giving all the emotion and feeling of electricity in the air at a hunt meet before the steeplechase jockeys are given a leg up, and then the race, all the possible outcomes: victory, or finishing in the middle of the pack, or falling and watching your horse, riderless, gallop on with the others as you achingly get up off the ground. The fire cast shadows on the wall of books, enlivening their bindings, tempting us to open them, bringing to life the literature and history of centuries of racing. The wind blew outside, rattling the window panes, making us feel warm and safe as we thought of the race horses quietly munching hay, lying down and getting up, sipping fresh water out of the buckets Tom had just topped off—twelve in the bank barn, the seven in the Charlestown barn, eight in the "Pretty Boy Barn," and Robert's seven up top inside the indoor track.

The fires—the fire in the living room fireplace, in the den, in Mimi's bedroom, in Elizabeth's room—he padded barefoot at night from one to the next keeping them all going. One winter, his bad foot hurt so much that the only way he could get the firewood up the steps was by crawling on his knees. And then, the spacious western fireplace in the studio, Frank Voss's studio with the wall-sized paneled window facing north and looking out over the "finish line field" letting in the northern light. Some nights, Tom would set that fire blazing, pour Mimi a glass or two of champagne, have a few sips himself, put on a good movie, but before watching it, he'd laughingly text me—just two miles away through the cold and over the snow-muffled woods, the ice-covered creeks, the bare frozen fields we knew every square inch of—a photo of Mimi luxuriantly stretched out on the leather couch, pointing out that I'd better get my act together if I wanted to keep up in our race since teenagers in this field of activity.

Snow, winter, cold—we loved it. Those few months in the winter when there were no steeplechase races, who would show at the door of my writing room at 7:00 on a Sunday morning? There he suddenly was, the door wide open, cold air blasting in, hands on his hips: "Come on, you've worked enough on that book. I've got a set tacked up and the alfalfa field harrowed." He knew I loved to gallop in the snow.

Twenty minutes later, I'd walk through the arch to the Pretty Boy Barn into the yard—tree in the middle of what would be a grassy mound surrounded by an asphalt walking ring if it weren't for all the snow. A short row of six stalls leads to the feed room in the corner of the backwards L, then there's a row of eight, all opening into the yard.

Horses look out over their webbings set at shoulder height. I hear a gravelly voice, "Patrick." It's Jack, the late Wassie's younger brother. The Ball family had grown up on Atlanta Hall when Tom's grandparents ran it. For most of our lives, Wassie had lived in the cottage across from the Pretty Boy Barn. "Got my stakes horse tacked up. Tom picked this saddle because you like the big stirrups."

"Morning, Jack," I say, as if I stepped into this arena every morning all week. "Pull him out." Jack, tall, in his late sixties, face toughened, leathery, criss-crossed with a spider web of red and purple lines, opens the webbing, and leads the horse out.

"Give him a turn?"

"Yes—please."

I relax by the mounting block, studying the horse as he walks. At the block, Jack stands in front of the horse while I check the girth and saddle, the sweet scent of Kentucky bourbon wafting over me. I step up on the block and ease myself into the saddle.

Instead of turning the horse loose before I have my feet in the stirrups, before I've tightened the girth and tied a knot in the reins, as many grooms do today, Jack is old-school. He walks the horse until he hears me say, "He's all right, Jack. Thanks." Knowing we'll be galloping in the snow and it'll be slippery—a horse could go down—I pull my irons up short. If his feet slide out from under him, I want to be able to step off.

Tom and Celeste are on their horses. Celeste is the top and longest serving exercise rider on the farm. She is bundled in gray 1970's ski pants and parka, thick scarf wound around her neck and face. Only her eyes are visible. She thinks she's twenty-seven, not fifty-seven, weighs a hundred pounds, and will willingly, trustingly, even blindingly, exe-cute—down to the most precise and torturous detail—exactly what Tom directs us to do. We're hacking to the start of the gallop, every step accentuated by the crunch of the snow. The night before, and then again at 6:00 this morning, Tom had been on a tractor pulling a twenty-foot wide harrow around the field.

We jog down the hill to the chicken coop we'd jumped head-and-head as children out hunting on Pepper and Queenie and decades later on Welterweight and Florida Law. Tom turns, and in an uncharacteristic move, drops the reins, lets his horse take off, daring us to go with him. I urge my horse on, and then I'm alongside Tom—Celeste has pulled in behind us—both our horses pulling, flinging their heads, wanting to go full blast, their hooves striking the harrowed snow making a crackling sound, packed clumps of snow jetting out behind us, Tom bowed over, picking up speed, the two of us together. And now what, I think, as I turn to walk back.

After the gallop, we hack home the long way, cooling the horses out, Celeste and I getting chilled but the cold doesn't affect Tom. He's riding in his old zip-up, leather-soled Kroops jodhpur boots—thin leather— while I'm in my insulated yet streamlined L. L. Bean boots. I have pulled a bandana over my head, around my ears, knotted it by the back of my neck, and plunked the Caliente Dickie gave me thirty years ago on top. Tom is wearing no helmet He has taken a fifty-year-old, itchy, moth-eaten, yellow and black wool pommel pad made of two knit layers, opened up the two layers and pulled it down over his ears.

We ride them right into the stalls, slide off stiffly, slowly—trying not to get that painful sting in the feet—onto the straw, pull off the tack. "I got him, Patrick," Jack says. "Go get warm," the sweet smell of bourbon combined with my frozen state bringing me back to galloping at Pimlico in the winters before classes at Gilman and then Hopkins. I hobble to the dark-stained, pine-panelled tack room, ribbons Tom's grandmother won in the show ring in the 1930's and '40s strung across one wall, old photos of Tom's earliest horses winning on another wall, a photo of Dougie Small, Dickie's older brother, a six foot jockey, his body honed down to sinew and bone, stirrups up short as a flat rider, looking classic, like a European rider—Lester Piggott—on Cookie in the winner's circle, Mimi and Godfather Gary by Cookie's head, smiling, Tom hiding behind them, grinning; dusty hunting saddles no one uses on their racks; and Tom, smoking, still in his parka and pommel pad for a hat, sitting at his big wooden desk covered with condition books, Racing Forms, envelopes holding horses' identification papers, half-smoked packs of Pall Malls, an open check book, ash tray, legal pad with notes, a battered leather brief case, sheets of paper with his signature scrawled over and over across them, and an "itcher"—a dollar bill folded into a small triangle, like a guitar pick, which he uses to scratch himself.

I sit on the collapsing couch, springs having no spring, my butt almost going to the floor. Pull off my boots, set them on the crackling iron radiator, wave irritably at Tom's smoke, rub my feet. He grins, pulls open the bottom desk drawer, shuffles through papers. "Damn, it's not in there. I forgot. Have to hide it from Jack."

I point with my thumb to the little room on the other side of the wall, behind me. "Is he still living in the back room?" A few years ago, Jack had taken all the "traps" out of the storage room, set up a bed, and he's been there ever since. "Yes. Where else would he live?" He stands, walks to a yellow tack trunk with black cross sashes, opens the top, flips through the tack, pulls out a fresh bottle, cracks the seal and takes a pull. He hands it to me. I take a swig. It goes down beautifully, smoothly, warming my chest, my soul, connecting us, connecting us to the farm, to Wassie, to my father, to our love of horses and racing, sealing off the outside world of modernity and computers and terrorism and cell phones and political correctness so that all that exists is the two of us 8:00 Sunday morning sitting together in a tack room with memorabilia from our youth—before our youth—all around, the radiators clanging, the air thick with tobacco smoke and the scent of saddle soap and Lexol and Neatsfoot Oil, the pungency of horse sweat rising up from the pile of dirty saddle towels and rub rags by the washing machine.

The door opens. The frigid air blasts in. Celeste laughs at us, then says, hopefully, "Got three tacked up."

He squints and looks at me.

"Let me get the boots back on."

Out we go and do it again. I never thought that one day I'd look back on these moments—irregularities in my normal schedule, irregularities that had become regularities over the past fifty years—as some of the most intensely pleasing and totally absorbing moments in my life.

I walk, march, trudge through the snow, talking to Tom, conjuring him up, envisioning him walking alongside me, hearing what he would say, this figure beside me—it *is* Tom, he *is* talking to me, he *is* alive. I trick myself into it. I step into my writing room, write a letter.

Dear Tom—Dear Partner, Brother, Cousin, Friend since birth, Godfather to my son Paddy, Father of my godson Sam, Fellow godson of our fathers' best friend Gary Winants,

You are here with me. You will always be here with me. Not a day has gone by in my life when I have not thought: ha—wouldn't Tom get a kick out of this! I could be teaching a class or feeding the horses and I think of you. Now, I still think of you—here, now, your presence.

I'm so glad I gave you the big kiss on your whiskery cheek and said "I love you" that last moment of our time together. I am thankful for that. I'll always remember that moment. You accepted it. Seated at the counter in the kitchen, you just kept staring straight ahead—with that gleam in your eye, Mimi across from you.

You know, a dream of mine was to stand up and give a certain talk in five or six years with you seated, embarrassed and audibly sighing, beside me. I wanted to give a rousing, rafter-rattling cele-bratory speech about your devotion to horses—the championships, the Eclipse Awards, your painstakingly hard work—when you were inducted into the racing Hall of Fame. And then walk out of the Fasig Tipton pavilion, over to Saratoga Racecourse, watch your horse win the A. P. Smithwick, stand in the winner's circle together, as we did with Cookie, with Mickey, with Brigade of Guards, with Anofferyoucan't Refuse, and celebrate on into the night.

In many ways, we know each other quietly—even telepathi-cally. For years you smoked Pop's cigarette—Pall Malls, and every morning, you and I crumple up a red or blue bandana and stick it in our in our right back pocket. I saw the simple things: the way only you drive into our entrance, swing right, close to the corn crib, spin the wheel left, and turn the car perfectly, fluidly, 360 degrees, bringing it to a stop. Where? You know I know: you execute the turn as Pop used to do, and you park in the exact spot where Pop always parked his car. Ready to go.

I can feel your spirit, strongly. You are strong. You command the attention of the room, and then walk through without saying a word. You and I both had our ambitions stoked, forged, in the stable of my father where we received the same training and lived by emulating the same principles. I went off to write; you stayed and polished and perfected your knowledge of the Thoroughbred horse, and met with plenty of defeats and deaths and losses, and you kept going. You understood and supported my ambition.

Who showed up decades ago at an awards ceremony on a dreary Sunday afternoon in Baltimore when I was given a check for $300 and a certificate for a story I'd written. You had a horse in at Laurel that day—ran the horse, jumped in the car, sped old-time racetrack style to the Enoch Pratt library, and when I rose to receive the certificate, I looked into the audience of one dozen, and there you were, with Mimi. You took us all to lunch, where you leaned over and quietly offered, " If you want to frame that check, I'll write you another."

Years later, it was April, your busiest time of year, and I was in the running for a book award. I was one of three finalists—the winner of the purse, much improved since that last one—to be announced in Lexington, Kentucky in just a few days. We were at your house after the Elkridge Harford races—at your party which you failed to attend. As we were preparing to leave, I walked into the kitchen and there you were, just back from the barn, dirty and scruffy, having concluded a long day of overseeing the entire point to point held on your farm, starting each race, and winning half of them with your own horses.

"Hey, when're you going down?" you asked, eyeballing me.

"Our flight's Tuesday night."

"Mine's early Wednesday morning," you said, looking away, your voice trailing into a whisper.

That's what I love about you.

It feels as if a physical, palpable chunk of me is gone—those early wild years, the riding years, sharing my father, sharing the striving, the sacrifices we made for our passions. The galloping head-and-head on our ponies, on Pop's horses.

The jumping. You were born jumping. When we skied, you jumped every mogul. When we rode Pepper and Queenie together, you sought out every chicken coop we could handle.

When we skated, you had to put bales of straw on the ice to jump. And when we started driving: oh boy—on the way to the Merrymans we schooled the Corvair, getting a foot of air over the bump on Cold Bottom Road.

Coming home with Tiger driving one night, Bobby Burke's big-engined Oldsmobile stood off too far at a bridge. We went through a tree and landed in a stream. It looked like our time was up, but this time I saved you.

You might have been a little too brave, too tough, too stoic—that injury this fall. You told me about the light-headedness, the falling down, the not telling anyone, the putting off going to the doctor. And then, on your last day with us when you felt sick and weak, you had to go out and work, plowing the entrance in the arctic chill. That was your way.

Those last days, you seemed so relaxed and pleasant and at peace. Happy with your family all around you. Even in death—I know that body on the bed this morning was not you.

This is you, this spirit I feel in the air. The power, force shimmering here, now, this love of animals and family and the out of doors, of steeplechasing and schooling young horses and giving them a pat on the neck after they've gone well, this going to the races, going there on a mission, willing the horse to win—like you did that afternoon after taking the gamble of a lifetime—you and Douglas putting up a quarter of a million to run John's Call, soon to be a ten-year-old, on Breeder's Cup Day against the fastest turf horses on the globe. John blazed down the backside at Churchill Downs with the leaders, and you and I were on the rail, by the wire. I was standing behind you and John was flying—my body felt on fire, John, old John, how could he hold this speed, how could he keep it going? Around the last turn, he was pinned in along the hedge. Then we were both jumping up and down as Jean Luc pulled him out wide at the head of the stretch and he was head-and-head with the other two. You were calling out "Come on John! Come on John!" and then Irish superstar Johnny Murtaugh on Kalanisi flew up on the outside. The four of them came battling down the stretch, Kalanisi winning, John third, beaten a neck for $2 million, having lost his shoe.

Those feet of his! You had to deal with those platter plates. If John hadn't blown that shoe off at the quarter pole—he would have won by a neck. He had the same guts and heart and drive as you.

What a laughably terrible dinner we had that night, but it was fun with your mother, wife and children all there.

Food and drink always tasted better with you: how about the kidney pies after hunting. Well, first the port—then the kidney pies. We'd be in our boots, laughing, warming up, the sweat and dirt still on our faces, your face with a bad scratch or two, Mimi on the other side of the kitchen counter, serving up the port and pie and laughing with us.

I'm glad we got in the hunting together on Welterweight and Florida Law. Ha—how I loved rolling along, letting'em tippy toe, and jumping that big coop on the racecourse head-and-head with you. How I enjoyed going to the meet, the hunt itself, and then, best of all, when you and I drove home together, sitting up in the cab, just the two of us. . . .

It was harder to accomplish as we got older—the just-the-two-of-us. First of all, you became more and more enamored with Mimi. Secondly, the kids came around, and then when you became a grandfather—well, it was impossible to extract you from Atlanta Hall. I'd have to stop by and talk to you between visits from a caravan of relatives and friends and workers—not to mention your constantly ringing cellphone—calls from grooms, jockeys, agents, owners. And the sycophants! How you savored that word for years. *"Sycophants!"* you'd say, after that one night twenty-five years ago we had it out. No blows exchanged. But that night I remembered the force of your body punches as a teenager.

* * *

I feel better now.

The writing helps.

I just stepped outside, relaxed, wrote my initials in the snow, as we used to do as boys when skiing or sledding or skating.

A.P.S. and *T.H.V.*

You know Tom, they're still carved in our dining room

window. They glow at sunset.

The sun is setting over the Griswolds' hill where I saw you hunting a few weeks ago.

"I've been hunting three times a week," you proclaimed the other night, and scowled at me. I'd been missing from the field and I caught your message. Then you admitted, "The last time my foot hurt so bad, I had to get off the horse in the middle of the hunt, call Gary and ask him to come pick me up."

The papers, the press, your thousands of followers—*Tom, you are having quite the write-ups.*

Still, so many people misunderstand you, but you don't care. You don't like small talk, and you tend to put your head down, light a cigarette and walk the other way at the sign of a phony approaching—Salinger's *Catcher in the Rye* being a favorite of yours. At work, you work. "It's in the details," you told me. "Pay attention," you say to your riders and grooms. You push all else aside and focus on each individual horse. No glad-handing, no chitchatting, no distractions.

Yet, you do enjoy striking up conversations with those who have no idea who you are. You like being incognito.

Two nights before John runs in the Breeder's Cup, we're in Louisville, driving back from the barn, stop at a tavern. We are staying at the legendary Seelbach Hotel, along with the stars of international racing. I'd thought we might hobnob with a few of them on this night.

"I don't know, Tom?" I say, as we pull up alongside a row of mud-splattered pick-ups parked in front of a dark, low-slung tavern.

"Ah, come on."

We sit at the bar. One rough-looking place. You light up a cigarette, start a conversation with the bartender. Four big construction workers are shooting pool. We've both stopped drinking as usual but on this occasion we have a beer which doesn't count. One more. The pool game ends. One of the players approaches the bar to order a round and you start chuckling.

You nod to him. "How you doing?"

He says, "Good, hey—what's so funny, pal?"

"I was just thinking, that game of pool could be put in the Guinness Book of World Records."

"Yeah, how's that?"

"For being the longest game in the history. . . ."

"Oh yeah," the guy says, laying one thick arm on the bar, and with the other waving the three at the pool table to come over.

An elbow pokes into your rib cage. My elbow. "Time to go Tom, let's go." I know you never back down.

In Orlando the night of my rehearsal dinner—you were the best man in my wedding the next day. We—you and my ushers—had been thrown out of a nightclub across the street from the police station. I was being held by two bouncers, worked over by another. Then this huge undercover cop was strangling me; I broke free and he was coming for me. Suddenly, there you were.

"Listen you big . . . , you touch my friend again and I'll kill you." That night, and any other night, or morning, or moment, I always knew, no matter what the odds, what the circumstance, you'd be there.

You're not afraid of anything: except snakes, sharks, heights, Mrs. Bedford, and Mimi when angry. And yet you relish experiencing fear and tension, *vicariously*. I got your text the other frigid, snowy day when school was closed: "*Vertigo* on at 2:00. " I remember that late night as kids we watched it in Ned's room.

You have a sensitive side—a love of children, of sculpture and painting, of well-written novels, of books on American history, of classic movies—especially Hitchcock. In life, you did have to toughen up. First, your father Eddie's death that morning we were having breakfast at your house, then your brother Ned's, my father's, your brother Jack's, our godfather Gary's, my mother's, Uncle Mikey's. Jonathon Kiser—most nervy and athletically gifted rider you've ever had, dies of a freak head injury caused by falls that occurred while water skiing and swinging from a Tarzan rope. Bob Witham—dies from a fall from a horse, not unlike ones we've all had. We got through them together. Suspendido, the timber horse of your youth—you retire him from racing. He's living the good life of a working stallion—hit by lightning. Florida Law, the timber horse of your mature years—you retire him. He's living the good life of a hunter—hit by lightning.

Remember when we were ten, before any of this happened, and we were shooting sparrows with our BB guns? You hit one. You picked it up, cupped it in your hands, and I saw a tear. We buried the sparrow, right there, outside our back porch.

You are a tender man. I see you holding your granddaughter Genevieve, walking through the creek in "The Meadow," teaching her, talking to her. I hear your voice, going lower and lower into a whisper when you are discussing something that touches you.

This letter is winding down.
It's time to feed and hay—
the horses are striding through the snow,
crossing the stream where we used to build dams
heading for the shed.
Do you think they need blankets tonight?

A quote from Hemingway comes to mind: "A man can be destroyed but not defeated."

In your case, Tom, we can top that. Our last night together, Jimmy Santoro and I brought up the time a horse kicked you in the jaw eight years ago. You attempted to continue training, directing your astonished riders to jog down to the "finish line fence," walk along the fence, turn, and school head-and-head over the first two hurdles, and then, "Each man for himself!"

Telling it to us, you laughed, "I didn't know it was so bad until Armando walked out, looked at me, and almost fainted. That's when they made me go to the hospital."

You thought about it, lying on the sofa in your living room, your foot raised as the doctors told you to do. You grinned and swung your feet to the floor. You stood up. "But I didn't go down," you said, and laughed, "I didn't go down."

Tom, you will never go down in my book. You can be kicked in the head, spurting blood, spitting teeth, but you will never go down. You will always be here for me, inviolate, steadfast, immutable, and for your children Sam and Elizabeth, your grandchildren Genevieve and Thomas, for this countryside you and Jack worked to preserve, for the Hunt and the keeping of its traditions, for steeplechasing and the racing you loved, and most of all for Mimi who will forever possess, and stoke the flames of, that passionate, wild love you had for her, and gave her, until your last moment.

Love,
"Your friend"

One More Run

Optima dies prima fugit.
(The best days are the first to flee.)

— Virgil

January 23
Dear Tom,

Snow day. No school. Snow and more snow. Wish we were going skiing. Remember the trip to "Blue Balls," that's what we called it—meeting your brother Ned and his great friend Harry there. You and I drove up in the Corvair through a blizzard. Schools had closed. Pop gave us a few days off from galloping at Pimlico; we left that night, against Mom's wishes. The car was registered in her name and she called the State Police to report it had been stolen. By the time they'd filed the report, we were out of the state and in Pennsylvania.

We flew past four-wheel drive pickups loaded down with firewood stuck in drifts and state snow-removal dump trucks releasing salt and gravel out the back, the plows in front skidding and scraping on the asphalt of the highway, shooting up sparks. You found a country-western station and we listened attentively to a favorite, Marty Robbins "El Paso." It was the full-length version that Ned had in his stack of 45's. "Out in the west Texas town of El Paso, I fell in love with a Mexican Girl. . . ." The narrator guns down another cowboy who is flirting with "wicked Faleena;" he feels terrible about it, and then steals a horse to escape. Tragic it was. He returns! "It's been so long since I've seen the young

335

maiden/ My love is stronger than my fear of death." A posse of the murdered cowboy's friends guns him (horse thief as well as murderer) down, and he dies in the arms of the "wicked Faleena," or, hallucinates that he does. So sad. Shaking it off, we discussed Marty's dual career: he was a singer/composer as well as *a race-car-driver*. This gave us hope: I could be a steeplechase jockey *and* I could do something else: travel, learn French, continue with my flying lessons, apply to the Foreign Service, join the CIA like my Uncle Ned, a World War II ace fighter pilot, on the Whitman side of the family. You wanted to be a steeplechase jockey *and* learn everything about breeding and raising Thoroughbreds; you wanted to travel to Ireland and England and France and Argentina and see how it was done there, and then to train racehorses. You wanted to be a *horseman*. So did I. We *were* horsemen. And we were both wearing our Irish wool "horseman" caps and both had red bandanas in our right rear pockets.

Onward went the Corvair—little car with big heart, my first, given to me by my grandmother Emma "Um" Smithwick, *our* first car which you and I learned to drive in, bumping through the fields of the Smithwick Stables racing farm at Hydes, splashing through streams, playing chicken with Speedy Kiniel on the tractor in the top paddock. We had grabbed a fifty pound bag of feed and tossed it on the back seat; I'd just sprung for snow tires on the back wheels; the engine was in the back sending its power directly to the rear wheels; and the Corvair would take us anywhere in the snow as long as it didn't bottom out.

As soon as we crossed the state line, we put on our serious, senior faces—tough to do at barely sixteen but you looked older than your age—pulled out jockey Dave Mitchell's draft card and bought a case of Iron City and a couple of bottles of red wine at a dingy liquor store, slapped the case of beer on the feed bag, tucked the wine bottles into the pile of parkas, gloves and hats, and sped through Pennsylvania to our motel where we got very little sleep, putting up with the antics and hijinks of Ned's friend, Harry.

The next day, whip-like leather thongs tossed around our necks, leather wine skins under our left arms, we skied in the below-zero temperatures into the late afternoon, one or two ski patrolman laughing and joking and skiing with us, until we were the only ones on the slopes.

The lift man at the bottom examined our faces for signs of frostbite. Then he asked, "Can you feel your fingertips? Can you feel your toes?"

"Yes," we lied, as he helped us onto the chair. We leaned back, pulled down the safety bar. Hands unfeeling in our gloves, we each fumbled with the mouth of the wine skin. Using our thumbs, we popped open a small button-like snap. Simultaneously, we each lifted the skin high with our left hand, held the nozzle with our right, squeezed the bulbous skin and watched the dark, red, essence of life, of earth, of a hot, dry day, on a hillside in the south of France as it came up out of the skin, was pressured through the narrow nozzle and arced, with clear definition, a thick purple ribbon, spiraling and lacing through the air—the universe in the background white: white snow, white trees, white snow-covered steel poles holding us up high—and then splashed onto our lips and into our mouths. That leathery taste, the musky magic: it rippled down our throats and into our bellies. High on the lift, exposed to the wind, looking down at the empty slopes, the cold now coming up through the ice-covered slats of the chair freezing our asses, you started singing, "I fought the law and the law won, robbing stores with a six gun. . . ." and there was nowhere in the universe we'd rather be.

The lift man at the top huddled in his glass-enclosed hut, smiled and waved to us and at the end of the day the ski patrolmen blocking the entrance to the slope laughed, gave in after we'd hollered through cheeks and lips so cold it felt like we'd been injected with Novacaine, "Another run. One more run!"

Blue Balls had the most God-awful lodge, an old Army barracks; everything was concrete, and steel, and cold, so as darkness fell over the mountain, we poled and skated past the lodge overflowing with families, past the garages and sheds holding the trucks, snowmobiles and snow-blowing equipment; schussed through one hard-packed parking lot, our bodies down low, in racing tucks; sped toward a snowplow-made bank, head-and-head, jumped together, and flew, holding our tucks tight, slapping down on the surface of another lower hard-packed parking lot; raced through it, straight to the Corvair, jamming in our edges, spraying snow across the door. We bent low and forward, struggled to pull up the bear-trap binding and to release our ice-encrusted, leather boots from the skis. We stood the skis up, checked the bottoms for gouges in the wood and loose or ripped-out edges

I pushed the button on the Corvair's door handle with my numb thumb and pulled the lever. Neither budged. I banged the rubber-coated handle of my ski pole against the button. Nothing happened. Turned around and, like a horse, kicked the door with the bottom of my ski boot, not too hard, several times. Yanked the door open, cranked up the engine. Gloves off, we set the skis and poles in the rack, pulled down the braces, our fingers sticking to the frigid aluminum. Feet blocks of numbness in our leather boots, fingers stiff, noses dripping, we hopped in the bucket seats, turned on the heater, waited for the ice to melt off the boot laces. We pulled the boots off, tossed them in the back, and as we accelerated out of the lot you reached back, grabbed two cans of Iron City, pulled the tabs off—*and I can taste it now, Tom; I can hear the Corvair's engine, air-cooled, and yes, its sewing machine-like surge.* We'd sing Tiger's drinking ditty—not having a clue what it was about—that began,

> Put on that old blue ointment,
> and to the crowd's disappointment,
> take a hot bath every other day.
> Oh, Jesus how it itches,
> but it kills the sonovabitches
> in that good old mountain way, ...

I see you fiddling with the radio dial, turning it to the Motown station we'd found. It might be the Supremes, "Look out for Bill, leave my Billy alone." You started singing along. You thought you were a great singer. We laughed at the half-frozen beers foaming up and overflowing onto our hands and wrists. Smokey came on, Smokey Robinson and the Miracles—"The Tracks of My Tears." We sang along:

> People say I'm the life of the party
> 'cause I tell a joke or two
> Although I might be laughing loud and hearty
> Deep inside I'm blue
> So take a good look at my face
> You'll see my smile looks out of place
> If you look closer it's easy to trace

The tracks of my tears
I need you . . . need you . . . need you

Outside—I'm masquerading
Inside—my hope is fading . . .

We toasted to another day of great skiing. We toasted to the
lift man at the bottom, to the lift man at the top, to the ski patrol.
The Corvair coming to life, the heater pumping in some warmth,
we were getting feeling back in our wool-socked feet. We lifted
the frozen cans to our lips, tasted the slushy froth and the steel
from the can and then the icy beer, a chunk of it banging around
in the stiff can. I pushed in the clutch with my left foot, put the
stick into first gear, let out the clutch and pushed the accelerator
with my right foot, let the wheels spin—snow jetting, pluming
behind us. Like a quick, light horse coming out of the starting
gate, the Corvair gathered itself together and we cruised out of the
parking lot, proceeding across sheets of ice, down into and back
out of deep ruts, and through foot-high drifts. "Do you believe in
magic, in a young girl's heart, . . ."

Wedeling down the mountain switchbacks, we opened fresh
cans of Iron City, laughed at the explosion of foam. We were
smoothly negotiating the switchbacks in the steaming Corvair, you
singing and keeping rhythm with your hands on the dashboard,
enjoying the feeling back in our toes, able to sing and talk without
having the garbled, mumbled sounds of a drunk man, the blood
pulsating fast now through our bodies, our fingers stinging and
lively and hot as if bees were buzzing around them, and the bees
were in our wool hats now, the wool itchy, the bees buzzing, our
heads hot, the blood pulsating through our ears, our ears hot. We
pulled off the thick wool hats, tossed them in the back. Without
the gloves, without the boots, without the hats, we were freed.
We could hear, we could feel, we could sing. Static on the radio.
We lost the Motown station. You turned the knob. Buddy Holly!
"Peggy Sue"! You turned the radio up higher. How you loved
Buddy Holly. You sang along, "Peggy Sue, Peggy Sue, I'm talking about Peggy Sue, my Peggy, my Peggy Su-oo-oo-oo...." You
opened the glove compartment, pulled out a new maroon pack
of Pall Malls and a lighter, unwrapped the cellophane, tapped
the pack against the dashboard a few times like an old-timer, lit

a cigarette. "Freeze out!" I yelled. (*Remember our "Freeze outs"?*)
I unwound my window, reached back and unwound the one
behind me while delivering one of my early diatribes, of over
forty years of diatribes to come, against smoking. You unwound
the windows on your side. Elvis's "Ain't Nothing but a Hound
Dog" came on. You belted it out along with Elvis. We whipped
past ill-fated vehicles that had skidded off the mountain into the
woods hours ago, red light-blinking trucks parked nearby, big-
bellied men in insulated canvas body-suits pulling out winches
and attaching them to axles and bumpers.

Flattening out, the switchbacks ending, we entered the town
of motels and bars and gas stations and liquor stores, men pumping gas, women outside the grocery store talking to each other
with their shoulders hunched and their bodies stiff. They stared
at us, our elbows on the door's edge, our hair blowing in the wind,
a summer tune playing, "Oh Happy Days, oh Happy Days . . . *it
was a bright, hot summer day,* . . . when Jesus walked...." right to the
motel parking lot.

Ned and Harry, looking neat and dapper, were standing out
in front of the cramped room the four of us shared. They were
holding up a fresh gallon of Early Times and bags filled with sharp
cheese and crackers, hot, spicy mustard, and smoked ham, cans of
sardines. We knew from their ridiculing us for continuing to ski
into the afternoon, that they'd retired early to the lodge, hoping to
strike up a conversation with some ski bunnies and invite them
back to enjoy cocktails in the room. They must've failed at that.
We laughed at the sight of them.

This wasn't the most sought-out motel—hardly any cars in the
parking lot, which was one large, snowy ice rink. It was tempting. You put your hands up on the dashboard, bracing yourself, released a deep sigh, and said, "Oh no, not this again." The
Corvair continued full tilt across the parking lot. Harry and Ned
were watching. We were headed straight for them. Harry had his
key in the door, and, looking over his shoulder at us, stepped into
the room. Ned stood there on the sidewalk, facing us, taunting
us. I jammed on the brakes, spun the wheel to the left, down-
shifted into second, floored the accelerator, sending the Corvair
into a spin, as if it were on a turntable, the front wheels in the center, the rear wheels pivoting us—arms and legs braced—around
and around, creating a vortex of jetting snow. Ned was laughing.

Harry, back out, was waving his hands and hollering at us to stop.

Tom—at this moment decades later I can feel my grip on the steering wheel. I can see the upward jetting snow, hear the engine, remember the wild, unreal spinning around and around, a perpetual motion 45 rpm Marty Robbins hit record that was never going to end. "Another run! Another run!" we had yelled to the ski patrolmen. I wish we could schuss one more time down the slopes, wedel one more time through the switchbacks, spin one more time a full 360 degrees in the parking lot. One more run, Tom. One more run.

Your Partner,
Patrick

No Andrew

January 24—Friday

5:15 a.m. No Andrew. I still haven't heard from Andrew. Not a call. Not a text. Not a message. I ache from this double loss. Tom, like a brother, and now Andrew, my son.

What to do? Get to work. Got to finish grading this stack of papers. Have to give them back today in order to push forward to the upcoming weekend assignment: "White Washing the Fence. Write a true or fictional account, using the techniques of Mark Twain we've studied in *Tom Sawyer*. Create your own modern version of how Tom tricks others into helping him white wash the fence. Topics will vary. Washing and waxing the family car. Mowing the lawn. In my case it was mucking out the big shed in the barn and raking the leaves."

We Never Went
to Wyoming

January 25—Saturday
Dear Tom,

We never went to Wyoming. Instead, most of the time, we worked. You won races. I wrote and taught. Oh well, you were doing what you loved. And you would have had those new Irish horses this spring and would have kicked ass with them.

I'd been thinking we might go this coming summer. I really wanted to see the Voss ranch and to get on a cow pony and ride for miles and miles with you across the western landscape. It was a dream of mine. One never to be fulfilled. There's a lesson here. I continue to learn from you.

Every day I have these brain-blips. For instance, after your mother's funeral a few days ago, at the wake, I got away from all the people, went back to her bedroom suite, a sun-filled room I'd always found relaxing, and sat down. I suddenly thought, Good Lord, where the hell is Tom—I haven't seen him here! And then, what a downer, I remembered:

The smoking. The foot. How I'd been after you to stop smoking, and more recently to do something about that foot. The poor circulation in the foot, then the infection, then the loss of blood and the strain on your heart, and the sitting around for three weeks—whether an embolism or a heart attack, I think it was all connected. "Do you have a brain?" I asked that last night, after discussing, first, your dealing with the veterinarian about the infection, and then, your refusing to tell anyone about the diverticulitis. "Do you have a brain?" Why did I ever say that? I saw that it hurt you. I don't like that I said that. I was so relieved that night, almost giddy—you seemed in good shape; you were on your way back.

I think that kick in the jaw ten years ago knocked you back a step or two. Others didn't notice, and you never mentioned it, but your speaking—the use of your lips—was affected. A slight slur. A *sibilance*. You became quieter, more modest; you listened more. And I think it slowed the firing of the synapses in your brain a fraction of a second. No wonder, a fourteen hundred pound horse wearing steel shoes kicking you in the jaw; it was incredible that it didn't kill you.

And now what do I do?

I couldn't help but chuckle to myself when I shook hands with that teary woman at your funeral, a few years older than us, who when we were teenagers, late one night while her husband was away, gave you your first . . . a-hem . . . treat.

Years later when I galloped horses for you, you took me on those fast-paced cross-country schools after we'd gotten the horses out. You were quiet. You never said a thing, but I knew you were doing it for me. Then, you added the polo. I wish I'd appreciated the polo more. The polo at the end of a long morning. Racing time—I was in a rush to get to the desk. I've been in a rush for too long. Another lesson.

The Breeder's Cup. You sent me to the racing secretary's office, to the jocks' room, to the cafeteria on errands so I'd meet the world's top owners, trainers and riders, making me a working part of the whole mission. You made a point of bringing me to Scotty Schulhoffer's barn, where we talked to Scotty as he grazed Lemon Drop Kid, about to run against the best horses in the world.

And now, what do I do?

Remember the time we snuck around in the dark the night before the Junior Hunter Trials and put the fences up? Now that's being young!

How about that night in Unionville, Pennsylvania You called me at the Skyways Motel, said to come on out to your "chateau" in the country for the night. You were shacking up with the house baby sitter—with whom you claimed to be having a good time on the trampoline—and she'd left you in charge for the evening. Taking the organic mescaline! Pulling the five-foot speakers out on the patio, going down to the wine cellar, you choosing a few of the best whites, I pulling out a few of the best reds, then up to the shed-size closets, flipping through robes and suits, and Gatsby-like, tossing shirts and pajamas on the bed, picking out what we wanted, the sauntering out to the patio, listening to James Taylor sing "Mud Slide Slim and the Blue Horizon," both of us thinking of that cabin in the woods, of no pressure—this was when I was preparing to ride Curator and would have to lose fifteen more pounds; you were preparing to ride Attic Action and would have to lose twenty—as the record spun round and round. We forgot about the track and losing weight and laughed and joked and talked about our dreams.

How about those wild adult years—winning at Laurel with Cookie, going back to the Milton Inn, celebrating with Gary—having that whole room to ourselves. Another blip, there I go—I was just thinking of asking you what the name of that room is.

And now, what do I do?

We never went to Wyoming. A lesson. Don't make that mistake again. I sigh. You're gone—forever.

Love,
Patrick

January 26
Dear Partner,

Another day without you drags by. Listlessly, sullenly, depressingly, (Do you know, Tom, that in order to be more direct and succinct, Gabriel Garcia Marquez never used an adverb?) I glance over the above letter. It is wrong. The ending is way off. You live on. Every day you live on through the example you set and the influence on people you had.

This has never been clearer to me than at your wake. "I arrived in Maryland with $26,000 worth of credit card debt," one trainer told me. "I was talking to Tom one night, relating my woes, and he said, 'See you at the barn in the morning.' Tom gave me that break I needed."

"I was just off the boat," an Englishman related, "I'd gotten too big to ride races in England but was light enough to gallop. There I was—completely lost at Saratoga, walking around the Annex one morning. Tom asked what I was doing. I told him

I didn't have a f-ing idea." 'Get on the van going to Maryland at the end of the week,' Tom said. 'Mimi'll find you a place to live. You'll be galloping for me.' "

"Tom saved my life," a middle-aged man from Concord, Massachusetts—owner of a successful paving and construction company—proclaimed. "I was twelve and going nowhere. My parents had just gone through a tough divorce. I was dropped off at Tom and Mimi's house when Tom was training at Rockingham Park. Every morning, 5:30 sharp, I heard, 'Boy, time to get up.' We'd have coffee, drive to the track without saying a word. Tom would bark, 'OK boy, get to work.' I was mucking out stalls and walking hots. In the afternoons, I came back, hayed and fed, whirl-pooled. I owe the success of my career to Tom; he taught me that with hard work, you can do anything."

(Not exactly how I remember Rockingham! We had some fun, didn't we?—at that house on the lake: sitting out on the dock having rum punches with Mimi and my long-legged girlfriend at sunset, shopping for a fan. There we were in the fan department, being helped by a clerk. "Now, this is a good fan; it is extremely quiet," he said. "Listen," you said, "we don't want that fan. We're renting a little rickety house, and any sound carries through the entire building. My friend here," you nodded to me, and I started to worry what you were going to say, "needs a fan that'll cover up all the noise his young girlfriend . . . ." Good Lord. I laugh to myself, remembering the shocked expression on the clerk's face, and the so-pleased expression on yours.)

Irish jockeys—some working in the U.S.A., others having flown over from the old country—quaffed their whiskeys and regaled friends with stories of you giving them their first shot and launching their careers.

You taught them how to ride a race without them knowing it and before they ever went to the post for the first time.

They learned how to train by your example—no short cuts—through an apprenticeship with the best.

By the time you were in your mid-thirties, freshmen were matriculating into Voss University—young riders, young grooms, kids whose families had thrown them out, boys who needed a second chance—and a few seasons later graduating with a Voss Degree in how to work hard and how to treat a horse through its entire career and life.

You didn't train horses just to win races—seven hundred and six in all, including thirty graded stakes. You prolonged the lives and careers of horses, transforming middle aged flat campaigners who had lost their speed into steeplechase horses going either two and a sixteenth over hurdles or four miles over timber. Upon reaching the age of twelve, these veterans segued into the good life of full-time foxhunters. When too old for this—it was out into the big field, "The Meadow," as you called it, alluding to "The Elkridge-Harford Hunt Crossing Atlanta Hall Meadow" by your great uncle, Frank Voss, where the pensioners would run free. Frank finished this painting, with his brother Ned in the foreground, in 1942. Today, just out of the frame of the painting, is the oak under which you buried Cookie and where we spread the ashes of his owner, our godfather Gary. Art, racing, fox hunting, family history, environmental work (the trees you and Jack planted along the creek to prevent run off are tall and healthy) all came together when you rode through The Meadow. If ever a man lived by the theme "Two Tramps in Mud Time," by Robert Frost, the poet you loved—

> But yield who will to their separation,
> My object in living is to unite
> My avocation and my vocation
> As my two eyes make one in sight.
> Only where love and need are one,
> And the work is play for mortal stakes,
> Is the deed ever really done
> For Heaven and the future's sakes.

—it was you.

Atlanta Hall Farm—You turned it into a state-of-art training facility. That was an advantage, and that was a weight on your shoulders, too. In the middle of January, on a late afternoon before a blizzard was about to hit, there you would be, grease all over your hands, under a tractor, hooking up a plow. Early July, on a sultry Sunday afternoon, you were on a tractor, watering and harrowing the indoor track.

One year, part of the "indoor" collapses. Another year, a section of the outdoor track washes out. The barn needs a new roof. The fields need mowing. The alfalfa field has to be harvested.

Owning your own training center has its plusses and its minuses. But then I remember the sign on your office desk, the office Mimi had designed and made for you in the old blacksmith's shop, out away from everyone, which you never used: "No Crybabies."

Loyalty—the trait J.B. stressed in his eulogy. Loyalty to your riders. J.B. spoke of Jean-Luc Samyn, the turf specialist who rode John's Call. After winning the Sword Dancer Invitational at Saratoga in 2000, and then winning the Turf Classic Invitational Stakes at Belmont, you were approached by one jock's agent after another, and urged by kibitzers, to switch to a Hall of Fame jockey for the Breeders Cup. But you stayed with Jean Luc and Jean Luc rode him brilliantly that day. (J.B. refrained from mentioning, that after the occasional trip when Jean Luc did not ride him so brilliantly, your *sobriquet* for him was "The Human Anchor.")

Bravery, "grace under pressure," and stoicism—the traits Turney stressed in his eulogy, reading a military report on an ancestor of yours who fought with distinction in the Civil War. By the time you reached your sixties, your body "hurt all over," you told me one night. Foot problems? Right foot with the big bunion will no longer fit in your riding boot? Simple, cut out a section and go hunting all day with four square inches of foot exposed to the sleet and snow. Running horses at a point-to-point in Maryland, a sanctioned hunt meet in Tennessee, and a turf race at Belmont Park all on the same day? You'd better have inherited some military leadership genes in order to plan, coordinate, and order the movements of your troops. And on this day, what might be your most enjoyable moment? Holding granddaughter Genevieve in your arms and teaching her how to watch a race.

Family life. The racetrack is not known for being conducive to a healthy family life. When we grew up, steeplechase as well as flat outfits moved from one track to the next, year around. Trainers didn't have a chance to watch their children's soccer, ice hockey and lacrosse games. Wives were separated from their husbands.

You chose to batten down the hatches at Atlanta Hall and to ship. You often had to leave but only for a day or two at a time. This plan was also founded on the principal that some might not know: which is that all your life, with the exception of August in Saratoga, you couldn't bear to be away from home for more than a week.

Master of Foxhounds—you loved foxhunting. Your grandfather, E. S. "Ned" Voss, was Joint Master of the EHHC for thirty-one years, you for twenty-one. Elizabeth learned the art of foxhunting from you and has been steeped in your methods of training. She will soon be a Joint Master.

History : The movie *Titanic*, based on *A Night to Remember* by Walter Lord, comes out. We bring Sam and Paddy to the movie. (During the tragic parts, the tough parts, you go outside and have a cigarette.) Later, we meet Walter—Gilman School alumnus, Class of 1935, whom I had gotten to know well through writing the history of Gilman—for lunch. You quietly, respectfully, knowledgeably asked questions about the *Titanic*, had your paperback copy signed by the renowned historian in his eighties, and asked about Walter's book, *The Fremantle Diary, A Journal of the Confederacy.*

Literature: the night of my fortieth birthday, you gave me a box of pencils, Classic Number 2's. I got your "point." I use them every day. You were under pressure and arrived at the party already having had a few drinks and clearly not yourself. I learned later you had just heard devastating news about your brother Jack's health. But you came to the party, and you stood and recited a verse from Kipling's "Gunga Din," which ends, "You're a better man than I am, Gunga Din!"

Giving—you were generous. Where did Baltimore County trainers go in February when the ground was frozen? Speedy would drive Mikey's van over. Mikey's top rider Kurt Rosenthal, riding long, would jog miles and miles. Mikey would be on the wildest horse, looking for logs to jump. J.B. would have a set. Vivian Rall, Turney McKnight and Peter Jay would appear. And there we'd be on your horses. Close quarters! Fingers and feet frozen, we'd be galloping one direction, and on the outside wall would be Mikey's jogging the opposite direction. The big door would open and close. Gusts of frigid wind would burst in. Horses would skip and shy away from it into other horses.

Saratoga: Every summer, we'd gear up to win the A.P.S. If you didn't have a horse that was a natural fit for the race, you'd pick out one or two with the race in mind, train them for it, and when the time came, they finished in the money. That's loyalty, giving, family, sportsmanship, friendship and skill as a horseman all wrapped in one package. That's you, Tom.

Thanks,
Partner

February 11
Dear Tom,

Mimi's birthday. I must stop by after work, leave her a card. Pop's birthday too, born in '27—if alive today he'd be turning eighty-seven.

And now, Tom, what to do with this aching, gaping vacuum in my soul?

What to do? Listen! Don't talk so much. Easier to do if not drinking. Listen—learn from others. Get to know Rob, Tom Whedbee, Reed, Tom Iglehart, J.B., Billy Santoro better. Pearce, Matt, Hank, Chip. Go see them. See more of sisters Sal and Susan. Develop good friendships with women—Sara, my young English department colleague at work, Madison, the young classics scholar from England. Give. Give!

Give up trying to change Ansley. Give up arguing. "What's the point?" you pointed out, "You're not going to change her."

"Love the one you're with." Love her as she is. Do not point out her minor faults, for I have great ones of my own.

Get romantic life revved up. Ha—those words of yours as I stood to leave the living room, the last night I spoke to you, the last night I touched you, the last night I listened to you: "How do you know?" you taunted me after I teased you, saying Mimi probably wasn't getting any loving—after all, the doctors had said you shouldn't exert yourself and there you were at home "convalescing." You stared me in the eye, "How . . . do . . . you . . . know?" you repeated, sitting there on the couch, your bandaged foot stretched out before you, an old National Steeplechase and Hunt Association yearbook opened to a photograph of me, gaunt—at one hundred twenty-five pounds—about to ride a race. You squinted at me—the exact way Pop used to do when he was deadly serious.

Where are your texts, Tom? Your winter p.m. texts.

"Hot dog in the bun."

"Muffin in the oven."

"Torpedo in the chute."

Our private competing ever since we both broke our maidens, you in a barn, me out in a cornfield—no one understands that.

It is now time to push off, Tom. It is time for me to begin to heal. It is time for me to put into action some of the ways I hope your life will inspire mine.

I want to make the best out of every moment. I am a man, not a machine. This calls for flexibility as well as self-discipline. Flexibility—go skiing once in a while or stop by and see friends.

Get back into the moment. Focus on the task at hand, concentrate on what I'm doing. Yesterday, I tripped twice on the same damn step, back porch, because I was not paying attention; I was off thinking of you and work and the horses and Ansley and school and the coming snow storm and wham, I hit the deck. How about driving home after work late the other afternoon, tired, sleepy, blury-eyed: I didn't even see that kid running the red light. Good Lord. I pulled out and there it was. He swerved, just missing me. I was off with you. I've got to focus on what I'm doing. As you say, "Pay attention!"

Love,
Patrick

Missing

March 7, Friday

Dear Tom,
Missing—
I think of you today
During the student performance,
You the student then,
Me the teacher now.
How I am teaching at your school,
And how this has meaning, this teaching, these students
    succeeding, doing so well,
        Putting in all their effort, trying their hearts out.

Missing—
I think of you,
Yesterday,
Home from work
I lay back, fell into a deep sleep.
Dreamed: Ansley was going out to lunch with "Tom Voss"
I saw those two words in Times New Roman.
You were alive,
And I awoke.
No.

Missing—
I think of you.

During the day of a big race
I would feel as if
I were living a parallel life,
And I'd imagine what you were doing
In the moments leading up to post time.

Missing—
Driving home from school,
I hear an extraordinary poem
On the radio
About a man's best friend
Who is alive,
But has left, cleared out, taken off
And is out there, living, somewhere.

"The inexpressible"—that is what a poem tries to express
Says the poet on the radio.

And I wonder, could the best friend
Be listening?

Missing—
Driving back to Atlanta Hall
In the old roaring six-horse van
After hunting,
Passing the port,
Tilting the bottle up, taking a sip,
Passing it to you,
Tilting it up, taking a sip.

Time going back—
To riding with Mom,
To mucking out stalls with Emmett,
To racing to Delaware Park at 4:30 a.m.,
To sharing a room with Pop at the Skyways Motel.

I am by my father's side late at night—
I have driven two hours in a car
With a smoking, clanging, metal-grinding engine
Fast—headlights slicing through the thick black night—

354 PART FOUR

80 mph,
90 mph,
From my newspaper office on the Eastern Shore,
Crying,
Unable to see,
Taking chances,
Not caring in the least
If the car careened
Off the road into a tree or telephone pole,
Hitting 125 coming down off the Bay Bridge.

At the hospital
Pop is in a coma—
I am by myself.
Then, you are there.
Your hand is on my shoulder.

—Never again your hand on my shoulder—

You wait. Remain still,
Then gently talk to me,
Reason with me,
Pull me away, drive me home,
Walk me into the house.

No one else could have
Taken me away
From that bed.

I see the look in your eyes in the photograph
Of us accepting the trophy
After teaming up and winning the Grand National
In our fifties.
You are totally focused,
Not thinking of yourself,
Looking at me,
Feeling, as no one else could,
What it meant.

Missing—

No texts
No "So and so toes up"
How odd—you die, you leave, you depart,
No one sends me a "toes up."
Did I expect
A text,
"THV—toes up"
Ha—I could see you sending that.
I bet you tried.

Missing—
I think of you as I drive home from school.
It's that knowledge of all the years—
As we sat that last night,
The steeplechase yearbook
In your hands,
Opened to a photo of me at eighteen,
In silks, in the paddock of Saratoga,
And you talked of galloping Arnold W in a chain noseband
For my father.
You knew I knew Arnold W.
What it took to ride him,
And to ride so many others.

Our legs had squeezed against the sides of this same horse.
Our arms had ached pulling on the reins.
Our hearts had banged as he leaped and plunged and we
Just barely kept him from running off.

You were in pain.
The foot hurt.
The infection hurt.
The knee hurt.
Your facial skin was developing folds
And was turning sallow.

Missing—
I'm trying to get it—
That feeling of communication without communicating:

Like breezing Welterweight in the rain for you.
Like hacking home after a hunt with you.
Ha—like that one long night before my wedding—
Beaten and bruised and exhausted and worried,
Looking across the jail cell at you,
And both of us suddenly laughing.

Like coming to the table,
The line of waiting book-buyers stretching out the room,
    over the porch and onto the driveway,
At the first big book signing of my life—you'd gotten me the
    Elkridge Harford Clubhouse.

The time printed on the invitations to give my reading had
    come and gone.
Guests were asking when I'd read.
I was drained from shaking hands,
Meeting old friends of Mom and Pop's,
Listening to their stories
And then writing inscriptions.

Coming to the table, you said:
"Sign the books faster. Don't take so long."
Then back, a few minutes later:
"You've got to do the reading now. People want the reading
    now or they're going to leave."
You rounded them up, got them outside.
When I arrived at my designated speaking spot on the
    porch steps,
You handed me a scotch, neat, and looked me in the eye.
"Drink this before you start."
You knew what was going on in my mind.
This was the book on my father on our youth on my love of
    my father
And you gave me confidence.

You gave me confidence
Standing beside me as I began to read
Through a sheet of emotion-driven tears.

Missing—
Your seven-days-a-week focus on the farm and the horses,
And it has led to this.
Ansley is right—you did get up, you did plow and work
    that last day
And that might have been what caused the embolism.
The farm, the racing, the struggle to be the best, to win the
    title,
To win to win to win,
Is that what did you in?

Missing—
That gentle sigh on the phone
Right before you sign off
That
    gen-
        tle
           sigh.

Missing—
The call from Saratoga—*When are you coming up?*
The text from out of the blue,
Got some shad roe. Come over at noon.
The jokes.
The laughter.
The sitting in Wassie's old cottage by the Pretty Boy Barn—
With Billy and Jimmy after hunting,
Away from our wives, our jobs, our responsibilities, our
    concerns
An interstice between late afternoon and early evening,
No one knows where we are.
Having a glass of Irish whiskey,
Cheese and crackers,
And laughing.
Time stopped.

Missing—
The galloping through life head-and-head.
Competing at times? Yes.
Perhaps—in younger years.

And maybe in later ones.

Missing—
Living Our Life together.

Death Be Not Proud

Death, be not proud, though some have called thee
Mighty and dreadful, for thou art not so; . . .

Thou art slave to fate, chance, kings, and desperate men,
And dost with poison, war, and sickness dwell,
And poppy or charms can make us sleep as well,
And better than thy stroke. . . .

— John Donne, "Death Be Not Proud"

April 4

It's a sparkling bright afternoon at the Elkridge Harford Point to Point held at Atlanta Hall. A few hundred vehicles—shiny new pickups, classic Land Rovers and new Range Rovers, European SUVs and coupes—are parked up by the paddock and close to the finish line. Men are in British wool jackets and Irish caps. Women in wool skirts, high leather boots and light jackets. The bright light reflects off the stirrups of the saddles, the bits of the bridles, the tips of jockeys' spurs as the horses and riders proceed to the paddock. I'm on the outskirts. Everyone is laughing and grinning and I know at least every other person. They wave, hesitate, wait for me to approach. I've just arrived and am going nowhere in particular but acting as if I have somewhere urgent to go. I'm thinking of Tom. There is no Tom here. First time in my life—since as kids we used to ride our bikes over—Tom hasn't been here. It was just two years ago he surprised me by informing me he was flying to Kentucky for the presentation of the Dr.

Tony Ryan Literary Award. Now, I am one of the judges and am scheduled to fly to Lexington on Tuesday to assist in presenting the award on Wednesday. Have my tickets and motel reservation, and am taking two days off from school. I am striding through the crowd at the races but I'm not at the races. I am with Tom in the airport when he teased and cajoled me in front of the security guards about my trophy in the phallic shape of a tower. I am with Tom here when he gave me a leg up on Welterweight and we went on to win. I feel Tom's presence beside me when suddenly a close friend of Dickie's heads straight for me, puts out his hand. We shake; he looks me in the eye and tells me Dickie died the day before. "He specifies in his will that he wants you, and only you, to give the eulogy."

"When's the service?"

"Wednesday at St. James. Will you give it?"

"Yes."

9 April 2014

I stand at the pulpit. Again. Here at St. James Church, a mile from our farm. Look out over the congregation. Surreal. Hadn't I just been here, giving Tom's eulogy? Hadn't we just buried Tom? Then, a few weeks later his mother Jen? And now, a few weeks after Jen, I am here again but Jen and Dickie are not here sitting before me as they were at Tom's. And yet, there are Dickie's sisters and brothers in the front row as well as the nieces and nephews I've heard so much about, especially Jane, now a veterinarian. Dickie's Gilman football coach, my headmaster, Reddy Finney, walks into the church, takes a seat way in the back; I feel his strength; it flows into me. I see Christine, who ran Dickie's shedrow for a few years; she loved working for Dickie. I nod to her. Tears streak her face. There's his big owner, Bob Meyerhoff. Andrea Seefeldt, who used to ride races for him, won stakes for him, and then became an owner, looks up at me. Retired jockey Vince Bracciale, who rode Broad Brush, takes a seat. Jockey Forrest Boyce is up front and dressed in mourning black, but what I see is a young woman in blue jeans, turtleneck and windbreaker at 5:15 a.m. in Dickie's tack room; she's got her tack on her lap and is ready to ride; and in her hand is a copy of Jack Kerouac's *The Dharma Bums*, on which she's having a test that day at the Maryland Institute College of Art.

The church is filling up. I search for José; find him in the back; try to catch his eye. I see a few more young women enter. So many on the distaff side of the racing world—an irony here: Dickie never remarried after that first false start.

My eulogy concludes with Dickie giving me his sheepskin shoes at the end of my last visit with him.

"I wore them to write in all winter," I recount. "They fit. And I have so much more that Dickie gave me: paychecks that helped get my writing going, the Caliente that saved my skull a few times, the custom-made Kroops galloping boots ordered through Charles Turner, a quiet support of and respect for my horsemanship, my writing, my teaching.

"Dickie gave to the hundreds of apprentice riders and young horsemen whom he mentored. He gave to his family. He gave to the hard-working and talented Mexican men and women who became his family. *He gave his life to his country.*

"The cliches break down with Dickie.

" 'He was a guy who always thought the glass was half full,' one might say.

"If you know him, you know that's wrong.

"*The glass was full, overflowing, brimming and bubbling over.*

" 'What you see is what you get,' another might say.

"No, what you see is not what you get.

"*You get, we got, a lot more.*

  Thank you, Dickie.
    —Pat"

Raging, Roaring River

April 30
Dear Tom,

The raging, roaring, rising current—brown, ruffled tree limbs being swept down, the river high, ripping and tearing at the edges of the banks, high, crashing and cascading against the pilings of the bridge, wide, broad, taking up the valley, flattening out what is usually a funnel of rocks and rapids, the lightning flashing, thunder crackling. I am walking in the middle of the road. The rain. It is different. The drops are big. I see them in the air, the individual drops. They batter against me. I don't have a hat on. I always wear a hat in the rain. The drops bang against my skull. I look at the asphalt. Am I seeing things? Am I hallucinating? The drops are walloping my skull. I walk up the slight incline, right in the middle of the bridge and I see: the drops are hitting and bouncing, the drops are hail. They are cold. They are hitting the old smooth thick boards and bouncing, hundreds, thousands, millions of bouncing hailstones. (*Remember that night we were way up-country in the Corvair, searching for the waterfall near Tiger's and it was dark, we'd been drinking bourbon, the rain came. It slashed through the trees, hit the crusher run turning it into a river, blinding us—the windshield a waterfall the wipers could not keep clear. We slowed. The rain stopped. We drove on, and then, the road was covered with frogs. Thousands of baby frogs! Thousands of hopping, green frogs. The crusher run had come alive and was bouncing and jumping. We might have smoked some pot. We couldn't believe our eyes. I had to drive through them. There was nothing else to do. For half a mile we drove through a sea of hopping frogs.*)

The lightning cracks! Who cares? Keep walking. Get hit by lightning. Killed. Another one gone. Patrick. He gave Tom's eulogy. Then he gave Dickie's, and now, how ironic … Is this *ironic*? I am double-checking, testing myself, wondering how I would explain it to my students. Patrick's gone. Who will give his eulogy? What will he/she say?

I'm not afraid. Really don't care. *Whack*! It's over. So what? I picture your stallion, the stallion of our youths, Suspendido. He's standing peacefully in the field, grazing, in the dark—a lightning bolt flashes across the sky, striking his "poll," right between his ears. Thirty years later: I see Florida Law, tall, arrogant, out in the field at night, refusing to go in to the shed with the others. The thunder rumbles around him. He puts his head up, up high, to watch—and zap—the bolt streaks across the sky, kills him instantly. I see myself, standing on this bridge, the highest point, metal rails on both sides of me, raging, flooding river below. If I were hit, I'd like to fall into the river and let my body go for a wild ride. I start to think about it. I have an urge to dive, head first, off the bridge and onto the rocks.

A minivan. I'm standing in the middle of the bridge. I walk to the side. The minivan slows. The driver lets his window down. Rain slashes in. His wife is beside him. His two children are in the back. They are safe on the thick rubber tires. "Are you all right?" he asks, staring at me in bewilderment. The kids in the back lean forward against their seat belts, stare.

"Yes, yes, I love it!" I exclaim, too loudly, opening up my arms, welcoming the rain and hail, the flashes of lightning.

"OK," he yells, pushes the button, up his window goes, and he drives on.

I must've looked crazy, but what the hell, I am feeling crazy. I'm out in the middle of this bridge, leaning on the iron rail, a perfect target, and just don't give a damn. I look up at the broad current sweeping down toward me; it is overflowing the banks and rushing out onto the road. Our canoe trips. . . .

My eulogy for Tiger—way back: the main metaphor: canoeing and "shoot for the V, head for the V." Eulogies! And you were there: The minister: "Keep it short and watch out for your friend there," he said, pointing at the urn holding the ashes. "You don't want to knock him over and have his ashes spill over the place." Wanting to knock over that damn minister! And, back in the pew, you beside me, your shoulder against mine, your voice—sure, strong, clear, "Get up there, give your talk, and make it as long as you fucking like." I can feel the muscle of your shoulder, clad in black pin stripes, against mine.

I walk to the other side—the water rushing away from me, this always reminding me of having learned of Mike White's suicide three decades ago, going for a run to this bridge, looking down the river, and thinking of it as Mike's life—going out, out to sea.

The water is rushing away from me, twice its normal speed. What it would feel like in a canoe: the sensation of a fast current picking up the canoe beneath us, the thrumming up through the thin-skin of the bottom, the thrill of it vibrating through our bodies, the wildness of it. Dropping down on our knees to lower the center of gravity, the speed, the yelling out—our old hunting call. *I think back on that trip when Paddy saved Andrew. We'd started late. There'd been a storm the night before, and as we came down the river at dusk, Paddy was the watch in the bow. He'd spot the downed tree, we'd prepare, slow, bump into the limbs, work our way through. But then it grew dark. When Paddy called out, it was too late. We crashed through limbs and leaves, and whammed into the downed trunk, the onrushing current spinning the stern around so that we were ducking under the limbs and the billowing waves were pushing us up against the trunk which we were leaning away from, our arms up, fending off the branches, the full power of the flooding river hitting the canoe broadside, digging under the canoe. We capsized. Paddy was fifteen, lithe and strong. Andrew was a boy of ten. Paddy and I were out from under the canoe. Andrew was under it. A vacuum had formed. The current was crushing the overturned canoe against the trunk of the tree and under its branches. The canoe was wedged in, hammered in, and branches ran from the trunk down to the rocks of the river and Andrew was under that canoe. I pulled. I pried. It was pitch-black dark now and I pulled against the vacuum and the branches with all my strength. It didn't budge. Paddy—maybe one hundred twenty-five pounds—grabbed the gunnel of the canoe, and yelled with all his might, releasing a primordial, painful battle-cry. The suction gave way, the canoe rose up out of the water, Paddy grabbed Andrew in his arms and pulled him out. . . .* Where is Andrew now?

I pull out my cell phone and take some pictures. Walk through the woods to the knoll where the boys and I used to watch storms.

Take more pictures. The rain slashes against my face.

Driving home, the pickup's windshield wipers break, again. The front window fogs up. I have to blast the defroster, making it hot. Open the windows. The rain pours in. Give up on the windshield, turn off the defroster, and steer the four miles home by hanging my head partway out my side-window and focusing on the pavement, the rain stinging my eyes.

At home, have a Smithwick's Ale. Follow it with a shot of scotch. Try to explain it to Ansley. She's distracted, receiving Oldfields emails and text messages, has to make a couple of calls. The electricity has gone out at Oldfields. What are they to do with the girls? "Are we ready?" she asks me. "Our electricity could go out any minute." I grab a couple of candles.

Eliza strides in. She has "had it" from work. She swoops by me and goes upstairs to change. I take out my phone, send messages and pictures to Andrew and Paddy. I don't send one to you, though, I am tempted. Your number is right there: "Tom Voss Cell." Instead, I send a message and photograph to Mimi. Paddy calls back. He gets it. No call from Andrew. A text from Mimi: "The Meadow is like the Atlantic Ocean. Tom would love it." Yes, you would love it. Yes. Yes. Yes. We would love it together.

Head for the V,
First Mate

Gambling With Speedy

May 2

The whole way to Pimlico, I'm thinking of having a big plastic cup of draft beer and something like a hot dog, pure race-track food. I can taste that beer, I can feel the cold cup in my hand. I never eat hot dogs, but I can taste the orange mustard, the crunchy onions, the sweet relish, the bland frankfurter. It'd been a long day of teaching. Speedy had called—he had to go to the races. I'd said no way at first, then at recess, had walked out to the pickup, sat down, called him back. "I'll sneak out early. Pick you up at three."

Now, cruising along, windows open, on the beltway, I tell Speedy I'm looking forward to a beer. Looking straight ahead, wearing his funky, customized sunglasses and purple straw hat, he states, "You better hadn't. No drinkin' and drivin' with me in this old truck. You know better'n that. You a bad 'nough driver as you is. Just the other day you slammed the door in my face."

"What're you talking about?"

"At Bob's, I got'n the truck and then you slammed the door in my face. Why'd you do that?"

Now, two weeks later, all he seems to remember of that day— which went from picking him up at 8:30 to returning at 4:30 to his apartment where he then had me working on an invention of his that included a condom, a rubber tube, and a plastic bag— is that I had slammed the door on him.

I thought back on that long day, the day of the Manor Races. I'd driven him to the hospital where he'd had his blood drawn. I

367

wheeled him over to the glaucoma specialist for a check up. He hadn't had anything to eat or drink since the night before even though I'd told him he could drink water. I'd taken him to a diner in Bel Air—walked him up a nice long ramp, gotten us good seats at a booth. Ordered myself eggs benedict and waffles and juice and coffee. He had a crab cake sandwich.

Walked him back down the ramp, got him in the cab of the pickup—no longer an easy task as he now has a fifty-pound feed bag of a belly which is difficult to pry into the seating space along with the long legs and long torso—and was preparing to head home, but no, I learned that we had to drive to a pharmacy to get his prescriptions filled and then he needed to "stop by Bob's," miles out of the way.

As I stepped out of the truck at the pharmacy, Speedy said, "And get me a pack of rubbers." I got back in, argued with him—"Why the hell do you need rubbers?"—pleaded with him. How I hate buying rubbers! It is so embarrassing and without fail there is always a young girl, a young woman, and a pretty one at that, behind the counter.

In the vast pharmacy, I walked up and down every aisle looking for CONDOMS, PROPHYLACTICS, RUBBERS, whatever the hell they'd be listed under, and couldn't find them, could only find pretty young women stacking things. Finally I spied a man walking around, pretending he was working. I asked him and he pointed me in the right direction. I walked over to the aisle. The rubbers were down low on the bottom shelf. I squatted down, looking for a good deal, and then a young woman pushing a baby carriage pulled up right alongside me. God, I had to get going! There I was with gray hair and checking out the rubbers and there she was with her baby, *a night of no rubbers*, checking out whatever was right beside the rubbers. And they came in sizes now, sizes she could easily see—there was a box with EXTRA LARGE stamped on it, and there seemed to be all types now, RIBBED, and TREATED WITH SPECIAL LUBRICATION, each promising great results. I grabbed a pack of what seemed to be regular old-fashioned rubbers, down the line, away from her, and dashed with my hand fully wrapped around the box to the checkout counter where there was a girl behind the counter, a couple of old timers in front of me taking forever, and a woman going through her coupons, spreading them out on the counter beside the old timers. I wanted to get the hell out of there. Behind me was a teenage girl loudly chewing gum and holding a bottle of shampoo, and behind her the young woman with the baby. I paid for the rubbers, got my discount with my special card, handed the girl Speedy's two prescriptions that were supposed to be ready, waited and waited, gave the girl Speedy's Medicare and Medicaid cards, got the hell out of there, back in the pickup, back to Speedy, thought we'd return to his place, that he might have gotten tired and forgotten his plan of visiting Bob, but no, it was "Bob, Bob, Bob." Receiving detailed directions from a man unable to see, I continued driving the opposite direction of his apartment, turned right at a stop light, passed three entrances on the left, "OK, now look for a big oak tree on a corner by a post-and-rail fence, you seet it?" took a left into a development, and drove half a mile down to the end of the cul-de-sac where Bob's house was on a hill overlooking a valley.

We sat on the deck. Bob was cleaning up—we'd just had a big storm. Limbs were scattered all over my fields and lawn, and here Bob, preparing for the birthday party of a grandchild, already had most of his lawn cleared. Speedy sat out on the deck sharpening his declamatory skills. Bob was being polite but holding his breath, waiting to get back to work. Speedy was enjoying the moment with his chauffeur/assistants both there. I finally hustled him back into the pickup, fastened his seat belt, and shut—*did not slam*—his door.

We're off the Beltway. Going up Northern Parkway.

"Winners Avenue, Winners Avenue, I tell you."

"OK, OK, listen, I'm just going to go the way I've always gone."

"You're going to go some way you used to go *one hundred* years ago with your daddy. All you do is go up Northern Parkway, take a left on Winners Avenue, go down to the dead end and take another left."

I don't see a sign for Winners Avenue. I take a left where you're not allowed to, as I'd done with Pop for years, and then later when galloping for Dickie, "OK, now we're driving along like I always used to do. The racetrack is on our left. The 3/8 pole is just thirty yards away." It feels like I'm going home. So familiar, like going to a family reunion. On the left is where Dickie's old barn used to be, and Mr. Small's before Dickie got the horses, the old long barn. I'd gotten a leg up on thousands of horses in that barn. First, when we were having some hard times, and Pop was just starting off, Mr. Small paid me a full-time salary to gallop his horses—including, every morning, the speedster Mr. Diz—before school, and he let me quickly get on one of Pop's horses between his own sets.

"Winners Avenue, I tell's you, but you jus' won't listen."

A stop sign is coming up, and the narrow road that runs along the outside of the Pimlico parking lot. "Winners Avenue, here it is. This is the exact same way I always go."

I take a left, drive down to the entrance, pull in. "I don't have a badge or a sticker. Wonder if they'll let me drive in. Just let me do the talking."

I pull in. No one stops me. I drive past the doors with ENTRANCE written across them, take a left. The parking lot looks full. I find a space at the far end of the lot, over by the row houses. Feeling victorious, I pull in, turn the engine off. Bantering, we get out. "What's that?"

"There's a bunch of kids playing on the porch steps of the row house across the street."

I step around to Speedy's left side, offer him my right elbow and we start walking. Slowly. "Where'd you park? You're supposed to leave me off at the entrance."

I look up. We have eight horse lengths to go. I tell him. "Damn if I'm ever going to let you bring me again! You should've left me at the entrance." He takes a few steps and stops. The late afternoon sun is baking the asphalt. There's no breeze. And it is hot. He's breaking into a sweat. "You need to drive me." I don't want to go back, get him in the truck, return to the entrance, unload, lose my parking space, then rush around looking for another spot. No badge and no sticker—I doubt if I'm even legal in this lot. "We're almost there. We're half-way there now Speedy, come on."

"I'll never come to the races again wi'chu. You just don't listen. I needs somethin' to drink!"

"I didn't have the slightest idea it would be difficult for you to walk this distance. I thought you'd been riding the bike."

"*Ridin' the bike ain't walking*! *I haven't been walkin'.*"

"Come on. We're almost there."

"Anyway, I tole'chu Billy stole my bike. Don't'chu remember *nothing?*"

We reach the entrance, walk in. There's a slight incline up to the turnstiles. "I know where I am now," he says. "This part is tough."

We walk up the incline, past the turnstiles. The large entrance hall is empty except for a big woman in a uniform sitting behind a long table at the top of the incline, and a man to her side who is selling programs and "cheat sheets"—lists of the top picks by the touts. I place Speedy beside the handrail that leads to the turnstile. He's bent over. "I needs' ta sit down. I needs' ta sit down *right now.* And I needs' a soda. An orange soda. My suga's down."

Everything is clean and shiny and there are no people around. I walk up to the long table at the top of the room looking for a chair—the woman is sitting in one, but she doesn't budge. The man is standing. "I have a chair," he says. "You can have my chair." He picks up his chair, brings it down to us. I set it down so that the front feet are facing down the slope to make sure that Speedy doesn't fall over backwards. Speedy lowers himself into the chair. Now he's sitting on a chair positioned just outside the line of turnstiles, where people exit the track. There's not a soul around. The carpet is clean.

I go in. The floor is polished. Where are all the brightly colored tickets on the floor? Where are the cigarette butts? The cigar butts? Where's the smoke? The hubbub? I traipse through four or five rows of chairs set up in front of a bank of television screens showing races all over the country. Below the screens is a long line of betting windows. Not one customer. I go to the snack booth. No, they don't have orange sodas. I get Speedy a diet Pepsi, ask about the beers. The woman behind the counter holds up two bottled beers. "Cold, these are really cold. Just came in and they were on ice. Feel them." I feel them but all along I had been imagining a draft beer in a big plastic cup, and besides, I don't really want it so cold you can't taste it. I feel like I'm letting her down when I order a draft. She pours it to the brim.

Back to Speedy. He's looking better. He sips on the drink. I sip on my beer. He stands, holds my elbow and we start our way toward the chairs in front of the windows. An older black man, on his way out, stops and looks at Speedy. "I recognize you," he says, smiling. Speedy smiles back. I tell the man that Speedy worked here for the Smithwicks. "I remember. I remember," the man says. I think of inviting him over to sit with us.

"A Smithwick had a winner here just the other day," the man says.

"Yes, yes—this is Patrick Smithwick," Speedy says, speaking more slowly than usual, clearly enunciating his words. We shake hands. "And that was Patrick's cousin Speedy, or D. M. Smithwick, *Junior* that won that race. Did you bet on him?"

"No," the man laughs. "He didn't look like much on paper."

"Next time," Speedy says, "Don't let that fool you. The Smithwicks know how to train a horse."

We're on the move again, Speedy asking me how much further. "Five lengths," I say, "three lengths." He lowers himself onto the chair while nonstop roasting me for making him walk so far.

I hear the bugler play the Call to the Post—well, I suppose it's a recording—and then, "The horses are on the track," and I can't wait to get outside and see the horses, see this track I've galloped around tens of thousands of times, watch the race. "Speedy, I'm going out to watch the race."

"OK, OK son. But first make a bet for me."

"All right, what do you want?"

"Here," he reaches into the right chest pocket of his overalls, pulls out ten or so greenbacks, neatly folded in the middle, and peels off the top two bills. "Number seven. Number seven—you got it. Put five to win and five to place on number seven."

"OK," I say.

He hands me the two bills. "These are both tens," I say.

He takes back one bill and tells me to go on and bet. Feeling light, fit, capable, unencumbered without Speedy gripping the crook of my elbow, slightly amazed at how quickly I can move, how I can see the chair in front of me, the man standing reading his *Racing Form*, the names of horses, their numbers, and their odds bright and blinking up on the big screen, I glide down the slope to the windows, bet, march back up and give him the tickets. He slides them into his left chest pocket. The senior citizen seated beside Speedy is studying a program. I ask if he could tell me the name of number seven. He has his program open to a different racetrack. He flips through the pages, finds the ninth at Pimlico. "Fortune Pearl," he says, looking up at me grinning. We both silently share a chuckle at the absurdity of the situation. A blind man coming to the races, sitting down after releasing a flurry of accusations and incriminations, out of breath, sweating, and then picking the horse to win in the race that has the horses going out onto the track at that moment, without looking at the program—or rather without having it read to him—without seeing the horses in the paddock, and without talking to any of the other bettors seated there who have been dutifully studying their programs and cheat sheets and *Racing Forms* all afternoon.

I quickstep up the concrete slope to the doors and out onto the asphalt. The gate is at the sixteenth pole, just up the stretch from the wire. I cut across the asphalt toward the gate. The infield is set up as if a carnival is about to take place. Tents. Stands. Buildings. There is no way I'll be able to see the horses go down the backside—nowadays, you have to watch that quarter of a mile on the jumbotron in the infield. There are only about twenty of us outside to watch the race.

The horses are loaded. Number seven is the last to go in. He doesn't look interested or excited. The bell rings, and they're off. The inside horses sprint for position. The jock on 7, Trevor McCarthy, is as relaxed as can be. He's standing fairly high and has a long hold on the reins. Looks like a jumping rider. "So pretty," as Speedy would say. Makes me crave to be up on that horse. He lets the other horses sprint to the front, eases in behind them as they head into the turn. He's last going into the first turn. I don't think this looks good.

McCarthy takes it easy going down the backside. I try to watch the race, but can't see through the vast array of tents and buildings, and the sun is reflecting off the surface of the jumbotron screen, but I can hear the announcer. Fortune Pearl is moving up. He's fourth coming into the turn at the three-eighths pole. They fly around the turn. I can see them now. I watch Fortune Pearl swing out wide using his momentum coming out of the turn. He's head-and-head with two others. The three are whipping and driving down the stretch. At the sixteenth pole, where I am standing, he blasts away from them and wins by three lengths.

We collect our money. We count it, and then we bet it all back, to win, on California Chrome in the Derby the next day. This is the main reason we've come to Pimlico today. Speedy needs to go to the men's room. We head up a steep flight of steps. At the top we run into amateur rider James Stierhoff and a beautiful young lady. They look like the perfect young couple. James, always exceedingly polite and respectful, is well-dressed in coat and tie—having just come from his investment banking office to place a bet on the upcoming Derby.

I introduce Speedy. He is the quintessential gentleman—sweet, asking them when they're going to get married, smiling, speaking slowly, clearly. I brag about what a great singer Speedy is, how the judges said he was the best at a recent Senior American Idol contest in Baltimore, but that he didn't win because he didn't sing a "standard." Instead, he sang his own song, "If Loving You Was Ice-cream."

"Sing some of it for these young lovers," I tell Speedy.

"No, I can't do that right now."

"Oh come on," I say. I begin singing, "If loving you was ice cream, I know what I'd do. . . ."

He puts both his hands up. "Oh my God—you're going to scare'em right out of this building. Now," he pulls himself up straight, reaches up and sets his hat at a rakish angle. He's got that cocky, on-the-stage expression on his face. He raises his eyebrows, and starts singing. His voice is clear; it is spell-binding; it reaches down into your soul.

Mimi Missing Tom

May 3
Dear Tom,

Friday late afternoon, I picked Speedy up at his new apartment and brought him to Pimlico so he could bet on the Derby—and on that day, being back on a track, I thought of both you and Dickie. I want to get back to that, my thoughts about the track, how I had wanted to go to many more races with you in the future, how comfortable I felt, at home, walking around the betting windows, walking out to the track to watch the horses run, watching them load into the gate, watching them being tacked up—oh, painful!—the three-year-old fillies were so sleek, so streamlined, so quick—kicking the back of the stalls, not "kicking" but rushing forward putting all of their weight on their front feet and them raising their hindquarters up and blasting the back of the stall. I watched the jock of Chucky Lawrence's filly hop four inches off the ground when that kick that would kill a man hit the back of his filly's stall. I wanted to be getting a leg up, to be light, honed down to muscle and bone, to hop on my right leg, have my left cocked, to feel your hand around my ankle, to go up, light as a feather, and to be there, in the moment, on the horse, ready to perform, but instead I was having a good time with Speedy.

On Saturday, I drive over to Elizabeth and Gary's, watch California Chrome win. Mimi has the television on loud—over the noise of the playing children. We have wine, beer. Elizabeth serves some hors d'oeuvres. Gary makes a pitcher of mint juleps,

375

pours one for me in a cold silver cup. Genevieve runs around. First she tries to get Frank, the black pot-belly pig, up and at'em. He's lying up against the wall. She prods and pushes him. He makes a big effort, rising to his feet—his belly is now only about half an inch off the floor! After that exertion, he collapses back on his pad. Genevieve laughs, sets up a course of jumps going from the kitchen into the living room: plastic play fences, a pile of pillows, a stack of books and magazines, whatever she can find; my loafers make a contribution. She puts on a small hunting cap, gets her whip, gives her imaginary pony a slap on the shoulder, trots over the two coming out of the kitchen, switches to skipping, gets on the correct lead, and schools over her living room course. Elizabeth and Gary take turns holding baby Thomas. I hold Thomas. Gary keeps replenishing my cup. Lots of action—continuing right through the race. Then, it seems like I've just gotten there and it's is over.

Mimi stands and announces. "OK, Patrick. . . ." I love the way she says my name. When she says *Patrick* it is as if she is celebrating part of you, "*Thomas*," and it is not all right for anyone including me to object because this *Patrick* is a part of Thomas and what I (Mimi) say goes. ". . . *Patrick* and I are going back to the house while Elizabeth gets the lasagna ready." Gary hands me my mint julep in a to-go cup.

I open the side door to the Jaguar. Mimi has to bend down low and swing those long legs in. Shut her door, go to my side. Swing my long legs in. "Watch this," I say. I put the key in the ignition. The steering wheel, making a nice humming sound, first lowers itself, then slides out a few inches towards me, at the perfect spot for my reach. "Makes it much easier for me to get in." I tell her this is the sort of thing you'd like, and in our old competitive way, ask if your Jaguar sedan did this. I joke about how when you first got it, we'd driven it to Johnny Merryman's funeral, and when you picked me up, you'd made a big deal out of the feather duster that came along with it, jokingly dusting my seat off, *caricaturing* the most obsequious of chauffeurs. We talked, as I backed up out of the driveway where Ansley and I had lived over thirty years ago, leaving the house with which you had lured me back to Maryland, charging us almost no rent.

We were out on Pocock Road, heading up the hill towards the upper entrance to the farm, the top down, and I was dying—not the right word!—I was looking forward to taking your wife for a drive, letting the Jaguar pick up speed, let the wind rush through our hair, hear Mimi laugh, but as we approached the entrance, she said she wanted to go back to the house. Something was up. You know what I mean?

We drove in, the sky huge, vast, infinite above us. I commented that the pine trees lining the entrance looked well. You must've heard that right after you left us, we were hit with a terrible rain, ice and windstorm that took trees down all over Maryland and that tore the branches off your pines. Mimi noted she had a lawyer working on the insurance company, which she felt was not fulfilling its obligation. We passed the spot where I used to park the truck and trailer in the shade, unload Riderwood, then take him out, with you coaching, for a school over hurdles.

At the schooling field, we followed the driveway to our right. How many times had I jumped young horses over all those logs under your supervision? You made it tense. You made it competitive, pitting one rider against another. "Oh, you're taking up the schooling logs," I said, and then, seeing a pile of big heavy new logs, realized my mistake. Elizabeth was taking up the old logs and putting down fresh ones.

We passed the one-story house, "Kurt's house," on our right, then, the indoor track on our left.

We headed down the long straightaway, up which you and I had hacked thousands of horses, on the way to the "indoor," or to the "polo fields," or to "Pocock Hill," or to the club, or to the "all-weather," and pulled outside the steps to the kitchen door. I said, "Hold on," and, showing off, pushed the button to have the roof go up. We got out. I had my Gary Murray-mint julep in my hand—the first cup of which had knocked off the top of my head.

At the kitchen counter where you always sat, Mimi poured a glass of wine.

We walked through the kitchen, past the wall-sized, imitation-Renaissance painting of the voluptuous naked beauties in the garden, past the bar where after a full day of hunting I had grabbed the $100 bottle of port and drunk most of it when we'd decided that yes, I would ride Florida Law in the Hunt Cup. We ducked under the low entrance to the dining room, through the wide hallway—the stairway on the right leading up to your dressing room I love with your hunting clothes and boots still spread out on the sofa, hanging from the closet doors, and piles of books here and there, and the soft light coming in the northwest-facing windows—past the spot in the hallway where you drew your last breath. You were leaving the den, bringing the dishes back to the kitchen, and it hit by the newel post to the stairway. Did you have a split second to realize what was happening? I don't think so because you would have called out to Mimi, twelve feet away, relaxed in the den with the fire going, as you loved, with a movie on, as you loved, with dessert coming up, as you loved, no one else in the old sprawling farm house. I think the clot flew up from the infection in your foot and killed you instantly.

It had darkened outside. The den was dark. Mimi didn't bother to turn on any lights. She held a long, black antique key, stuck it in the top of the wrought iron door lock, turned it. The door opened and we came out of the dark room into the natural light seeping in from the open front and sides of the awning and brightening the stone floor. There was a new table to the left, a glass table surrounded by iron chairs with bright green cushions. On the right was a sofa against the wall, and lounge chairs facing it, all with blue cushions decorated with red and green *arabesques* (the same swirling, dancing patterns that dominate Arab art and which my students have been replicating on their Islamic prayer matts). OK, OK, patience, what's your rush? I'm getting to it! Before us, on three sides, *green green green*, the green of the pasture on the left, the green of the lawn in front of us leading to the yellow barn, and the green of the lawn to the right leading off to the spot at the top of the knoll where Florida Law is buried.

Mimi sat on the couch.

"Patrick, I've been good, I've been in good shape, but the last few days have been hard, very difficult. I've been thinking of Thomas all the time. I miss him. I miss him. I don't know how I can go on without him. . . . You know, about four months before he died, I told him, 'I don't know where you end and I begin.' "

I pictured you and Mimi as one, as one spirit.

"I was raised as a Catholic. It was drummed into me. Everything, and I believed it. But I don't now."

She was crying and she looked at me, "I don't believe in God. I don't believe in the afterlife. It makes it all so difficult. . . ."

"But you believe in love and goodness, the power of love and

good—which *is* God," I said.

"Yes."

"And you believe in your love for Tom and the power of his presence; he is with you forever."

"Patrick, I've been so good. I have no one to talk to. You loved Thomas. You have Ansley."

"Yes, I do." I put my hand around her shoulder.

"Last night," she said, starting to cry, "last night I couldn't help it. I'd been reading, and I turned the lights off, and l thought of his shoulders," she put her hands up, as if she were placing each hand on one of your shoulders, "those broad strong shoulders the children all have, and I thought of his upper arms," she ran her hands down your biceps and triceps, "the tattoo on his arm, THV." (I thought of that, back when Hep sewed those tattoos on you. Your own initials! You're supposed to put your mom's name, your girl friend's name, a symbol for the Army or Navy or Marine Corps, but no, at sixteen, you take a dare. What will it be? "I don't know—how about my initials.") "I ran my hands down his arms, not in a sexual way, to his hands, those strong big-boned hands that I love." She smoothed your hand, one then the other, in the air, over and over, healing your hands, wiping out the cuts and scratches and scrapes. "I loved those hands, Patrick." She looked at my hand on her knee. "I thought of his belly, I loved his belly and the scars from the operations, the big scar running across the bottom of his stomach," she smoothed and soothed your scar in the air, "and then his thighs, those powerful thighs, I loved his thighs."

I thought about your body. I pictured it when we were teenagers and riding races and you had it down to 155 and looked pretty good. Then I saw it when you got it down to 140 and you looked absolutely terrible with hipbones puncturing the skin and then remembered when we were kids and swimming and you were pudgy. I saw us sitting naked on a bench in the locker room of Lou Rutenberg's club up in the middle of nowhere in Pennsylvania, wet bathing suits by our sides, pulling on shorts and shirt, preparing to go out with Lou and play some golf. We'd just come in from the pool. There was a high diving board; you had gone up it. You had sat on the end of that diving board, feet dangling. A long line had formed at the bottom. You couldn't really stand up, turn around, walk back down the board and go down the ladder. How humiliating. I sat on the side of the pool, feet in the water. I called up to you but stopped as the line at the ladder lengthened and my encouraging seemed to create more pressure. I sat there chanting to myself, Jump Tommy, Jump Tommy, and finally you did. Instead of the long line acting like jerks, they gave you a tremendous applause. Then, there we were changing in the locker room when four boys walked in, local bullies. What were we doing at their pool? They made a few negative remarks about the high diving board. You sat there, relaxed, staring at them. "How old are you anyway?" one asked.

"Old enough to know better," you said.

"Old enough to know better than what?" one of them asked.

"Old enough to know better than to take any shit off of you, asshole," you said as calmly as could be. Goddamn! We were, alone—two against four, and I wasn't looking too daring or muscular. Just then Lou walked in, asked why were we taking so long, and took us out to the golf course. That was the pudgy stage, I know all the stages, even the last decade stage—when we shared a bed, a shower, a car at the Seelbach Hotel in Louisville when John's Call ran the race of his life and you were in the powerful body stage with the broad shoulders, the thick arms, the strong thighs and the belly Mimi so liked on its way.

I don't know any other male's body in that way. Remember when you'd ride your bike over in the summer. We'd pick out a couple of spy novels from my collection, ride our bikes down to Sidney's, and hike down the creek until we came to the peninsula with the swimming hole on the downstream side. We'd toss off our clothes, jump in the water, cool off, and then lie on our towels on the peninsula, the creek on three sides of us, reading our novels of adventure and intrigue, duplicity and deception. After a few moments, you'd go over into the shade. That fair skin didn't do well getting sunburned.

"Not in a sexual way," Mimi said. She went through it again, feeling the images she sketched out in the air, "his broad shoulders" her hands held high, "the tattoo and then those strong arms," she ran her hands down your arms, "his hands, I loved those hands." She looked at my hands, not so battered and beaten and big-boned as yours, my finger nails not blackened and broken. "At night, I used to lie like this," she turned away from me, "and he'd rest his hand right here on my hip." She placed her hand on her hip. "We'd read at night—you know how he loved to read—and sometimes I'd turn to go to sleep, and he'd rest his book here on my hip. I can feel it now, his hand on my hip. Oh Patrick, I miss him. I miss him. I don't know how I can go on."

Tom, I told her, "You've got to go on, but you've got to live your own life. You can't live just for your children, just for this farm. This farm wore Tom out. Here he is living in this house right in the middle of everything, no let up, day after day. Look— how he died—just hours after plowing out the driveway."

"Yes," she said, "you know, he wanted to retire. He was going to stop and we were going to travel. He used to hate traveling. Every time I planned a trip, 'Oh please don't make me go,' he'd say. The time Barbara and I went to Thailand, 'Oh please don't make me go,' he begged. Jack didn't go either. Neither of them would go. But recently. . . ."

"That trip on the Queen Mary—that's what did it."

"Yes, that was a little long for him, but that's what did it. He enjoyed himself. He loved it. And we had a great time in London. We were going to go to Rome."

She started crying. "You've got to have something to look forward to," I said.

"You have Ansley," she said.

"Elizabeth has her children, her husband, her youth," I said. "Sam has his new girl and the excitement of an upcoming marriage—if he ever proposes. They're fine. You have to take care of yourself. You're not a trainer," I said.

"No, I'm not a trainer."

"You can't just stay here to hold down the fort."

She smiled, "I like holding down the fort. But I'm going to travel. I want to go to Italy. I want to go to India. I want to see the world. I had wanted to do it with Thomas."

By this time, the rain was pouring, splattering, hammering on the canvas porch awning, some of it spewing in through the open sides onto us. My body was tight beneath my polo shirt, tight and shivering. "Do you want to go inside?" I asked.

"No, no."

We sat there. The rain poured. And we talked and thought about and missed you, Tom.

"It didn't have to happen," Mimi said. "It wasn't a heart attack, as the papers said. Thomas wasn't going to have a heart attack. His heart was as strong as can be. It was an embolism. The doctors told him to keep his foot up, to be still, to not do anything, day after day, and then one day they told him he could do some work. He checked on the horses and plowed the entrance, and that night it hit. They were wrong. It makes me feel guilty. It didn't have to happen."

Keep your heels down,
Patrick

Beauty

I'm having an amazing and inspiring time teaching poetry in both my English and Creative Writing classes:

Today, I cleared the white board and wrote the word, "Beauty." My stable of poets took off, some writing sonnets, many writing poems that would find their way into *Young Voices*.

It was quiet. My legal pad lay atop a rubble of vocabulary tests to grade, syllabi to hand out, essays to read. I pushed the pile to the side and let the pen ease across the page:

Beauty
For Ansley

Beauty gives you pause
It takes your breath away
It sends you to the heavens
It lightens and heightens your day
It makes you feel better in every way

Beauty makes you look twice
It makes you wonder
It can hit like a clap of thunder
It can astound

But more often
It comes to you gradually—
Or does it?

I remember that first look—
That face
Those shoulders
The hair pulled back
The enigmatic smile—
Soon the first page of our book

Beauty is something you desire
It can stir your fires
It inspires you to seek more
To dive in
To become a part of it
To require—or rather—
To possess it

When engaged with beauty
One is out-of-body
Out-of-mind
Ethereal, spiritual
One is unlimited
One will live forever
There is no beginning or end
Only beauty

Amen

PART FIVE

. . . All things fall and are built again
And those that build them again are gay. . . .

— William Butler Yeats, "Lapis Lazuli"

Just an Accident

I was revving up. It was a mid-Saturday morning in late June and it'd taken me a while to get going. I'd pulled on a heavy sweat suit and vest, fed the horses, mucked out the shed, rowed the rowing machine, pedaled the stationery bike, stretched, taken a hot shower, all in an effort to loosen up my back and get the glue out of the gray matter. The day before I'd driven the pickup and Rice Trailer up to my distributor's warehouse in Pennsylvania, loaded one thousand books that the distributor was overcharging me to store, driven back, unloaded them into the barn, and my back was locked up between the shoulder blades. After accomplishing this carefully orchestrated and secret mission—I didn't want Ansley to know we had one thousand unsold books or that I was keeping them in the barn to save money—I celebrated by ordering a couple of bottles of wine out to dinner with the Sweetheart and Eliza. A romantic time afterward with the Sweetheart. I was still not running on all eight cylinders, but I was getting there: at desk, pen in hand.

Bzrrzrrzrrzrr—goes my phone over on the counter. The ringer is off but the damn vibrator was still on. *Bzrrzrrzrr*—"Speedy Kiniel New."

I pushed the green button.

"Hello, hello," he said, "Who's this?"

"Patrick, this is Patrick."

"Oh, hi sonny, wha'chu doing?"

"Working, I'm writing."

"Could you come over," he said in a strong whisper, "bring me to the doctors?"

"I'm in the middle of writing."

"What're you doing the rest of the day?"

"Got to go to Oldfields with Ansley," I lied.

"Just bring me up to the doctor so I can get a prescription."

"What's wrong?"

"It's my throat. It's all swollen up and I can't swallow."

"You sound all right, now."

"It happens after I eat. Can you just come on over right now?"

I never should have answered it. I am not a brother, son, mother, grandson, nurse, girlfriend. I am not "on call."

"Bob's out of town, and Annie was going to pick me up but now she can't."

"I don't think I can do it. Let me check with Ansley and I'll call you back."

I walked to the house. By the time I reached the porch, I realized I had to do it.

I talked to Ansley—too busy to go. Called him back. Yes, I'd be there. I bustled around. I'd normally take the truck—it had a good grip above the door for Speedy to grab onto as he swung himself into the seat, and it was the most spacious for his large frame and growing belly. But it was still hooked up to the trailer.

I collected wallet, cell phone, keys to Ansley's car. She was on her computer, writing an Oldfields report at the kitchen counter. She helped me locate the doctor's office using Google Maps. I dragged around feeling sorry for myself.

Then, suddenly, quickly, wonderfully, she was up from the counter, in the shower, and in the car—ready to go.

At Catholic Charities, walking out with Speedy on my arm, we meet a wonderful black woman, Becky, who loves to read. She greets Speedy, chats with me, asks about my writing, cheers me up.

In the car, we start driving, with Ansley navigating.

"Angie, can you make a call for me?"

"Sure." Speedy hands his phone back to her. "Just look up Annie. You'll see it."

Ansley finds the number, pushes it, and hands the phone to Speedy.

"Annie, Annie, this is Speedy. You don't have to take me to the doctors now. Angie and Patrick's taking me. We's on our way.

Thank you."

"She was coming over?"

"Yes, there's no need now that you're taking me."

I ask about Becky, why doesn't he get to know her better.

"Becky—she's fat. She sat on my lap and almost killed me. She keeps askin' if she can come by and give me some company at night. I knows what she wants. Yes sir I knows and I'm stayin' away. She might kill me. She's eighty years old."

"That's impossible."

"No it ain't," he laughs, "and she's let me know she's still frisky as a young filly."

"All right," I say, "enough on that."

"Anyway, she's fat."

"No, she's not fat. She's a good looking woman."

"Don't tell me. I felt her wrist and I can tell. Plus she sat on my lap. I had to push her off."

We find the doctor's office, a small building between a used car lot and a vacant lot. "I'm so glad we not in that truck."

"Why's that?" I ask, bending over him, undoing his seat belt.

"You know why! Something in that truck burning up. You better hadn't be driving in that truck with Angie. . . ."

"OK, let's get out. The truck is fine now. I got it fixed. You were right. The front disc brakes were seizing up—that's what was making that burning smell."

"I tole's you. When will you listen? We could've been thrown right through the windshield."

I guide Speedy up a ramp into the office. We wait.

Then, we're in with the Indian doctor—an attractive, fit, but weary and rumpled, woman of fifty.

"How's your throat, Speedy?" she says from behind her desk, as if to an old friend.

"Well, it's better now. But it's been sore. After I eat, it's been sore."

"But you think it's getting better?"

"Yes, but it gets sore and my throat's swollen. I need's some anti-bodies."

"OK Speedy, the only thing I can give you is a Z-pack. I don't like giving these out. People are taking antibiotics for everything now. It's not good for you. Do you understand, Speedy?"

"Yes, I do," he says smiling. "What'chu think of that plane

goin' down and all those people bein' killed?"

"You mean the Malaysian plane over the Ukraine?"

"That's it. Shot down. The Russian rebels shot it down."

"Terrible, that was terrible," she says, writing out the prescription. "You know," I'm sorry I didn't call you back. I've been working long hours. I was here until 9:30 last night and just didn't have the time."

"That's all right," Speedy says, smiling. "You got to make all that *big money*."

"Big money, ha. I see seven or eight patients a day. Spend an hour with each. If I wanted to make the big money, I'd have a receptionist and I'd see as many people a day as I could. That's not the kind of doctor I want to be." She folds the slip of paper, hands it to me. "Now Speedy, you take two of these the first day, then one a day afterwards for four days. That should knock out any infection. All right?"

Here is my opening. "Let me ask you one thing, Doctor Bhambani. Would it not be good for Speedy to lose some weight?"

"Yes, Speedy—you need to lose weight."

"Ah no, I feels just fine.

"Speedy, you used to be a fit man," she says, looking him in the eye. "Just two years ago, you came in here and you were thin. You were active."

"I been riding the bike."

That's the invisible bike in his apartment, I think.

"Yes, but you used to work with the horses every day, and since you've gotten glaucoma, you've suddenly put on all this weight."

"Not that much. And I ride my bike."

She looks at me. "How much do you weigh?"

"One sixty."

"And how old are you?"

"Sixty-three."

"Speedy, you should look like him," she says. "He's fit and the right weight."

"My throat's swollen. I needs' the anti-bodies."

"If you were his weight, you'd be just right," she says, eyeing me.

Back in the car. I go on about his weight and the strain it is putting on his heart. Ansley taps me on the shoulder. I drop it.

We go to the pharmacy. I want to tease about the rubbers, tell him I'm very relieved he hasn't used up his pack of Trojans, but don't with Ansley there. I order the drugs. Wait.

Back in the car. He says he's hungry.

We pass an outdoor barbecue place on the side of the road. I make a quick U-turn. There's one narrow spot and I have to back in. I hesitate.

"What'chu doin'?"

"I'm parking."

"Ain't nobody ever parked a car by having it sit still."

Instead of turning my back, I twist my whole torso around, back in.

"Pshew, you's the worst driver I ever seen. I takes my life in my hands every time I drive with you."

After lunch I feel better. It's a beautiful clear day now. I'm back. Joking with Speedy. The windows are open but he wants them up and the AC on. I'm driving down a road, two lanes on either side, lined with used car lots and fast food stores and stoplights. I put the windows up and the AC on—but don't like it: can't hear what the other vehicles are doing. I feel disconnected.

He wants to go to Royal Farms for chicken. I can't believe it. Wants the chicken for later on tonight. The closest Royal Farms is miles away. Nothing but 7-Elevens and fast food joints and strip malls. Suddenly, we're up on a hill. The area looks familiar. Are we there, is this where we turn left at the light to go to his apartment? But I'm also thinking of going straight if he insists on the chicken.

We're slowing in a line of traffic at the stoplight. Am I too late to get in the left lane? I glance in the mirror. No one in the lane. Looks fine.

Speedy's talking about another invention for which he wants to get a patent—I'm taking guesses at what it is, preparing to turn into the left lane, laughing but irritated that he's saying he can't trust me with the invention, that I'll tell someone.

"Who am I going to tell?"

"You be running your mouth talking to J.B. about the horses and then you'll tell him."

We're poking along. "Yes, this is it. This is the road," Ansley says. I want to turn around to my left, check the "blind spot," and be sure the lane is clear, but my back and neck are too tight so I look in the raised indoor mirror to my right and the driver's side outdoor mirror to my left as Speedy brags about his invention that is is going to make millions. "Well, if you don't trust Patrick with it, who will you trust?" Ansley asks. I'm relieved he's stopped insisting on the Royal Farms chicken. Yes, this is where we turn left. We're creeping along, two miles an hour. I turn the steering wheel, head in, gradually, to the left turn lane. I ease into the lane, *WHAM*!

What the hell? A car is attached to my door. It's right front bumper is mashed into the front of my door. It is very strange. The car is up against us. Cars shoot by on our right. I'm disoriented—Kafka's Gregor with an apple suddenly stuck in his back.

"Look to see if the driver is all right," Ansley says.

I strain to turn around, look over, through my tinted window, out into the heat, and through his tinted window. I open my hands up, questioning him, and he nods OK.

Speedy starts up. "What's happened? What's happened? We've been hit. Lem-me out. Lem-me out."

"You can't get out, there're cars flying by."

"Lem-me out!" He shakes the door handle. "My neck, oh my *neck*!"

Ansley opens her back door part way, squeezes out, goes around and talks to the man in his car. She yells to me, "He's going to call the police. He says everything is going to be all right. It was just an accident and the police will be here soon."

"Police, Police! Lem-me out!" Speedy bangs hard, loudly, against the door. "I'm going to cut you open if you don't let me out. Open this window!"

I open his window a few inches. Cars swoosh by.

"I'm goin'ta sue. I'm goin'ta sue. My neck. I needs a neck brace, we have'ta get a neck brace. I won't be able to sleep tonight. Oh it hurts, it runs down my neck into my leg. I wanna talk to th' police."

The doors are on lock. He tries to open the door. I tell him he could get killed if he steps out into the traffic shooting by. I can't budge. I have Speedy's huge belly to my right and this guy's bumper jammed up against me on my left.

"I'm going to sue!"

Ansley and the driver come around. He's a tall, fit, handsome black man. Ansley sets a pad near my window, asks me questions—driver's license number, insurance company, insurance company's phone number—while talking to the man, and writing down the information.

"Who's that? Who's that out there?"

I wave to Ansley to back away from us. I wave and make faces, trying not to look crazy to the driver.

"I wan' ta to talk to you!" Speedy hollers to the driver. "I'm goin' ta sue.'"

"What?" he says. "What are you saying?" He peers in through my window at Speedy.

"Get me the police! I gots' a pain running from my neck down to my leg. I wants' ta talk to a policeman."

The driver puts his head down into my window. It will only open two inches.

"Who are you?" Speedy asks. "Are you the driver?"

"Yes."

"He's blind, he can't see," I explain.

"You the driver? My neck's killing me. I hurt my back. Lem-me out' a here."

The driver stares at Speedy.

I grimace at Ansley. She walks the driver away, back to the door of his car.

She tends to more paper work, returns. "The police will be here soon," she says.

"Police, police!" Speedy yells.

The police arrive. There I am, stuck. Can't get out. Ansley talks to them.

She gets back in.

"I'm going to sue."

"You can't sue. That means you'd have to sue us," Ansley says.

"Well, that don't matter. My neck hurts and I'm goin' ta sue."

That was it. *That* was it for me. *Here* we are, bringing him to the doctor's, then back from the doctor's, and he is going to sue us for it.

"Speedy," Ansley says in a stern voice, "You can't be hurt. We were barely moving. I'm sitting back here and I'm not hurt. If anyone is hurt, it'd be Patrick." She says this crisply, sharply.

I've had whiplash three times. I've been in too many accidents. I have no serious injury. My back is aching, but I sure as hell am not going to mention it.

"I'm hurt, I'm telling you, and I'm going to sue."

This is the end, my friend.

"Speedy, you're not hurt. You're just making it up. And if you're going to continue talking this way, this is the last time we're going to drive you anywhere."

True, true, that's true, I think.

"There's no way you can be hurt," she asserts.

We limp back to Catholic Charities. I do not talk. No one talks. I park in front, with a group of retirees sitting outside beside the front door, watching. I can't open my door. I grab the top of the window, force it—screeching and tearing against metal—down with all my strength, and climb through it. I smile and nod at the retired group as I walk around to Speedy's door, hold it open. He chuckles. Chuckles again. "That was some joke, wasn't it, Patrick. Some joke."

I do not answer. I am with a human who is the incarnation of disloyalty. Everything is becoming gray. It is like one of the times I have given blood, have not listened to the phlebotomist, have hurriedly left the Red Cross center, driven home, tacked up and gone for a ride—beating the system. Feeling good. Don't need to rest. But then, suddenly, on the hack home, when slowed to a walk, in the February cold, in the late afternoon, the breeze picking up and going through my jacket, the sun setting, I have shivered, everything has turned gray, and I've wondered if I would make it. On this occasion, everything is gray and getting darker, but I do know that I am going to make it.

Get Over It

The past is never dead; it's not even past.

— William Faulkner

July 4
Dear Tom,

I just got a text from Mimi on how much you used to like to watch the fireworks from your place. And that she hopes to win the A.P. Smithwick this year. She tells me that she misses every square inch of your anatomy. I texted her that I can hear your voice right now, and I can smell the tobacco and horse sweat on you. Ha—I can also see the puzzled expression on your face if you walked into this writing room at this moment—all windows open, pups by feet, fan on, and me sitting here in shorts and flip flops and no shirt. "What're you doing inside on a beautiful morning like this? I have one tacked up and ready to go."

And, I'd do it. I'd have that old feeling wash over me, as it has hundreds of times before: The galloping, the race horses, the feel of a fit horse between my legs, the smell of the leather and horse and hay and straw and your damn cigarettes—all so foreign from the fishing trip with Hank and the boys on Lake Champlain I've just gotten back from. You might like the peace and quiet and intense focus of fly fishing, and that strong right arm and powerful wrist of yours, that punch you can get out of that arm, would adapt perfectly to casting.

I am casting. I am casting this line of words, the above words are the line going back, back, looping whipping flying back

397

behind me until I can feel the rod bend slightly, and these upcoming words will soon be changing direction, whipping forward, releasing, unspiralling before me. I am casting my thoughts out to a point just behind that one rock, where I hope the fly will land, and catch my idea. What I am aiming for is beneath the surface.

I have noticed, with the exception of Mimi, people don't really want to hear me talk about you. That's also with the exception of Ansley and Eliza.

(Suddenly I see how your foxhunting is similar to fly-fishing. The term "to cast" is even the same. You cast the hounds—send them into the "covert" to flush out the fox. You cast the fly—to catch that trout.)

I cast again. I'll be at a dinner table with friends, mention an anecdote about us, and there won't be any feedback. There's just silence.

I feel as though they are thinking: that guy is pathetic. I don't want to hear this. It's over. Tom is gone. I never could understand him, I couldn't understand his and Patrick's relationship. Furthermore, didn't he bring it on himself? Look at all those cigarettes. Look at that weight he gained. Going to the vet, give me a break!

He reaped what he sowed, they're thinking.

The fly has drifted. I snatch it out, cast again: plop—even those very close may give me that look of sympathy that is not sympathy. It is *pity*. I cast, and they don't bite..

I get the feeling that some people thought you were arrogant, grumpy, narrow minded—thinking only of race horses—and self centered. You're gone and they don't want to hear about you, they're done with that subject, I should be too, and they're moving on, man. Get over it!

That's what you told me. It was a Sunday. We planned to drive over to visit Jimmy Murphy at the hospital in Laurel—an hour and a half away. One of Pop's best friends, one of the last ones still alive, and a strong supporter of you. He was in his last days. You were to pick me up. I hopped on the Farmall, started mowing the front paddock, keeping an eye out for your car coming in the entrance. I called you. No answer. Mowed some more. Called. You answered.

"What're you doing?" I asked.

"Just finished harrowing the indoor."

"Harrowing! We were supposed to go see Jimmy today."

"Was that today?"

"Yes, it was. He's only going to be around a few more days, and I've got to go to school tomorrow. Today is the day."

"Well, it's too late now."

"Christ, I don't believe it."

"Get over it."

Your fucking arrogance! What else is there to call it? It got us in so much trouble. Well, maybe not, maybe it wasn't all your fault, there was the time . . . , now that I think of it, the fights were often brought about by your companion: walking into the Dukehart's, some older college-aged guys there, I said something not so complimentary as we walked through. Seconds later, you came in, there was a misunderstanding, they thought you had made the comment. They provoked you, which didn't take much, and when I returned with a couple of bloody Marys, there you were with four guys on top of you. Same thing at Reed Huppman's one night. Though this time you brought it on yourself. Now, the incident in Middleburg, at the Red Fox Tavern—that was my fault. We'd both ridden in a hurdle race. You'd been reducing—we'd driven down in a "hot car," dressed in layers topped off with rubber sweat suits—and then you'd had a fall and a concussion. We were in my old black Falcon, after the last race, leaving the Glenwood Park course. There was a bottleneck going out the entrance, so we took off down the dusty roads and up and down the hills, going cross-country, headed for Dot's farm. On the way, we sped past a pack of local farm boys drinking beer in the woods and using the cans for target practice. They yelled something nasty. I yelled something back. They fired off a few shots and jumped in their trucks. I knew these back dirt roads, and the Falcon flew down them like a bootleg roadster during prohibition, skidding around turns, rear wheels shooting out the gravel, splashing through the creek, passing Dot's barns and house, clouds of dust billowing up behind us as we flew out to Sam Fred Road, and before you knew it we were in the parking lot of the Red Fox Inn. Victorious! No one could have kept up with that pace. I hopped out, headed in to get us both seats at the bar. You stayed behind to pull off your britches and boots. I was seated at the bar with some Middleburg girls when you entered, bloody nose, face all scratched up, hair disheveled. They'd followed us, waited until there was only one of us, and jumped you. Since then, I've never left anyone alone in a parking lot.

The altercation outside the bowling alley at Ligonier on our families' annual ski trip. J.B. brought it up the other night. What a memory he has. I'd forgotten those bullies encircling us when we left the bowling alley. We were just thirteen or fourteen, and we gave them a run for their money.

And the two of us, didn't we have some interesting fights against one another, though I never threw a punch; I resorted to my old Gilman wrestling moves, either got behind you or took you down. What was that inside you? What caused that fire? I think it was anger, anger at your upbringing, anger at your father's early death, anger at your older brother Ned giving up on life and drinking himself to death, anger at your younger brother Jack: he had been given good looks, incredible smarts, a lively, sharp wit, intensely natural athleticism; you loved him but you thought he never fulfilled his potential. When he did settle down, focus on his career and family, became productive and began to reel in some impressive accomplishments, he became ill, very ill; he died.

All your life you stifled the anger deep inside you, and the hurt, the pain, of being the child in the middle and not paid attention to by either parent.

This from eighth grade:

September
Dear Patrick,
How are you? I'm here at McDonogh. Everything is going OK. Every morning a loud gun goes off outside my room. Then we get up and march. We wear hot, itchy wool uniforms all day.
I went out for the football team. At first I thought I'd like it. I was playing quarterback, but now the coach says they need me in the line. All I do is run into people all afternoon. The coach yells at us.
I'm looking forward to seeing you soon, on Thanksgiving vacation. We'll go riding together. I can't wait to ride Pepper.
Yours truly,
Tommy

I can't imagine a worse place for you at that age.

Tom, I had dinner with George Fenwick the other night. He

said he always had the greatest respect for you. "He had balls," George said. "I hated it there. I hated boarding at McDonogh, the guns, the wool uniforms, everything about it. I was talking to Tom one day. He said he felt the same way and he was leaving. I asked, 'What do you mean?' 'I'm leaving,' he said. And the next day, he walked out. He just said, 'Fuck it,' and walked out. That took some balls."

Your leaving McDonogh had always been a mystery to me. It wasn't until a couple of decades later, we were having some drinks—after our wives had booted us out of our houses for the night—that I learned what happened. We were at the bar of our hotel. I asked about McDonogh.

"I walked out."

"What do you mean, 'walked out'?"

You turned to me, frowned. "I walked out the driveway, out to the road, took a left, and started walking home."

You had another sip of your stinger, took a pull from your Pall Mall and stared ahead. You could be a pain.

I waved the smoke away. You took another pull and obnoxiously blew it in my direction. "Christ," I said. "When are you going to stop smoking?"

"When you stop galloping those crazy horses at the track that are going to kill you any day."

"Well then, what happened?"

You made that sigh, and in a low voice, explained that you were on your way home—a twenty-mile walk—when the school station wagon picked you up, brought you back. They called home, but your parents were away. They decided you were acting crazy, so they drove you to Sheppard Pratt Hospital, which at the time was synonymous with "Looney Bin" or "Nuthouse" to us kids.

By now, the bartender had elbowed his way in, and a couple of other men who most likely didn't have such good experiences in school were leaning our way. You chuckled and stood up. "I was in this room, you know, like a hospital room. There was nothing wrong with me and they told me to get in the bed and stay there. Meanwhile, there were these other patients walking up and down the hall. They were clearly not normal. Finally, the hall quieted down, but I could hear a boy crying in the room next to me and other kids talking to themselves and a whacking sound like someone was banging his head against the wall. They turned the lights down in the hallway. Each room, including the nurses' station, had a window at about this height," you held your hand at your hip level, "and below that was a solid wall. So, I thought, this is simple. I got out of the bed, pulled on my clothes, stepped out into the hall, ducked down low"—you bent down, below the height of the bar, and arms hanging down, cigarette in mouth, snuck down the length of the bar, by this time, everyone at the bar, listening to the story"—and I scooted down that long hallway, past the rooms, past the nurses station, to the stairwell, down the stairs, out the door, and started to walk home again. . . ."

You didn't tell any more. Later, I learned you called home, your parents were off on a trip, and Vera came and picked you up about five miles north of Sheppard Pratt. Vera. For years, she was always there. "Vera, toes up," was a text you sent me a while ago. Vera—the wonderful black woman who lived in your house and who much of the time was responsible for raising you and Ned and Jack, and who was like an aunt to me.

Saratoga Redux

The alarm goes off at 5:30 on Wednesday, July 30th. Pop's memorial race is the next day, Thursday, first race at Saratoga Springs: the Grade I A. P. Smithwick Memorial. $125,000 purse. Elizabeth Voss is running a horse just a few weeks off the plane from Ireland. It takes most trainers ten or twenty years to reach the level where they have a horse of the quality required to enter a Grade I stakes race. The majority of trainers train for their entire life without ever entering a horse in a Grade I stakes race. Elizabeth has been training full time and a half since the day her father died. It's been six months. And now she has a horse entered in a Grade I stakes race. The Voss stable is the only stable in North America that has run a horse in the A. P. Smithwick every year since its inception.

The alarm is not the type you can punch in; you cannot push a snooze button, you cannot unplug it, you cannot put it under a pillow. Barking, yapping, tearing around the kitchen. It is our new puppy, Winston, a Yorkshire terrier Eliza picked out, in the kitchen with poor Alfie. This is his preferred time to arise.

Pull on robe. Walk sideways down to the kitchen. Open door to back porch. Winston and Alfie fly around the wood-stove, bumping into each other, their feet skidding and sliding on the floor, leaning in going around the turn. They straighten out, jetting through the doorway across the porch down the steps onto the lawn barking and yapping and wildly happy to be alive. Push the button on the coffee machine. I'd put the grinds and water in the night before. I'd set my bags out two days before, laid my clothes on the bed, picked through them trying not to bring everything in my wardrobe. Running shoes for bicycling. Bicycling shorts. Goggles and ear plugs for swimming. *Unbroken* by Laura Hillenbrand. *The Inferno* by Dante. And the day before, I'd narrowed down my writing supplies: one reporter's pad, one legal pad, three pens, no computer, which meant no emails, no facebook, no social media—I'd be living in the present. I'd ironed two shirts and a pair of linen pants. I'd sat out on the back steps in the late afternoon sun and shined my leather lace ups and leather loafers as Tom and I did when I stayed at his house in Saratoga, and for a full second, I pictured Tom alive and well out on his deck, shoeshine kit by his side, doing the same at the exact same time.

Make the coffee. Feed dogs, horses, cats. Carry bags down. Lower back is still sore from moving the books, and now, left shoulder blade and left side of neck is knotted up from the car hitting us. Eliza's white sedan is drenched in dew. Open trunk, toss in the bags. Eliza's bag—heavy. Lug it down the stairs. Heave it into the trunk. Finally all bags in. Or are they? Anyway, it's time to set up the bike rack. Can't wait any longer. If I do, they'll be standing around impatiently waiting for me, and Ansley will be offering unwanted advice as I make the last-minute adjustments. I shut the trunk, pick up the bike rack. (Old memories—memories of putting this on the back of the 1987 Volvo 240 DL station wagon, the best family vehicle we've ever had. Five forward gears. Thirty miles per gallon. Superior to anything made today. I'd have two bubbles on the roof, then tie the rack onto the back, hang Esmerelda, then three children's bikes. Lash it all down with bungee cords and baling twine, and off we'd go for a two-week vacation to Florida, or Maine, or the Adirondacks and Saratoga. It floods over me: carrying the half-asleep children out of the house, gently setting each on the sleeping bags and pillows I'd laid out the night before. The quiet. 3:00 a.m. Sometimes, I'd load up at midnight and drive through the night.)

I've had a practice run tying on the rack. Didn't want to be catching a lot of flak—"Dad, do you have to bring the bike?" "Sweetheart, can't you just borrow a bike when we get there?" "Patrick, is that going to scratch Eliza's car?"

This is an old timey bike rack; I get the buckles and the nylon belts and the braces all situated just right. Set thirty-five-year old Esmerelda, only bike on the road today with a classic leather saddle, on the arms of the rack. Tie her down. Out they come with more stuff. "I'll have to put that in the back seat, " I say, bracing for an argument. No argument. I'm delighted.

Dripping sweat. This is good. Loosening up the back and neck. Hop in shower. Hot as I can handle. Let the water drill into my left side. Turn it to icy cold. Let it drill into left side.

Chase Alfie and Winston around. Grab blanket and pillow for Eliza. Pat the pups. Shut door. Start engine. And, we're off—it's 7:30, not bad! We're off and running for Saratoga Racecourse.

Everything going smoothly. My insistence the night before that we leave early in the morning had initially met with resistance. Smoothly. I want it all to go well, especially for Sweetheart; she hasn't been to Saratoga in a few years. My plan is to head up the road in the early morning, arrive after lunch, have time to go for a bike ride, see the town before going to the National Steeplechase cocktail party and then to dinner.

All's going well. We're almost through Pennsylvania. Ansley's navigating. My phone rings. The insurance company. The adjustor is filing his report. There is rust on the hood—when did this accident happen?

I want to get this over as quickly as possible. I do not want Ansley to be reminded of the accident, do not want this damn accident and the damn insurance company to intrude on our drive to Saratoga, do not want us to be reminded in any way of Speedy's threats to sue us.

I explain that the rust was from an accident that happened in March. Backing the pickup out of the garage in a snowstorm, I had run into the hood of Ansley's car. While the car was at the body shop, we wanted to get the hood repaired too.

They would repair the door but the adjustor was not certain about the hood.

Mark, from the body shop calls. Can he get started? We're all straight about the door, I tell him; go ahead and repair the door.

Another insurance agent calls. I explain the situation and add that we've already been given the go ahead on the door and the body shop is working on it as we speak. This agent is not so happy to be made irrelevant. She prissily and self-righteously points out that there is a problem with the second claim. After I explain about backing up into Ansley's car, she informs me that her department does not handle this sort of claim; she has already sent it up to her "superior." I'd have to talk to him.

Mark calls. The superior calls. The superior says there is something unusual about this claim; she has to send it to another department. Ansley grabs the phone.

"Listen, what's the problem? We pay our insurance. We've paid our damn insurance to you for thirty years with no major accidents. We had an accident the other day, and while the car is in there, we decided to get the hood fixed—that was from another accident. What's the problem? Is there a statue of limitations? Isn't this why we have insurance? What the hell! This is frigging ridiculous. We're on a family trip and we're fed up with you giving us the run-around. I have no more time or willingness to deal with your unbelievable inefficiency and incompetence. Let me talk to someone who can take care of this right now, this minute. And do not put me on hold." Sweetheart gets the job done.

We arrive at our motel. At first, all I see is a long, low-slung building in the midst of a vast tarmac parking area. Pull car right up to room. Unload. Ansley hands me the key. My God, I haven't seen a key like this in years. It is a wide flat key and attached to it is a triangular piece of worn, yellow plastic that looks exactly like the old Skyways Motel key Pop, Tom and I used to have for our room at Delaware Park.

It's sunny out. Only 2:00. Haven't had lunch. Unpack. They decide to go off to Saratoga. To shop! I can't imagine it. I go to the front desk, find a big dispenser with snacks, pull out a bag of peanuts, a box of peanut butter crackers, a bottle of cranberry juice, ask how far Saratoga is. The receptionist points to the highway, "That's Broadway. It goes right into town. Just a few miles." Back in room, strip off clothes, pull on shorts, step onto a deck, feel the hot, splintery wood under my feet, lie back, let the sun soothe and warm and heal me. Eat the nuts and crackers, drink the juice, delighting in the quiet and solitude.

Back to the room. Have received two calls from insurance agents. Standing out on our little deck, I call both back, swearing to myself not to take any more during this entire trip, and not to tell Ansley about these two. Pull on running shoes and T-shirt, bicycling gloves. Set old sun-dyed and cracked helmet on head. Switch glasses for sunglasses. Push bicycle out of room, throw leg over it, and off I go.

There's a wide shoulder but these aren't ideal bicycling conditions—cars and trucks speeding past me on a two-lane highway. I get in a rhythm. In places, it seems as if I am going eerily fast. I glide down into valleys and there's no wind resistance, the bike just flies. In no time, I'm riding along with SPAC (Saratoga Performing Arts Center) on my left—trees and a park and then signs for the Gideon Putnam and memories: first, Mike White and I as teenagers driving out this way to find restaurants that weren't so expensive, just the two of us having dinner together, like adults. And back further, swimming in the gigantic pool at the Gideon Putnam: Mike and I would ride our bikes out and swim all afternoon, diving for pennies, nickels, dimes, daring each other to swim through the legs of adults. We'd get our nerve up and jump off the high dive.

In Saratoga now. Pulling up at lights. Riding between cars. A long line of cars on Broadway. I ride up outside the line, slow, pull over to the crosswalk, cross, ride back to the road and continue on, taking in the city, looking for Eliza and Ansley, breathing rhythmically, steadily, inhaling the action, the excitement, the traffic, the pedestrians, the sunlight pouring down, splashing onto the asphalt. Everyone looks happy. Drivers have their windows down, elbows out, they're laughing and chatting with the passengers. Adults on the sidewalk are licking ice cream off cones, pushing prams, joking with their kids, pointing at clothes and art in store windows. Here they are! They're merrily pacing down the sidewalk side by side, swinging their bags. They're smiling and happy. They're shopping and in their element. I call out. They wave. Off I go, up Broadway, to the final light. Ride up the hill, the sky blue, not a cloud. Space. No traffic. Big, beautiful mansions—painted bright colors—on either side with sprawling lawns and ornate gardens and views looking down on the town. Broadway is wide here. I pedal, one hand on the handle bars, lollygagging along, not having to be anywhere, no cell phone on me. I am alive and pedaling and working up a sweat and just over that way, through the campus of Skidmore on the way to the polo fields, is where Tom and Mimi's house is. I am flowing through space and time and my legs are effortlessly going around and around and I'm changing my grip on the handle bars to relieve the pressure on my back and the A. P. Smithwick Memorial is tomorrow and Tom has two horses in it. No, Elizabeth has two horses in it.

I ride to the top where there is a mansion on the right and then Broadway disappears, becomes a rutted, gravel farm road headed into the woods. I do a U-turn, start back down. But won't this be boring? Coasting all the way down Broadway. Lean in, bank to the right, sail up a driveway into the campus of Skidmore, pedal up the hill, take a left, start on a loop around the campus I know well from my running days and from the college tour with Paddy. Rolling now. The pedaling is effortless. Keep getting in these patches of space and time that are like being in a vacuum; the bike magically picks up speed without me telling it to. I'm twelve. Bicycling off for an adventure with Mike. I'm eighteen, bicycling to the rec center to do pushups and sit ups and pull ups and the duck walk and sprints, sweat pouring off me. I'm wearing waffle-patterned long underwear, turtle neck, sweat shirt, sweat pants, and I've got to pull five more pounds to ride Arnold W the next day—making 130.

I'm up on Esmerelda, and I'm 29, I'm 36, I'm 46, I'm 52—it's the day before the A. P. Smithwick; Tom has a horse in the A. P. Smithwick; I've galloped and schooled the horse that morning, and the next day we have every possible thing in the universe set in motion so that that horse will pull away from the pack at the last fence and win the race. And every one of those years, at 29, 36, 46, 52, we do win it.

The quarter-mile track with the springy, spongy surface is coming up on the left. Paddy and I had run around that track together when he'd looked at Skidmore and I'd loped around it—four times, a mile—many a time during cross country runs when visiting Susan, whose house is a mile away. I'm coasting, floating, and I see the figure of a tall, fit woman long-striding on the sidewalk ahead of me. It's a familiar figure. Can't be? But probably is. What a coincidence. All is going well. This is going to be a good trip. I'm parallel to her and yes, it's Mimi. I think about passing her while maintaining a stern, serious, focussed expression as I knew Tom would in this situation, but I can't resist. I lean in, pull up beside the sidewalk, hop off the bike and give her a big kiss.

We talk about Tom. What we miss. She explains how she is coping. It's her thirty-ninth anniversary and she's going out to dinner with Elizabeth and Gary. Laughing deeply as we walk along in the sunlight, she relates the details of her "wedding day": Tom drove her to the Towson Courthouse, grabbed someone walking by, pulled him in as a witness, and they were married by the clerk of the court.

I ask how Elizabeth is doing. A week earlier a horse of Elizabeth's had been beaten by a nose at the wire in the Jonathan Kiser—a memorial hurdle race in honor of Tom's best jockey (who won the A. P. Smithwick on Brigade of Guards twenty years earlier), and a race the Vosses like to win. It looked like a dead heat. Many thought the Voss horse had won. To spectators, it appeared his body was further forward than the body of the other horse, but the other horse, at the precise split second of reaching the wire, was at the point in his stride when his neck was fully outstretched, his nose extended. He got the money. "She's tough. She's Tom. She just keeps going."

We long-step through the campus. She takes a right to head back to her house. I throw my leg over Esmerelda, take a left and head for the motel, ducking and dodging through the traffic as I used to do as a kid. Then, I'm out in the open, cruising down the shoulder of Broadway, past SPAC. The shoulder disappears and I ride along the white line on the edge of the road as tractor-trailers roar past, the bike no longer flying on its own power. I'm pedaling now, pushing it, wanting to get the hell off this section. Then I'm unlocking the door with the Skyways-like key, picking up the bike, parking it by our bed.

The girls return. Everything speeds up. We three shower and dress in the small room. Drive to the National Steeplechase party at the Reading Room. Have good time seeing Kip. I'm talking to him about racing, Eliza approaches—and he switches leads and ratchets his enthusiasm level up a full notch: he's asking Eliza what she's up to; he's listening; he's inquiring; he's focused. Those two are "two peas in a pod," as Granny used to say. Lots of Maryland people there.

Reiley McDonald approaches; says he'd been looking for me. "I saw Reddy recently." (Reddy Finney, Gilman's legendary headmaster.) "He said he really liked your book, 'but Reiley,' he said, 'there's one thing.' " Reiley is lowering his voice to a hushed gentle voice, 'I just don't see why. . . .' " and at this point I know exactly what he's going to say. Reddy made the same comment about the first book. I wait knowingly for it "he has so much about sex." We laugh.

I tell him that Reddy was the first person I met when I walked out of St. James Church after giving Dickie's eulogy. "It made my day," I say. "He'd driven over by himself. He waited for me and shook my hand, congratulated and thanked me for the eulogy. That meant a lot to me." We swap Reddy stories. I think about the thoughtful handwritten letter Reddy sent me after Tom's funeral—specifying times at hunt meets when Tom had been helpful and generous to him, apologizing for not being able to make Tom's funeral, and asking if I'd mail him my eulogy.

I've gotten a drink at the bar near the table where Eliza and I had had the book signing at Sonny Via's party. I'm free for a moment, relaxing, taking in the scene. Or, putting on that that's what I'm doing. Eliza takes me by surprise, laces her arm through my arm. "How ya doing, Dad?" she asks with a big smile.

"Good, good," I say.

She looks into my eyes. My face starts to crumble, the mask to come off. "You thinking of Tom? The book signing?" Yes, yes, I nod. It seemed moments ago, there we were at our table, no one paying any attention; Tom sauntered over, started signing and handing out books and soon we couldn't sell them fast enough. "I am, too. That was so fun, wasn't it! Tom would want you to remember it and to enjoy this party now."

Cocktail party fizzling out. Out to dinner with Susan and her beau Stephen. It's one of Susan's favorite restaurants, and she treats. Afterwards, on the way home, stop at Sperry's for a nightcap. Back to the motel, pull out the 'Skyways Motel key,' and hit the hay.

The morning of the race. I don't go to the track. This is the first time in my life I have not gone to the track the morning of the race. I hop on Esmerelda, ride around town, buy a *Racing Form*, pick up a *Saratoga Special* and order a ham, cheese and egg bagel at Uncommon Grounds on Broadway. Sitting out at a table on the sidewalk with the parade of excited gamblers, horse-lovers and tourists streaming by, I read about the race and study the past performances of the horses. Before I know it, it's time to get going. Back at the motel—close quarters—we're changing and laughing and showering and bumping into one another.

We get to the track early. We're in the paddock. Our unwieldy herd of friends and family is there early. Then, there's Elizabeth.

She's calm, doing three things at one time. She's balancing Genevieve—bigger now, clutching her—on her hip. She's talking to the grooms. She's talking to owners. She sets Genevieve down beside Gary and tacks up the horse, Makari. She's laughing and beautiful and stylish and acting as if she has been doing this all her life. She has poise. I give her a hug and a kiss; she looks me in the eye, hugs me back, says, "What do you think Dad would say?" "He'd love it," I say. "He'd tell you the horse looks like a winner."

She's standing beside her jockey, Jack Doyle, an Irish lad as tall as she, discussing the race. "Riders up!" Jack cocks his left leg, hops alongside the walking Makari. Elizabeth is bent low, walk-trotting with him just as her father used to do. She grips his ankle and he flows up onto the horse in one fluid, releasing motion.

The A.P. Smithwick. One of the great steeplechasers of the decade, Divine Fortune—the favorite, two-time winner of the race, trained by Hall of Famer Jonathan Sheppard—tires second time around and drops back. Soon Makari is up in the front. Then, it's Makari and Demonstrative, the second-favorite, racing down into the last. Demonstrative jumps it "in hand," slightly ahead, an old pro. Jack's having to drive and scrub and whip—Makari rockets through the hurdle, a little low, but he lands running all out. They battle it out going down the stretch. The announcer calls them, back and forth. From our box, ten lengths before the wire, it looks like Demonstrative has won. Jack does not rise up quickly out of his tuck as a victorious, celebratory jock does. The two horses gallop out together, the jocks talking, neither knowing who "got it." We trot down the steps to present the trophy. The stewards are looking over the film and the photo finish. We're a little down. Elizabeth's horse has just been nudged out again. Two in a row . . . not good luck . . . hard to keep going . . . Then, the announcer calls out, "Makari!"

McLean, Susan, Eliza and I present the trophy. We're in the photo with Elizabeth, Genevieve, Gary, Mimi and Jack. I'm crying and trying to make myself look presentable as the pack of photographers snap away. I'm holding the gold trophy—a historic trophy originally made for the Tom Roby, a race which Evan Jackson, one of Pop's best friends, was the last to win. Evan, alive and well, donated the trophy to the race thirty years ago. I'm grinning and we're joking and a waterfall is cascading from my eyes. Elizabeth is modest, gracious. A circle of reporters surround her, holding their microphones out, asking her questions. She answers them as if she's been doing this for decades.

We're being escorted by a Pinkerton to the Saratoga Room, what we've always called the Trustees Room. A handsome middle-aged man in a suit drops in with our entourage, walks alongside me, instantly reminding me of a sensation from when I was a teenager riding here: being escorted by the Pinkertons back to the jocks' room, and racing fans fast-pacing along, either congratulating you or asking questions about the race, or asking you to sign their program—and it had to be right where you were listed as the rider. "Are you the one that wrote the book?" he asks.

I grin, "What book?"

"The book that starts off all about this race?"

"Yes, yes, I am."

"Good book, good book," he says. "I'm reading it right now. I bet you're happy about this Voss win."

"I sure am. I really am."

"When's your next one coming out?"

"Soon, I hope."

Then, he's gone. Instantly, I wish I'd brought him along with us.

Into the Trustees Room. Into the *air-conditioned* Trustees Room. What a release—to breath the cool, dry air. My old friend is no longer here who used to circulate with the tray of bubbling glasses filled with champagne. But the tray circulates. A throng of us watch the race over and over on the overhead television.

Someone asks Susan if she bet on the race. "I don't bet, and I don't eat at McDonalds." We laugh and laugh.

Before we leave, I want to thank someone. I ask who's in charge, and meet Maude Walsh. I shake her hand, tell her what a wonderful job they do year after year.

Spend the afternoon at the races. We're a group. Two great friends from our earliest days of teaching at Bollingbrook School in Petersburg, Virginia have come. James has brought his husband David. Wendy has brought her husband Jamie. Out to dinner at The Mouzon House—a French restaurant in an old Victorian house, we're laughing and talking about old times, and I'm signing and giving Wendy and James books. Susan and Stephen are having a great time. (They are a couple out of a Marquezian novel celebrating the magic, resilience and staying-power of love. Enchanted by each other in their early twenties, fate and circumstances pulled them apart. Three decades later, after raising their separate families, they are back together and rejoicing in the miracle of it.) Jamie has just been on 60 Minutes. He is an expert on restoring historic and extremely valuable paintings—and is often called upon to give his opinion on the authenticity of a painting, if forgery is expected. He asks me about racing. I ask him about paintings, and art dealings, and how he tells an original from a forgery. It is fascinating. I explain I've been inspired to learn about Vermeer and forgery through teaching the young adult novel *Chasing Vermeer* at Harford Day.

I'm sitting next to McLean and am not drinking. I am sipping out of McLean's pint glass—he's becoming a beer connoisseur and has ordered a dark and biting ale.

Mimi is at a nearby table with her riders and owners, and Elizabeth and Gary. Gary comes over and whispers something to Eliza. Eliza breaks out laughing. The jockey, Jack, would like a kiss. Gary told him right before the race that if he won it, Eliza would give him a kiss.

She laughs, goes to their table, gives the Irish lad a kiss. We're having a good time at our table, even though we're not discussing anything to do with racing. I think of giving a toast to Pop. His face, his being, his smile, his body is suddenly there with me. It is overpowering me. In preparation, I talk to the waiter, discuss just what type of a scotch "neat," I'd like, and he brings me the softest, most luscious, most delicious single malt I've ever had. I'm listening to Jamie. I'm joking with Minter about our old tennis playing days. I'm giving Susan a kiss—she looks so beautiful and happy with Stephen—and I'm thinking of Pop when a pianist sits down, warms up with a few Sinatra standards and then sings Louis Armstrong's *What a Wonderful World*, which always reminds me of Pop. I'm melting now. Images of galloping for Pop at Saratoga, of standing in the paddock alongside him. I see Ansley talking to the pianist and he starts in on Louis Armstrong's *Mack the Knife*. She's asked him to play it, for me. *What a Wonderful World* sent gentle, wispy images through my mind. *Mack the Knife*—Pop's favorite—jolts me. Makes me feel Pop is there. Makes me want to erupt in crying. Makes me wonder why he isn't there. I see him taking Mom's hand. We're at a big party under a tent. There's a dance floor in front of the band. I see him take Mom's hand and head for the dance floor.

Ansley has gotten some spoons, not the small ones with the table setting. Bigger ones. Soup spoons. Now we're in for it. She puts on a serious, far-off look, crosses her legs, warms herself up with a few flourishes, checking out the sound, the concussive power, the feel, the heft of the spoons, and then she's playing the spoons along with the pianist. Susan can't believe it. The pianist looks over at Ansley, nods, acknowledges her. They go head-and-head. Everyone at the table is picking up spoons and trying to keep up with Ansley. She stays totally focused, looking far-off, playing them on her knee, rippling them down the fingers of her open hand, playing on one leg then the other, rippling them down her side, clacking them between the palm of a raised hand and her thigh—she's off, in another world, with her father; she's beside him and he's not weakening as when she last saw him; he's young, healthy and strong. He's fully into it, playing those spoons better than anyone; he's got the serious face, then he has the painful expression, he switches off to the mournful look, then he opens both eyes wide and looks out at his audience while performing a virtuoso technique, the spoons going impossibly fast, the clackety-clacks speeding into one powerful, increasingly fast tempo, yet his head still, his eyes steadily looking out at us, eyebrows raised, as if it is a walk in the park, and he's daring anyone else to give it a try. Daring. Daring. She's off, in a trance.

In the morning, I ride my bike to Uncommon Grounds. Order a coffee, walk around, searching for the usual stack of *Saratoga Specials* in the newspaper stand. The stand is still filled with the previous day's *Specials*. I like this place, but it is not the most efficient. I remember seeing a package outside the front door. Step outside, there is a bundle of *Specials*. I break the plastic tie, carry them in, set them on the stand, purposefully not looking at the cover. I pull one off the top, sit at a table. There is a full-page photograph of Makari jumping the last fence head-and-head with Demonstrative. Demonstrative is a neck in front and on the outside; his jockey is playing it cool; the horse has jumped it well and has his landing gear—front legs outstretched—ready to touch down and speed to the wire; on the inside, Jack Doyle is down low, riding all out, driving Makari who might've "gotten in" a little close to the hurdle; he's shooting through it low, his head up a little high, as if he's just whacked "the box," his ears pinned back, and his knees still tucked up. Behind his hind feet you can see the gap he's made in the brush. Right above Makari's raised head, Jack's lowered head, is the headline, "For Tom," and in smaller letters, "Makari jumps to Smithwick win." I take a deep breath.

Open the paper, flip through first few pages looking for article and come across a photo of Mimi and Genevieve, in their racing finest, walking down the horse path and headed into the paddock. Emblazoned across it: "Photo of the day." It's by Todd Marks and it's an attention getter for "Kip Elser's Kirkwood Stables." I find the article by Joe Clancy. A couple of paragraphs down:

> Six months after her father, veteran trainer Tom Voss, died at 63, six months after she decided to manage the stable, six months after she said she was going to Saratoga's Oklahoma Annex with a stable of horses the way her father did, she won a Grade 1 steeplechase at Saratoga.... "It's not sinking in, it won't sink in for a while," Voss said. "What's it been, 11 years since we won this race? ... the A. P. Smithwick was always one my dad would talk about...."
>
> Tom Voss called Paddy Smithwick ... a second father. Smithwick's son Patrick and Tom Voss were lifelong friends. Tom Voss would aim for a sharp Smithwick runner every year at Saratoga and won the race four times—with Cookie (1980)), Mikey Free (1987), Brigade of Guards (1997), and Anofferucantrefuse (2003).

I hold it in. I sip my coffee, look at the photo on the cover and the headline and hold it in. Taking one step at a time, I walk to my bike, throw my leg over it, go for a twenty-minute ride up around Skidmore and over to Susan's.

Two hours later. I am back in Uncommon Grounds. I am in a stuporous, delirious, delicious, peaceful state with all of Saratoga and the whole glittering universe and thousands of years of life out there before me, waiting to be experienced, but first I have to have something to eat. I'm a little shaky. I'm hungry. I need some protein.

I cannot make a decision. "Well, let's start at the beginning," the pretty young woman says. "Now, what type of bagel would you like?" She hands me an order sheet: Number "212" at the top, and lists of every possible ingredient below—twenty items, three lists, how would I ever decide? I ask if we could discuss the order. "Yes." She guides me through the order: we decide on a sesame-rye bagel with everything on it. We decide on an iced tea. I take the tea and sandwich to a table out onto the sidewalk where my bike is parked.

Go back in. Ask for some paper. The same smiling young woman hands me several order sheets.

Back out: I scratch out some notes on the back of the five-by-seven sheets, wanting to remember:

Susan and Carrie go to work. They are clearing "chakras." Working on meridians. Creating "cross-over energy lines." Pressing on "key energy points," rustling around, one at my head, one at my feet, and then a hand is under my back, another on my stomach, and they are whispering to each other to do this, to do that, and I don't know what the hell they are doing, I am flying flying. . . .

I am high up and I look down and there is the stretch. The turf stretch—from the last fence to the wire. At Saratoga. I've got plenty of life left. I have that and more. But the point is: "Ride from the last fence to the wire like your life depends on it." As Pop said. "Open up on the field. Also, the future is Open. I see the future—out there: space, lots of it. There's lots of space and I am flying over Saratoga, I am flying over the young female trainer whose filly died at the races yesterday, over Ansley, over Tom, over Cot Campbell who is gearing up to win the Whitney with Palace Malice, over Iraq, Sunnis, Shiites, over Iran, over Afghanistan and everything is going to be all right, the future is going to be good. Then, I go into a whirl. It's like the swirling colors in Van Gogh's Starry Night. *I am on some sort of flying material, yes, a flying carpet out of* Arabian Nights—*a somersaulting flying carpet, diving, then pulling out of the dive, flattening out and shooting over the land, and soaring back up. At the top of the whirl, I prepare. Starting to dive again, I bank sharply, trying to pull out of the somersaulting-flight pattern. The centrifugal force is pulling against me, but I hold it, hold it—and I jettison out of the spin and am speeding over treetops, over thousands of acres of trees. Ecstasy Bliss. Freedom.*

GONG! GONNNNNNGGGGG! GONNNNNNGGGGG! *Susan strikes a brass gong and the sound waves reverberate through my body, shooting me out into the open universe. There's a bright yellow speck. It grows larger and larger until it fills everything and explodes.* GONG!

There's another splotch of yellow paint. It grows larger and larger until it fills all space and explodes. GONG! It happens over and over.

Then, there is a long hallway in the sky. I am looking down it, into infinity. It is narrow. Greek columns on both sides. It is floating in the sky. Blue-gray. Peaceful. Pop, Tom, Mikey, Mom are telling me there is plenty of future and to Open Up. OPEN UP. Open up after the last hurdle, leaving the others behind, and open up in life. Pop is telling me this. Open up to new ideas and interests.

I feel this easing of tension. They are all OK. Pop, Tom, Mikey, Mom are O.K. There is a new concept. It relaxes me. It is that the social animal in me, the out-in-a-crowd me is not the writing me. Compartmentalize. There's me—talking to someone at the races. And there's me at my desk writing. Those two are different. They can be different and for some reason this relaxes me. Is it that for so many recent years at Saratoga, I have been the "author" selling and promoting his books, going to book signings. And now it's, "What's next? What're you working on now?" Yet this time, I see a way of separating the two and setting Myself the Man free from Myself the Writer. I am free to live, to fly-fish, to ski, to ride, to go to the races, to place a bet, to go on trips with the family, to love Ansley, and I am free to sit down and write.

The long hallway with the Greek columns and the voices now of Pop, Tom, Mikey, Mom, Bob Witham, Mike White, Dickie, Brian Hickey, Emmett, Tanza, Scotty Schulhoffer dissolves, the gray hallway and columns becoming smaller and then a speck of bright iridescent blue appears in the distance, the speck becoming a spot becoming a splotch becoming a parallelogram the shade of lapis lazuli, the lines perfectly parallel, the corners sharp as those on a diamond, growing larger and larger until it fills all space, and suddenly, it is out. Gone. It starts again, this time a tiny spot of faded red, light years off, and it is speeding towards me, a crimson parallelogram orgasmically exploding in my mind, obliterating itself, wiping the screen clean, and starting over again as a tiny faded red, a rose color red light-years away coming towards me . . . .

Open up after that last hurdle. I have plenty of the race left. Ride it all out. Write when you're writing. Live when you're living. Open up to all of life.

After the treatment, after lunch—I take off for an afternoon of bicycling:

I feel high. I stop, talk to people, tell them I feel high—I have an LSD high, and they look at me as if I'm crazy, and I am, in a way. I'm crazy-high.

I bicycle all around the backstretch of the main track. Leave note for trainer Barclay Tagg. "Seems like yesterday we were talking about Tom Voss and Dickie Small. See you around. —Patrick."

I bike to Yaddo, the artists' and writers' sanctuary just to the east of the track. As kids, Mike White and I used to ride our bikes on the gravel paths through the gardens, up and down the driveways, and on the smooth, dirt paths through the woods. There are all these new signs—you can't go here, can't go there. Well, how the hell do you get to the office if you don't go up the driveway? I pedal up through the woods toward the main building. I can hear a golf cart stalking me. I pull the bike up at the office, the same office I'd entered ten years earlier and had been greeted by a friendly receptionist who encouraged me to apply for a residency.

This time, as I enter, a pale, severe-looking woman in her late twenties sitting behind her desktop computer looks up in shock, and stares at me as if I'm ET stepping out of my space ship. She does not stand; perhaps she never leaves the desk, the room—has never gone outside into the sunlight. I hear the crunch of a golf cart's wheels on the pea gravel outside, the whine of its engine, and then there's sudden quiet.

"Hi, ha, you don't have to worry. I just wanted to pick up some info on the residency program for writers."

She stares at me.

"I was thinking about applying to the writing program." A young man—cheeks flushed—steps into the room behind me, walks around me, stands at the edge of a counter, two arm lengths away, and stares at me with his eyes popping out of his head. He's a few inches shorter than I, and is wearing a tight T-shirt showing off his weight-lifting pectorals and biceps.

"The deadline was today," Miss Sunshine says.

"I don't mean for this year. I mean for next year."

Muscles is staring at me. I'm ignoring him. He has bullets shooting out of his eyes. "Did you see the sign?" he blurts out.

I turn my eyes towards him. "Yes."

"Then, why did you come up the road?"

"I wanted to stop by the office."

"But you saw the sign?"

"Well, how are you supposed to get to the office if you can't go up that road?"

"You make an appointment," Miss Sunshine snaps.

I think back on the wonderful receptionist here a decade ago. She gave me a note about Mike Damsi wanting to meet me at the $50 window. He used to ride in the "hot car" with Pop. Also, she had rented us her house and had gotten to know my mother. Wouldn't I stop back again? She hoped I got a residency; it would be great for my writing. . . .

I ask Miss Sunshine with the porcupine needles now bristling if I can pick up a brochure or pamphlet about the program.

"It's all online."

He's moving towards me. He's twenty, thirty years younger, and he's well built. My adrenalin starts to pump. It is kicking in. It is not fight or flight. It is fight. This jerk is getting ready to usher me out. He had better not touch me.

"My book just won a $10,000 literary award," I say, "and the first hundred pages are set in Saratoga, some of it right here. So I thought I'd look into a writing residency." My voice is cracking. I'm frustrated it is cracking. I'm sounding whiney, going into a higher octave. I'm trembling. I'm thinking of fishing here with Mike before these two were born and lying in the shade on the bank listening to the great Fred "Cappy" Capossela of "It is now post time," fame, call the jumping race. I see that one huge fish that broke my line. I feel the reverberations of my bike and the rattling sound as Mike and I fly down the steps in the garden between the statues of nudes.

"This is why we have the No Trespassing signs up," says Muscles. "So the writers won't be interrupted."

This is my place. I've been coming here since I was twelve. I used to fish here with Mike. I knew the woman who worked here and she knew me. "My name—my father's name—was all over the papers yesterday and is all over the papers today and if anyone deserves to come to this fucking writers' retreat it is me and you can go to hell." That's what I wanted to say, that's what I didn't say.

I leave, and it gets me down. I walk around the magnificent rose gardens, ride out, up toward the main track, and instead of turning left by the three-eighths pole of the track, take a right into Horse Haven, trying to forget about it. Screw them. I bicycle over to where Pop was stabled for a few years, including the year Tom and I galloped for him. Bike over to the Annex, where the steeplechase horses are stabled. See Elizabeth, pat the winner of the A.P. Smithwick, whom she is grazing. Talk to Jonathan Sheppard, ride to the rec center where Mike, Willie and I used to watch Speedy fight; and bicycle back to the motel.

That night, I consider going up to the Adirondacks with Susan, Ansley, and Eliza the next day. Eliza is shocked. Why? She asks. (Earlier—I'd been pressing to go to the Whitney on Saturday.) I don't tell her it is this "opening up" I'd experienced that is pushing me. No, she does not want to go to the Adirondacks. What am I thinking? We are going to the Whitney—one of the biggest races of the year. *Come on, Dad.*

In the morning: Eliza and I drive over to see Thomas while Susan and Ansley walk. Mimi is out. It is just Rita—the lively and giving Italian who has worked for the Vosses since godson Sam was a baby—Thomas, Eliza and I. We have a peaceful, quiet time with Thomas—one year old. Eliza is cute and gentle, at ease, happy to be there, in the moment, with Thomas. I also feel peaceful with him.

Back, Eliza and I shower and change for the races. Ansley returns from a two-hour walk with Susan. Ah-oh. Eliza talks Ansley into going to the races with us. It is hot, and it is humid—even steamy.

We don't have a box or seats and we are on our feet the entire time. I do everything I can to make the races enjoyable for Ansley, but nothing is working.

We leave the races, walking a good distance to the car. I want to resurrect the afternoon. I tell them we've got to go to the Fasig Tipton cocktail party—one of the biggest parties of the year. They do not want to go. Ansleys's feet hurt. Eliza says she's sweaty, looks terrible and wants to go home to clean up.

If we go home, we'll never make it back to the party. Both are accusing me of being selfish—dragging them to this party. I know if I can just get them there, they'll have a good time. We walk from the track to Kip's, where we parked. Ansley insists on returning to our house. She doesn't want to stand at a cocktail party. "Why did you park so far away? . . . Why are you so set on this party? . . . All you think about is yourself."

We're in the car. I crank up the air conditioner. There's a long line of cars on the street going towards town, in the direction of our house. I back out, go the opposite direction. "Where are you going? This isn't the way." I don't say a word, drive in and out of the back roads I know from childhood bicycling, dodging the traffic, end up over by Tipton Avenue, very proud of myself. They drag themselves out into the heat. They need to use the ladies room.

We do have a few blocks to walk. I stop and joke with two cheerful women having cocktails out on their big porch. It is exactly the kind of conversation Tom would have enjoyed and would have engaged in at a time like this, partially to exacerbate his entourage. I'm hoping the good cheer will rub off on the girls. It does not.

We arrive. First, I find large, clean, nice bathrooms. Then, I find them a bench. Michael Finney—proprietor of Yoicks—looking young and healthy, appears, starts talking and joking and drawing them out, cheering them up; he's saved me. He's opening a new store—equestrian art, English upper scale outdoors clothes and equipment. I sold lots of books at Yoicks, when it was in Maryland. Go to the bar, a martini for Ansley, glass of wine for Eliza. Bump into Elliot Letchworth, a bloodstock agent ("Horse thief," would be a better title, Tom once told me), who says he wants to meet my wife and daughter.

Elliot, mid-forties, devotes all his attention to Eliza, asking her about design, fashion and going to the London College of the Arts in the fall. He gives us the lowdown on a new player in the steeplechase business, McKelvie Fullerton—who is buying yet another farm. Says we can come look at a horse he has picked out for McKelvie to buy—just over there in stall 69—for $200,000. The girls are gaining interest. He explains how he found most of Tom's best horses.

Elliot's from Warrenton, Virginia. As a youth, had hunters, rode some in point to points. "When Tom was getting started he'd come down in his brand new Imperatore. All the latest equipment. Shiny boots and new leather leggings and three perfectly turned out hunters. Arrogant. He was so arrogant. He'd get out with his fedora pulled low over his eyes and wouldn't talk to anyone. Brand new tack, the brass on his shanks glistening. . . ."

Elliot had an agenda. I remembered now. He had said the exact same thing in an article; it had pissed me off and I had told

Tom so. This wasn't true. Most of the time Tom was using a combination of Pop's tack—which was new since he had just gone into training—and old equipment of his father's and even his grandfather's. He'd have one assistant with him, Emmett, and these horses he was running certainly weren't hunters—some were rogues and this Elliot Letchworth couldn't keep one leg on either side of them for more than thirty seconds. If Emmett had ever heard him talking this way about Tom, he would have said, "Don't say another word about *T-a-u-m* unless you want to step into this stall with me and see who steps out."

"That's not so. . . ." I say. "He wasn't like that. . . ." I was remembering Tom working around the clock but I didn't have any fire in it. I was weary of defending him. Tom was simply being professional, focused. Yes, the horses looked sharp. Yes, the tack was well-oiled. Yes, he looked good. Furthermore, he was reducing. He was doing light—and it hadn't been easy losing those thirty natural pounds of muscle. He was down to business and wasn't going to be walking around gabbing and glad-handing like Elliot was doing at just this (*adjectival epithet removed*) moment. He was developing the disciplined training habits that would one day make him one of the best trainers in the country. By the way, he never wore a pair of leather leggings in his life.

We move on—talk to Jack Doyle, the winning rider. He's smoking—partly to stunt his appetite, to lose weight—exactly what caused my father to die from cancer at the age of forty-six and a half. I consider lecturing him but don't. I introduce Ansley and Eliza to Stowe Burke. His grandfather Bobby Burke and John Coales are coming up from Virginia the next day. We're just going to miss them. We talk to Terrence Collier, Fasig Tipton's lead auctioneer. I tell him how I took Paddy, age seventeen, to the sales one night; he saw Terrence up there in the limelight with gavel in his hand, auctioning off million-dollar horses, and he said, "Dad, Dad—I saw him last night. That's the same man who was up dancing on the piano at Siro's!" A woman steps in to our group, shakes my hand, congratulates me on *Flying Change*, tells Terrence he has got to read it. She goes on and on. Ansley shows signs of boredom. Then, I'm saved: Terrence politely asks Ansley what she does. Ansley gives one or two of the titles she holds at Oldfields. Terrence, I remember, is a Francophile. I brag about my wife teaching French and chaperoning twenty student trips to France and studying Russian through a French-speaking professor when she was a student in Paris. That does it. Oh, she was going to be so miserable at the party. Now she is speaking French with Terrence, head of sales for Fasig Tipton, talking about Paris and about the French, inquiring about London, asking if he could introduce Eliza to anyone in London, Eliza will be going to graduate school at the London College of the Arts ....and *wanting another martini.* When I return for the second round, I go to the same bartender, a middle-aged man doing this on the side. Chat with him and leave him a good tip.

Soon, we're meeting Susan and Stephen for dinner at a restaurant in town. The server is late with our drinks. I go to the long polished bar. A quiet man in a checkered shirt tells the bartender, "Next round's on me." He buys a drink for everyone at the bar—twenty or so—and buys our round. I wait for our drinks, chat with him. "It's the least I can do," he says, "to thank this wonderful town, this incredible race meet, this glorious sport."

After dinner, we drop Eliza off at Sperry's. Out back, outside, the music is loud and there is a mob of people, hundreds. I see a fellow Maryland country boy, a trainer in his fifties, from Harford County—his farm not far from my school—staggering, looking lost. I ask what he's doing. "I've lost my wife." I laugh; he grips my arm at the elbow, reminding me of Speedy, and I lead him through the throng to his wife sitting at a booth inside. "Thank you, Patrick, thank you, Patrick," he says—his bright blue eyes blazing into mine, his thick youthful blonde hair perfectly combed—as clearly as the most sober man.

I leave Eliza with a tall, handsome young jumping rider related to my old Merryman girlfriends. I'm worried.

She gets in at 3:30. We're up at 6:30. Drive to Uncommon Grounds. Eliza remains sleeping in the back. Ansley and I have coffee and egg, ham and cheese bagels at a table outside. We order a bagel for Eliza. Then, we're buckling our seat belts, ready to head home. I start the engine; Eliza awakens, asks for her bagel. I've forgotten to pick it up. I return to get it. Walking through the tables on the sidewalk, I spot my bartender from the Fasig Tipton party sitting down for breakfast. On the way out, I ask what his plans are for the day. Ansley's standing on the sidewalk, "Come on, come on," waving to me.

It's hard to leave Saratoga. It is impossible to leave Saratoga.
I jog to the car.

Speedy's Birthday

---

14 August 2014

Speedy's birthday. Seventy-five today. He won't be driving in, asking for his birthday present. I don't call him, asking if he'd like to go out. I don't get him a present.

The Undertow

"Do you see him? Do you see the story?. . . It seems to me I am trying to tell you a dream—making a vain attempt, because no relation of a dream can convey the dream-sensation, that commingling of absurdity, surprise, and bewilderment in a tremor of struggling revolt, that notion of being captured by the incredible which is of the very essence of dreams. . . . No, it is impossible . . . to convey the life-sensation of any given epoch of one's existence . . . its subtle and penetrating essence. . . . We live as we dream—alone. . . ."

— Marlowe in *Heart of Darkness*

August 17

A week after returning from Saratoga, after working from 6:00 a.m. to 6:00 p.m. every day on the farm, and then throwing a lively, even raucous, going-away-to-London crab feast for Eliza, Sweetheart and I are in the Jaguar, and out of there—top down, accelerator down, wind blowing through our hair, sunlight on our necks.

At the beach, there are warning signs. STRONG UNDERTOW. BE CAREFUL. I wade through the waves—tough here near Fenwick Island north of Ocean City. They roll in, build up a crest, then suddenly crash. They roll in, roll and roil, building strength, gathering height, then at the peak develop the warning, the white spewing crest which no longer rolls like a line of barrels, as it does at the beaches in Florida with their long gradual inclines, but instead crashes down and rushes in, all power, the white water pushing and pulling and whirling, knocking you forward, knocking you down. Just as suddenly, it withdraws, sucking

426

you back so you'll be properly positioned to be creamed by the next oncoming wave that initially looks so benign and negotiable sweeping in from the depths, then gathers power and height as the former wave is sucked beneath, and crashes down on the outgoing current.

A wave builds before me, higher and higher, about to break. I dive into it, come up on the other side, swim out a few strokes, turn, check on the life guard stand, and start down the coast, headed south, leaving thoughts about Saratoga about Tom on land, doing the crawl, bringing my elbows up higher and at a sharper angle out of the water than usual, taking a breath on my right side with each stroke, keeping an eye on the beach, trying to swim parallel to it, not wanting to go too far out.

A wave picks me up, crests, drops me. I'm too close to the shore. I switch to the breaststroke to see where I am. I cruise along, check—there's the lifeguard stand, and it's the one with the beautiful, blonde and very fit girl in the dark blue bikini, and I'm passing her now. I'm out where I should be now. I'm in a trough—right before the waves build and break. I slow, try to touch down. No bottom. A little spooky. I think of the dolphins I saw early that morning swimming just another twenty yards out. Wonder if there were any sharks following the pod of dolphins and envision Louie Zamperini punching the shark in the nose in *Unbroken*—could I do that?

I swim hard, twenty, thirty strokes, the sting of the salt, the glint of the sunlight on the waves, the rhythm of my strokes and harder-than-usual kicking propelling me away from the nightmare of the crash and Speedy's reaction, and see by a big wave coming, dive to the bottom, skim along the sand like a skate, surface.

Switch back to the crawl. Have a rhythm. Cutting through the water. Feel like a fish. My arms reach out, dig into the water, power through, come out with elbow high and dig sharply back in. I kick harder than in a pool, and let my torso rotate more than in a pool so that with each stroke I roll slightly to that side while my feet kick hard to steady me. My butt is up out of the water. This is different from a pool or lake. I don't have to use energy to keep afloat. My butt is up, buoyant, and my feet are up near the surface of the water. The waves pick me up, let me down and I just keep the same rhythm. The waves knock into me, slam into me. I continue slicing into the water and angle further out, away from the shore. I look up. I'm past the beautiful lifeguard and half way to the next lifeguard, tall, skinny, short blonde hair and a prominent nose—a male. I'm not the least bit tired. I keep my arms wheeling around, digging in, coming up sharply with elbow angled out of the water, then slicing in. Without knowing it, I let my kicking ease up, then realize it and pick up the pace, and the kicking powers me forward, keeps me steady. I do wonder—does this churning of my feet attract sharks. Time does not exist.

I power down the Eastern Seaboard. Can't get over the distance I'm covering. Ease up, do the breaststroke, glance over at the tall, skinny male lifeguard. Had planned to stop here. Maybe just a little further. How about a big push here? Count the strokes. Thirty strokes and then ease up. Here are some boys, out in the waves. Good, it's not too deep. I'm happy to have company. I head out a little deeper so we don't collide. They're laughing and smiling. The sunlight and water is splashing off their faces. I'm in a world to myself. I am a fish. I slice through the water, pass them, ease up and do the breaststroke.

Now, I'm half way to the next guard stand. Two guards: the dark-haired, dark-skinned, more amply developed, rather perfectly developed girl and the very slight, very young, very blonde boy who is the runner. He can run all day. He's like these sandpipers. I see him running down the beach carrying a sandwich to another guard. I see him running from station to station. I see him jogging across the hot sand, to the dunes, the deep sand not slowing, his body not sinking in, his economic sandpiper steps taking him across the hot sand, up to the path between the snow fences and up over the top of the dunes. Soon, he'll be carrying something back, jogging down the beach. He must be a cross-country runner. Andrew was like that as a kid, could run all day. How I loved those years of his running cross-country, going to all the meets, running alongside him, cheering him on. OK, thirty, give me thirty strokes: I'm running beside him at the championships. I'm stroking hard, fast, focused, but I'm not swimming, I'm running. The finish is up a steep hill. Runners are caving in. Crumpling. Going from a fast pace, to a jog, to a crouched-over crab-trot. Andrew is grimacing. He doesn't quit. He doesn't crumple. He doesn't give in to a walk. "Pump those arms! Pump those arms! Quick short steps, Andrew. You can do it. You got it. We're almost there." We pass them. Pass runner after runner. Finish strong.

Ease up. Let it go for now, I think. Let it go. Do the breast-stroke, check my bearings. I'm past the cross-country runner and the well-developed lifeguard. I do have tingles in the fingers in my right hand. Both feet are numb. I have a strange feeling in my left foot, right across the arch. I picture a crack going through the bone. It feels like your foot feels after a horse steps on it for the briefest second. The waves are battering me. I look down and can see a light sandy color. I've drifted in too close. I stroke my way back out, past where the waves are breaking, a little further than I like. I go back to freestyle. My form is off. Concentrate on it. Pull it together. Get my rhythm. Go hard and steady, not counting, not thinking about anything but the swimming and the oncoming waves and where I am in relation to the shore, hard and steady, I'm the ocean, the fish, the sky, the sand, I go on and on, sleek, fast, streamlined, and then, like a plane banking, I suddenly turn to the right, downshift into the breaststroke, and glide in.

The bottom. The beach. I stand, lean forward, trying to go forward. The water is rushing back, pulling me back at the knee-caps. A wave smashes into my back, knocks me forward. I barely stay up. The water begins to rush back. Raising my knees high, pumping my arms, I run stiffly out of the surf.

The firm beach beneath my feet. Vertical now. Hard firm beach below, blue sky above. Water rushing off body. Full day ahead. No encumbrances. Nothing to carry, nothing to lug— physical or mental. Free. Out of myself—*ekstasis*. Part of the beach and sunlight and water and sky. Streamlined. Body hard, fit. Out of time. Could be twenty, could be forty. I am sixty plus. I'm alive! Feel twenty, but don't think this, just feel it. Glance up the beach. Past this lifeguard, past the next, past the next, look-ing forward to the long easy walk back to Sweetheart. Amazed at how one can cover a distance in the water, I start walking back up the East Coast.

Fenwick Island Hunting
August 19
The race at Saratoga in honor of Tom is scheduled for Thursday, 21st.

There has been a serious mistake. Here Tom is—young, handsome, face smooth and unwrinkled—up on a horse at our place just outside the barn in his hunting clothes, all just right: black coat, hunting cap, stock, and pleasantly grinning. I'm talking to him.

Where've you been?

He looks so peaceful. He's up on Time, Mom's filly whose full name is Just In Time—Tiger Bennett saved her life. We were waiting and waiting for Fini, her dam, to foal. We'd checked her in the big shed at 10:30 and we were giving up, heading to bed. Tiger said, "I'll go out and check one last time." And there she was, only part way out, needing us, two men and a boy, to pull as hard as we could to get her out, and then to open up the sack so she could breathe.

Handsome. Fair skin. Unblemished. Eyes fully open. Riding around. This is unbelievable. This is wonderful. "Where the hell have you been?" I ask. He doesn't answer. Just walks around on Time.

Is he waiting for me to go with him? Is that it? Well, maybe I will. Isn't this incredible. Tom's fine! He's here with us. Look— there he is—as physical, as palpable, as meaningful, as real as I am standing here outside our barn, our big red barn on this very green grass and his skin is smooth and fair—blonde hair pokes out of his hunting cap by his ears. Some people are meandering around. They're not paying any attention. It's almost as if they don't see him. I try to draw them over to look.

The trailer—it's our Rice trailer, gray-blue, smaller than the long, overkill, customized, silly trailers they make today with everything but a Jacuzzi and cocktail lounge. It's our Rice trailer and it's brand new and it's hooked up to Mom's Ford Fairlane with the big V-8 that can outrun anything on the road. It's in the upper field, an unusual place, in the field by the driveway entrance with the ramp down waiting for us. Tom is waiting for me. That's it.

OK, I give up trying to tell the people about him. I duck into the barn to get a horse. It won't take long. I'll catch a horse, put him in a stall, run into the house, pull on britches, boots and hunting coat, run back out, tack up and load up. "OK,"—I look up at Tom. "OK—hold on."

This is the life. My life as it should be is back. It is healed. The grass is green. The sky is a wonderful early morning deep, timeless blue with the promise of a great day of hunting ahead of us. Tom is up on Time and he's in a nice hunting saddle, not a racing saddle. Hey—that's my old hunting saddle he's using. Time is calm. He's letting her walk around, graze a little. The barn is a deep, rich, blood red, and the time of this day, all of the future, is stretching out ahead of us. The energy is there. The energy at a meet before the hunt. The air is filled with it—a frisson, a shimmering, sunny, electric charge.

I walk to the big white sliding door opening to the central aisle of the "bottom barn"—the stalls and shed. Step into the feed room. Scoop feed with a metal scooper into the freshly painted steel bucket—top half painted dark blue, the bottom half light blue. Step back outside the opening to the sliding door to bang the scooper against the bucket and to watch them jog in and to talk to Tom.

Onto the green grass, the corncrib—the same blood red as the barn—before me. The door to the red corncrib has been freshly painted white. I have the scooper raised, and am about to bang it against the bucket and ask Tom where the meet is: Isn't this great! How I do love hunting with Tom, as we've been doing since we were five years old, he on Pepper, me on Queenie—not knowing what the day will bring, the excitement of that atavist feeling, not knowing where we will go, what time we'll come in, what will happen. Feel at ease. Myself again. All of myself is here, now. A part was missing but I'm now whole. My wrist is about to bang the scooper against the sides of the bucket and to swish the feed around; my senses are ready to hear and watch the horses trot and gallop excitedly, licking their chops, up to the gate; but now there is no one there: red barn, green grass, deep blue sky, and a vacuum, just space, where Tom had sat on Time, loosened his hold on the reins, and let her pick some grass.

I search for witnesses. There are some out in the field. A congregation of them. "Didn't you see Tom?" I ask. They don't reply. They look at me like I'm losing it. Well, they are the ones who are crazy. "He was just here, didn't you see him?" I insist.

No reply. They don't even look me in the eye. There are now other trailers and vans pulling in the driveway and into the field. "Where'd he go? Did you see where he went?" I ask. The trailers and vans keep rolling in the driveway, up the hill side of the barn where Tom had just been on Time, across the space he had filled, through the gate and into our top field. The meet is at our place. I am upset, perplexed—all these vans and trucks and trailers rolling past me. I toss and turn. Open my eyes. I'm in a bed opening my eyes expecting to see light and feel air wafting in the two front windows of our bedroom facing the front paddock and to hear the dogs barking and the horses grazing and some geese honking but instead there is just this steady humming sound of an engine, an air conditioner, and darkness: dark wall in front of me. I'm in a big bed by myself and I don't know where the hell I am. Then, click, I remember I am in a bed in a motel room at the beach.

I turn over and there Ansley is beside me in this vast bed. I'm relieved. So glad. Incredibly grateful. I snuggle up to her, gently lay my arm around her waist, and look around. The curtain is pulled tight against the wall-length sliding glass doors. There is a thin vertical strip of bright light at either end of the curtain. Bright light trying to get in.

Fenwick Island Stairs
August 20—one day away from the race in honor of Tom.

I am climbing up a stairway. Each stair is made of a new, light-colored, thin strip of pine. I am climbing, stepping, faster and faster, going up, trying to get through the top where there's a trap door like the new one we just put in the exact middle of the hayloft. I am young, yet it's difficult. The steps are becoming escalator-like, coming towards me, going faster, and I have to increase my speed. Have to jog, picking my knees up, to keep up with the downward spinning steps. I am making progress, heading up, about to go through the trap-door opening, but then the escalator suddenly stops and jolts forward, speeding up, going away from me. My feet start to go out from under me. My feet are being carried up by the speeding wooden steps and my torso is falling back. My head is about to slam into the thick oak-board back of the trap door opening. It's going to hit hard—with all of my backward flying weight. I call out, "Tom!" I call out, ""Tom!" I know he's there. I know he's right behind me. I picture him—between twenty-two and twenty-five—long blonde hair combed back; fair skin. "Tom, Tom!" I call, worried, yes, as I become weightless, falling back, my feet rushing up the relentlessly speeding escalator, my mind picturing what will happen if the back of my head slams into the oak barn boards, but in my core, deep down, I know he'll be there. I know he'll be there and that he'll catch me.

August 22—the day after Tom's race

> Across the beach and into the waves
> Laughing and joking into the spray
>
> Sun on our backs
> Her hair astray
> Flowing in the breeze
>
> Ball of blazing fire above
> Sand between our toes
> Icy water taking away our breath
>
> Then out—cold plump droplets
> Like tiny puffed-up pillows
> Sliding down goose-bumped skin
> Her hair straight back
> Scooped away from face
> Suctioned between shoulder blades to spine
>
> She laughs, leans back, shakes her head,
> Runs fingers through sea-soaked hair
> Flinging the ends up, freeing them
> Her back straight, shoulders broad,
> Chest deep
> Breasts bold in the cold
>
> Why not a hug
> Why not a kiss
> This is a chance
> Not to be missed
>
> Then—
>> Walking down the East Coast
>> Stride
>>> by
>>>> Stride

                    Hand
            in
        Hand

Strong
Linked together
As one
Looking forward to the future
To the afternoon
To the fun—a game of chess
Pawns fall
My knight saves her Queen
Her Queen captures my castle
And King and Queen meet in the tower high
    above the keep

Seven stories up
The windows open

The tapestries rippling
The waves crashing outside
The sun baking the sand

The portcullis is down
The bridge is up
Guards in mail, swords on their hips
Patrol the parapets

While blinds from Venice clatter
White sheets and pillow cases are clean and cool
Skin is sticky, quick to the touch and tastes of salt
Clammy pepper-and-salt grains of sand dry in the heat
And spread through the bottom of the sheets

And the Venetian blinds clatter
The tapestries gently ripple and slap against the walls
The drapes billow
The waves break outside and the sun bakes the sand

Until we lie back

Hand in hand
Pull sheets up over our chests
And travel far off into our distant lands

And awaken in the gloaming
Knowing that the night is not far off
Slate black sky speckled with stars

Out to dinner
Candlelight
She in low-cut white
Skin reddened
Becoming tan
Across her arms and chest

Bottle of red glimmering

Dessert—light and sweet—for two

We sail back
North now
Under the stars
Up the East Coast
Up the glistening walk-way
Convertibles, radios turned up loud, stream by on our left
Waves to our right
Dark and breaking all night

We sail along,
Tacking upwind
Into the light Zephyr
Caressing and cooling our hot sunned faces

She takes the elevator at this hour
I walk up to the top of our tower
Ten steps up, then turn right
Ten steps up, then turn left
One-*two*/one-*two*/one-*two*/one-*two*/one-*two*, turn right
Enjoying the rhythm of it, the meter
Reminding me of something

It's one line of iambic pentameter then another
        Going up
             Going up
      Spiraling up
             Until the Seventh Floor Door
      Out of the stairway—onto a balcony
             The kingdom safe and sleeping below

Through the entrance into our chamber

Waves still crashing
Wind still blowing
Drapes still billowing

Into the white sheets
My arm around her waist
Her hand cupping my hip

And the moment of bliss
Lying together as one
Before going deep, deep
Into luxurious sleep.

Changing Vets

August 29

I've decided to change vets. This last one has been too expensive. Why not use Ginny Gillam, the mother of my advisee Rosemary who graduated last year, and the mother of Louisa, whom I'll be teaching Medieval History this year. I give Ginny a call and she comes the next day. We narrow down the number of shots the horses need—and she saves me $100. She asks about Speedy. At first I think she means my cousin Speedy, Mikey's son. So we end up talking about him. He and his wife Eva have moved up from Kentucky into the family farm, Sunny Bank, just outside Middleburg, Virginia. She tells me he has horses at Pimlico and Laurel, and is maintaining a tough schedule commuting to the Maryland tracks from Virginia, but—he just won a stakes race the other day. Yes, we agree, he can really train.

We switch to discussing Speedy Kiniel. She'd worked with him every day during her youthful years of riding at Mikey's, and he had "been so helpful, taught me so much." Feeling guilt, I say I haven't seen him in a while. I tell her about missing his birthday for the first time in years. She says she'll call him the next day.

Brief Encounter

September 3

Andrew suddenly shows up at Paddy's in Denver. He's been doing a lot of long-distance driving from California, and out to the Dakotas, Virginia, Georgia and back; from California, and through Kansas, to Virginia, North Carolina, and back; and was passing through on his return to California. We get some fun facebook photos of the two brothers pouring buckets of water on each other. We're talking to him, trying to persuade him to move to Denver, hike, ski, camp, meet all the fit women, get a job with hip, positive young people at a ski shop. Get settled and move into something more serious. We're excited. Then, Andrew has too much to drink one night, goes wild, becomes violent. Paddy is forced to call the police. Ansley and her brother Graham, a Marine veteran, fly out. The police put Andrew in a psychiatric unit. This is our chance. We hope we can get him some help. Ansley calls the police station, calls the psychiatric unit, explains over and over about Andrew's Post Traumatic Stress Disorder, about his paronia, about his dependence on drugs, about his losing job after job. Andrew spends the night; the next morning he meets with a psychiatrist and is released. He takes off. Again, we have no idea where he's gone.

The Speck in Your Neighbor's Eye

<hr />

Back in the classroom—I'm having a lively, provocative and inspiring time teaching Medieval History. Each year, I've added another layer to my knowledge of the fascinating characters who marched, sailed, crusaded and rode through our pages. I'd discovered that in order for the students to understand the influence of the Catholic Church on the one-thousand-year period from A.D. 467 to 1400, I needed to review the origins of Christianity.

I was teaching the Sermon on the Mount. Focused on the Beatitudes: Matthew 5. 7 "Blessed are the merciful for they will receive mercy."—in preparation for teaching Islam and for directly juxtaposing Christianity and its origins with Islam, Jesus and his life and work with Mohammed's. I assigned each student a parable to present to the class in the form of a skit. Except for two Catholics in the class, they'd never heard of parables.

We performed a few each day. The Parable of the Prodigal Son—forgiveness. "But while he was still far off, his father saw him and was filled with compassion; he ran and put his arms around him and kissed him. . . ." I thought of Andrew. We'd find him. We'd been having our differences but he'd contact us soon. I softened. I felt warm and comfortable inside. I imagined throwing my arms around him. I'd have to reach up. I'd wrap my arms around his chest, give him a bear hug. I would feel his sternum, where it protruded, push against my chest.

I read Matthew 5. 38–42 to the class; "You have heard that it was said, 'An eye for an eye and a tooth for a tooth.' But I say to you, do not resist an evildoer. But if anyone strikes you on the right cheek, turn the other also; and if anyone wants to sue you and take your coat, give your cloak as well . . . do not refuse anyone who wants to borrow from you."

". . . if anyone wants to sue you," I thought of Speedy.

". . . do not refuse anyone who wants to borrow," I thought of Speedy.

Matthew 7. 1 "Do not judge, so that you may not be judged. . . . Why do you see the speck in your neighbor's eye, but do not notice the log in your own eye?" I noticed the speck in his eye, but was I seeing any more clearly than he?

It had been three months; I hadn't visited him all summer.

I pictured the two of us sitting in the cab of the pickup outside the 7-Eleven, me reading, Speedy—concentrating, staring straight ahead—reciting John 3, Verse 16, Speedy.

I felt the weight of his Bible in my lap, the heft of it in my hands. He knew Jesus. He loved Jesus. Jesus was not a dreamed up figure in a book of fantasy and wished-for occurrences. He was an acquaintance, the real *son* of God, and he was alive.

At night I was reading *Unbroken* by Laura Hillenbrand. I was reaching the end: Louie Zamperini has survived imprisonment, mistreatment, and torture by the Japanese during World War II. He returns to the States and his life starts to unravel. Horrible nightmares about being tortured. He drinks more and more. But then he goes through a conversion inspired by Billy Graham, halts his drinking, forgives his torturers, and the nightmares cease.

I have felt this pleasing warmth ease through me in the afternoons as my students read and performed their parables and the language of the Bible fills the room, reminding me of the warmth and comfort with my grandmother Emma Smithwick, "Um," when she read the Bible to me. The same Um, who, when she was in her late-nineties and needed to go up or down the steep and twirling steps of her house, was carried by Speedy.

How could Louie possibly fly to Japan, meet the sadistic prison guards who had beaten, starved and humiliated him, light up with a huge grin and run down the line hugging them? How could he forgive the "Bird"—who had tortured him over and over, igniting the nightmares that had almost driven him into alcoholism and insanity. But he did. He did it, and he lived on.

Tom would say, "Get over it. Go and see him." I pictured

different ways of doing it. I had the fob. I could get into the building. After work one day, I'd walk through those double doors, walk down the hall to his room, knock. "Who's that?"

"Patrick," I'd say, with a sigh.

I'd listen as he got out of his chair and tapped his way to the door. "Well, how ya doin' sonny-boy, how ya doin'?"

I'd step in and we'd talk and joke. I'd tell him to come on, let's go for a drive, get a bite to eat. We'd pick it right up; he'd ask about the family, about Andrew especially.

But I was *busy*, and school had me hopping—a new administration with all kinds of new To Do's: goals to write up, committees to form, meetings to attend, a new website through which to communicate, our classes were to be visited and evaluated by the new head and by the division head and by who knows who else—why not a child psychologist? Well, in fact, that's not so far-fetched: the new school counselor—who wore skin-tight, "spray-on" (as Andrew once called such clothes worn by Miss Martia, his day-care teacher who drove a souped-up Camero to work) stretch pants along with waist-hugging blouses that had the male teachers' heads spinning when she walked by—would be visiting the classes of students who were having trouble, and I'd been finalizing plans for a book signing in Minnesota with a riding teacher who was always "out of pocket," as she expressed it, meaning too busy to set any plans.

In Minnesota, at the book signing—called "Luau on the Lake" of all things, and held at a Yacht Club—I showed photos of Speedy in the power point. He was also prominent in the video. Seeing him, hearing him, feeling his hand gripping my elbow, I felt like the biggest hypocrite.

Back from Minnesota. Earned a nice check. Sold a good number of books. Another busman's vacation with the Sweetheart. But for three days, each morning I felt disoriented, in a fog. All was going fast. My class was visited by administrators. Alumni had a day off from public and Catholic schools and poured into my room. I was told to plan another field trip. Piles of papers to read, maps to grade, Islamic prayer mats to display.

In English, I assigned a short story called "The Moustache" by Robert Cormier. Not one student gets the central point. I reread it during a free period before class. A boy—just old enough to drive—visits his grandmother in a retirement home with the name of Lawnover. She goes in and out of reality, hallucinates, and partially due to the moustache that the boy is sporting, she thinks he is her deceased husband. The boy learns that his grandmother early in marriage had accused her husband of having a relationship with another woman. This accusation undermines their marriage. Soon afterwards, the husband is killed in a traffic accident, and his wife learns that he never had the affair. But it's too late. He's gone. And yet, now—here she is, old, fragile, hallucinating, and she thinks the grandson is her husband. The grandson gives her a kiss goodbye; she feels relieved after all these years, forgiven; the grandson, the boy—now a man—leaves, his life changed, after changing hers.

I spelled this theme out. Guilt is a repetitive note at the beginning of the story. The boy feels guilty at the outset: he'd rather be going to the beach with his girlfriend than visiting his grandmother. He soon discovers his grandmother's guilt, and he leaves the hospital awakened to the realities, some of them dark, of life, wondering about his parents: do they have secrets like this? The class was quiet. The students thought about it. I thought about it: the boy's initial guilt, then, the impossibility of the grandmother ever having *her* guilt assuaged. But finally, even if in a hallucinatory, unreal manner, she does receive forgiveness.

That Thursday afternoon Brian Belt, the blacksmith, came. When the horses were in training, he'd had a great time shooting the bull with Speedy. There he was, a "captive audience," Speedy on the shank, Brian with the horse's hoof between his legs and Speedy talking about women between his legs and horses and racing, gambling, music, politics, and President Obama, of whom he was increasingly knowledgeable and extremely proud.

As Brian trimmed Charley's beautifully formed feet, he cheerfully asked me if I'd "heard anything from Speedy." I told him about Speedy threatening to sue me and that I'd cooled off on my visits.

After Brian left, I rode both horses. Gradually coming into focus in my mind was the image of stopping by Catholic Charities. The thought of it was a relief. Pleasant. Soothing. Sunday. Why not drive over Sunday afternoon? Again, he'd be gently gripping my right arm at the elbow. Again, around my tendon just below the bicep, I'd feel the smooth, soft skin of his long individual fingers.

Was Blind, But Now I See

Friday, I'd been tough on my students in the early moments of my last study hall. How I dislike study halls. I suffer through them. Feel like a lump. Feel I should be teaching, doing something to earn my keep. I'd been scolding those whose attention was drifting. Mainly to get out of the room, I had dashed down to the kitchen, put on a kettle of water, dashed back to grade a paper, then rushed to the kitchen where the kettle was boiling and whistling and spouting steam and drawing the attention of other teachers who were leaving their rooms to take the kettle off.

I was returning from making a cup of tea. Quarter of two. I like a cup of tea in the afternoon, and on this day especially with the Eighth Grade Speeches coming up, I knew a dose of caffeine would help prevent me from getting woozy. I was walking down the long empty Friday afternoon hallway (everyone tucked away in their study halls dutifully and blankly staring at their books and taking sneak peaks at the clocks over the doors) and was wishing Bob Witham were still alive so I could tell him how I'd finally come around to enjoying a cup of afternoon tea in the afternoon, though *Irish* tea, I'd tell him, teasing, just to get him going, "Not that sissified English tea you can't taste." Just the thought of Bob—his smile, his laughter, his relationship with Tom. "Patrick, I went to Tom's health club with him last night. You should see what he does. Have you ever wondered where that big tub of nice rub rags comes from? It's just disgraceful. It's highway robbery, I tell you. The man has no conscience. He's irredeemable. I saw him do it last night. He's incorrigible!" "Do what," I'd asked, laughing, as we jogged off together on the outdoor track, preparing to gallop, Tom up on top of the hill, puffing on a cigarette, watching us like a hawk. "Do what? What do you think? I watched as he stuffed two of those nice towels with the blue line running down the middle into his clothes bag, this just a week after winning a $100,000 stakes race at Belmont." Down the hallway, I turned into my classroom holding the hot mug of Irish tea and the most wholesome, straight-A, all-around athletic boy in the entire school, Arthur, walked up to me, "Mister Smithwick, Mister Smithwick—your phone rang," he said urgently. "It was Bob House. Bob House called you," he said, trying earnestly to be helpful. "Are you going to call him back?"

"You should not be looking at my cell phone," I barked—like a jerk! Then, I looked at the phone. "Bob House." Who the hell was that? House? Sounded like a television show. "No," I self-righteously declaimed. "I don't know who that is."

I finished the mug of tea. Looked up. Friday afternoon—sunny out! The poor students—soon we'd be packed into the dark, gloomy field house. The students would be sitting on the hard basketball court floor, after being told to "Be still," "Be quiet." I'd be standing in the back, doing isometrics and stretching. And we'd be listening to speech after speech. I grabbed the Frisbee under my desk, stood up, announced, "Let's go! Outside!"

Out, out, life's *not* a brief candle, life's *not* but a walking shadow, life's *not* a poor player that struts and frets . . . . We were outside and it was a bright, sunny day, the air was fresh, you could taste the air, it was air I looked forward to riding through, air I would pull Charley out into and feel his power and high spirits transport me through the sunny oxygen-rich substance, across the fields, transform me from teacher at a desk to rider on a horse, rider part of a horse, turn the horse and me into horse-rider flowing through nature, becoming a part of nature, *horse-rider-field-woods-grass-gallop-speed-fast-chilly-air-fast-past-ears*. It was Friday, it's been a glorious day of teaching and laughing and now we're outside in the sunlight.

The orange Frisbee was flying and winging and spinning through space. The girls were laughing. Bradford, tall, taciturn, thin, who played basketball year-round, who bounced a basketball from the moment he got out of the car in the morning to the moment at dismissal when I shook hands with him, *who was turning into a basketball*—laughed, tossed the Frisbee with eloquent skill, with *elan*, and the girls played jokes on us and we ran and played and celebrated the day—Friday!

The bell rings, we jog to the gym to hear the Eighth Grade Speeches, the speakers do a fantastic job, and then before you know it, the speeches are over and I'm packing students into their mini vans and mega SUVs, merrily sending them off for the weekend. I am enjoying being myself instead of the "teacher-self," it is only 3:30, the shadows are lengthening but the sun's rays are still warm and bright and I will soon be out of here, driving home, going for a ride. I had been been thinking of breaking my impasse with Speedy today, but I decide to go on Sunday when I'd have the time to drive him around and do some errands, hear his stories and get him an order of hot "black like me" coffee, spare ribs, cole slaw, mashed potatoes, corn bread, orange soda, and what the hell—a big bag of pork rinds to go.

Three students still waiting to be picked up. Sixth graders, sitting on a bench together. I joke that they might have to come home with me. Katy Dallam asks if they know how to muck out stalls. I say one could ride, one could muck out, one could clean tack. I feel the biceps of the two boys. Then, Louisa is there, sister of my past advisee Rosemary, daughter of Ginny, now my vet. She is walking around in the sunshine. So cute. So mature. An old soul. She must've been through this life at least a couple of times, and here is her mother—exactly the same but older and taller. We're all clumped together—Katy, Ginny, Louisa, the three girls waiting for their parents, and I. I'm speeded up and telling Ginny how well Louisa is doing in class, mentioning her just-completed map. Katy is listening and nodding. Ginny says that Louisa enjoyed learning geography the year before, but Ginny's not focused on this subject, doesn't seem interested, is looking at me in a funny way. Katy, knowing something, steps away. We slow down, like autumn leaves that have been blustering, blowing across a sunlit lawn and the wind suddenly fades and they flutter to the ground. Like automobiles on a highway hitting eighty roller-coasting down a mountain in Pennsylvania with tractor trailers all around. You'd better keep up. You're flying. Eighty-five. Peterbilt behind. Kenworth in front. You're on the ball, looking in the mirror, keeping an eye on the long stretch ahead, looking for radar traps, police cruisers, and then you're putting on the brakes, you're going slower, you're looking to see how the Peterbilt behind you is doing and you hear the air brakes kick in, hear the engine downshifting, the air brakes whistling, *Pfffffff*—and then *whine* go the air brakes of trucks. *Whooosssh* go their engines as they sigh and slow. Speedy could do these sounds. Ginny is frowning, looking up into my eyes. *Whooosssh.* Katy is looking at me in a concerned and empathetic sort of way. *Pfffffff.* Louisa is walking away. Ginny is looking right into my eyes. "Did you hear about Speedy?"

I brace myself. I doubly brace myself. All my life: "Did you hear about what happened at Devon?" (Show ring rider killed jumping a fence.) "Did you read about what happened to Shockey Gillet?" (This—last fall at the dentist's. He was the dentist's patient. Rode off for a cross country ride at the age of seventy-seven and never came back.) "Did you hear about the galloping boy at the Canadian track?" (Killed galloping a horse last summer.) "Did you hear about the horse in the Czechoslovakian steeplechase?" asks a teacher at school. (Killed jumping the liverpool, a hurdle/water jump, just a week ago.) "Did you hear about the Australian jockey, the young woman?" a friend says in an email from Wisconsin. "Click this link to read about it." (Killed riding a flat race.)

I know Ginny has a new job requiring her to go to the track every day. I know my cousin Speedy has horses stabled at Pimlico, is racing at Laurel, and has been winning races. Ginny gives me a report on him every time I see her. I picture Sunny Bank Farm—2,000 acres—in Middleburg, Virginia, and I see Cousin Speedy, tall and energetic, fast-paced, positive (received his name for being born two weeks early)—out on a horse, out by himself in one of those 100-acre fields, popping an older horse over stone walls, spurring a younger horse around a herd of cattle, and then, I picture the tractors, the equipment, all the ways to get hurt on the farm. I think about those long commutes to the tracks he's been making. I picture the curves and sharp turns on the narrow roads from Middleburg to Laurel, driving back on them after a late race, in the dark, the lights of oncoming trucks in his eyes. "Speedy? No." I cringe inside.

"Didn't you get a call from Bob?"

I envision Bob Witham, alive and well, for a split second and then imagine him on his deathbed in South Carolina. That was five years ago. I'm all mixed up. No, I sure as hell didn't get a call from Bob. . . . Oh—Arthur! I wish I hadn't scolded him. *That* Bob! *That* Speedy! I picture "Black Speedy" as we called him all our lives when we had to differentiate between him and "White Speedy." I picture that Bob, whose two numbers I had listed under "Bob House" and "Bob Cell." I hear his deep, baritone, radio-announcer voice.

The parent of one of the three girls pulls up. Katy walks past us with the girl, opens the car door.

"I didn't get the message," I tell Ginny, as Katy walks back, past us, eying me worriedly. "I had to go to the assembly."

"Well, you'd better call Bob."

"You know what it is, why don't you give me the message."

"No, Bob wants to tell you."

"I'd like you to tell me," I say, by this time, feeling it might not be good, this news might not be positive, and she is such a wonderful, considerate woman. I'd like to hear it from her. I am staying calm. I am ready to return to action. I am ready to stop by Speedy's apartment on the way home today, I am ready to drive straight there, right now, right now . . . .

"Speedy died in his sleep last night. He died in his sleep."

Too late. It's too late. I took a break, and now I'm ready to return. It's too late. The door is shut. Locked shut, and bolted. Click. The massive portcullis to the castle of death—thick oak beams bolted together with black wrought-iron hinges and armored bars—has slammed down, shaking the earth, and he is on the other side. I can't hear him. I can't see him. I can't listen to him. There is no longer any point for me to study and research ways for him to get around better. I will no longer be able to read passages from the Bible to him and hear him memorize and recite God's messages one moment and the next hear how he had the most amazing sex with so and so, the grand dame of American steeplechasing, the holiest and highest of socialites, right in the tack room and the sounds she made and what she asked him to do, and I'm saying, "Enough, enough, I really don't want to hear about all that and I don't believe it anyway."

"Ohhh, she loved it. Ohhhh, she couldn't get enough."

"OK, that's it. No more for me."

"What's a matter. We's just two men. Can't we talk like two men?"

Five minutes later. Back to the Bible. Back to Reverend Popoff! Back to his plan of going all the way to Medjugorje, splashing holy water on his eyes, being instantly healed, being able to see again, because he is so pure and good, and what comes around goes around. . . .

Ginny looks me in the eye. I ask commonplace questions. Heart attack, the doctors think it was a heart attack. I leave Katy with the last two students to load up, knowing she'll handle it. Dozens of times, she'd given me permission to leave early to take Speedy to the hospital, to a doctor. And she often asked how he was.

On the way home, I catch Ansley in her office:
"You did more than anybody. You did everything you could. It might be all for the best. He couldn't see. He couldn't do any of the things he loved. He couldn't work with horses. He couldn't do his art. He couldn't be Speedy. There's a reason he was called Speedy."
I keep driving.
"High blood pressure. Diabetes. Glaucoma. Blind. Look at the quality of his life. What could he do?"
"Talk. He could talk."
"But he was running out of things to talk about. . . ."
I feel better. Paddy calls me from Denver. Eliza texts me from London.
Andrew knew him best, worked with him for a year. No call from Andrew. I call Ann, an art teacher who was preparing to do a show of Speedy's drawings and paintings. I call Bob. What to do? Cremation? Funeral? Contact his sister? Contact his wife?
Blind, trapped in a room, unable to paint, unable to rub a horse, build a fence, muck out a stall. Steadily gaining weight— no wonder he was a grumpy.

Home. I've been crying. I'm in a sweat. I don't know what to do. I jump in the shower. Savor the water beating down on my face. I put my face in the stream of water. Turn it hot, hot as I can stand it until my skin's on fire. Then cold, as cold and hard as it will go. "I'm alive! I'm alive! I'm alive!" I chant, rubbing my chest and arms and hopping up and down, my skin tingling and sizzling. "I'm alive!"
Let Alfie and Winston out. Pull on work boots. Walk out to the barn through the late-afternoon air, look down at the posts along the board fence we had reinforced that hot summer day, beads of sweat dripping off our chins, backs tired, ground hard— "With your brawn and my brains, we can do anything."

Glistening, the world is glistening. Everything is crystalline. *I can see, I can see*—I think as I look down at the slanted rays of sunlight hitting the wet tips of the blades of grass and of the fall leaves, sparkling; they are sparkling. It is fall, how beautiful it was to drive along Deer Creek, in the early fall, to that depressing apartment. The sunlight would dance and twinkle on the rapids, exploding firecrackers of silver on the rushing, churning water; I'd think of ways to describe it, to make it come alive for him.

I walk up the bank to the top of the barn, prepare to open the small door built into the huge sliding door and I look down at the cement we'd laid on that steaming hot summer day. J. S. K. Who would ever take notice of this? I had thought, watching him painstakingly write his initials in the wet cement. I look now and feel and hear the scraping of splintery wood against wet cement. I smell the chalky grittiness of the cement.

I step into the top of the barn, the loft. Empty. Clean. Vast. Capacious. You can see the bones of the barn, the long hand-hewn chestnut beams. Shimmering ribbons of light illuminate the half inch space between the vertical boards lining the walls. I throw down twenty fresh bales of hay.

Walking down to the lower barn, I look out at the back field. In my imagination, I see the big "straw ring" which we made on the coldest day of the winter. I look out at the back field, super-imposing the image of the straw track onto its rolling contours. I blink and it's gone. I closely examine the field: the straw and the manure has decomposed into the soil, and now there is not a trace of the track.

The pups are in the barn, barking and yapping at the cats; they're running and sliding on the cement floor, looking up at the cats stealthily and confidently maneuvering along the edges of the high stall walls. I walk down the aisleway. Passing the tack room on my left, I look down at the footlocker on my right. *Sit down, he said. I sat down beside him. He took my hand in his. It was swollen, throbbing, aching. He took my hand, poured rubbing alcohol on it, massaged it between his warm, soft, dark, long-fingered hands. He made a cross over it, closed his eyes, lowered his head in silent prayer. We sat quietly. I could feel a warmth flowing through my palm, an easing of the throbbing pain. Then, suddenly, he sat up. "OK, that's it," and walked away, towards the van, preparing to clean it out. The swelling was gone.*

I can see! *I can see*! I automatically think, as I have for two years when I wondered how he was doing. I look through the tack room door at the intricately-made knee bandage—an Arab-tasseled decoration for a sheik's war horse—hanging from a nail, and then at Warfield's tail: he was so sweet, he made two fly switches—thick, beautiful, chestnut—from Warfield's tail after he died, drove over and gave them to me, and there they hang. He made this handle to the feed room. He and I put this window up in the feed room. He fixed the crack in this old wall box of Pop's, using a piece of scrap wood and some screws he found in the garage. He took Mikey's old down vest, and gave it new life; I was giving up on it, and he sewed a new zipper into it, patched up the holes: "Mikey Power." The sole was peeling off Mikey's old insulated work boots and there was a hole in each boot where Mikey's bunions, and then mine, had rubbed through. He took them home, cut out patches from an old tire, applied glue and patches, and brought them back as good as new: "Mikey Power."

Speedy, the inside of the lower barn is dusty. Cobwebs. We've cleaned out the entire top of the barn—preparing for some parties for Paddy and Eliza. An expert barn man has vacuumed and swept and chiseled away the dust and dirt and bat droppings on the barn floor, some of which has fallen through the floor cracks into the stalls below. Where are you and your blower? You could clean this whole barn out in one hour.

I continue walking down the aisleway to the shed. It's early. Charley, outside, sees me, thinks I'm going to feed him, relaxes, stretches out, lets his phallus drop, relieves himself. I do the same. *And Speedy, I can hear you laughing! I can hear you now: "He lookin' a'chu, looking at what you got, at that little white worm, and he's thinking: so pitiful, so pitiful."* I'm reminded that I need to have the inside of the horses' sheaths cleaned out, and for a second, remembering Speedy said he could do it, even blind, I think: one less worry, I'll just get Speedy to do it. That is, to have a bucket of warm water and Castile soap by his side and to bend over by the horse's hind legs, reach up, pull down the horse's sheath, go up in it and remove the "bead," as he called it. He taught me how to do that. He showed me the gob he'd pull out of the tip of each horse's phallus.

I feed Charley. Feed Riderwood. Get out a currycomb, stiff brush, soft brush, rub rag, hoof pick—and work on Riderwood, then Charley—chanting Charley's name over and over, as Speedy did—currying, brushing, rubbing each horse until he glows and is jumping around trying to get the hell away from me.

He's no longer blind, I think. *Speedy's no longer blind. His spirit has flown off. He's off riding motorcycles with Quinsel waiting to get into the gates of heaven. He's riding: he's galloping Neji, Mako, The Sport, Ancestor across the ridge of the big field at Hydes and picking up speed as he approaches the gates of heaven; he's riding bareback alongside Quinsel his brother and Alfonso his nephew—three part-Cherokees, part-Africans; three all-American young men, as American as you can get their family trees going back hundreds of years before the Mayflower, before Columbus, before the Vikings, a shank snapped on one side of the halter and the end tied to the other.*

It's a full moon and they're flying across the top of the 100-acre field, schooling head-and-head over the three hurdles. They used to get themselves fired up on a bottle of bourbon, pull the horses out at midnight, school and race them, put them back in the stalls. The next morning Mikey would call out, "Speedy, Speedy—look at this. These horses got all upset about something last night. Look at their coats—they were hot. Did you hear anything last night?"

They don't need the bourbon any more. All they need is the sharp feel of the withers in their groins, the ribs between their knees, the whipping mane under their hands, the wind whistling past their ears, the feel of flight, of freedom as they fly head and head across the ridge, the moon over their left shoulders, the hurdles coming up....

Speedy's spirit is off and running. He's with his creator and he is creating! "Yes!" *as he says it,* "Yes-s-s-s-s!" *stretching the word out and stressing the sibilance.*

He is seated at a long dining room table in the late afternoon with the heaven's northern light coming in a big window that looks out over a green field with a stream running through it and chestnut, bay and gray horses galloping down to the stream and jumping across it.

He's out of the basement from hell and he's in heaven now and the light shines in the big north-facing window and he has an image in his head, a message he wants to deliver. A box of used and worn crayons are by his right hand and he can see them clearly, he can make out every color, the nuance of every shade, they are worn down to the nubs and this is how he likes them. Before him—an old spiral notebook a galloping girl who'd given up on college had given him that he has filled with bright, energetic drawings alluding to Gauguin, Van Gogh, Native American carvings and sculpture, African art, pagan art—the back and front of the pages are covered with naked men and women in Biblical scenes, Garden of Eden scenes, animals, symbols, all this mixed in with drawings from the racetrack. He pushes these old notebooks away and opens the large format sketch pad from heaven with cotton-infused textured paper: clean, clear, no blue horizontal lines of a spiral notebook, no red vertical lines, and he can see the scene he wants to create: bright and lively and with morals—he might just write the moral to make sure it's received—lessons from the Bible, the Bible by his side that he can read, the words on the page are large and jump out at him with life. He reads aloud and when he gets to an important word he calls it out. The words are alive when he reads them and he translates them into what he sees in his mind and then can see on the page, the people, the animals, alive and breathing. He draws, colors, sketches—fast. He's Speedy. He knows the Bible. The characters come alive for there he is in heaven and he's Speedy and he's going to beat the odds, he's alive in heaven and may hop on a motorcycle like the one he once had at Saratoga and take off through the clouds with Quinsel.

He's drawing a Baptism scene. He's thinking of Jesus—of God—and he imagines himself being "held under by Jesus's hand"—held under in a river, a deep river in Egypt by "Jesus," blessed by "Jesus," saved by "Jesus." And Jesus is black! He hums. He hums and as he draws the humming breaks into singing.

Take me to the water
Take me to the water
Take me to the water
To be baptized

None but the righteous
None but the righteous
None but the righteous
Shall be saved . . .

I'm going back home, going back home
Gonna stay here no longer
I'm going back home, going back home
To be baptized.

He's driving a souped-up black Ford Mercury outfitted with glass packs on the dual mufflers—blblblblbbl-splutttter blblblbl-spluttter—he's flying off, he's on the road between gigs, it's 2:30 in the morning and the sedan's cruising at eighty-five through the clouds, along a Southern highway, no cops in sight, all the rest of the band sound asleep. He has no worries of being pulled over and thrown up against the side of the car by a fat white man in a uniform and being called "boy." He has no worries of there being no motel they can sleep in, no restaurant they can eat in, no restroom they can use. This highway is long and straight and now the sun is coming up and the band is awakening and the Mercury is cruising. Speedy's got one hand on the steering wheel and in the other a hot black coffee laced with vodka and they start singing. Not the rhythm and blues they'll be singing that night at the jazz club but gospel, the gospel they grew up with. As the sun is coming up over the clouds on the eastern horizon, he starts humming Amazing Grace, *the sun's rays are shooting through the clouds, the Mercury is flying, the glass packs are purring* pbbbpblllll pbbllblllbbbbb ppppp *and they take it away, harmonizing, Speedy leading, the car safely flying into the West. No Georgia, South Carolina or Virginia state troopers threatening them if they pull over, threatening them if they drive through the town, threatening them if they do anything beside walk straight to the jazz club. Speedy's voice is soaring higher and the Mercury is flying higher. The Mercury is lengthening, becoming limousine-like and Quinsel's in the back now, Alfonso too; Wayne Gaither has joined up though Speedy never trusted him and knows he robbed my grandmother for years, and Junior Tibbs—his old sparring partner, William Gaskett, the sweetest man who ever worked for the Smithwick Stables, Buba—an old friend, and even Sonny—Sonny Thorton, the only black steeplechase and flat jockey of his time, Sonny who died riding a race at Charles Town—"I told him to hang it up! I told him he was getting too old to ride those bad-legged, raggedy-ass, doped-up Charles Town horses, but he wouldn't listen."*

They're packed into the sedan with the members of Fat Boy and the Comets before they became The Soulations, and they're singing. They're flying safely through the heavens with an Army motorcycle escort now, big Harleys, sparking white Harleys on both sides, black Military Police soldiers with brown boots polished to such a shine that they're shooting off sparks, and in front, leading the procession, is the Commander in Chief, President Barack Obama, "a black man, son, a black man!" on a Harley and ain't nobody going to bother them now, they're free free free . . . Rrrmmmmooooonnnn Blbblblblblblbl Rrrrrrmmmmoonoon Blblblblblblblblbl. . . .

Amazing Grace, how sweet the sound,
That saved a wretch like me.

I once was lost but now am found,
Was blind, but now I see.
T'was Grace that taught my heart to fear.
And Grace, my fears relieved.
How precious did that Grace appear
The hour I first believed.

Through many dangers, toils and snares
I have already come;
'Tis Grace that brought me safe thus far
and Grace will lead me home ....

Speedy's wearing a black suit lined with purple; he's up on the stage, he's snapping his fingers and he's easing his voice higher and higher, showing off his range, hitting that pitch, that high note that has the women and girls screaming, "Speedy! Speedy!" Oh, he's loving it, bringing it back down, lowering his hand so the band will know, slowing it down, and the dancers are slowing, feeling romantic, hugging and laughing and kissing and he's in heaven singing his own songs now, "If loving you was ice cream, I'd. . . ." He's thinking, "This is so nice. So nice." Marvin Gaye is in the wings. The great Marvin Gaye is in the wings back behind the curtain and Speedy is supposed to do a couple of short numbers, then step off, let the great man on, but the audience loves him; he plays with them, brings his voice way down, lets it soar high high, higher than Marvin can reach and he starts to walk off the stage, the girls are screaming, "Speedy! Speedy!" He just can't make himself go off. He strides back to the center of the stage. Marvin Gaye's handlers are in the wings waving to Speedy, waving for him to come off. Marvin is pacing—would he have to get rid of this upstart, stealing the show, not what you want with a warm-up band. Marvin is waiting to go on and waiting outside the auditorium is one of Mikey and Pop's top men, not the top man, he's up on the stage, but one of the top men who will soon be telling Speedy, "You got to come back. Mikey says he needs you. It's Saratoga. We've got some good horses but the men don't know how to handle them. Mako's got a knee. The Sport's old tendon is flaring up. Mikey says you've got to come back. We got this new colt, a rogue, who needs some training. Almost killed William in the stall the other day. . . ." But he's not telling him that yet. Speedy's on the stage and the women are ooohing *and* aaahing *as he slips into a Smokey Robinson number, and they're melting, they're running their hands up and down their sides and shimmying and swaying and swooning as he sings, "People say I'm the life of the party/ 'Cause I tell a joke or two."*

He's young and fit and strong and fast. He's Speedy. He's up high on the canvas ring at the rec center at Saratoga and he's moving. He's dancing. He's bouncing off the ropes. The sweat is glistening on his black muscles. His arms are long and strong as steel and they whip out of nowhere at his Italian opponent who has his elbows held up high and is fighting peek-a-boo style and who throws a right hook. Speedy dodges the punch by simultaneously snapping his head back and backpedalling. He lures his opponent in, tempting him, convincing him to go again for that right hook which throws the Italian off balance and that split second Speedy moves in on him jab jab jab with the left, a right to the body, jab jab jab with the left, a right to the body, jab jab jab, a right to the head, a flurry of punches, a blitzkrieg of shots to the head and he's standing over the would-be brawler.

He's in heaven now and he is victorious over his opponents of a lifetime: poverty, little education, diabetes, pain and arthritis in his right shoulder from decades of rubbing, really rubbing, horses; pain and a steel rod in his foot from a warmblood stepping on him; glaucoma, operations on both eyes, blindness; weight gain from not being active, not being Speedy; the constant, always-present tension as well as danger of dealing with prejudice and bigotry in a racist country for an entire life, being called "nigger" by his white landlord; and lastly, death—he's looking down victoriously at the one-time bragging Italian pugilist now trying to regain his breath on the floor as the referee goes through the count-down. . . .

"I holds nothin' against him," Speedy is thinking. "It says in the Bible—'do not judge so that you may not be judged.' He's a man; I'm a man. That's all there is to it."

He is victorious. And hell, he's got to get back to the barn, water off, feed. His big horse is in tomorrow. The Sport. Getting some age on him. He's got to check on him. He's going to beat his entry, the favorite, the champion—Bon Nouvel. Gots' to beat him. Will beat him. Against all odds. But he'll do it. Paddy Smithwick is going to go out there on The Sport and show that young rider Tommy Walsh a thing or two.

He looks down at the defeated fighter on the mat.

"What comes around goes around," he thinks, and then he doesn't think but rather hears, in a powerful baritone from above, "If you forgive others their trespasses, your heavenly Father will forgive you."

He extends his glove and lifts his opponent up off the mat, onto his feet, and then he's out of the ring, back at the barn checking on The Sport who will challenge Bon Nouvel in a historic, blistering duel down the back stretch, around the turn, over the last, and win.

His Neck and Head Across My Shoulders

I drove in the driveway, returning from school, hoping, praying he'd be better. I was envisioning him on all four legs. He'd be grazing out on the knoll—beneath where his old buddy Warfield was buried. I'd step down out of the truck, slam the door—knowing they'd hear it. I'd walk toward the back porch, giving a carefree glance out toward the back field, and I'd see him raise his head. He'd watch my every move. Then, he'd start ambling in—his walking stride smooth, graceful, having the potential at any second to break into a gallop—for his afternoon feed. Riderwood would be nearby, and he'd follow Charley in. They'd both be licking their chops.

I'd caught something from the students. They were dropping right and left. I had a fever. Had to blow my nose every three minutes. Developed a sinus infection, a sore throat, a cough. Sneezing: my students were planning to video me rapid-fire sneezing and send it to Ripley's Believe It or Not.

I parked by the barn, left my lunch bag, jacket and satchel plump with papers to grade in the back. Yes, there he was in his favorite spot, up on the knoll in the back field, on the other side of the stream, in the early-fall sunlight. He picked his head up, pricked his ears forward, looked at me. "Hey Charley!" I called, trying to make it sound as it had on all the other afternoons over the past ten years. "Hey Charley!" I stopped and focused: looking at those legs, willing those legs to move. Again, he had all his weight on three legs, none on his right front. He stood with his right front knee bent, his toe pointed.

I long-stepped to the tack room, grabbed a leather shank,

proceeded down the hill to the stream crossing, up the hill to Charley. He did not move.

I snapped the shank onto his halter, gave him a rub on the star between his eyes, a pat on his neck, and a quick, deep massage on his left shoulder. "Come on Charley." Pulled on the shank. He didn't budge. Pulled on it harder. Instead of moving forward, he stretched out his neck and head. "Come on Charley." Gripping the shank, I pulled hard. He hopped forward on three legs, leaving his right front hanging. I continued the pressure. He hopped forward again. "Come on boy!" Now he was moving. Now he was ahead of me, hobby-horse cantering on three legs, building up his momentum. I jogged alongside his shoulder. We crossed the stream; he cantered on three legs up the hill toward the barn.

I got him into the stall. Gave him a scoop of feed. Riderwood ambled over. I put him in the stall beside Charley, gave him a scoop of feed.

Grabbed a clean bucket, rushed to the house, ran the water seemingly forever until it was steaming hot. Filled the bucket. Carried it back out. Poured two cups of Epsom salt into the black rubber feed tub on the floor of Charley's stall, and then poured in the hot water, sloshing and stirring it. Dragged the rubber tub to his foot. Reached down, gripped his ankle right above that suspicious scar—marked by a two-inch line of white—(Again, I wondered, had the nerve to the "toe" of this foot been taken out? Had he experienced an injury to this foot years ago, in Germany? In France?) and gently set his foot down in the tub.

He had his foot in the tub but no weight on it. His knee was bent and the toe of his foot was just barely touching the bottom of the tub. I flicked away the flies with my bandana, rubbed him between his eyes. He lowered his head and pushed against me, rubbed his face against my hip. I rubbed and massaged his neck, shoulder, and back on one side, ducked under his neck and rubbed, massaged his neck and shoulder on the other side. Standing on his far side, I leaned into his shoulder, taking some of the weight that would normally be distributed to his right front. He relaxed onto me. I moved closer, placing my shoulder under his neck. He lowered his neck, easing more weight off his left front. I changed my standing position from legs straight and back bent, to legs bent and back straightened, though at a forty-five degree angle from my hips to my neck. Braced each arm against my knees so that I was forming a Gothic arch—arms one side of the arch, back the other side, weight coming down where the sides were joined at the cornerstone, my shoulder. I would tell my medieval scholars. I felt Charley sigh and relax, his weight from that quarter of his body now off his good foot and on my back. My legs, the strongest part of my anatomy, began to tremble. I thought of Santiago in the *Old Man and the Sea* arm wrestling through the night until blood came out of his fingernails and in the morning, with a surge of strength and willpower, pinning his opponent; I thought of him fighting the sharks through the night and in the morning cutting his hands to keep them from cramping, and I willed my legs to stop trembling. Drops of sweat dripped off my nose. I'd had the worst leg cramps a few nights earlier that I'd ever experienced; the cramps surged simultaneously through the hamstrings of both legs, and then they attacked my calves, over and over, until I wanted to die and then I was vomiting but I couldn't kneel over the toilet, I couldn't bend my cramping legs. I was vomiting and cramping, and Ansley got me through it, only she in the entire world of millions could have gotten me through that night and I knew it was from pushing it too hard, drinking too much coffee and tea at work, not resting when I got home, holding Charley up every night, night after night, with the sweat pouring off me, and finally, doing the most stupid thing, taking some antibiotics that the blacksmith (and there I'd been criticizing Tom for consulting veterinarians about his health!) pulled out of his truck and said would wipe out my illness. I might have the cramps again, but no matter. I wasn't thinking about that. My body was in the shape of a Gothic arch and I was holding Charley up. His neck was over my shoulder and now he relaxed his head so that his neck was stretched out, lengthened, resting loose-muscled on my back. He was a part of me; I was a part of him. His health, his life was in my hands. Forty-five minutes until the vet arrived. Then an hour or so of work, of digging at the abscess, of setting up the X-ray machine, of taking the X-rays, of examining the X-rays. And then?

* * *

It had started two weeks ago. I had thought one day he was "a little off." I watched him walk in to be fed when I got home, and yes, he was "off." Brian came, trimmed the foot. He pulled his razor-sharp blacksmith knife with the curved tip out of his leather chaps, and cut a dime-sized hole in the toe. Some puss oozed out. We thought we had it. Just a normal abscess. I got out the duct tape, plastic diapers, Ichthymol, plastic bag, Epsom salts. First I soaked the foot. Then, facing backward, I set Charley's foot between my legs as a blacksmith does, gobbed the Ichthymol all over the foot, wrapped two plastic diapers around the foot, pulled on a plastic bag, wrapped an old bandage around that. Finally, I wrapped duct tape around the entire package.

Late afternoon after late afternoon, I returned, made a mug of tea, and worked on Charley's foot. It got worse. I got worse. He was on three legs. I couldn't shake the sneezing, the infection, the fever. I called Ginny, the vet. She dug deeper into the toe, released more puss. It'll be all right, Brian had said. It'll be all right, Ginny said. J.B. stopped by, "A.P., you have to let nature take its course."

Horses get abscesses all the time. A microscopic particle makes its way up into the foot, starts working its way out, an infection begins. You cut a small hole at the location of the infection, the gook comes out, you soak the foot in Epsom salt, slather Icthymol all over it, wrap it, keep it dry and clean, and it clears up in a week. Sometimes the particle travels up through the hoof and breaks out at the coronet band. Riderwood had had plenty of abscesses. Charley had never had one; he had the best, most perfectly-formed feet on the place. When he stopped racing, I took the shoes off him, and we never put another one on. He went wonderfully barefoot.

*   *   *

I crouched in the stall, Charley putting more weight on me. Maybe he was taking a snooze. I crouched, arms and back in Gothic arch formation, Charley's neck and head warm across my back and shoulders, a part of me.

Heard the crunching of the crusher-run, the hum of a SUV— Ginny. Silence. Then louder crunching of the crusher-run and the roar of a truck engine, the crushing and the rumbling coming closer, and stopping—the veterinarian with the new X-ray machine Ginny had enlisted. Silence.

I extricated myself from Charley. Gradually straightened

out my arch, met Ginny and Marianna. We X-rayed the foot from every angle and then studied the X-rays on a computer screen. Marianna pointed to a gray, fuzzy area in Charley's foot, explained that he must have broken a bone there when he was young. We could see the complex puzzle of pastern , coffin, navicular, and pedal bone. The pieces joined into a cone-like shape, the tip of the cone pointing down towards the front of his hoof. The cone-shaped puzzle of bones were surrounded, supported, and protected by a shock-absorber of cartilage and ligaments. The infection was eating away the support system. Marianna drilled a hole in the top of the hoof and one in the bottom, flushed out more puss.

She could treat it, she explained. She could drill more, flush out more of the puss. He'd be stall-bound for a month. He wouldn't be able to put any weight on it. And there was no guarantee. I would never be able to ride him. The coffin bone could gradually rotate, and one day the entire bone could go through the bottom of his "frog," his foot. She left.

"Patrick," Ginny said, "I don't know if this is really what you want to do, but it's your choice."

"I agree. He can't live like this. He's not himself like this.

I snapped a shank onto his halter. He trusted me. I led him out of the stall—he made it across the shed and then, trusting me, he hobby-horsed-cantered down the aisleway and out of the barn, up the bank, streaks of fading sunlight receding behind the hills west of us where I had galloped him hundreds of times. I stood him in front of the big sliding doors, one of his favorite spots on the farm, where he loved to graze on the rich clover.

Eight years ago, I'd held him on this spot, letting him graze, on a spring afternoon. First Speedy arrived, then J.B. The sun was still out, all was bright. "I can fix this knee," Speedy said, feeling the swelling. "Don't you worry about it. But—don't you take this horse to no more hunt meets without me. You hear! You hear!" We were back from the two-hour drive to Blue Ridge where we'd won a timber race. J.B. was patting Charley, "I like this horse. I liked this horse the first time I saw him in the paddock. This is my Aunt Betty's kind of horse." Riderwood, in the back field, whinnied and tore around. Everything was sharp-edged, clearly lit, crystalline—we were on a roll.

I loosened the shank and let Charley graze.

Ginny was at her truck, preparing the needles. Charley rubbed his forehead against my side. He was alive, fully alive. He stopped rubbing and looked directly into my eyes.

Two and a half weeks ago, at this time of day, the sunlight dimming, I had tacked him up, ridden him out, across the Hunter Trial Course, to his hill where he had stopped, stared at his green light. I'd laughed, relaxed on him. We'd cantered out of the Hunter Trial course over a double-log, down into the valley, then galloped up the hill and jogged along its crest, down through the woods, over a few logs. Pulled up, walked across the wide cement-floored bridge that crosses the Little Gunpowder. We both looked down at the river meandering through this flat area. Between it and the Pike a half-mile away, you could just barely make out the oval outline of a racetrack from long ago. This was a bad area for Charley. Did he sense horses racing around that outline? Did he sense crowds and cheering? Did he hear the bell of a starting gate? Nearing Hess Road, which bisects the Pike, he started to misbehave, throw his head, stop and shake, side step and jig up the hill, away from the traffic, towards the edge of the woods thickly lined with briars and multa-flora rose. I released the reins, let him gallop full tilt up the hill. Once on the other side, the ghost of a racetrack out of view, he calmed down. We waded across a wide section of the Little Gunpowder near the Hess Road bridge. He stopped mid-crossing, splashed and splashed—the silver drops flinging high, catching the yellow-red rays of the setting sun. I squeezed my legs to urge him on. He put his head down, nose into the water, splashed more, acting as if he were going to roll, then powered through the creek, his shoulder and rump muscles churning up the steep bank.

Walking home on the tractor path in the gloaming, half a mile from the farm, tall ready-to-harvest rows of corn on both sides, Riderwood's high-pitched whinnying rippled out to us. Charley's muscles tensed. Closer, we saw Riderwood's silhouette—tail streaming straight out behind him—galloping down the fence line. Charley whinnied, fought against the bit. I pulled on the reins. He bundled his body up beneath me, then released it, diving forward. "Wo-a, wo-a, OK Charley, OK." I let him jog right up to the gate where Riderwood stood pawing the ground, both scolding and greeting us.

And now, holding Charley, I listened. I heard Riderwood pacing along the fence on the other side of the barn. He couldn't see us. I heard him break into a canter, his feet pounding the ground, going away from us, down to the stream crossing. Then I heard him thundering back and skidding against the full metal gate by my writing room. The chains that secured the gate to the post rattled and the hinges squeaked as he banged into it. He let out a long, frightened, whinny. Charley raised his head, turned in the direction of Riderwood, pricked his ears forward, and whinnied back.

Afterwards, I opened up the trunk with the winter blankets, pulled out Charley's favorite, slung it across him, and then Riderwood's blanket, so that he was fully covered. It was dark. Chilly. The stars were out.

Checked on Riderwood. Called him into the shed. Patted and talked to him. Walked slowly to the house, slowly poured a Smithwick's Ale, tilting the glass so that there wasn't too much froth, picturing Charley leaning over the fence by my office the first time his new owner, Winky O'Keefe, met him. Winky rubbed him between his eyes on his star, held up her pint of just-poured Smithwick's, and he slurped the froth right off the top. His future—the hundreds of cross-country rides, the wild fox hunts and finally that one hunt when he settled down; the wins, over timber, over hurdles; the riding him up to tables of food and port and champagne at hunt teas, old acquaintances of his stepping forward in disbelief at his relaxed stance just five horse lengths away from drinking and talking and bright-colored party-goers, and patting him; the win over hurdles in Virginia, finally able to keep him settled, able to control him, able to gallop along behind that frontrunner; and the feel going into the last fence, the feel of acceleration, the ecstatic, all-in-the-moment, this is it, this is everything, out-jumping the frontrunner, then getting down low, hand-riding him, waving the stick along his neck, not hitting him, I'd never hit him again, waving it so he knew it was there, his stride lengthening, his head lowering, and we were running, flying, under the wire, in front, then the pulling up, the easing up, the fulfillment—all that he had given me, this being a part of him and him being a part of me, this future was yet to come.

I poured a single malt into a crystal glass, pulled on godfather

Gary's suede jacket, walked outside. Folded the blanket back, as you fold back a bedspread before lying down, off Charley's head, neck and shoulders. I lay down with him, my shoulder blades against his right shoulder, the concave, inward curvature of my neck comfortably supported by the convex, outward curvature of his neck, my left arm stretching up into his thick mane. Nothing, nothing, could pull me away. I was where I wanted to be. I was looking up into the infinity of the black sky and at the hundreds of bright—extraordinarily, miraculously bright—stars. I called Paddy in Colorado. We talked. It was wonderful, soothing, pleasing, to have him there with me.

The next afternoon, I tacked up Riderwood and headed out. It was getting dark.

I had no plan of where to go. First, we ended up in the Griswolds' schooling field.

We found ourselves cantering over the post and rails. Heading into the triple log, I laughed to myself. I'd just gotten Riderwood, had only popped him over a few small fences. Andrew was eighteen and I wanted to take him out fox hunting, but he was far too big to ride Warfield. I gave him a leg up on Riderwood, telling him, "He doesn't know how to jump. We're not going to be jumping him today. OK?"

"Sure Dad. No problem."

And there I was galloping along through this field at the back of the pack of foxhunters and I had looked up. There Andrew was ahead of me. Following the lead horses. Up and over the big triple log they sailed. The run was on. I jumped the log. Andrew was way ahead of me and I watched cringing as they galloped full tilt into a board fence. Up and over he flew.

Riderwood and I jogged through the woods and out over a chicken coop onto the Hunter Trials course. Riderwood was clearly puzzled when, at the top of the hill, I pulled him up, made him stand still, and we looked down at the light changing from red to green, and the stream of white lights heading north on the Pike. We jumped out of the course, retraced the path I'd last taken on Charley

Heading home, we crossed the Little Gunpowder up by the Hess Road bridge, and he cut loose, holding a one-horse party, splashing in the river, soaking my boots and jeans. Five-eighths of a mile from the farm, over the last hill, he suddenly threw his head one way with his thick, powerful neck, then the other, and flung himself forward, trying to take off with me. I couldn't settle him down. I stayed as relaxed as possible. "Wo-a, boy, wo-a Riderwood." Kept my hands down and my legs loose, as if I weren't there. We jigged along. An eighth of a mile away from the back gate, he began whinnying. He threw his head, yanking the reins through my fingers, stretched his head down and away from me, then bucked, kicking his hind end up high, landed, and reared up.

A sixteenth of a mile from the back gate, he stopped. His entire body, every muscle, started to shake, tremble. He threw his head to the side—crazily tilting it so that the flat cheekbones were parallel to the ground, started cantering in place, whinnying. I brought him to a halt; he bundled up all his strength and energy like a horse that "freezes" and then might do anything, throw himself down, leap wildly forward, take off. I pulled my feet most of the way out of the stirrups. Loosened my hold on the reins. Loosened the girth a hole. He careened into the corn field, through one row of corn, then another, the stalks slapping and slashing against us, the ears of corn hard as they whacked my legs and elbows. Came back out onto the tractor path. Careened into the other side of the corn field. I got him back on the tractor path, kicked him hard. Cantered to where he could see over the corn stalks to our back field.

He stood still in the middle of the tractor path, instantly stopped trembling. He pinned his ears forward and was looking, seeking, trying to find, waiting, anticipating a dark, sleek horse letting loose a buck and a fart down by the stream, rearing up, holding it, holding it as only he could do, playing, up on two legs—How does he do that?—then coming down and sprinting, galloping, long mane flying, tail straight out behind him, to the back gate, jamming on the breaks, pressing his chest up against the back gate, nostrils flaring, eyes wide open, and, so was I, so was I.

There Is Nothing
But Immortality

I swear I see now that every thing has an eternal soul!
The trees have, rooted in the ground . . . . the weeds of the sea have . . . .
*   the animals.*

I swear I think there is nothing but immortality!
That the exquisite scheme is for it, and the nebulous float is for it,
*   and the cohering is for it,*
And all preparation is for it . . and identity is for it . . and life and death
*   are for it.*

— Walt Whitman, "To Think of Time"

September 19
Dear Tom,

Y ou know by now that I dedicated my power point presentation at school on riding and writing to you. I had a hard time not choking up while explaining some of those slides of us together. How I did enjoy looking through the sheets of Mom's slides and seeing us together as children and teenagers, over and over, skiing, riding, skating and standing proudly beside our just-purchased cars. The presentation went well. I did it for you, at your school—the only school you ever liked, and I did it in your honor. How incredibly drained I was afterwards. I said the hell with the back-to-school faculty party, drove home and went for a ride.

This week, each day, we came closer and closer to the 19th of September, your birthday, a day of celebrating you even if it meant

466

just dropping by and giving you a kiss on the cheek after you'd had a meat loaf dinner with Mimi and the children, or if it meant a big party like the one Mimi threw when you turned fifty, and the next day you and I, again, had to look death in the eye when we discovered our godfather Gary on the floor by his woodstove.

Later in the week, we drove back to Gary's house, tried a couple of doors. Locked. You gave me a leg up onto Gary's roof, I pried a window open, shimmied myself in and unlocked a door for you. We prowled through the house, examining his memorabilia (Yes, I remember galloping your horse of that name) as you, the born detective, loved to do, seeing and feeling Gary's soul, and each of us taking one item of clothing.

What a kick Gary would have gotten out of it! The hell he would have raised, but he had no children, and we had premonitions of his relatives descending on the house. We knew we wouldn't be included. I took a suede jacket—I think of Gary every time I pull it on. You took the tweed overcoat. We looked at the pictures of his winning horses, most of them of Cookie. We breathed him in, as no one else would have, could have. He loved you, unconditionally. He'd deliver full rants, four-letter word spiced diatribes on your lifestyle and training; he'd knock the whole steeplechase world, the entire world of racing, the entire universe, but the next day, there he'd be, best friend of our fathers, by your side. *Remember the night we shipped Cookie up to the Meadowlands? You, the trainer; and I, the groom; and Gary, the owner; and Peter, the journalist, flew up in a small plane. We were in our drinking stage of life. They were mad at both of us. Cookie ran under the lights. Bill Martin—"the slasher," as you called him—was in the tack. Peter was being the dutiful journalist, taking notes for a day-in-the-life-of story on you, the Youthful and Successful Trainer, and Cookie won, yes, we won.*

This week, I drove to school, the radio off, thinking of you. Today, on your birthday, I stayed away from Pocock Road, which passes Atlanta Hall. I took a detour that would be easier on the emotions, I thought, but then found myself driving down the gravelly Turner Road and past Mrs. Graveur's—the high-peaked Victorian house on a hill where we'd gone to kindergarten together. The classes were up in a spacious loft, and you'd been Zorro in our spring play. You performed the Errol Flynn, stuntman part of leaping off the stage, a big drop, to the floor while waving your sword. *Remember? I see it vividly. You were always* quiet, perhaps intimidated, to yourself when in a school building, but not this time: waving your sword, you tossed your cape behind your back and leapt off that stage with great panache. All our lives we've made inside jokes about Zorro. Just last winter, a new movie—Zorro—was on, and I texted you about it.

Upon arriving home each day this week, I did not put my feet up, read for a few minutes, and fall asleep—"Take ten," as Emmett used to call it. My "ten" had been turning into twenty and thirty, which had been leading to a low-energy grogginess upon awakening, and I had decided I was not going to fall into that habit for the school year. I kept going.

Out of the car, I strode fast toward the house. Opened the door. Out Alfie and Winston burst. Put on a kettle of hot water. Made strong hot tea. Fed the dogs. Grabbed an energy bar and the mug of tea. Took the pups for a long fast walk. Up, up, on top of the hill down which one winter evening a decade ago I had skied into a valley-covered bottom of geese, Sawyer, our golden retriever, sprinting ahead—we sped downhill, into the geese and thousands of them spiraled upward, honking and swirling into the sky. Later at dinner that evening, you told me you'd been out hunting with Turney, had been in a blind in a corn field for hours, had not seen one goose, and then had seen this majestic sight, this vortex, helix of geese wheeling into the sky—and out of range.

The geese had been hunkering down in a protected area, "the Wideners," as we still call that valley where your father years ago built the cow barn, the back of it facing the steep hill and woods, the front looking out on the low fields and the creek. We camped near there one night, on a little peninsula jutting out into the creek.

Remember the night we hiked, out away from your mother's barn, over the hill, into the Igleharts' field? We made a fire, heated up some hot chocolate, got in our sleeping bags, fell asleep. The awakening: We looked up and there were thirty cows, thirty gigantic, spooky, dopey heads of cows hovering over us, staring at us, sniffing us, two arm-lengths away, crowding in to see what the hell we were. You leapt up, yelled a few choice words, let it be known to me and the universe just what you thought of this, my great idea to camp out on a hilltop under the stars where there was such a nice cool summer breeze. The cows charged away, ground rumbling beneath us. You led the fast-paced way back to the barn where we lay our sleeping bags down in the hayloft, above Emmett's room.

Every day all week, I was high energy on arriving home. Went for a ride or rowed on the machine. (Just finished *The Boys on the Boat*, all about rowing and a long shot crew from Washington State making it to Hitler's Olympics and kicking ass, winning it. You would've enjoyed this book by Daniel James Brown, perhaps as much as you did Laura Hillenbrand's *Seabiscuit* and *Unbroken*.) But on the day of your birthday, a Friday, I planned to take Ansley out for an early dinner.

I read about Co Co Chanel in *The New York Review of Books*, taking interest in her amazing career in fashion, and planning to cut the article out and send it—until I came to the part about Co Co collaborating with the Nazis—to Eliza now enrolled in the London College of the Arts. Ansley arrived. I hopped in a hot shower—neck and upper back between the shoulder blades were stiff from standing on my head for my new students—had Ansley rub on some Amish ointment. Fired up the Jaguar. Put the top down. Pulled on Gary's suede jacket. Had it all planned, but didn't tell her. Didn't want to give her any choice or even the chance to say it was getting late, it was chilly, we should do it another time—because I was doing it no matter what. We were driving towards St. James Church and Academy. Not the way to get into town. Instead of going past, I told her, "Let's drive through the old school." I parked outside the chest-high stone-wall. Ansley got out. I turned the key off. Hesitated. Took the keys out. Just to be safe. Couldn't help it after a lifetime of taking them out when you might be around. You'd like nothing better than to slide into my leather seat, turn the key, drive off. You weren't around; I rationally knew it. But, I took the keys with me anyway. The last time I'd left the keys in the Jaguar, the top down was down and it was parked outside your kitchen. You had left the not-so-exciting party, lowered yourself into the driver's seat, lit a cigarette, found the keys under the mat, started the engine, honked the horn a couple of times and taken off. I came running after you. Hands on the top of the door, I'd jogged alongside —as I used to jog beside Florida Law and Welterweight waiting for you to give me a leg up—and had vaulted into the passenger seat; you were laughing, knowing you had picked the one thing to set me on edge, and off we flew.

Ansley and I walked into the graveyard, down the gravel walkway and between gravestones to your site. I had imagined myself standing before your tombstone: your name, your dates before me. Irrefutable evidence. Forever. There you'd be—beside your father Eddie, your brother Ned, your brother Jack, your mother Jen. I had walked down to this spot and had watched the interment of each of them here. I had carried your ashes here. The hole was deep and the minister had said he'd set the urn in the hole for me, and I'd said, no thank you, I'll do it. I had kneeled on the small rug over the fresh dirt, and had leaned forward, and had lowered your ashes into the ground.

I knew this spot well. There was your brother Jack's stone, March 6, 1952 to May 14, 1996; your brother Ned's stone, November 6, 1947 to April 8, 1977; your father Eddie's stone, December 23, 1926 to December 27, 1965. Memories of each death swept through me.

I was standing by the handsome stonewall up onto which you and I as St. James students used to jump and then run the entire perimeter of the graveyard. There was a strong, healthy oak between the tombstones and the wall. Just down from us, in another row, was stone after stone: your grandmother, your grandfather, great uncles, great aunts.

There was a bare spot in the grass between the tree and the stones.

Cars pulled up on the other side of the wall. Children jumped out, calling and laughing, sprinted across the parking lot and down the hill to soccer practice. Mothers stepped out a beat slower. Their doors shut. They spoke to each other and to younger children as they made their way down the hill. A few of them would've caught your attention.

Behind me was the church where we'd been nervous acolytes together. To my left was our school. In the foyer hangs a portrait of your father, one of the founders, along with J.B's father, and another handsome one of Jack, who initiated the environmental program and who oversaw the planting of hundreds of trees in the fields surrounding the campus. First through third grades— we were inseparable. *Remember sneaking around, at the end of the school day, to the back where there were those low-slung horizontal windows at ground height that let light down into the basement? Remember lying there in the grass, watching the girls pull on their leotards? Ha— grounds for detention, demerits, suspension, expulsion, shipping us off to the psychologist and psychiatrist, and loading us up with drugs in this day and age! We'd lie there, whispering and laughing, our sides touching.*

Before me—I looked out. I couldn't see the playing fields, the view of which was blocked by the wall, the fields where we'd stood together and watched Paddy and Sam play soccer and lacrosse. My sightline swept over the spread of playing fields, over the valley in which they lay, over the tasseled heads of uncut wild grass and flowers in the field on the other side and to the woods we had hunted through, galloped through, one behind the other, on Pepper and Queenie, on Welterweight and Florida Law. To my right, down the hill, was the show ring where we had circled, then pulled our horses up, took off our hunting caps and leaned forward in prayer during the minister's Thanksgiving Blessing of the Hounds. This was the show ring where we'd ridden our first pony classes. Mom and Pop were there. Jen was there. I don't remember your father coming to a show. Wassie Ball would be there. He loved you and trained you and bestowed upon you everything he knew about horsemanship.

It was peaceful standing up on that hill—church behind me, our school to the left, playing fields straight in front and then the wheat field and the woods, our old show ring where we'd ridden in our first lead line classes to my right. Out of sight, children called to each other. I stood there and did not have my preconceived reaction, which was to be looking at your name and dates, and the tears to be pouring out, and to be talking to you, and a spate of memories to be surging through my mind, sweeping over me, swamping me with the force of the Deer Creek rapids battering me against that boulder, wrapping the canoe around me, sending me to meet my maker—until you pulled me out. I had thought I'd experience a purgation of emotions, a release, a catharsis while staring at your stone, and this might open up a fresh, new, brightly lit path to the future.

There was no stone.

I paced, trying to figure out where I had set your urn. Ansley returned; we studied the hard-packed dirt. No stone for Jen either. There wasn't much spiritual or mystical about it. The tombstones were heavy and permanent. Eddie and Ned's were covered with a mossy, gritty, greenish algae. Jack's was clean and white on the bottom two thirds and then the algae took over. I tried to rub it off. Your's? Was that where it would go, beside Jack? But, here was the bare spot in the grass—five feet from the tree. Would it go here? Or, could it be my memory was inaccurate—that I was conflating your burial with your mother's of a few weeks later—and you were over here, in the spot where I had thought Jen was?

It might have been all for the best. Instead of focusing on your stone and burial site, I looked into space. Instead of staring in shock and disbelief at the finality of your name and numbers carved into stone, I wandered, listened to the children calling and laughing, watched the leggy mothers lithely stepping out of their cars, felt this odd emptiness—of you gone, me there.

Your body and presence and laughter and joking, all our memories, not there. And no signifier, no standard, no symbol. Where were you? I had nothing to grasp.

Air—fresh, clean fall air; we'd driven up with the top down and the fresh air pouring in. I pull up the zipper on Gary's jacket.

Trees—early fall, leaves still green.

Ageless, indestructible two-hundred-year old stonewall.

Sky.

Clouds.

Children are playing. Ansley has discreetly strolled off to another section of the graveyard, giving me some breathing room. Soon we'll be heading to dinner. You loved a good dinner. You were a different man once lured, pushed, dragged, hustled, forced off the farm, away from the track. At a restaurant you would relax, laugh, joke, get outside yourself, have a Coors Light, or in earlier times, a margarita, get up two or three times, go outside, light a Pall Mall, take Ansley with you, and back you'd both come, chuckling, conspiring, sharing a thought.

On this night, in the St. James graveyard, beside the school we attended, up on the hill overlooking the fields and woods of My Lady's Manor we'd ridden through, I have been thinking you'd come back.

Where are you? What are you doing?

You're gone. You're at peace.

You've had enough and you are with your brothers and you are at peace. Your spirit is here—hovering gently over this graveyard; it is here in a peaceful manner. It isn't anchored by an urn of ashes that is either under this bare spot or that one. It isn't limited. You aren't limited. You aren't finite. Your spirit is here and it is at Atlanta Hall Farm with Mimi who is preparing meat loaf for your children and grandchildren. It is over there, twenty gravestone rows away, with Ansley. It is at our farm where you spent much of your youth and where J.B. and I, just last week, spread some of your ashes. It is with your son Sam and daughter Elizabeth and your grandchildren Genevieve and Thomas. (Mimi told me that after Thomas was born, you'd asked her, "Is it possible? Is it possible that I have enough love in me to love Thomas as much as I do Genevieve?" Yes, you did, and you found out.) It is over by the artificial track you put in and it hovers above the hurdles in the finish line field. It has a strong presence in the indoor track to the point where riders galloping, whipping, flying around those sharp turns sometimes imagine your forceful presence there, hands on hips, your piercing look, studying the horse, taking in every movement, your mind thinking, plotting, training, putting yourself inside the skin of that horse, figuring out how to make him a better, faster, quicker, stronger, happier race horse than anyone thought possible.

Your spirit will be at all the hunt meets this fall. It was strong at the Hunt Cup last spring. I felt it in the paddock when the announcer dedicated the race to you. It came down and squeezed me; it took all my emotional essence and squeezed me like a lemon; tears came out, tears and memories of the years and pride in what you meant and stood for with all these people listening, at this race you loved to win. Your spirit was palpable, physical, graspable at the A. P. Smithwick in Saratoga this August when Elizabeth's horse took that one long nod and won the race.

Your presence was strong last Sunday. I was alone. Ansley was at Oldfields. I wrote most of the day. I was drained. I took Winston and Alfie, for a walk. It was Winston's first cross-country walk. You would have enjoyed it. We gave chase to a herd of deer in the woods, and up on the high hill that looks out all the way over the valley to Atlanta Hall, we spied an arrogant coyote, who didn't move, didn't budge, as the dogs barked and came closer and closer, and then finally, we they neared, turned and loped back into the woods.

The weather had been strange throughout the day. Early on, it was cool and damp and looked like rain. Then, it cleared up and got hot and muggy. I thought I'd mow. I went outside. Big black thunderclouds were rolling in from the south, the wind was kicking up, and there was some rumbling of thunder. I'd be too good of a target for the lightning if I were up on the tractor mowing the back field, which needs it badly. I decided to compromise. I pulled out the lawn tractor, the seat of which is not so high up, started mowing the lawn. The clouds dissipated. It never rained. I continued mowing for three hours, thinking of the last time I'd seen you in action. I'd been in my writing room when suddenly a couple of hounds were sniffing and running around the barn just outside my door, trying to catch a scent, happy as can be, and then a few more jauntily jogged by and then the whole pack of them swept across the back field, under the fence and through the hedgerow, into the field of winter wheat. I watched as the huntsman and whip in their Pink coats arrived on the scene, and then, the rest of the field, led by a master in a Pink coat who I could see without a doubt was you. And I was thinking, while mowing, that your spirit was out there, galloping through that field; I could see you galloping along, floating above the winter wheat.

After swimming laps in the neighbor's pool, I sat out on the patio and perused a section entitled "Later Poems" in a collection of Yeats' work. We were studying "Lapis Lazuli" in my Creative Writing class and discerning how different its theme, "All things fall and are built again/ And those that build them again are gay," is from the famous line of Yeats' younger years: "Things fall apart; the centre cannot hold."

I got up, poured what was left out of a bottle of red wine— Argentinian, you'd be interested to know—into a glass, tossed crackers, nuts, and a few leftover slices of cheese on a plate.

I sat, relaxed, drained, looking out at the back field. Sipped the rich red wine. There was nobody there but Riderwood grazing a few feet away—I'll have to get another horse, a friend for Riderwood; J.B. has had mentioned he might have a good one— and the pups scuffling around beneath my feet.

I sipped the wine and re-read the ending of "Lapis Lazuli."

. . . Two Chinamen, behind them a third,
Are carved in lapis lazuli,
Over them flies a long-legged bird,
A symbol of longevity;
The third, doubtless a serving man,
Carries a musical instrument.

Every discoloration of the stone,
Every accidental crack or dent,
Seems a water-course or an avalanche,
Or lofty slope where it still snows
Though doubtless plum or cherry-branch
Sweetens the little half-way house
Those Chinamen climb towards, and I
Delight to imagine them seated there;
There on the mountain and the sky
On all the tragic scene they stare.
One asks for mournful melodies;
Accomplished fingers begin to play.
Their eyes mid many wrinkles, their eyes,
Their ancient, glittering eyes, are gay.

Sitting out on the patio, overlooking the stream, the field, the knoll where Warfield's buried, the hedgerow, the cornfield—corn now taller than I—and the woods in the background, I listened to the birds singing and calling to one another. I listened to the frog croaking, making his pronouncement to the world, down in the stream, and I chuckled remembering that day the meet was at Atlanta Hall and we'd overheard Sebastian Cromwell say to a visiting female rider who had told him he was in her way, "Excuse me. Do you know who I am?" Later, during a lull, with Sebastian a little too close for comfort, you'd laughed and repeated it over and over— "Excuse me. Do you know who I am?"—making it more *supercilious*, more ridiculous with every repetition: The next day, I'd stopped by on the way home from school and handed you a poem by Emily Dickinson we'd been studying:

I'm nobody! Who are you?
Are you nobody, too?
Then there's a pair of us—don't tell!
They'd banish us, you know.

How dreary to be somebody!
How public, like a frog
To tell your name the livelong June
To an admiring bog!

"Yes," you'd said. "That's one thing I know: I'm just a big fish in a little pond."

Watching Riderwood graze, I wondered what the glistening six-foot black snake—that had whipped out from under the large, floppy-eared leaves of hosta when I was mowing, and slithered fast as hell ahead of me—was doing, and thought of how I could catch him and play a trick on you—

But never met this Fellow,
Attended or alone
Without a tighter Breathing
And Zero at the Bone.

—then caught myself. The pups banged against my feet, jumped up on my knee wanting a treat.

Half a mile away, the neighbors' children were having a ball, laughing and playing and calling out to one another. I looked that direction, to the northwest. The entire sky was cloud-covered with the exception of one long swath, Key West sunset blue at the top, purple-violet rays shooting upwards out of the bottom.

The children's laughter and yelling grew louder. There was the high-pitched, ecstatic recess-scream of a girl. The wind had shifted and the clouds were moving from the north toward me, rolling, gathering strength, gathering darkness, increasing the barometric pressure. I could feel it. It darkened overhead but there was still that wide strip of bright blue and the bottom of violet-purple rays shooting upward. Then, the bottom cloud started moving with more force and clarity towards me, and an incredible rumbling/roaring noise, like an unceasing roar of thunder, swept over the farm. Louder and louder. The barometric pressure grew stronger. I finished the glass of malbec.

A section of the lower horizontal cloud cover started snowballing up on itself. It balled up into a head, and then there were shoulders, and the head was approaching me along with the roaring, and the shoulders were separating from the clouds so that there was a head on a set of shoulders, growing, developing. There was a face—a nose, fairly sharp, a face with lines and cracks that had experienced the fullness of life, a strong jaw, and these big shoulders—the features coming together, coalescing, while the noise was now relentless, blocking out all else, and the pressure was so high the air was about to explode into water drops, and it was you.

Your presence rumbled towards me, closing in on me, the noise blocking out all sounds but one: your voice. It was loud, it was deep, and it was clear as a bell: "Push it, Patrick. Push it. Make the most of it."

I stared and then the roaring began to dissipate. I didn't realize until that moment how powerful this pressurized noise had been. The sound weakened, flying off. It must've been a jet. Couldn't have been a jet. Must have been a squadron of jets— the National Guard sometimes they flew over, low. But if so, why couldn't I have seen them? I could hear again the laughing and yelling and screaming of the neighbor's children. I could hear the birds singing, the frog croaking, the insects chippering and chittering and zinging. I took my eyes off you for a second, looked out at Riderwood now splashing in the stream. I brought my eyes back, and there was just a low-slung cloud with one puffy balled-up protuberance, and the upper cloud was coming together with the lower cloud, and then, they were joined. The sky darkened. Big fat cold widely-spaced drops of rain plopped onto the hot stone of the patio. *Push it, Patrick. Push it*, echoed in my mind. "Make the most of it."

I will, Tom. I will!

Acknowledgments

I am extremely thankful to a large number of insightful read-
ers and generous patrons for their contributions which made
publishing *Racing Time* possible.

Ned and Rachel Owen, Harriet Iglehart, and Cynthia
McGinnes provided valuable advice and feedback, and strong
encouragement, on the manuscript. When publishing time came
around, they became the keystone triumvirate of support, the
foundation upon which a structure of patrons was built.

John Egan, Larry Haislip, Maureen Henderson, Lucy Howard,
Tom Iglehart and Candida Lancaster reviewed and discussed
early unwieldy drafts. Carl Gold, Billy Santoro, Larry Smith and
Margaret Worrall supplied additional insight and encouragement
on the next round.

Jeff Christ, Cynthia McGinnes, and Madison Briggs read the
text of the late, more polished drafts in stages, while furnishing
a detailed analysis and engaging me in productive discussions
at the conclusion of each stage. English teaching colleague Sara
Jameson boosted my confidence in sections having to do with
teaching and poetry, and inspired me to re-read Walt Whitman's
Leaves of Grass. My Middle School Medieval History, Creative
Writing and English students at Harford Day School were a daily
inspiration, an uplifting force and cheerful, life-affirming presence as we studied literature and history together; they injected
youthfulness and exuberance into their teacher while he lived
through, and wrote about, the experiences in these pages.

Cary Woodward strongly supported me throughout the
whole project, as did his former Gilman School student J.B. Secor,

who often visited my writing room in the barn, releasing in a firestorm of energy, intense, even tearful feedback on some chapters, and hilarious, free-flowing, unbowdlerized amplifications of others. Randy Lewis spurred me on by texting lengthy entertaining and emotional responses as he flew through the chapters. John Russell completed an interesting fact-checking of literary quotations, and a painstaking, line-by-line edit of the manuscript, the week before I sent it to the publisher.

Patrons were essential to the success of *Racing Time*. Thank you Frank Bonsal, Perry Bolton, S.A. "Skip" Brown, Joe Davies, Charlie Fenwick, Ben Griswold, Lucy Howard, George and Mandy Mahoney, Irv Naylor, J.W.Y. "Duck" Martin, Greg Ryan, Caroline Stautberg and Mimi Voss for your interest and generosity.

Will Dixon provided his marketing skills, coming up with the first draft of a "prospectus." My daughter Eliza sharpened Will's initial draft, and designed a portfolio of illustrations and text that was critical in securing our publisher. Eliza performed the behind-the-scenes work of designing flyers and invitations, building the website and Facebook platforms, and often, calming and reassuring her father.

Wayne Dementi, publisher of Dementi Milestone, was professional, knowledgeable, patient and considerate, and he has the most wonderfully-soothing, southern-Virginia accent to hear on the telephone early Monday morning when one is under deadline pressure. Fellow Hollins College Creative Writing graduate Robin Traywick Williams introduced me to Wayne. Wayne introduced me to Aynsley Fisher who performed her duties as the copy editor with a sharp eye for the smallest details as well as a full comprehension of the big picture; her sense of wonder and excitement for the book raised my spirits and injected me with confidence as we headed to the printer.

Gerard Valerio called on his years of book design experience, his career as an artist, his attention to detail, and his passion for the themes of *Racing Time* to design the cover and every page of this book, the third we have worked on together. His assistant, Sherri Ferritto, was the epitome of grace under pressure, as she received emailed files of illustrations from the artist, copy from the author, and instructions from Gerry right up to press time, and calmly, accurately laid out the pages and assembled the files, which became this book.

Sam Robinson—it all began with me visiting Sam's studio, stepping away from the other guests admiring his paintings, flipping through a sketchbook on his desk, and discerning how with a few strokes of the pen he could capture the action and mood of a scene. The next day, I mailed Sam a manuscript of *Racing Time*. As he read, he started to fill pages with deft drawings of scenes from the book. Soon, the sketches became full size, two-color oil washes; then the oil washes became full-color 24 by 18-inch oil paintings.

My wife Ansley maintained a high degree of patience with me not telling her, as the book was under construction, what I was feverishly working on seven days a week for five years. I didn't hand her a manuscript until I had it as polished as I could get it, at which time she provided indispensable comments. (As a writer, there is absolutely nothing more nerve wracking than lying in bed, reading *Moby Dick,* and beside you, your wife is propped up, noisily flipping the pages of your manuscript, occasionally emitting a guffaw, at other times a noncommittal "hmmmm," and then, she's quiet, too quiet, and you look over, not knowing what page she's on, and she's crying.)

More importantly, Ansley supported me every day, since the dark, bone-chilling afternoon of January 22, 2014 when I returned from a frenzied hike through snow-covered fields and began "holing up" in my refurbished milking parlor in the barn at all hours of the day, all days of the week, sometimes staggering out with watery eyes, in another world—far off with Tom, Dickie and Speedy, and with Warfield and Saitensohn—unable to communicate with live, earth-striding humans and horses, dodging my dearest friends and closest colleagues, writing the main body of *Racing Time*, which poured out after I tapped a vein and penned the first two words—"the acorn" I tell my students—which sprouted, developed and grew, with a great deal of pruning and weeding by those thanked above, into this book:

"Dear Tom"

Patrick Smithwick
Prospect Farm
Monkton, Maryland
1 May 2019

Design and production
by Gerard A. Valerio.

Typographic composition in
Hermann Zapf's Palatino
and technical production
by Sherri Ferritto.

Printed and bound by Jostens
on 60 lb Finch Opaque.